C0-DAX-230

URBAN NETWORKS
—
NETWORK URBANISM

RENEWALS 458-4574

DATE DUE

WITHDRAWN
UTSA Libraries

Research Programme Network Cities, Faculty of Architecture
Delft University of Technology

URBAN NETWORKS
–
NETWORK URBANISM

Gabriel Dupuy

Compiled and edited by

Jeroen van Schaick and Ina T. Klaasen

Techne Press / 2008

Library
University of Texas
at San Antonio

Design/**Science**/Planning

Editorial Board:
Prof. dr. P. Drewe, Emeritus, Faculty of Architecture, Delft University of Technology, The Netherlands
Prof. ir. J.J. Jacobs, Faculty of Industrial Engineering, Delft University of Technology, The Netherlands
Prof. dr. P. Roberts, Department of Civic Design (Regional Planning), University of Liverpool, United Kingdom
Dr. T. Poldma, Associate Professor, School of Industrial Design, Faculty of Environmental Planning, University of Montreal, Canada
Prof. dr. A. van der Valk, Land Use Planning Chair, Wageningen University, The Netherlands

Urban Networks – Network Urbanism / Gabriel Dupuy
Compiled and edited by Jeroen van Schaick and Ina T. Klaasen

Keywords: spatial planning, urban planning, network urbanism, network theory, technical networks, network territories, network operators, ICT, digital divide, automobile system, car dependence, Cerdà, Broadacre City

ISBN: 978-90-8594-019-7

Translation and language editing: Philip Dresner (Chapters 2, 3, 4, 5, 7, 8, 12, 14, 15, 16, 17, 19)
Lay-out: Jan Willem Hennink
Editing assistance: Ana María Fernández-Maldonado, Wendy Tan
Cover photo: Buenos Aires electricity network (Ina Klaasen)
Cover design: Iwan Kriens, Jeroen van Schaick

Published and distributed by Techne Press, Amsterdam, The Netherlands
www.technepress.nl

This publication was produced within the frame of the research program of the Delft Center for Sustainable Urban Areas and financed by the Chair of Spatial Planning and Strategy at Delft University of Technology.

Copyright © 2008 by the author and the editors, unless otherwise stated. All rights reserved.

No part of this publication may be reproduced or stored by any electronic or mechanical means (including copying, photocopying, recording, data storage, and retrieval) or in any other form or language without the written permission from the publisher.

For the images used in this volume, the editors have consulted with artists or copyright holders to their best avail and acknowledged their work as well as possible. Those who feel that their images have not been recognized sufficiently or have been used inappropriately, are invited to contact the editors or publisher.

Contents

Part I   Networks: Past and Present Challenges for Urban Planning

Part II   Network Territoriality: Golden Age and Crises in Cities Around the World

Part III   Motor Cars: System, Network and Dependency

Part IV ICTs: Interconnections and Divides

Part V New Tools for Planners

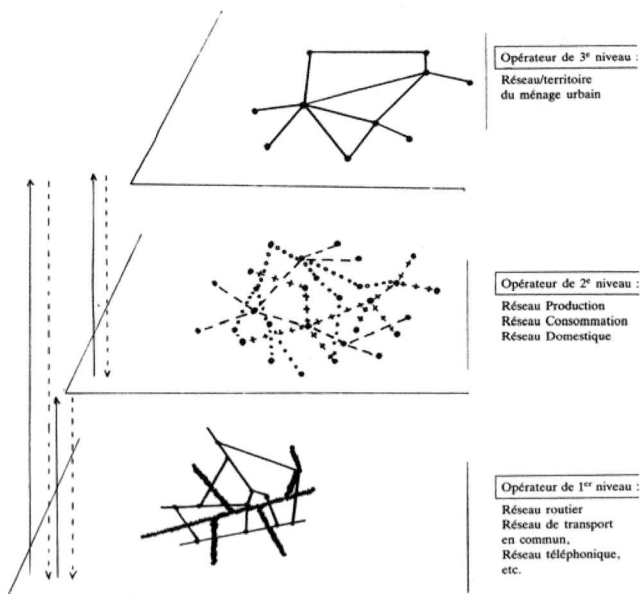

Opérateur de 3e niveau :
Réseau/territoire
du ménage urbain

Opérateur de 2e niveau :
Réseau Production
Réseau Consommation
Réseau Domestique

Opérateur de 1er niveau :
Réseau routier
Réseau de transport
en commun,
Réseau téléphonique,
etc.

Illustration 0.1   **Dupuy's triple-layered framework as it was published originally.**
Source: Dupuy (1991a: 119)

Urban Networks – Network Urbanism

Foreword

The work of Gabriel Dupuy has been a source of inspiration for my research and teaching at Delft University of Technology and elsewhere. We first met at the *Ecole Nationale des Ponts et Chaussées* with the 'Réseaux' multidisciplinary research group, which is closely related to the *Laboratoire Techniques, Territoires et Sociétés* (LATTS). Later we both became, and remain, members of the scientific panel of *FLUX, the International Scientific Quarterly on Networks and Territory*, which was founded by Dupuy in 1990.

When I read *L'Urbanisme des Réseaux* (Network Urbanism) it was an eye-opener for someone like myself, working in an environment of conventional urbanism and architecture practice. Based on a re-reading of the classics, the book introduced the three fundamental characteristics of modern networks, i.e., the topological, kinetic and adaptive criterion. Working in our Design Studio 'The Network City' focusing on ICT and, in particular, on the Internet, we discovered that Dupuy's triple-layered framework (illustration 0.1) was perfectly suited for analysing the new technology and its networks: the network city, a 'new old way' of thinking cities in the ICT age. The three interacting levels correspond as follows in the case of ICT: the Internet infrastructure (level one), the 'Internet industry' (level two) and the actual traffic on the Internet, as revealed by traceroutes (level three).

Gabriel Dupuy too has turned his attention to the topic of ICT and the Internet. Recently he has even tackled the thorny question of the so-called digital divide (see Part 4). But before doing so, he focused on the automobile system and on automobile dependence (see Part 3), thus providing a link to the Charter of Athens, old and new, and to the work of Nikos Salingaros, an applied mathematician and physicist who has extended Barabási's 'new science of networks' to the complex networks known as cities (Salingaros, 2005). This kind of thinking is relevant to today's still largely unresolved urban mobility problem.

Ultimately, Dupuy's work has paved the way for thinking on – and the design of – a new urban form: an urbanism of new networks that extends beyond a hierarchical configuration of space and time in the city.

L'Urbanisme des Réseaux was published in 1991. It is a rather long way from that book to the present publication. First, there was a nine year wait before an abridged adaptation of the Chapter on the historical background was translated into English and Dutch (included in this book as Chapter 1). But now we have this book, which, through the eminent example of Gabriel Dupuy's work, proves that France, after all, is more than just a favorite destination for Dutch tourists. Battling the language barrier, the Netherlands, having become something of an Anglo-Saxon country, needs more boundary spanners – especially in the realm of spatial planning.

Prof.em.Paul Drewe, June 2008

Introducing *Urban Networks – Network Urbanism*

Jeroen van Schaick and Ina Klaasen

Gabriel Dupuy: an oeuvre

It is not easy to boil down the work of 30 years in a single book. Gabriel Dupuy's fascination with the relation between the technical professions and urbanism started early, exemplified by his doctorate thesis and first book *Urbanisme et Technique, Chronique d'un Mariage de Raison* (Urbanism and Technique: Chronicle of A Marriage of Convenience) from 1978. During the 1980s he became interested not only in the role of techniques (e.g. calculating size and structure of conduits, modelling traffic, simulating urbanization), but also in the role of technology in urbanism, i.e. the role of physical networks in urban development. Using the notion of networks, the work of Gabriel Dupuy has broadened over time in the sense that he has treated a network not just as a physical object, but also as a concept. Moreover, he has shown that network thinking is a necessary element of urban planning in the 21st century.

The work of Gabriel Dupuy has gained considerable depth over the years because of three things mainly. Firstly, his work radiates a thorough understanding of historical developments, as illustrated by his integral treatment of the 'coming into being' of networks, the development of underlying concepts through cross-sectoral and cross-border knowledge transfers and the changes in physical structure of networks. Secondly, his in-depth dealing with case studies, sometimes holistic, sometimes to illustrate specific concepts and arguments, has enriched his theoretical groundwork. Thirdly, his detailed study of both the automobile system and ICTs links his theoretical work to the policy agendas of today and tomorrow.

Until now though, much of Dupuy's publications were only available in French and Spanish. This book aims to introduce his 'network thinking', in its depth and its width, to an English-reading audience.

1990 was an important year for Gabriel Dupuy. It was the year that he founded the magazine *Flux*, a journal that "is especially concerned with the ways in which networks are designed, regulated and operated, as well as the relationship between networks and the territories they serve". As such, *"Flux* is one of the few academic publications in French which specializes in the field of town planning." (http://latts.cnrs.fr, accessed July 2008). Moreover, 1990 was the year that he wrote *L'Urbanisme des Réseaux* (Urbanism of Networks; Dupuy, 1991a). In that book, Gabriel Dupuy translated his work on technical networks into a study on network thinking in the field of urbanism, reacting to what he perceived as a crisis in the field of urban planning.

The crisis that Dupuy signalled at the start of the 1990s has not been overcome. The conflict between urban planning based on an areolar conception of space (i.e. based on zones, boundaries and edges, see p.65) and urban planning viewed from a network-based conception of space is still very much alive. Networks, both as object and as concept, are still not seen as part and parcel of mainstream urbanism. However, since 1990, some things have changed. It seems that a shift in spatial planning is taking place towards 'relational thinking', i.e. towards network thinking.

A shift in spatial planning

In 2007 the Dutch newspaper *De Volkskrant* developed a list of 50 subjects-every-Dutchman-should-know-about-science-and-technology. One of those 50 subjects – published in 2008 in book edition – was *Techniek en Stadsontwikkeling* (Technology and urban development). Van Kleef (2008) explains that nowadays technology is still often invisible in urban designs and plans, despite the real, although intricate relation between the development of technical networks and the development of the city. But this is not the only reason to re-examine networks in light of urban design and planning.

In addition to this view of networks as physical 'things' that re-organize time and space – a viewpoint commented upon by Dupuy (2005: 120-122) – Albrechts and Mandelbaum (2004: v-vii) show two other important strands of network thinking in relation to spatial planning. On the one hand, network thinking can be seen as a new paradigm – as far ranging as shown by the term 'the network society' – that confronts spatial planning with a challenge for fundamental change in light of a new context. On the other hand, network thinking has direct implications for the way planning processes are organized requiring governance styles that include a range of stakeholders organizing themselves in networks. However, Albrechts and Mandelbaum also show that physically-oriented thinking, paradigmatic thinking and social network-oriented thinking are sometimes as far removed from each other from each other as zonal thinking and network thinking are in spatial planning (see Chapter 1).

Moreover, authors on network thinking seem to be split up in, on the one hand, a group that sees a new kind of society developing based on new networked structures and, on the other hand, a group that thinks of networks as fundamental structures in any society rather than as something recent. The former sees networks as an organization form with characteristics such as foot-looseness and virtuality that is replacing 'old' organization forms. The latter emphasizes the durability of physical structures. There are also those in the middle that see networks as fundamental to human society and at the same time see dramatic – partially technology-driven – changes in the intensity, scale, multiplicity and complexity of networked organization forms. This standpoint implies that there are strong links between the three different types of network thinking. However, literature that bridges the gaps between physically-oriented thinking, paradigmatic thinking and social-network-oriented thinking is scarce.

Where then can we place the work by Gabriel Dupuy? Three issues are important to understand his position. Firstly, Dupuy's background in planning is grounded in engineering. Secondly, "France has a long-standing tradition of spatial planning for regional and urban development (…) carried out by the central government or by local governments" (Ministère des Affaires Étrangères, 2006: 50). Thirdly, France is known for its tradition of prospective research and scenario development (Drewe, 2008). From this perspective, Dupuy clearly takes the stand that network thinking is not limited to either seeing cities as physical networks or to seeing urban planning as interplay of numerous stakeholders. For Dupuy the development of networks in relation to territorial development hangs very much together with parallel changes in organizational structure and stakeholder involvement.

The structure of the book

Urban Networks – Network Urbanism consists of five Parts. A number of the core Chapters of Dupuy's book *L'Urbanisme des Réseaux* (1991) have been selected for Part 1. In these Chapters the history and theory of network thinking in the context of urban planning are addressed supplying the theoretical basis for this book. In the first Chapter the focus is on the history of network urbanism: a re-examination of urban planning classics highlighting the way their authors dealt with network thinking. Also attention is paid to a number of people outside the world of urban planning who developed some of the early urban technical networks. While explaining what these networks meant for urban development, in this Chapter a first step is taken in developing a network concept for urban planning based on the concepts 'topology', 'kinetics' and 'adaptivity'. In the second Chapter a theory of network urbanism is built that provides grounds and arguments for urban planning in the network age. The concept of network operators is developed and the three levels on which they operate are defined: physical networks, functional networks and household networks. The third Chapter introduces the concept 'network territory'. Dupuy argues here that technical networks have "introduced into our societies a new, predominant form of territoriality that urban planning, as a rule, failed to acknowledge", without claiming that this is the only remaining form of territoriality (p. 66). The final Chapter of Part 1 elaborates on the problems connected with the use of network maps. Using examples from the early days of computational visualization tools, it explains that there is a fundamental conflict between network maps and their usability for urban planners.

The Chapters chosen for Part 2 – adaptations of articles mostly predating 1991 – illustrate the lines of thought leading to the Urbanism of Networks idea. In this part of the book it is shown that network urbanism needs to be seen in the context of territorial development. It extends the concept of 'network territory' from Chapter 3 on the basis of four case studies: the encapsulation of Andrésy – an outer suburb of Paris – in regional networks, the development of the French road system in light of American traffic models, the collapse of networks in the Buenos Aires region and the way this is dealt with, and the cross-border development of the Eurovision radio and television broadcasting network.

The Chapters in Part 3 and 4 – written between 1995 and 2007, after the publication of *L'Urbanisme des Réseaux* – have been selected to give more depth to the implications of network thinking in urban and regional territories by focusing, respectively, on the automobile and on ICTs. After a Chapter that develops the metaphor of the 'universal adapter' for the automobile system, Part 3 elaborates on the concept of automobile dependence; how it works, how it varies between national, regional and cultural contexts and how to deal with it. The Chapters in Part 4 address the rise of ICTs. Chapter 13 and 14 explore the conditions of an ICT-'miracle', respectively as it developed in Iceland and – in contrast – as it did not in Saint Pierre et Miquelon, a number of small French islands – an overseas department – close to the Canadian coast. Whereas in Part 3 automobile dependence as a societal problem is explained as being inherent to the automobile system itself, in Part 4 the digital divide as a major societal problem is attributed to the rise of ICTs. The Chapters on ICTs show how the digital divide is related to other types of divides, in particular focusing on the digital divide as a geographical problem as well as a problem of scale.

In the two Chapters of Part 5 the focus is again on the broader question of urban planning, revisiting the original ideas about an Urbanism of Networks as set out in Part 1. The conditions under which network urbanism has to operate in the 21st century are summarized in Chapter 18. A number of challenges for urban planning are pointed out: changes of scale, continuing technological progress, the development of two-track cities and the reality of deregulation. Chapter 19 subsequently sketches the contours and possible ingredients of network urbanism for the future by elaborating on a number of key concepts.

Concluding remarks

All Chapters, except for Chapter 19, have been previously published, albeit some in an earlier version and/or in French and Spanish. So the book has not been written as a monograph and should be read as a collection of articles. Still, cross-references between Chapters may help the reader to see that the Chapters are strongly interrelated. In view of this interrelation it was decided to put the references together at the end of the book instead of at the end of each Chapter.

Throughout the book the reader will find a number of text boxes. These white texts on dark backgrounds showcase ideas – citations – from authors who have influenced Gabriel Dupuy's way of thinking. The attentive reader will see that they refer to some of the key concepts used throughout *Urban Networks – Network Urbanism*. In addition, numbered boxes inside the Chapters function as particular illustrations and are referenced in the text.

As said, the goal of this book is to open up a mainly French oeuvre to an English-reading audience: twelve of the nineteen Chapters are first-time English translations. So *Urban Networks – Network Urbanism* should also be of interest to readers who came across publications by Dupuy in English before and would like to get a better understanding of his views on urban planning. In addition, the French flavour of the case studies - and the mix of Anglo-Saxon, Hispanic and French references - might help in discovering the richness of the French discourse on geography and spatial planning.

Part I

Networks: Past and Present Challenges for Urban Planning

1   A Revised History of Network Urbanism*

The zoning approach has dominated urbanism to such an extent that very little room has been left for other approaches regarding the organization of urban territory. In particular, the idea of spatial organization based on networks, which appears to be a relevant organizational form in present-day cities, has hardly been developed. However, this does not mean that throughout the history of urbanism there have never been any network-based approaches. They have been produced on several occasions and in various forms, theories and utopias, although rarely in implemented projects. In whatever form, these network-based approaches have been, in different ways, simply marginalized. Their authors were completely ignored by the world of urbanism, occasionally even aggressively ostracized. Some of them succeeded at self-censorship, returning to orthodox doctrines. Others have been recognized and even praised for other aspects of their work by critics who neglected their contribution to the study of networks.

Therefore, it is necessary to re-read these authors, in order to rehabilitate them with regard to their approach to networks. Evidently, the point of departure, when re-reading, has to be the modern notion of networks. This analysis aims to enrich the current approach to the city and does not pretend to be a comprehensive historic approach.

The notion of networks is ancient. The origin of the word might be lost, but its metaphoric usage appears during the 18th century to describe a physiological aspect (e.g. the circulatory system or network), a physical aspect (e.g. the hydraulic network) and even a military aspect (e.g. the network of fortresses to defend a territory). However, it is not through these historic concepts that I am studying urban planning and design concepts. Of importance is the relevance of certain past theories for present and future urban reality. My analytical perspective is that of the modern notion of networks. Using cars or the Internet as examples seems more appropriate to illustrate an ideal, a virtual reality or a utopia, than the cool observations and technical examples of roads, cables and pipes running through the space of our daily life. For the car (see Part 3) as well as for the Internet (see Part 4), what matters in the first place is the individual. The user configures and re-configures the network depending on whichever contact, with other people and places, he deems useful or desirable.

The network, in its modern notion meaning, is characterized by three main criteria:

- *Topological criterion*. The search of direct connections between points and the ideal of ubiquity characterizes the topology of a network.

- *Kinetic criterion*. Instantaneousness, homogeneity of speed and the importance of rapid transportation and flows without time losses or interruptions; defines the movement or kinetic aspect of networks.

---

*   This Chapter is an adapted version of an article previously published in Garritzman, U. & Nio, I., 2000, eds, *Oase # 53 Netwerkstedenbouw – Network Urbanism*, pp. 3-29, which was a shortened and adapted version of « Réhabilitation des Doctrines Urbanistiques Favorables aux Réseaux ». In: Dupuy, G., 1991, *L'Urbanisme des Réseaux: Théories et Méthodes*. Paris: Armand-Colin, pp. 81-106. Included with permission.

- *Adaptive criterion*. The present-day meaning of the word network includes the notion of multiple choices with regard to connections, both in space and in time. These connections may require a permanent support, a fixed infrastructure. On the other hand, ideally, the network has to be able to constantly adapt itself to new user requirements.

From Haussmann to Riboud, and from Cerdà to Hart, the network thinkers constitute an odd group.[1] Nevertheless, I will try to describe the essential contributions of personalities such as Arturo Soria y Mata or Henry Ford, according to the three dimensions of modern urban networks: topology, kinetics and adaptation. I will then concentrate on the ideas of I.Cerdà and F.L.Wright. Both are undoubtedly urban designers and approach networks in their relationship with urban space in a broad sense (in contrast with sector-based approaches limited to, for instance, transportation networks).

From Cerdà to Virilio: the topology of networks

The typical network topology, so clearly different from the zoning approach of orthodox urbanism, is seen for the first time in the work of Cerdà. From the end of the 19th century this concept is also found in the work of other authors. The network establishes a relationship, a maximum connection; if possible a direct and multiple connection between points in a space, independent of their location and across barriers and borders. In this way, the network makes urban space accessible and stimulates decentralization. It is an inherently discontinuous extension of urban space because the network only connects points. The network replaces linear discontinuities in this space based on historic, administrative or urban borders, with a built-in type of discontinuity. This erases, in a way, the geographical space except for the nodes and the links, thus creating a specific network space.

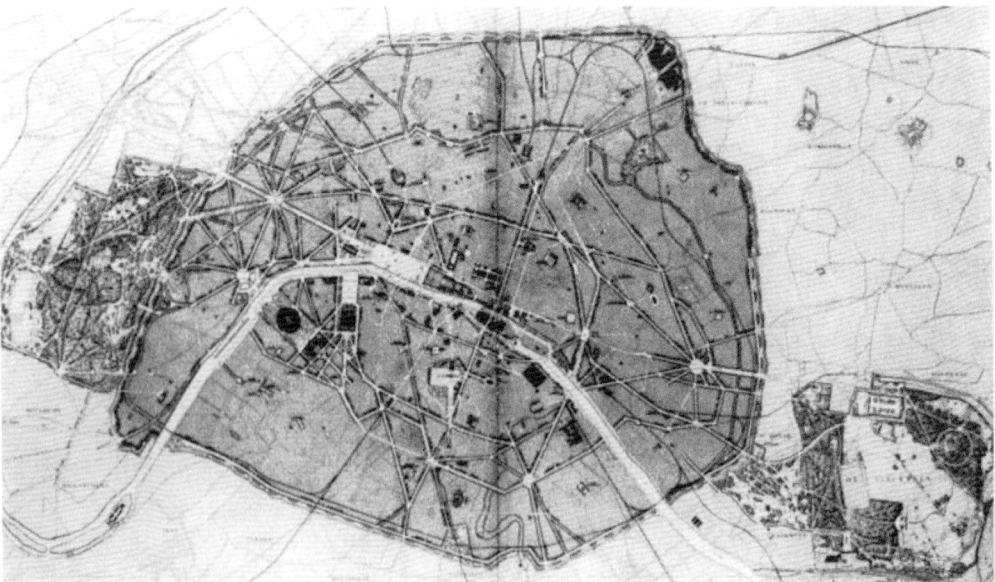

Illustration 1.1   Haussmann's transformation of Paris (Alphand, about 1867). Source: unknown

Haussmann cannot be considered an adherent of networks, in the modern sense of the term, because he still had an ambiguous approach to the topology of networks. The Prefect of Paris was looking for a way to supply abundant fresh water to the different parts of the city; a city that he considered a collection of fragments to be linked. In the same way, he wanted to link, through a network of drains, a large number of points in Paris to the sewerage. But the topological limitations of the Haussmann network appear very quickly, whether it concerned water, drainage, roads or public lighting. Haussmann conceived a strict hierarchical network, from the sewerage to the collecting drain in a building, from the aqueducts to the local water mains in a dwelling. The top dominates the base and the centre dominates the periphery. Furthermore, according to Haussmann's idea of regulation, the network is limited by the administrative borders of the city, due to the resistance of landowners outside the city borders. There is an interior and there is an exterior (Haussmann, 1879). The fortifications constituted the borders of the city, the place 'where Paris ceased to exist' (Haussmann, 1893, illustration 1.1).

Arturo Soria y Mata, an urban planner and designer from Madrid, proposed the *Linear City* project in 1886 (illustration 1.2). Although the very simple design of this city does not immediately evoke the topology of the modern network, the basic principle of the *Ciudad Lineal* is precisely maximum connection. The author tries above all to answer a question that he poses in this way: "In each agglomeration (...) the fundamental problem (...) is that of connecting buildings" (Soria y Mata, (1913) 1979). The linear design brings all connections together into one axis, enabling them to function in a much better way.[2]

Illustration 1.2   **The connection of the *Ciudad Lineal* in Madrid (460 m wide and 5.2 kilometre long) to the tramway network of Madrid.** Source: Soria y Mata ((1913)1979: 37)

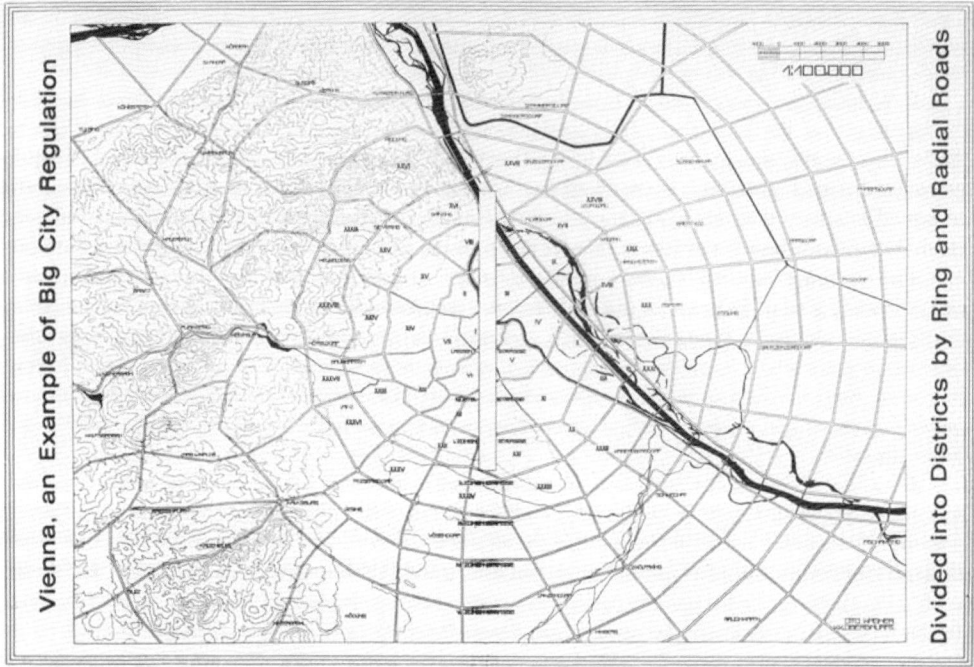

Illustration 1.3   **Survey plan of Vienna from the study *Die Grossstadt* by Wagner (1910/1911).**
Source: Kristan (2002)

In 1892, the realization of the *Ciudad Lineal* commenced. One year later, Otto Wagner proposed a regeneration project in Vienna, also based on a modern topology of networks (illustration 1.3). The project relied heavily on the idea that new means of transportation would be the key of the future urban development, and in opposition to the 'classic' urban plans, Wagner's project deliberately did not provide for an *a priori* distribution of the different urban elements in the geographical space. Industries, residential neighbourhoods, offices, and so on, were supposed to arrange themselves inside the networks according to their own topology and without having to take a zoning of the urban territory into account (Schorske, 1984).

Samuel Insull was neither a proper urban planner nor an engineer (Hughes, 1983). Director of the Edison electricity company in Chicago until 1910, he was the brilliant secretary of Edison, appointed to head a small electricity enterprise, one of twenty that served Chicago at that time, in order to develop it by taking advantage of the regional possibilities. He succeeded in his task beyond all expectations. In 1910, his company was the only supplier of electrical energy in Chicago and the largest enterprise of electricity in the world. The Chicago Edison Company even became a sort of model that numerous cities in the world attempted to imitate. How did Insull achieve such a result? He did this by using a modern concept of networks. He wanted to link up as many points as possible by means of electricity connections. All power stations were interconnected. The network served whatever and whoever

Number of apartment customers	193
Number of hall-lighting and garage customers	34
Average number of lamps per customer	12
Kilowatt-hours used per year	49,620
Customers separate maxima	92 kw = 6.3% load factor
Maximum at transformers	29 kw = 20% load factor
Annual income per customer	$18.34
Diversity factor	3.2

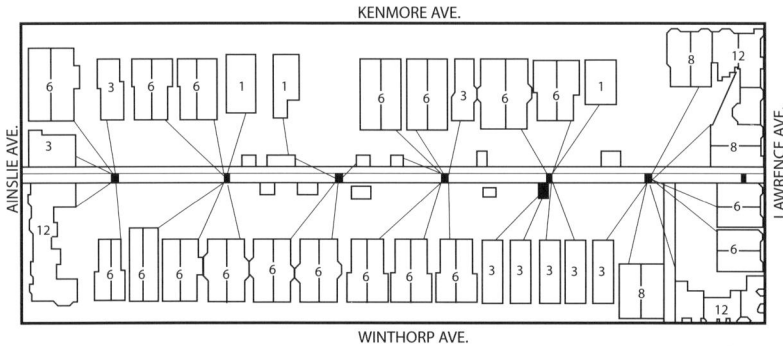

Illustration 1.4   **Diversity of demand for electric service in a block of apartment buildings, Chicago.**
Source: Hughes (1983: 218)

that might need electricity: public lighting, the metro, the tramway, all sorts of manufacturers (from brickyards to ice cream makers), offices and private dwellings (illustration 1.4). Insull rapidly went beyond the borders of his original area, connecting to rival networks, which he simply bought out. All of Chicago became covered and soon after that the suburbs, the far away periphery and the region. Insull used a topological network strategy, in which connecting everything to everything became the primordial condition for the development of his company.

For two reasons the example of Insull is interesting. On the one hand, such a strategy has to have repercussions for the organization of urban space. Selling electricity is not the same as making urban plans, but unquestionably the extension of the network had consequences in terms of economic activities, transportation and even urban development. Insull's strategy ran counter to the principles of urban zoning in Chicago at that time, reducing the possibilities of the municipality to control urban development and land use. At some stage, people started to realize that. Attempts to bring Insull down in the end succeeded and he left the company in 1910.

On the other hand, the example of Chicago, though specific, is an archetype of the construction of new networks, in cities all over the world: networks for electricity, for gas, and especially for water, but also for transportation. The growth of networks often comes about through the more or less conscious application of this topological network model, connecting and interconnecting everything that can conceivably be connected; creating its own territory beyond administrative barriers that try to oppose this, with obvious effects on the possibilities to control urban developments (see Chapter 5).

In French cities as well similar projects appeared at that time, all based on the same topological idea of networks. In this way, the city of Nantes projected its water network beyond its municipal limits and built a monumental reservoir in the small community of Chantenay where the highest point of the Nantes agglomeration is found (Pinson, 1987). The relevance of this example has less to do with the

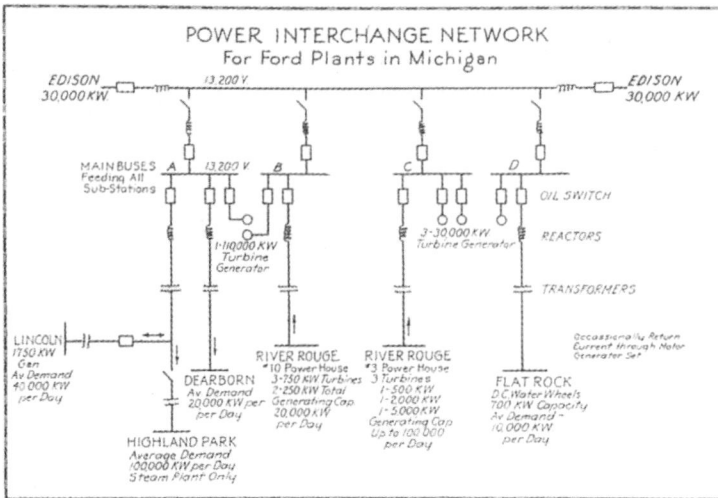

Illustration 1.5   Ford's electricity network in Michigan. Source: unknown

topography than with the topological significance given to the whole operation. The obstacles of the municipal borders had to be overcome to allow for to the topology of Nantes' network.

One of those who used the possibilities of the new electricity networks was Henry Ford. He tried to decentralize the industry, notably the automobile industry, which he knew well. He also wanted to reverse the harmful effects of the city on the lives of workers. Ford's goal was to enable people to work and therefore live in villages, by installing small production units in the countryside, which were linked to a main factory. Electricity was considered the means to make this ubiquitous connection possible. Ford proposed to supply energy by way of hydraulic systems, and to produce electricity locally (illustration 1.5). Towards 1925 he succeeded in having several dams constructed in Lake Michigan, which allowed him to realize at least part of his project.

Thanks to electricity, the modern network topology dominates this project, overcoming the fundamental division between town and countryside. The extension of the networks beyond traditional urban borders questions essential aspects of towns and cities, especially density and concentration. Through its new topology, the network redefines these urban issues.

In France, the rise of the automobile was perceived by most urbanists as a threat to the city, as a tide that had to be contained. From Le Corbusier to the French versions of the Buchanan Report, the official doctrine was that traffic had to be steered and channelled. At the same time, public transportation was strongly promoted. The message of American urbanists, such as Clarence Arthur Perry (1929), who analysed the automobile phenomenon in a very comprehensive way and who drew original conclusions related to urban development, was not well received in Europe.

Through the convergence of Information and Communication Technologies (ICTs), the French telephone network became one of the most modern in the world. It provided new services such as screens; automation and remote control, by which artificial communication became possible, enabling interactivity. The Internet network, even with its current imperfections (the long waiting times and its unfinished deployment), presently constitutes a worldwide outcome of this development.

Urban Networks – Network Urbanism

This same idea is extended, in an allegoric way, by Paul Virilio. He announces the end of vertical density, horizontal communications, radial-centrism[3], and the advantage of the centre over the periphery. Virilio predicts the historical shifts from activity to interactivity (Virilio, 1987), and from 'central' to 'nodal'. He foresees the development of a generalized decentralization, of an endless periphery, the symbol of the demise of the industrial urban form (ibid.).

Circulation and communication: the kinetics of networks

The second dimension of the network, in relation to its modern territorial meaning, is the kinetic one. The network defines space and time simultaneously. It establishes a new relation between the two based on circulation, flows, speed, and tending towards instantaneousness, or 'real time', to borrow an expression from the ICT domain.

The notion of a specific network time, dissimilar from 'ordinary' time and measured differently, manifests itself wherever networks exist. As the railways and the telegraph systems developed this awareness gradually gets trough to urban planners and those responsible for urban facilities. As mentioned by Jean-Pierre Williot, the spreading of electric illumination contributed to this transformation. The act of lighting up became instantaneous. The fact that public lights when switched on start to work immediately and simultaneously everywhere unifies urban space (Williot, 1990). In the long term, the entire society, beginning with the urban society, changed its relationship with time due to the expansion of industrial activity. But the network will always be ahead in this regard. This is a new territory, defined from the beginning by a new temporality of flows, by the measurement of speed and especially by the importance of kinetics.

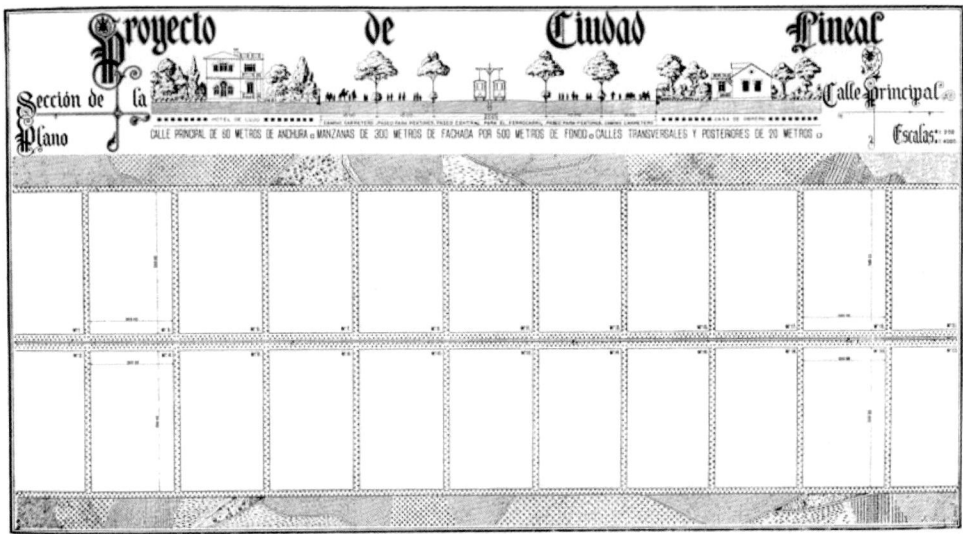

Illustration 1.6   **Profile and plan of the *Ciudad Lineal* in Madrid, with a central axis of 40 metres and transversal and backstreets of 20 metres wide.** Source: Soria Y Mata ((1913) 1979: 15)

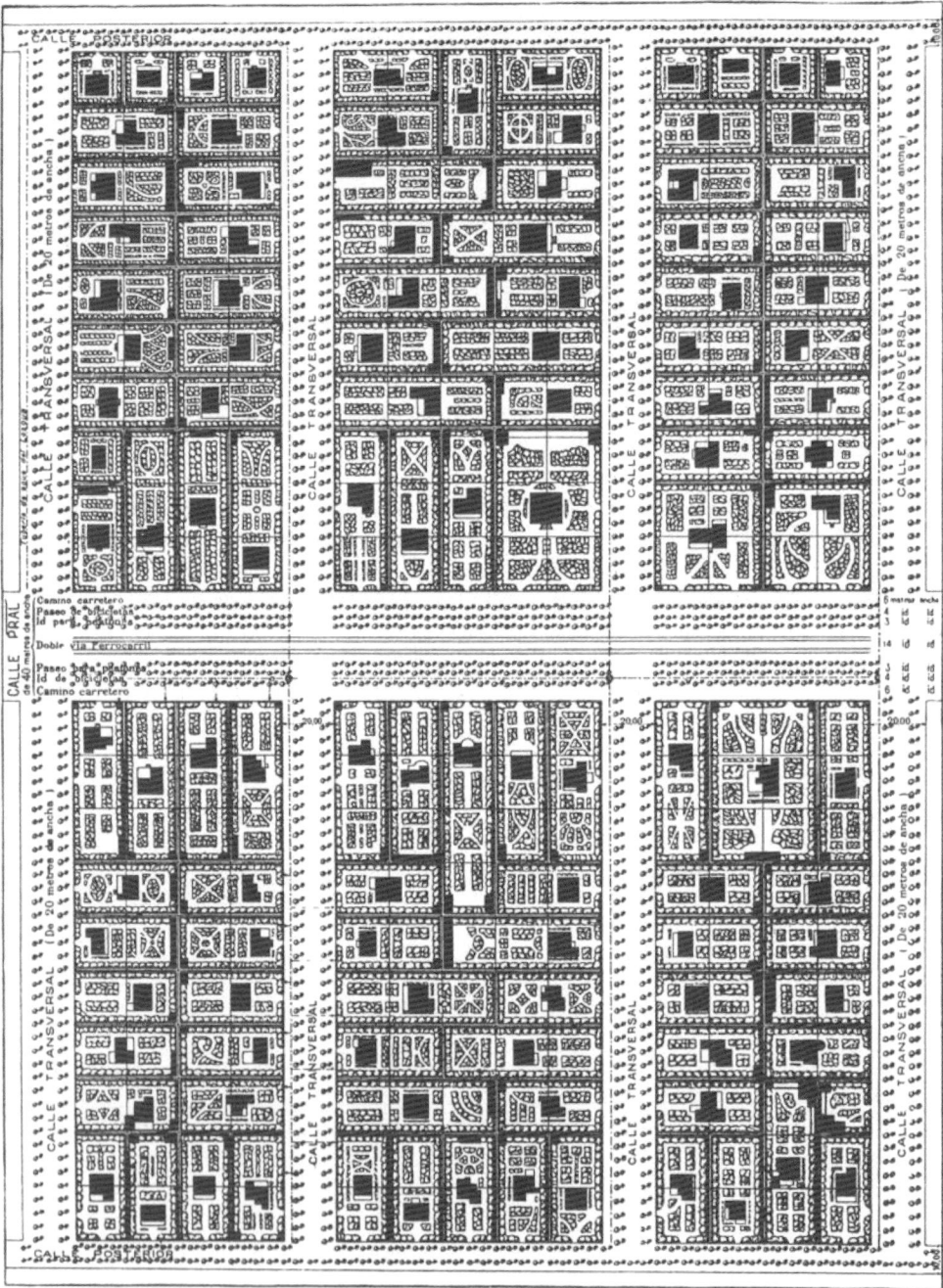

Illustration 1.7 **Layout of streets and lots in the *Ciudad Lineal* in Madrid.**
Source: Soria Y Mata ((1913) 1979: 14)

Soria y Mata also reasoned according to a kinetic criterion when he conceived his *Ciudad Lineal*. "The shape of a city is or must be a shape derived from the necessities of locomotion ... [it] will reach perfection when the amount of time spent to go from each house to all the others will be the lowest possible: such is the case in linear cities" (Soria y Mata, (1913) 1979). It is true that the scheme that he conceived rests entirely on the shortening of the distance along the linear axis where the circulation is accelerated. The *Linear City*'s avenue is 450 meters wide. The longitudinal axis comprises a tramway line and a 40-meter-wide road divided into seven lanes according to the different types of traffic (illustrations 1.6 and 1.7).

Soria y Mata was not just interested in transport. He also paid great attention to the kinetic dimension of networks to promote the passage of all flows. He wanted to deploy networks channels, railroads for transportation of goods, wide and well-paved roads, electric cables, public lighting, and telephone and telegraph systems. Circulation was not only intended for people, but also for goods, services, energy and information. All these must be delivered with the speed required by the modern city.

The wish to impose a new rhythm on traffic was present everywhere. This could be seen along the main roads but also at the 'junctions' and in the 'centres', the switches and current distributors; everywhere there were changes in direction and places where new connections were made. Cerdà was passionate about junctions. Wagner hoped that the 'wonderful modern means of locomotion' would penetrate Vienna without encountering any obstacles. To serve the suburbs of Chicago, Insull developed converters capable of transforming electricity from direct to alternating current without hindrance. Henry Ford used the new water and electricity networks to separate industry and manpower, which previously had to be in close proximity.

The concept of speed changed, and is still continuously changing (Gökalp, 1988). Cars and telecommunications strengthen these phenomena. Jacques Riboud wrote in 1971: "It is the journey time that counts and not the distance" (Riboud, 1981). In the most extreme case, travel time simply does not exist anymore. In the car, one can forget the travel time by linking up with other 'faster' networks. According to B. de La Rochefoucauld (1982) the car becomes an "abode where the hours lost in traffic jams are spent 'at home', with the radio, the telephone and probably soon television". According to Virilio (1988), we would eventually get to a point where we can travel without actually moving. The vehicle would be an image on the computer screen, becoming transformed in 'real time', i.e. creating the illusion of time without the delay of having to travel from one place to another.

It is always in the network that these transformations in the relationship between space and time take place. It is not just the technical progress in the field of mobility that matters. Those quoted were not so much interested in the pure speed of the vehicle, the signal, the rocket, the impulse or of the light ray. What mattered to them was the possibility to use this speed everywhere; without being restricted by obstacles like bifurcations, connections, and so on. The kinetic dimension of the network is, therefore, strongly linked to the topological dimension, as well as to the adaptive dimension that we will discuss in the next section.

Adaptive networks: the 'systemic' vision

The ideal modern network is capable of adapting itself in time, of evolving by enabling the new connections required by its users, generated by the transformations of the 'environment' of the urban system. This concept appears, however little they are reread from this perspective, in the work of a large number of authors, all of them relatively marginal personalities in the history of urbanism.

This concept might not be present in the work of Haussmann, who thought the city to have an almost perfect and definitive form. Neither might the adaptive aspect of the network always be explicit in the writings of Cerdà. However, in the case of Soria y Mata it is the foundation of his projects. The Ciudad Lineal allows for alterations of the patterns of movement (at least when they are linked to the central axis). It also allows for an almost unlimited development of the city, while still preserving its advantages, by branching off the linear axis. Soria y Mata situated the extremities of the network at Cadiz and Saint Petersburg or at Beijing and Brussels. Meanwhile, he projected a *Ciudad Lineal* of some eighty kilometres in Madrid. Although he only managed to realize five of them, the principle behind the project was that, if the need to expand the city presented itself, adaptation was possible. Wagner equally hoped that transportation networks in Vienna could keep developing. He took into account probable changes in the modes of transport, as well as the development of new urban centres. Therefore, the network had to be adaptable in two ways: with regard to the technology and with regard to the urban structure.

Taking into account the particular nature of the electricity network, Insull elaborated a real theory on the adaptation of the network. He advocated that the network should be adjusted to different temporal scales. He wanted an almost instantaneous adaptation of supply to demand: this was the work of the 'dispatcher' for which Insull designed a regulating system. He also included estimated necessary adaptations by extrapolating statistical series: the network had to respond to the demand of a given day in the year, based on the experience of the previous year, the weather forecasts, and so on. On the long term, the network should be able to adapt to the changing nature of the demand, beginning with the public demand (e.g. lighting), followed by the industrial and later the domestic demand. Besides this temporal adaptation of the network, the network can be spatially adapted by extension and diversification. For that matter, the spatial adaptability largely conditions the temporal adaptability. Following Insull's lead, many network operators based their work on the same principles. The operation of Chantenay also aimed at making the Nantes' water supply system adaptable. Situating the reservoir in Chantenay, the highest point of the Nantes agglomeration, the network could, in the long term, cover the demand of new expansions and new connections without the need of a rigid plan.

The development of electrical networks, car traffic and more recently telecommunications on a large scale, convinced authors as Hart and Virilio that these networks should be able to adapt very rapidly. Hart (quoted by Hughes, 1987), but also Ford, considered the network as a possibility to interconnect small communities, both existing ones and new ones. According to Virilio (1991), the speeds reached at present will be overtaken by the arrival of communication systems that are based on speeds that are close to the speed of light. Still higher speeds would turn the world upside down. The object becomes less important than its trajectory, which becomes in itself instantaneous. Before, the territory, which consisted of geographical places, was discovered and perceived through movement – for example in neighbourhoods and towns. Now, the territory would be located around the immobile individual. The latter perceives the world not any more through physical mobility, but through interpreting a large amount of data that he gets by means of ICTs. The city, if it can still be called a city, is a space of instantaneous choice, always modifiable, which through its virtual multiplicity defines an extremely evolving system.

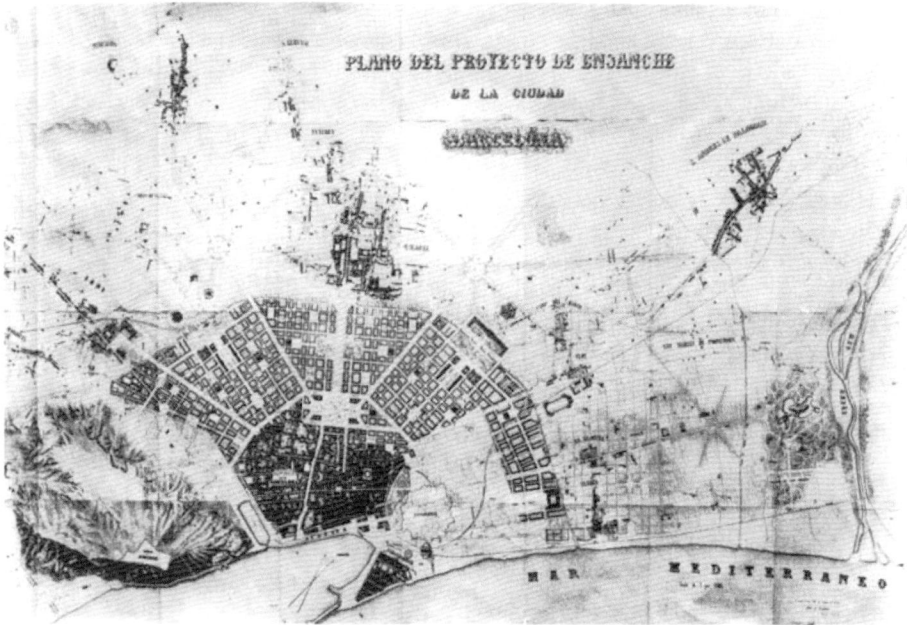

Illustration 1.8   **Plan for the expansion of Barcelona by Antonio Rovira y Trias, 1859.**
Source: Cerdà ((1867) 1979: 20)

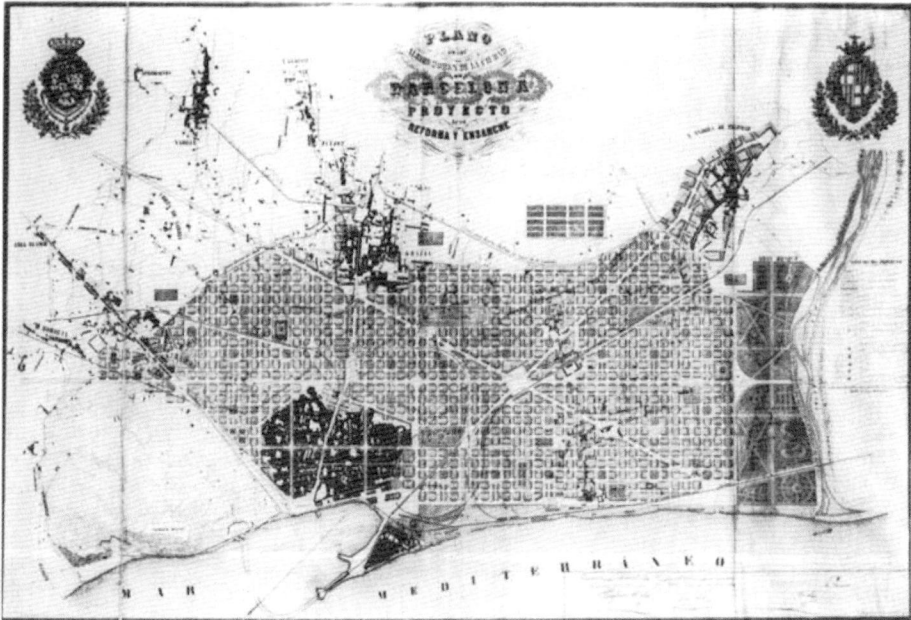

Illustration 1.9   **Plan for the expansion of Barcelona by Ildefonso Cerdà, 1858.**
Source: Cerdà ((1867) 1979: 21)

In the end, the network's ability to adapt seems to refer to the possibilities of transforming the nature or the structure of the connections. In the short term, the network should aim at maximal utilization of all possible links at each moment. This can be compared to the way the telephone book works: at each arbitrary moment, anyone can look for all possible telephone numbers. In the long term, the network must also be able to adapt to major morphological changes, by the creation of new supports for the new links and by the projection of new points likely to be connected. To extend the analogy with the telephone book, it is essential that each year the updated numbers and/or addresses of existing subscribers appear in the book. But the phone book must also contain the names and the numbers of new subscribers, the 'new points' that are linked by the network.

In the history of urbanism, two personalities best illustrate this modern vision of networks, characterized by a new topology, by kinetics and adaptability in relation to the city. Ildefonso Cerdà and Frank Lloyd Wright granted networks, at different times but in the same way, a deciding role in the city. They had a comprehensive perception of urbanism, integrating their work with the technical networks available during their time. They deserve to be presented in some detail, since their thoughts have been underestimated, misunderstood or pushed aside by the dominating schools of thought in urban planning and design.

Cerdà: urbanization and networks

In 1854, a *coup d'état* in Spain brought a liberal progressive government to power. The city of Barcelona took advantage of the occasion to revive an ancient claim: the demolition of the city walls of Philip V. The wall formed a tight circle around the city, preventing its expansion and producing the densification of the habitat, very profitable for the property owning bourgeoisie, but unbearable for the working

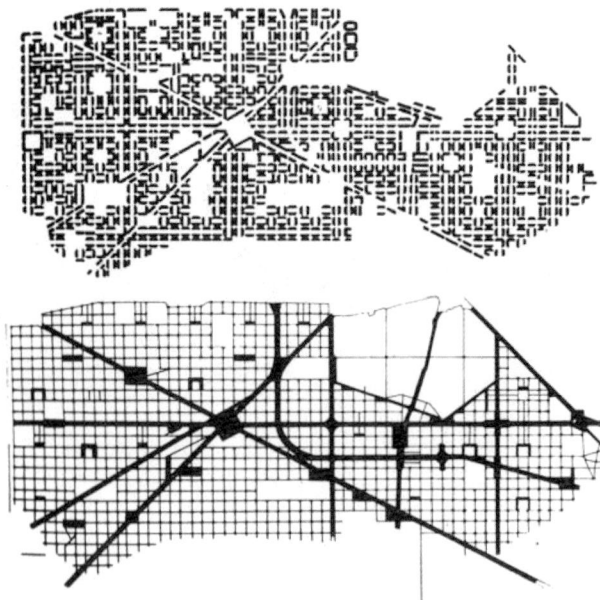

Illustration 1.10 **Building mass and circulation space in the plan of Cerdà.**
Source: Cerdà ((1867) 1979: 27)

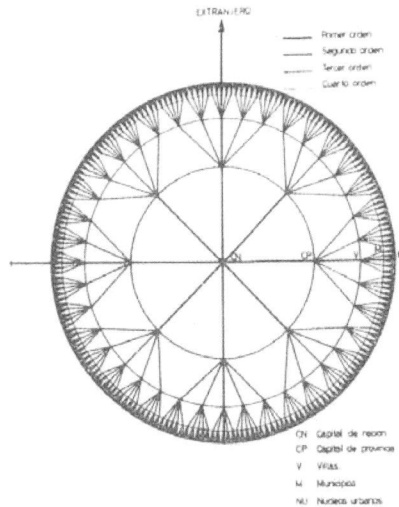

Illustration 1.11   **Scheme of the universal *vialidad* within a nation-state.**
Source: Cerdà ((1867) 1979: 124)

classes. When the walls were demolished, an expansion plan became necessary. The municipality launched a competition won by the architect Rovira, who proposed a classic plan to expand the old city (illustration 1.8). Meanwhile, in Madrid, the minister for public works appointed another architect, working at that time as engineer in the section of *Bridges and Roads*, to make a topographical survey of the zones around the Catalan city recently made available for urbanization. Ildefonso Cerdà extended his topographical work by establishing a expansion plan, the *Ensanche*, a plan that Barcelona was forced to adopt instead of Rovira's, under pressure of the central authority in Madrid. While the Rovira project consisted basically of drawings, Cerdà's work was accompanied by an enormous report in three volumes, entitled *Teoria General de la Urbanizacion* (General Theory of Urbanism), which supported his proposal (Choay, 1979; Cerdà, 1867) (illustration 1.9).

Cerdà's theory starts by a reconstruction of the entire history of the human habitat. It considers the city the necessary combination of shelter and circulation (illustration 1.10). This fundamental couple, representative of human nature (would one not say 'human territoriality' today?), stems from the distinction movement/dwelling. This couple can be found on all scales. In the city, the block corresponds to the dwelling, the route to the movement. The city itself is defined as "a gap of habitability in the great system of the universal *vialidad*" (illustration 1.11).

For Cerdà, this concept of *vialidad* – difficult to translate from Spanish – even expresses an absolute imperative: the possibility of constant and unlimited movement, of rapid, direct flows without bounds. Within this logic, the network is not the main thing, but it has considerable importance as the most convenient method of organizing urban roads to make the city accessible, to satisfy the imperative of *vialidad*.

The street system included a physical and material aspect that Cerdà, as a good topographer, did not neglect. But the relevance of his contribution is not in his treatment of physical and material aspects of the street system. It is in the idea of 'communicativity' [4]: to give all places and all residents a possibility to link up with the *vialidad*. The *gran vialidad*, which Cerdà considers as universal, must be able to penetrate the city everywhere. The city should be 'permeable', 'through all points of its periphery'. The *gran vialidad* carries the benefits of communication to the entire population, up to the most distant points. The mobility network must be extended to all residences, workplaces, warehouses and other areas of urban economic activity. Each urban road is part of the universal 'communicativity' and should, therefore, have numerous 'nodes' that relate it to other roads. This is why, specifies Cerdà, "each system or combination of roads is called a road network".

Particularly the network's topology is studied by the author of the *General Theory of Urbanism*. The hierarchy of roads, the multiplication of junctions, aims at facilitating what our modern specialists call 'general accessibility'.

Today, as for Cerdà, "all is movement, all is expansion, all is communicativity"; the network as he conceives it has an open character. It makes it possible to reach everything that the city's inhabitant can gain from contact with others around the world, almost to infinity. For this reason, Cerdà calls the main routes that assume this function, *transcendentales*. It becomes clear that everything that hinders this linking up with the entire population, which is a 'necessary, indispensable part of life and essential for each locality', must be rejected. Cerdà, therefore, condemns with great firmness all possible obstacles. 'The system of city walls, ditches and barriers' [5], considered until now a necessity, harms the communication of the *urbe* with the universal *vialidad*. "Problematic circulation at doors and gates, and the limitation of the period they are open severely undermines the interests of contemporary man, who relies on all hours of the day and night to do business. Since the electric telegraph has been made available to all, time is no longer measured in days and hours, but in minutes and seconds. Along with the telegraph, the trains respond to the same demands, except during the few hours of the night when they don't run."

The topological vision of the network introduced by Cerdà contains a kinetic dimension as well. A new time has come for urban life: a time of networks, of railways, and of the telegraph, of which the author of *The General Theory of Urbanism* has already grasped the importance, but also of future networks capable of ensuring rapid communication. "The man in the street quickly tries to find the object he's after." Apart from that, Cerdà includes in the road system everything that the citizens require: drinking water supply, solid and liquid waste disposal, the transport of goods, of energy, of information, and so on. Vaults, pipes and cables, of different dimensions, situated at varied levels beneath the streets, allow for the city being fed with electricity and with different kinds of fluids.

The adaptive dimension of the network is also taken into account by Cerdà, even though he does not deal with it explicitly. The adaptability of the network in the long term is evident from his commitment to universal *vialidad*. All that changes outside the city (if outside is still an appropriate notion) necessarily participates in the overall communication system, which implies adapting the network. This is precisely what Cerdà proposes to do, starting with the failing road network of old cities. The adaptability in the short term can be demonstrated by the way in which Cerdà deals with the issue of junctions. These network nodes, which serve the topological redistribution of movement, were subjected to a meticulous analysis (illustration 1.12). One should take into account all kinds of movements, all the possible connections that there are to choose from, and, with this objective in mind, one should try to design the most flexible junctions possible. "The different ways of transportation, the diversity of directions, of speeds, of destinations, this huge multitude of things so different, so heterogeneous, that use the road, require, in public interest, solutions suited to the way each of the elements functions, corresponding to the nature of each movement." This approach is the opposite of the blind channelling of traffic flows advocated later by progressive urbanism.

In laying out junctions, one must reconcile habitability and viability. This task obviously presented Cerdà with problems. He devotes numerous pages to these problems in the *Teoria*. But he doesn't quit the task of organizing a true circulation network, that much is he convinced that only this network could make his contemporaries enter the system of universal communication.

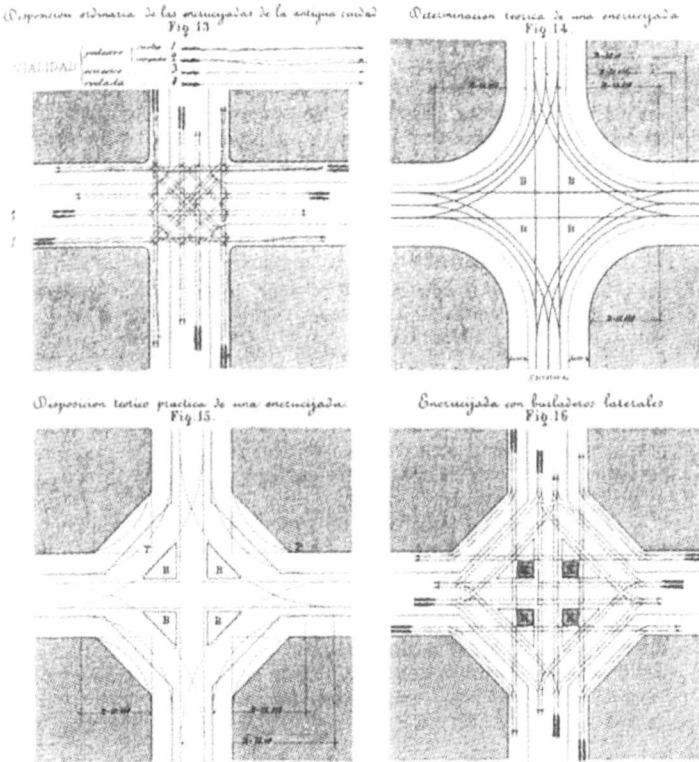

Illustration 1.12   Some of Cerdà's studies for junctions. Source: Cerdà ((1867) 1979: 155)

Cerdà's work is particularly interesting because it introduces an almost modern network concept early in the history of urbanism. His foresight is astonishing. What forces inspired Cerdà in his quest for the new network? An explanation can be found in Cerdà's militant involvement in social issues. He was concerned with social problems to the extent that he himself researched the living conditions of workers in Barcelona. He was enraged by a living situation that he thought stemmed from the inability of the Catalan city – enclosed as it was by its city walls – to adapt to contemporary life and to new methods of transport and communication that he knew (e.g. railways and telegraphs) or imagined (e.g. electric tramways). He was convinced that all of this could change and had to change. He decided to place himself in the service of this cause, a cause to which he devoted his entire life. This (almost missionary) involvement with urban matters has *vialidad* as its ultimate goal, universal and transcendental, in Cerdà's own words. To achieve this goal the network is the project to be realized. The network will prevent a divorce between the city and modernity, and will give back the citizen his humanity, his urbanity.

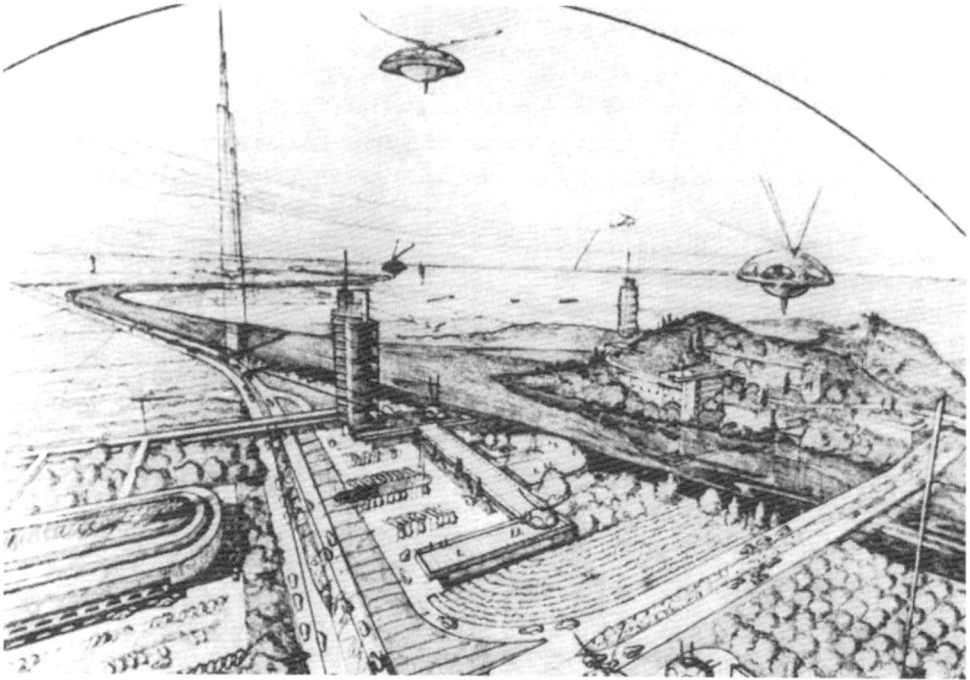

Illustration 1.13   **Bird's eye view of *Broadacre City*, including road and telecommunication networks.**
Source: Wright (1958)

F.L. Wright: Broadacre City

Broadacre City is literally a utopian landownership vision (illustration 1.13). Like Ildefonso Cerdà, Ebenezer Howard and Arturo Soria y Mata, Frank Lloyd Wright attempted to eliminate the bad consequences of landownership in cities, in particular the far too high density of cities. *Broadacre City* allowed the urban population to have at least an acre[6] per person at their disposal. Wright calculated that in 1939 the United States had ample geographical space to apply this principle: one single State, Texas, was enough to accommodate – according to *Broadacre's* norms – the entire American population. *Broadacre* disperses, practically unlimited, urban population and industry: family houses, factories, offices and farms are totally decentralized and located in such a way that everyone has the good things of nature at one's disposal and can benefit from them, and that everyone can enjoy a maximal freedom to act as one pleases. Wright's utopia is not that of Étienne Cabet's (see Choay, 1965). He does not propose the retreat of the urban population to self-sufficient rural communities. A return to nature, in the twentieth century, cannot be imagined without the preservation and development of the communication systems that are a necessity of modern urban society. Neither did Wright advocate the pursuit of production increase, popular in progressive urbanism circles at that time. On the contrary, the author of *Broadacre* rejected this trend and positioned himself in the larger perspective of general social communication.

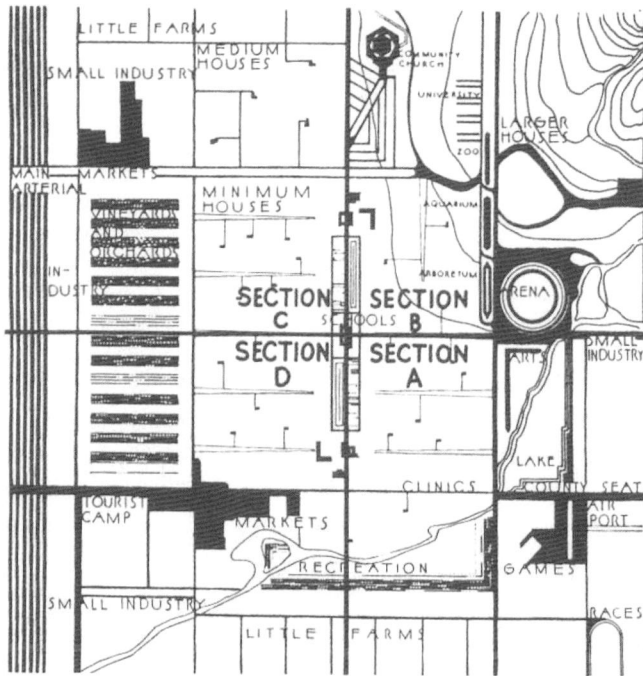

Illustration 1.14   Plan of *Broadacre City.* Source: Wright (1945)

The isolation of inhabitants and of activities in *Broadacre* can be lifted at any moment. In this respect, Françoise Choay made a good analysis of the significance of *Broadacre*. "Everyone is connected to the collective space; all directions are equally open for exploration" (Choay, 1965).

The metaphor that drove Wright's quest in this way, appeared in his writings: "the monster displays itself in space (...) thousands of acres of a cellular fabric displayed (...) a network of veins and arteries that radiate in obscurity (...) moving down there with a threatening and deafening rumbling (...) non-stop activity to the needs of which all conform (...) this fabric connected and reconnected and interconnected with an efficient and complete nervous system (...) with delicate fibres to feel the pulse of its own organism which reacts in a dynamic impulse, and in all that circulates, the electric stream of human life (Wright, 1953)". Ubiquitous connection, secure vital flows, permanent regulation; the biological images that Wright uses reflect the three dimensions of the modern network: topology, kinetics, adaptivity. *Broadacre City* is created, in the first place, by an unlimited road network. It is a grid of highways that cross each other, making any agricultural, industrial or residential unit accessible by car (illustration 1.14). One should fully understand the new nature of this accessibility. Robert Fishman has shown that *Broadacre City* is not an ordinary suburb (Fishman, 1977). Wright's critics have failed to understand that he has explored the limits of suburbia. The extension of highways that start out of the city centre, will lead to an increasingly diminishing accessibility and an ever-growing dependence on the periphery.

For Wright, the role of the automobile in modern society implies radical decentralization, dissolving the traditional borders that separate the city from the countryside. The new city has neither centre nor periphery. The place for social contacts is not the centre but each unit in as much as it is linked to the others by the highway grid. The cultural and commercial areas are located at each highway crossing, ensuring equal accessibility to all, and independent of its position in the grid. The American *Central Business District* loses its attraction power. The highway nodes are henceforth potential sites for just as many business centres; but the multidirectional choice offered by the network prevents nodes from becoming predominant. *Broadacre City* is the city of 'everywhere and nowhere', a utopia in a new meaning of the term. Contrary to Howard, who saw in transport a way to alleviate and improve circulation in a traditional fabric, Wright and Soria y Mata, foresaw that the new modes of transport, especially the car, would generate a completely different fabric that would expand towards an unlimited space.

"The mechanical movement characteristic for the automobile absolutely differs from that of man who moves on foot or uses animal traction. This new standard should be applied to a general concept of space for the planning of the new city and its new residences." (Wright, 1958)

The new standard no longer measures distances, but time, in minutes and seconds.

"Let's imagine these functional units integrating one with another in a way that each citizen can, according to his choice, have at his disposal all forms of production, distribution, transformation and leisure, in a radius of ten to forty minutes from his residence. And that he can have all this in no time at all, thanks to his car, his personal plane or public transport." (Wright, 1953)

Wright not only reasoned according to the potentials of the automobile. He also assigned a special role to the service station. As a first step towards the decentralization of the city, the service station becomes a node in the new network city. But the airports and air transport, the train stations and railroads, the ports and the steamers fully participate in the functioning and in the symbolism of *Broadacre City*. All modern means of transportation and all forms of transmission are activated to make *Broadacre* a city of communication. In his last writings, Wright was very aware of the tremendous expansion of transportation and communication means, also outside the traditional city: "Today, I do not know any small farmer who does not possess a car, or even two... anyone without a telephone. They all have radios." (ibid.) People, goods and information must circulate or be accessible according to a system of kinetics and topology that can be, in Wright's words, summarized in, 'in an instant and everywhere'.

As for the adaptivity of the system, obviously several gradations can be distinguished. The communication network is conceived to allow the inhabitants to choose destinations and connections. The highway grid, the airports and the telephone network are only supportive in making each person's 'connections' possible. In the long term, the possibility of expanding the networks while preserving equivalent potentials for additions, ensures adaptation to varied new developments.

Like Cerdà, Wright elaborated a scheme that positions networks in the organization of a city. The significance that Wright gave to these networks surely precedes the way in which the citizens at the end of the twentieth century take networks for granted. However, many failed to understand the message of the author of *Broadacre City*. In the United States, he was blamed for willing to spread a form of suburbanization of which urbanists were starting to be aware of its drawbacks. In Europe, for those few who knew of his work on urban planning, he is considered a supporter of the anti-urbanism of Jefferson. It is true that *Broadacre City* allowed for residential neighbourhoods in a natural environment, but Wright's utopia is definitely urban. He advocated spreading but simultaneously he connected by means of networks. Wright never suggested the return to nature-based communities, so convinced was he that this type of life was outdated. *Broadacre* proposed an urban way of life. Wright simply considered, in 1923, that "The big city is no longer modern ... at the age of electric transmission, of the automobile and of the telephone, the urban concentration becomes a congestion without reason: it's a curse." (Wright, 1923)

It has also been said that the *American way of life* powerfully effected Wright's mind (Randle, 1985), which is undeniably true. This does not justify though why, when in Europe networks are everyone's business, we continue to refuse to acknowledge Wright's way of thinking about urbanism. It is even less acceptable that we condemn it in the way L. Benevolo does, who only attaches importance to *Broadacre* as an inspiring allegory, whereas "considered [as] a concrete programme, *Broadacre* can only lead to confusion and to sustaining the dream of an escape to nature, diametrically opposed to the tasks of modern urbanism." (Benevolo, 1979)

Epilogue

Wright, Cerdà and many others deserve credit for observing and predicting the emergence of networks, at a time when their development took off. Moreover, some of these urbanists have understood, at least in part, the significance networks would carry for urban society. It is now time to listen to their message.

Today, the emergence of networks is a fact. The car is already a century old and has spread all over the world in an astonishing manner: a billion vehicles give people access to the global network. Electricity is an indispensable element of our daily life. The network city is neither fictional nor utopian: it is a reality. Urban planning and design cannot base its doctrines and its practices on ways of thought that neglect or reject this reality.

Stuck on an approach that gives privilege to zoning as a way to fight urban anarchy and real estate speculation, in urban planning and design the network approach has been ignored for over a century. One has hardly listened to those who, from Cerdà to Wright and from Soria y Mata to Wagner, advocated a network-oriented approach to the same end. It is about time for the networked cities of today and tomorrow to overcome this cautious attitude and to admit that a new track should be followed, i.e. that of networks.

Notes

Note 1   Remarkably, none of the writings of the authors in question appears in the anthology presented by Françoise Choay in 1965 entitled: *L'Urbanisme, Utopies et Réalités, Une Anthologie*. This confirms that the urbanism establishment did not take them seriously. It is useful, however, to consult the remarkable work later published by the same author on urbanism of the nineteenth century (Choay, 1969), especially in respect to Haussmann, Cerdà and Soria y Mata (and also Hénard).

Note 2   The idea of the *Linear City* has inspired several urban planners and designers. Soria y Mata's approach, for whom the linear design is a condition in a reticular topology, is nevertheless very specific. It can not be compared with that of Miliutin whose linear city is constructed according to the principle of the assembly line and subjected to the objectives of industrial production (Miliutin, 1974).

Note 3   Radial-centrism is a spatial organization model found in European cities. The radial-centric model comprises a centre that polarizes the urban space and axes that converge towards the centre, like the spokes of a wheel, which direct mobility flows.

Note 4   *Communicatividad* is the term Cerdà uses.

Note 5   Including barriers built for fiscal reasons. Cerdà blames them for making the city impermeable to universal communication.

Note 6   An acre represents about a half hectare.

"In the *Broadacre* plans ... Wright foresaw what I take to be the essential element in the structure of the new city. It is a city based on time rather than space. Even the largest of the old 'big cities' had a firm identity in space. It has a center which was the basic point of orientation – the Loop, Broadway and 42nd Street, and so on – and a boundary . Starting from the center, sooner or later one reached the end of the developed area. In the new city, however, there is no single center. Instead, as Wright suggests, each family home becomes the central point for its members. They create their own 'cities' out of the destinations they can reach (usually travelling by car) in a reasonable length of time. Indeed, we customarily conceive of the new city in terms of time rather than distance. A supermarket is not four miles away but ten minutes away in one direction, a mall thirty minutes in another direction, and a job forty minutes by yet another route. The pattern formed by these destinations represents the city for that particular family of individual. The more varied the destinations one chooses to reach or is able to reach, the richer and more diverse is one's personal 'city'."

From: Metropolis Unbound: The New City of the Twentieth Century *by Robert Fishman, in* Flux, N° 1, 1990

2   Urban Planning in the Network Age: Theoretical Pointers*

Redefining the position of urban planning in relation to networks is no easy matter, given the major stumbling blocks created by decades of misconceptions and specialization. It calls for comprehensive and solid reconstruction. Pioneering thinkers like Soria y Mata or Frank Lloyd Wright remain as relevant today as ever. But the first step is to determine the scope of urban planning in a realm now dominated by networks. Does the urban planner have a specific role to play here? With what limits? And what means? And why does the traditional conduit network model fail to live up to the demands of modern urban development? This is neither the time nor place for rushing to judgement or jumping to conclusions. A theoretical detour is needed, including an attempt at defining the nature of a network, in order to establish the true place of all concerned. Next, we shall present the tools and a few examples of current approaches. Some experience has been gained in this area. The examples we shall be looking at may lack the purity of theoretical analysis, but they are far enough removed from conventional wisdom to illustrate the network approach.

Virtual networks, real networks

Fundamental to the network concept is the need to acknowledge an underlying, spatio-temporal, diversity. One must be willing, as Raffestin (1980) puts it, to identify 'points' that are more than mere geometrical abstractions, with the social and geographic substance to make them the 'manifestation of any individual or collective ego'. Those points can be the villages, towns, capital cities or metropolitan areas with which geographers have long been familiar; or the homes and housing units better known to urban planners. But there is no reason why they should not also include factories, dams and electric power or water purification plants. They amount to what could be described as 'territorial nodalities or points of reference or power', i.e. discontinuities in the spatial or spatio-temporal continuum. Each point – or node – differs from the next in that they pertain to distinct entities, diverse intentions and dissimilar powers.

Such diversity is axiomatic, and no network can exist without it. A fir tree plantation or seedbed cannot be described as a network because it, on the contrary, asserts the identity of the trees or seeds and the places where they are planted. That said, it is easy to see why pioneering theorists like Christaller and Lösch might have adhered to such an idea given that they began by singling out spatial points of differing levels or functions: theoretically diverse and hierarchized hamlets, villages, towns and cities.

Next, one must be ready to recognize the existence of 'projected transactions' based on Raffestin's conception of points. What does this mean exactly? A point is not an abstraction but the 'manifestation of an individual or collective ego', i.e. the place where an actor maps out a future course of action. The point can become the source of an individual or collective desire to forge a relationship – a potential link, involving notions of interaction and communication (Claval, 1981) – with another point, i.e. another actor: what we shall call a projected transaction. In so doing, the actor introduces that other point into

*   Previously published as « Les Réseaux pour un Nouvel Urbanisme: Éléments de Théorie ». In: Dupuy, G., 1991, *L'Urbanisme des Réseaux: Théories et Méthodes.* Paris: Armand-Colin, pp. 107-126. Included with permission.

his, her or its territory, since "a space is turned into a territory by the actor's aims or intentions (...) The actors are not adversaries; they take action and consequently seek to maintain relationships, to perform duties, to influence one another, to monitor, block or green-light one another, and to distance themselves from – or come close to – each other" (Raffestin, 1987). These relationships thrive on the differences between the points; and any given actor can have any number of them.

The points and projects – projected transactions – all evolve over time, developing their own identities in contrast to the others. A transactional project cannot exist without its differences, but those differences may emerge from the relational plans. There is what Amar (1988) describes as a 'recursive definition' of a network, involving two concurrent attributes: the *uniqueness* of the points, and the *stability* of relations between them.

In order to bring the as yet planned transaction to fruition, its architect must have the power to incorporate another point into his/her/its territory, and to establish the desired – projected – relationship in time and space. Theoretically, though, individual actors do not have that power. Imagine I want to link my home up to a spring located some distance away so as to secure my daily supply of pure, fresh, drinking water. The spring belongs to the owner of the land where it flows. How do I persuade him or her to allow me to tap into it? How do I then ensure the reliable delivery of the water to my home, and ensure the spring's long-term purity?

This kind of projected transaction needs to be considered in the light of the idea developed by Cottereau (1969) with respect to the urban planning involved in building the Paris metro system, involving a range of different actors galvanized by projects that not a single one of them had the power to implement on their own. The only way to realize each individual project was through *collective* urban development. Some time ago, the French press ran a story about a Middle Eastern prince granted the right to build a private access road from his second home to the A13 motorway. The reason why it made the papers is probably because it was such a rare case. As a rule, other – collective – actors tend to be the only ones with the capacity to carry out a transactional project under their own steam. But this new brand of actor, which we shall refer to as the *operator*, does not work on behalf of a single individual. It groups together a number of different transactional projects, pooling several requests for interlinkages to be established between various points through a sort of collective delegation of authority. This cluster of projected transactions is what we shall call the *projected transaction network* (PTN).

A PTN has two key characteristic features. Firstly, it falls by definition into the realms of desire and imagination. The actors dream of – and dream up – transactions without necessarily turning their attention to the technical means or even to a codification of the transactions. Nothing can prevent me from dreaming of a direct, instantaneous relationship with others. What is to stop me from imagining that I have a fresh water source within my reach, or that the friend I want to meet is right here, right now? Secondly, PTNs belong to the world of the virtual not the real. What matters most to the actors concerned is the ability to capitalize on the full range of transactional opportunities a PTN might be able to offer. One particular point would need to be linked up to another in order to enable a particular transaction today. But links must also be forged with other points in order to pave the way for transactions that may or may not prove useful tomorrow. More than just a relationship, what is being planned here is a range of potential linkages to be brought into play if ever and whenever the circumstances so require. The history of urban transport networks in Canadian cities illustrates this well. Almost as soon as the first public transport systems were up and running, everybody wanted services that would be comfortable, offering unlimited capacity and running in every direction, at any time of the day and night, at the lowest possible price (Armstrong & Nelles, 1986).

These two characteristic features of the imagined and the virtual tend to make the PTN – known to network planners as a network of 'desire lines' or 'affinity matrices' in the respective fields of urban transport and telecommunications (Curien & Gensollen, 1989) – into what Bouley (1990) calls a 'maximal network' in his exposé of the excessive demands placed on the French railways, demands that they could never hope to meet. The body of individual projected transactions can conceivably pave the way for the emergence of a body of point-to-point links. The actors would each regard their PTN as a *maximal* network: I want to be linked directly to my source of drinking water, but my next-door and, indeed, my other neighbours each wanted to be linked to theirs as well; and what is more, I – and they – would also like a direct link to all my/their neighbours as a back-up in the event of a cut in our supply. Each and every actor, if given the choice, would 'opt for the maximal network of the most direct links possible' (Raffestin, 1980).

This 'maximality', however, has its limits. Territories are not systematically defined with a view to capitalizing on the potential for relations, communication and movement, i.e. for 'transactions' between 'points'. The transactional territoriality model may well appear increasingly prominent in our modern-day societies, but it has not put an end to formerly predominant – and at times still quite robust – forms of spatio-temporal delineation: frontiers, boundaries, grids and chronologies that have nothing to do with the priorities of directness and speed. As a matter of fact, those older forms of territoriality continue to hold PTNs and contemporary technological potentialities in check, as seen in the case of the Eurovision broadcasting network being hampered by national sovereignties (see Chapter 8). The actors' plans, even in the realms of the imagined and the virtual, do not provide for every possible link that can be forged instantly with every single point. Long-standing or newly emerging boundaries preclude some points, timescales and tempos, thus creating 'insider/outsider' dividing lines that the transactions would never stand a chance of crossing.

This results in the scaling down of the actual transactions and their range of possibilities, and makes it necessary to tone down the term 'maximal' for a PTN. A *maximal* network is not an infinite network; and as the PTNs develop in modern societies they tend to be characterized, if anything, by a maximalist tendency. This kind of network can be called a *virtual network* (de Radkowski, 2002).

Finally, a PTN is by design a territorial network. As the collective project of a body of actors, it reflects the territoriality that an operator is expected to produce. In the face of the various technical, economic and political restraints involved, however, the operator has to strike a balance between the imagined, 'maximal', virtual network, the available means and the real-life conditions on the ground (Raffestin, 1987). This compromise serves to crystallize what the French call the 'technical' network, i.e. the actual infrastructure network.

Let us illustrate the point with two examples. In the first, the operator may be likened to the public authorities in that it advances a political rationale; and in the second, the operator is a company whose economic rationale is what holds the PTN in check.

The prominence of the political rationale can be seen in the water supply system of ancient Roman cities, as set out in the writings of Marcus Vitruvius (Bonnin, 1984). Urban consumers never had a direct connection to the drinking water network. The water was first stored in a reservoir then allotted and delivered to three categories of consumers: private homes, public fountains and cisterns, and bathhouses. Each category was granted an equal share. Once the share-out had been decided, the water was channelled into three separate reservoirs. Any surpluses left over from supplies to private homes and bathhouses went into the reservoir for public fountains and cisterns. So there was not only a physical limit to consumption due to the storage capacity, but also a *de facto* prioritization of public uses (fountains and cisterns) not granted to private consumers (homes) or concessionaires (bathhouses). This extremely hard-to-implement conception of a network reflected the clear political will of the authorities to curb inequalities in the use of a scarce and vital commodity whose supply could be highly unreliable.

As for the economic rationale, the operator of a large public transport network may need to strip the PTN of desire lines between urban centres (see illustration 2.1) in order to secure its economic feasibility, as in the case of the nineteenth-century Canadian tramway system (Armstrong & Nelles, 1986).

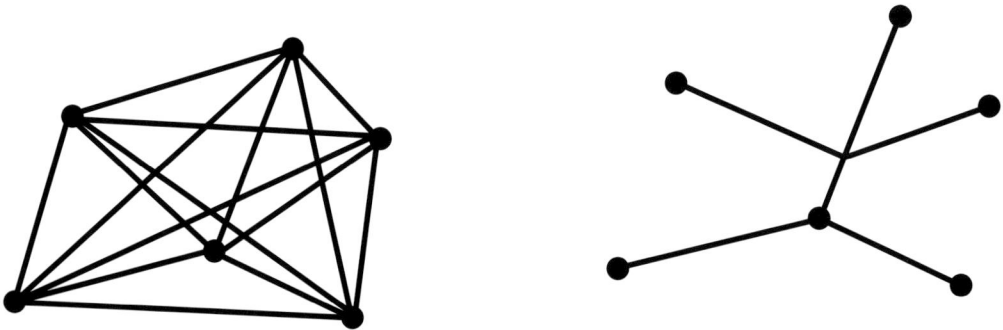

Illustration 2.1   The simplified network (right) serves the same points as the network on the left

Both of the above examples were chosen because the restrictions on the virtual network – and, hence, the PTN – are clearly not of a technical nature. The picture is not so straightforward in the many other cases in which technology creates a somewhat harder to decipher combination of differing constraints (Claval, 1987; Dupuy, 1978). Most modern networks – public transport, water, power, telecommunications and so on – fall into this category. With the urban road systems developed in the 1960s, for example, the original PTN embraced all of the various desire lines representing the journeys of city residents. Then came a complex modelling and planning process that culminated in our, now familiar, modern road system (Dupuy, 1975; see also Chapter 6). The transition from the PTN to the actual infrastructure network can only be understood by pinpointing the many decisions both combined and obscured by the mathematical dimensioning and planning tools used. The resulting impenetrability has led to that transition being attributed to the technical side of the procedure. Which is probably why the French have been so quick to call the infrastructure network a *technical* network – a term that passes muster only so long as one bears in mind that the procedure is never purely technical, but subject also to the above-mentioned economic and political constraints. To avoid any confusion, we shall now refer to it as the *real network*.

A real network is a collectivizing structure that exploits and, at the same time, homogenizes diversity. Initially, the collective project starts out with a variety of different points and a host of projected transactions and, hence, links. For the sake of feasibility, however, an emphasis must be placed on standardization in the rationale of the actor in charge, i.e. the network operator.

What rules serve to guide the operators in their work? We have seen how critical the political or economic criteria can be; and recent history offers some interesting insight into how they go together in modern networks (Jacobson, Klepper & Tarr, 1985; Dupuy & Tarr, 1984; Dupuy, 1978). In actual fact, while the current rules governing network expansion generally tend to stem from efforts to make the most of restrictive circumstances, the influence of the past and the heritage of existing networks continue to play a key role. Sometimes the rules are straightforward. The county urban development services in the Lille area in Northern France, for instance, stipulate that dead-end streets on local housing estates should never be more than 50 metres in length – a measure that grew out of, and continues to be sustained by, the need to tackle the unhealthy blind alleys of the past. The RATP public transport operator's plans for changes to the Parisian bus system limit the distance covered by a single bus line to what it – based on its extensive experience in running that system – regards as the ideal number of kilometres. The Parisian urban heating company adheres to the principle that it will connect a new subscriber applying for P megawatts capacity and located at a maximum distance of D metres from the network only if $P > P_o$ and $D > D_o$, where P_o and D_o represent the thresholds established according to the cost of connection, the prospective user's estimated consumption, the going rates charged by the company, the expenses incurred through investment and so on. Although the economic criterion appears predominant here, the calculations made at each stage have tended to hinge on another set of factors altogether: public service provision, public loan rebates, the ban on selling electricity to prevent cogeneration and increases in the cost of heat production, and so on.

For other networks, the rules are less specific and far more complex. More often than not, though, it is still possible to detect an economic rationale counterbalanced by obligations to provide public services, all combined with some highly tenacious technical imperatives, realities and restrictions.

What becomes of the projected transactions in the constitution of a real network? While the operator cannot avoid having to collectivize and standardize individual projects in order to achieve its goals, those projects do not necessarily end up being completely watered down or eroded. Standardization is bound to have its limits, i.e. in the power of the operators compelled to yield at times to the demands of the occasional powerful actor seeking to ensure that the network layout works to the advantage of their own transactional projects. Other projects, however, cannot be taken into account. Some points, despite having figured in the virtual network, will be sidelined from the real network.

The water company in charge of implementing my plans for a connection to the fresh water source will build a network to serve hundreds of my fellow residents. Understandably, the end result is not the kind of network we each of us had in mind. It is a more of tree network starting at the source and lacking any direct links between the various residents. Some interlinkages may be introduced in order to ensure continued delivery in the event of a broken pipeline, for instance, but the company refuses on economic grounds to supply applicants located too far away. On the other hand, the network is extended to other domestic or industrial users regarded as potentially large-scale consumers.

When the original spring proves unable to meet the additional demand, the network ends up having to draw water from the river and to combine the two sources according to seasonal fluctuations in their availability. The water must be treated to comply with sanitation restrictions, because of the time spent in the pipeline; and pressure levels, for instance, need standardizing in order to keep the network running properly. In the course of this transition from a virtual PTN to a real infrastructure network, the actors have nonetheless managed to ensure that the latter upholds some aspects of the former: regular supply, water quality, key consumers served regardless of distance, cut-price rates, and so on. Meanwhile, a closer look at the real networks reveals how some of the points have managed to influence the overall design: industrial consumers have had a relatively significant say in the layout of the EDF French electricity company's network; the extremely intricate web of RATP bus lines in the suburbs of Paris stems, by and large, from almost two hundred years of changes to the original lines as a result of the various municipal authorities demanding that they serve a particular area or take a particular detour; and drinking water systems in various cities of France have been expanded and operated in such a way as to meet particular sets of needs.

Infrastructure networks, therefore, are never fixed and unchangeable. Adjustments can be made when a powerful actor so demands. That said, there are limits to the changes. A collective actor's infrastructure network often seems complete and set in stone because it is the end product of a hard-negotiated compromise on which the operator would be ill-advised to backtrack in a hurry. The network secretes its own organizational procedures. It standardizes in order to function to the best of its ability on a collective basis with the greatest possible long-term stability (Ribeill, 1986).

It is in the course of this process that the differences become apparent between the virtual network and the real network. The fact is that the virtual, imaginary, PTN – an eminently open-ended collection of spatio-temporally heterogeneous and, in comparison to the more technical infrastructure network, ill-assorted projects – should provide for a host of direct opportunities, for spatio-temporal availability, and for every kind of link needed to meet the varied and changing aims of the actors. As mentioned earlier, it is by design a territorial network. But it is not a model with which the real network generally tends to comply.

On the contrary, real networks seem sometimes to strive to create their own territory, with the operators seeking to secure spatio-temporal control based on the lines and nodes of 'their' networks. But "it is the networks that ensure control over – and within – a space [and] every network is a reflection of the power of the dominant actor or actors" (Raffestin, 1987). The delegation of power definitely affects network territoriality during the transition from the virtual to the real network. There is a difference – and the potential for conflict – between the territoriality of the virtual network and that which the real network is likely to establish, via its operator, to the benefit of the leading actor or actors involved in the compromise inherent to its establishment and management. So the divergence between virtual and real networks generates tensions leading to changes concerning the points, the transactions and the operator. Alongside the recursive definition of points and relationships seen earlier, that divergence acts as a mainspring of the network's future development. The various processes involved can be represented as in illustration 2.2.

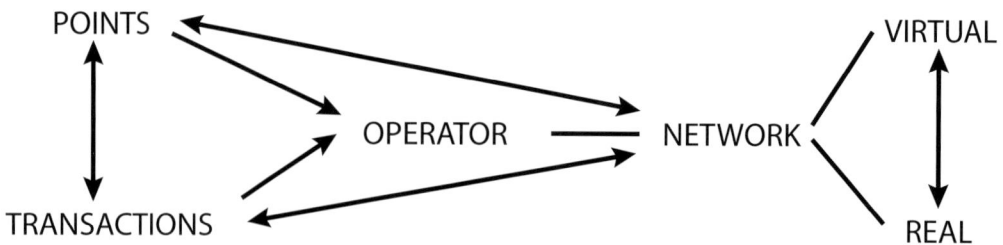

Illustration 2.2   Definition of an evolving network

Is the city in the hands of the network operators?

If we now turn our attention to 'localized' actors – individuals, households or industrial establishments – we see the divergence between the virtual and the real network in another light. There are times when not every transactional project is assured by the real network actually set in place. Each operator has specialized its network. Yet one mode of transport, for instance, cannot necessarily replace another; and a telecommunications network may help launch a transaction but not bring it to fruition. What is more, a real network always falls short of the original aims in terms of the desired relationships. Individual actors genuinely determined to see their projects implemented are therefore going to have to offset the shortcomings. But how? First and foremost by using their organizational powers to supplement what they are offered by the real networks.

The mechanics involved in this are quite complex. Fishman (1977) provides some outstanding insight. Having long studied the work of Frank Lloyd Wright, he came to regard *Broadacre City* as more of a prophecy than an allegorical utopia. *Broadacre*, in his view already exists today and the bulk of the American population is living there. It is the fruit not of urban planning but of millions of economic actors – families – choosing to relocate their activities, their living spaces and homes, and to reorganize it all into networks. City centres have become almost meaningless. It is no longer a matter of suburbanization, which implies that a suburb maintains a distant yet strong reliance on the centre. The new city, in the United States at least, is something else altogether. In the *Broadacre* model the true centre is located not in some central business district but in individual residential or economic units, which each piece together their own individual cities with themselves at the centre. This unique form of urban development involves the various actors using their albeit limited organizational powers to make all of their projected transactions reality in the shape of networks. They cannot, of course, produce the large-scale infrastructure and the broad-based community services provided by the operators – which can be described as *level-one* operators. They are just the users or rather 'stakeholders'. But it is up to them to use what they are offered as a basis upon which to forge, by every means within their power, relationships that come as close as possible to the true nature of the virtual network. Fishman (1990) notes how this results in the construction of three sets of what can be described as *level-two* networks:

- *Production networks*: more or less akin to company logistics networks of suppliers, subcontractors, customers, and so on, together with an additional layer of relations with the labour market, and all of the linkages required for a company's informational needs (Bressand, Distler & Nicolaidis,1989);

- *Consumption networks*: what Fishman (1990) calls the *mallopolis* of shopping centres, distribution channels, brands and franchises – together with leisure facilities – that increasingly enable consumers to see a product in one place, to check out the price in another and to make their purchase in a third, bearing in mind that we are talking about the same product and brand;

- *Personal networks*: made up of all of the points crucial to one's personal life, including close family and parents' friends, for example, together, in the case of households with children, with crèches, schools and various children's activities located in various places.

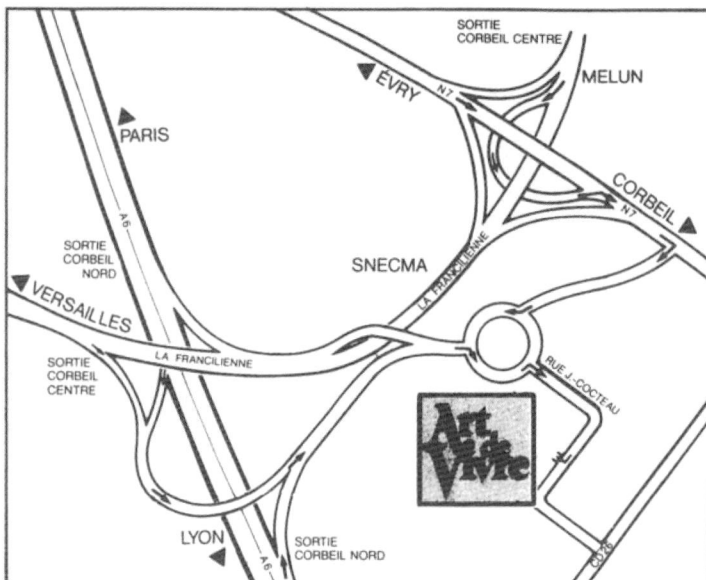

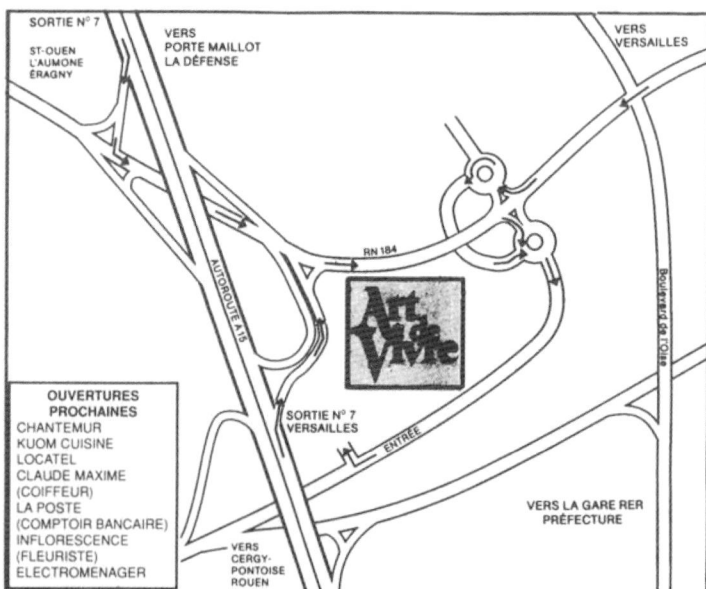

Illustration 2.3   French-style *mallopolis*. The major retailers adhere to a spatial rationale that has seen their consumption networks based increasingly on the road infrastructure systems.
Source: France-Soir, special Art de Vivre advertising section from the 1980s

Urban Networks – Network Urbanism

Each of these three sets of networks has its own spatial rationale. Neighbourhood primary schools are located in places within walking distance for the school-age population. Offices are built at the nodes of the road or public transport network. Shopping centre sites are selected according to road networks and customer catchment areas (illustration 2.3).

Each urban household, using every means of communication provided by a *level-one* operator, must, according to Fishman (1990), "make the necessary connections among the three [*level-two*] networks on [its] own in such a way as to draw that complex pattern of multidirectional journeys that constitute each person's city" (see illustration 2.4). Furthermore, aside from having neither a centre nor outskirts, the new city has no fixed boundaries or any clear dividing lines between the areas where people work, live and shop. Yet it still boasts its own distinctive structure that staves off the chaos into which some are keen to see it descend. This can be described as a *level-three* network structure.

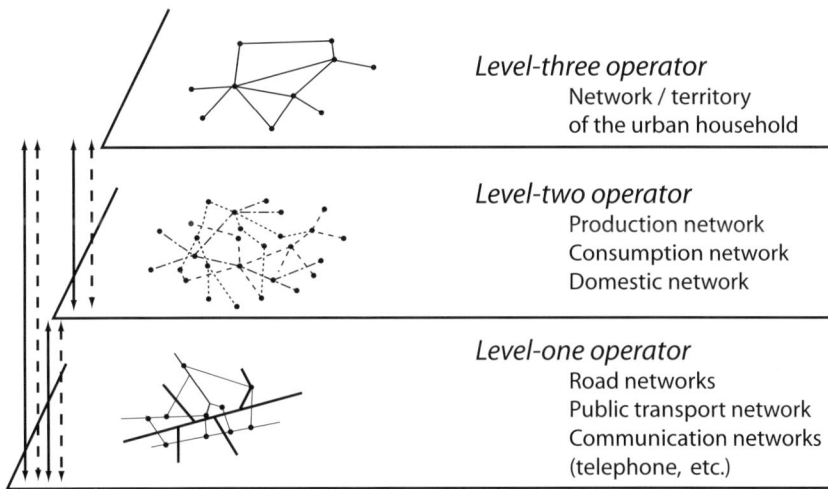

Level-three operator
  Network / territory
  of the urban household

Level-two operator
  Production network
  Consumption network
  Domestic network

Level-one operator
  Road networks
  Public transport network
  Communication networks
  (telephone, etc.)

Illustration 2.4   The three *levels* of network operators (re)organizing urban space

Even though Fishman's theoretical vision may play down the continuing influence of city centres, especially in Europe – although to some extent in the United States too (Goldfield, 1988) – it sheds valuable light on the interconnecting roles of *level-one*, *level-two* and *level-three* network operators in contemporary urban policy. Interestingly, he comes close to the thinking of such precursors as Giovannoni (1931), and concurs with the comments of Moles (1987) on the quality of life in the so-called wired city, which is underpinned increasingly by the 'system of connections between individual social units and the network sources'. Ultimately, this particular version of the network city – intricately designed and the best possible realization of a given actor's virtual network, based on a specific point – is built by the individual actors themselves, playing the role, in a sense, of a *level-three* operator.

How does urban planning fit in with this new approach to the city at a time when the founding principles of the erstwhile, strictly boundary-based, bourgeois city and industrial urbanization are giving way to urban connectivity and reticulation systems? Is it not a strategic challenge for planners to adapt to ICT development and the changing shape of the city (Gibelli, 1988)?

The first question to arise here concerns the legitimacy of urban planning initiatives when the theoretical model presented above would appear to suffice. Operators at the various *levels* described, if properly regulated, seem capable of filling the roles that might otherwise conceivably be allotted to urban planners. Have urban planners lost their place then? Do they have no alternative but to fall back on the increasingly questionable and ineffective doctrines of zoning and delimitation? The answer is that there are perfectly good grounds for urban planning in the network age.

Here are just three of the many strong arguments in its favour.

1. The above theoretical model may not address the matter of areolar territorialities, but they still remain in place, in spite of the networks, at various scales and on legal, historical and cultural grounds. The three-layered network arrangement must come to terms with the territorialities long recognized by urban planning. Urban planning can be the art – and the planner the artisan – of such compromises. Indeed, past and present planners have occasionally played that role on a partial or sector-specific basis. Ildefonso Cerdà (1815-1876) managed to reconcile habitability, i.e. the territory of human settlements, with the *vialidad universal*. Eugène Hénard (1849-1923) strived to expand efficient road networks in a city without challenging its territorial boundaries. The French government's master plans for urban planning and development, introduced by the country's land laws, provide for a toing and froing between desire lines, traffic estimates, road network schemes and urban zoning (Merlin, 1984).

    In the new city in America, urban planners have come up with some interesting combinations of various types of delimitations and networks. In France, official traffic and, moreover, urban journey plans are expected to seek such compromises in conjunction with land use plans (Faivre d'Arcier, Offner & Bieber, 1979; Lassave, 1987); the development of cable television networks has managed to dispense with some boundaries and to promote research into the possibilities for inter-commune development; and the sanitation sector has become the focal point for research aimed at making rainwater drainage networks part of the restructuring and enhancement of some urban spaces (FNAU, 1987).

2. The findings of analysis of *level-one* operators – showing, for example, that having more than one car, telephone line and television set may be regarded as an attempt on the part of a household-operator to adapt its real network to the virtual PTN of the micro-community it represents – can to a large extent be transposed to *level two* and *level three*. The role of network operators at each of the three *levels* has its limits, which can be detrimental to parts, if not the whole, of the urban community.

    Level-one operators inevitably tend to specialize or divide their networks into sectors. A water company or department considers its duty to supply drinking water. But it fails to grasp the communication, information and symbolism-related sides of the water in the tap, even though these are probably significant factors in the mind's eye of urban society (Sansot, 1984). Splitting transport into very separate modes, each with its own distinct technologies and *modi operandi*, further illustrates this limitation, whereas urbanites are more concerned about the overall matter of journeys or connections.

    In the extreme, when a network is divided into sectors whole rafts of social desires or demands that lack a *level-one* operator end up being ignored. One such example can be seen in the arduous task of setting up reliable and accessible remote alarm systems for the elderly and infirm. And the more market-driven increase in the consumption of mineral water has exposed a continuing failure on the part of the water supply network operators to cater to a social demand.

Meanwhile, *level two* is often dominated by one-dimensional economic or administrative rationales. Decisions regarding the site for a shopping centre depend on the road network, and access remains a real problem for people travelling by public transport, by bicycle or by foot. The French education system tends to favour pupils walking or taking the school bus to school, and almost completely ignores the opportunities provided by the telecommunications networks. There are plenty of other examples to show how far *level-two* operators are from "consistently and deliberately devising, organizing or planning [their networks] for social uses"; and their sector-oriented rationales definitely ought to be "reined in and tailored to such uses instead of striving to meet production or management-oriented needs" (Devillers, 1988).

3. The level-one operator model does not preclude the risk of double-dealing. Public service networks appear to have a reassuring public image in France. They seem to guarantee fair and impartial treatment for every citizen and localized actor, and are expected to remain non-political. A tight rein is kept on commercial concerns and the technology is tempered by a worthy sense of humanism. Yet the operator has a considerable amount of power. Even though it may be delegated, some actors are more influential than others. How many operators do not have a dedicated department for dealing with 'special subscribers', 'big accounts' or 'major customers'? Moreover, the tendency to crystallize the network and centre it rigidly on easily manageable technologies and hard-to-renegotiate compromises is utterly inherent to the operator's role.

Some of the many examples of this kind of double-dealing in other countries have been well documented. Soughir (1984) shows how a water conveyance system in Sousse (Tunisia), under cover of a project to introduce adequate technical solutions and tight management procedures, was used to help the tourism industry, to the detriment of market gardeners and ordinary citizens. Whitt (1982) describes how some companies' head offices benefited from the design of the San Francisco Bay Area Rapid Transit system, to the detriment of other, socially more pressing, needs. Anderson (1981) reproduces transcripts of discussions in California highlighting how a seemingly innocuous decision to apply the principles of marginal cost pricing to a local electricity company would affect the most underprivileged members of society. It led to the operator, allegedly for the sake of good management, prioritizing major users over those consuming no more than they had to in order to meet their basic needs – and who would have had their electricity cut off for being unable to pay their bills had the policy been implemented. Similar stories have emerged in the case of telecommunications and broadcasting networks. In Quebec, for instance, subscribers to the cable TV network, which, in the early 1990s, already figured among the basic urban networks, were given the choice of either signing up to a new sports channel and paying a higher price or losing their subscription altogether.

Rouge (1953) had already warned of the "growth and proliferation of all-pervasive networks making huge profits and exposing humanity to equally significant risks because of the increasingly intricate mechanisms they were putting in place"; and hoped that the new field of 'spatial management' would be able to curb those risks.

Bardet (1947), aware of the scale of exchanges and keen to improve the networks and nodes, believed that the technology was too quickly stealing a lead over urban planning, and that it was paralysing decision-making – in the development of the metro or mains drainage systems, for instance – thus rendering it restrictive and open to question. Oddly enough, Hirsch (1990), after heading the project for the construction of Cergy-Pontoise new town, agreed with that view, saying that the experience had taught him to be wary of the inflexibility of infrastructure networks in the face of the necessary changes involved in urban development – and reserving his most scathing criticism on that score for the urban heating system. Bassand and Rossel (1989) condemned the pretentiousness of a 'technocratic flow management strategy' claiming to represent the 'common, general good'. And Neuschwander (1988) feared that the networks would play their increasingly central role in national and regional development according to a 'hierarchical structure' rather than their inherent 'biological structure', stressing that the cumbersome French administrative and political procedures would always sway the operators' rationale in favour of hierarchization.

Communities must not be exposed to the very real dangers of political, economic and technological abuse of a network at operator level.

So the grounds for urban planning in this field are twofold: firstly historical, since bona fide planners have granted networks a key place in their conception of the city from the early days of urbanistic thinking right through to the present day – and the fact that this side of Cerda or Wright's work was obscured by another school of thought in no way detracts from the sharpness and relevance of their analyses, and even their suggestions; and secondly social, since the construction of the networks actually organizing the modern city calls for action to regulate and monitor the operators on the community's behalf. Which leaves the matter of where exactly urban planning should focus its action vis-à-vis the networks. Let us expand on some of the answers suggested above.

First of all, urban planning definitely should play a part in the networks' operating processes. This, of course, is the crux of the matter. Acting in parallel to those processes, on a different place from that of the operators – a field compartmentalized and restrained by the principle of boundary-setting – has been seen to confine urban planning to the fringes of urban life and the modern city. Specialization of the kind adopted in France during and after the struggles for control of the city between urbanists, hygienists and engineers – which left the urbanists in charge of planning and the members of the *Association Générale des Hygiénistes et Technicians Municipaux* in charge of water and sanitation networks (Claude, 1987) – are unacceptable when the city is being reshaped before our very eyes through the convergence of actor-operators working on the networks at the various *levels* described above.

Urban planners cannot intervene at *level three*, where the urban household is, according to Fishman (1990), building its own network city. No matter how tempted they may be to do so, it is too late to turn the clock back.

Functionalist zoning has sought to lock the citizen into an areolar territoriality which, given the widespread coverage and significance of the networks, is no longer feasible. Millions of individuals, families and economic actors have, as Fishman points out, overcome such endeavours by using the networks in their own way, and by developing a new space of connections beyond that of municipal, administrative or urbanistic 'boundaries'. There can be no question of taking back those spatio-temporal development micro-powers with which individuals are creating a new form of urban life.

Basically, what is at issue here is the bona fide participation of the citizen in urban planning. This indulgent trend has, according to some, been blocked by a lack of interest on the part of the general public. But it is hardly surprising to find citizens turning their backs on a participatory role granted on subjects rooted in the conventional orthodoxy of bounded spaces when genuine participation in urban planning lies elsewhere, i.e. in the combination of networks that individual or collective actors and households can each develop for themselves, thereby equipping themselves with spatio-temporal links to the world and the means to create their own city. For this is what allows people to live in one place and to work in another, to drink mineral or tap water rather than well water, to be informed, to talk to friends located anywhere in the city or beyond, and to be a 'stakeholder' with near-instant access to a multifaceted and ubiquitous urban society, all within their own territory established through multidirectional connections at the various network *levels*.

The advent of the networks could be said to have irredeemably deprived professional urban planning of a share of its development power to the benefit of a genuinely individualized form of urban planning, which, although largely unknown and empirical, has nonetheless become a fact of life that must be taken into account in any professionalized, network-centred development action.

Level-two network operations – production, consumption, education and personal relations – correspond quite well with some traditional forms of urban planning. Utilities grids have, in line with an areolar principle, sought to lay down rules governing access to the various services required for what Fishman calls 'personal life'; industrial estates and enterprise zones have endeavoured to gain control over production plant siting; and so-called commercial planning has strived to tie its action in with the spatial rationale of the major retail chains.

Here too, urban planners have clearly lost – or, in some cases, failed to gain – a share of the development power that orthodox delimitation-based planning believed it could grant them. Economic actors – together with other actors in the education sector, e.g. French private schools – have managed to acquire some such power in the real-life city of today. They can put into practice strong rationales specific to their own networks without entering into inflexible plans that appear ill-suited to the situation on the ground. Evidence of this new balance of power can be seen in France in the use of the country's highly flexible mixed development-zone procedures and its special commercial urban planning laws.

Once again, there would appear no way to turn back the clock and to give urban planning direct control over the production, consumption and domestic-sector networks. On the other hand, it is possible for it to intervene at this level. Indeed, it is already doing so, and its action could be enhanced and made more efficient if planners were willing to understand the rationales of the various actors' networks, and to refrain from clinging to untenable orthodox positions. In practical terms, it will mean having to identify the key nodes of those networks. These tend to be interface, intercommunication and interconnection points – such as seaport or airport nodes, multimodal stations/platforms or teleports (Chaline, 1989; Dézert, 1989) – that no single *level-two* operator can really handle on its own. Given their importance to the urban community, urban planning needs to pay special attention to their development, and to regard this as a significant field of action relevant to the new forms of territoriality. The demand exists and has become increasingly apparent. But suitable approaches must be adopted so as to avoid previous mistakes made in the case of multimodal platforms (Dupuy, 1991a). The development of a station, platform, teleport or large shopping centre does not amount primarily to a matter of zoning. It is a question of ensuring sound network connections, of enhancing the respective node vis-à-vis the various networks, and of combining different linear and areolar territorialities. Urban planners will earn recognition for their role if, through working in close cooperation with the operators, they can provide original solutions in this area.

Furthermore, their role in dealings with *level-one* operators is not just possible but necessary. A country like France, among others, has a tradition for public intervention in urban networks. Local authorities sometimes build and manage the network themselves. Or else they can delegate either or both of these functions to private-sector actors, while retaining the right to a say or to regulate them, and so on. Rather than the actual intervention of urban planning, then, what is at issue here is the fact that it has, in the past, been kept away from such matters by extreme sectorization and specialization. So one must be willing to accept that urban planning has the capacity to intervene wherever a real network is being developed in order to help incorporate the virtual network, to promote interrelations with operators at the other levels, and to improve the overall inclusion of infrastructure networks whenever the community believes it to be of benefit.

Urban planners can undoubtedly intervene in several areas, the most obvious being in assisting the usual local authorities with their responsibility over areolar territories. The advantages and limitations of such interventions are well known. The greatest difficulty arises over their role with respect to networks organized at a very different scale. This is especially the case with two major networks: the telephone and electricity networks. But there is also the road network. Hall (1988) shows how a genuine automobile system was put together in less than a century based on small-scale technology used by amateurs on an ill-suited road network. At *level one*, the network operator managed to find the financial and technical means to create a network suitable for vehicles. At *level two*, nationwide networks were deployed providing service stations, followed by restaurants, hotels and shops designed for access by car. And at *level three*, drivers established their own user networks. None of this could be confined to within local authority boundaries. But the intervention on the part of urban planning absolutely must scrutinize those networks or else lose any chance of coordination with the other operating *levels*.

A higher level of network coordination, as part of a general holistic, open-ended and adaptive approach may prove necessary when users are experiencing serious difficulties with urban public services – due to their complexity or an inability to grasp the issues and the real opportunities on offer, for instance, as has been the case in urban engineering (Calatayud, 1989). And another authority may useful at a time when local government, in Latin countries at least, appears to lack the required scope and standing (Martinand, 1986).

Having identified how and where urban planning can intervene in the realm of networks, the next task should be to specify the methods and approaches, bearing in mind the need to identify and work on the nodes, links, connections and regulatory processes according to the topological, kinetic and adaptability-related requirements.

"It is platitudinous to say that information has become a commodity. And yet it is a platitude from which one has to draw a very sad conclusion: individual empowerment is ever-more reliant on access to that information. While renewable and non-renewable resource allocation stems from non-human – climatic, pedological or geological – factors, the dissemination of information stems from human decisions [and] the fact that there are now data-rich countries and data-poor countries (…) puts information at the heart of all policy-making. Societies are *territorialized*, *deterritorialized* and *reterritorialized* depending on whether or not they have access to information: signalling systems can enhance or depreciate, build or destroy, make appear or disappear. Distributions of workers and capital are determined by a new informational logic formulated in primate nodes yet propagated by ever-more abstract networks.

Without the network, information is nothing. Information, when all is said and done, hardly matters at all. What matters is the network to communicate and disseminate it.

Christaller's celebrated central place theory, dating back to 1933, shows nodes to have been relatively more important than links after the industrial revolution, but they have been superseded since the 1950s by the networks, as seen in the information theory devised by Claude Shannon.

The territorial system and the *territorialization-deterritorialization-reterritorialization* process through which empowerment is gained, lost and rediscovered are now governed by communication theory.

What is lacking now is a network theory to round off central place theory."

From: Repères Pour Une Théorie de la Territorialité Humaine *by Claude Raffestin, in Cahier du Groupe Réseaux, 7, 1987*

3   Social Scope of Networks[*]

The user as a stakeholder

An opportunity for immediate, direct and ubiquitous relationships, yet the freedom to chose the time and place ... that, apparently, is what people have come to expect from the networks. Over and above its functionalities – carrying liquids, signals or passengers – a network's value as a common good hinges on its ability to live up to that new ideal.

Two particular examples will help make better sense of this. The first one regards what is without a doubt the quintessential network from the point of view of the above, i.e. that of the telephone, which, although relatively recent in France compared to other countries such as the United States or Sweden, has been the subject of much qualitative sociological and anthropological research. The second example, on the other hand, is one of the oldest networks, i.e. the one bringing running water to the home – the most basic functionality, which the collective psyche has also come to regard in the light of that modern ideal.

From the mid-1970s in France, the telephone soon became a tool accessible to one and all at the office, in the street – through public phone booths – and especially in the home. Ubiquity was now the rule. It became almost abnormal for anybody to be unreachable by phone, as reflected in the tremendous technical and economic efforts put into the development of paging, radio-telephony and the mobile phone.

To begin with, the telephone was considered expensive, strictly for business and emergencies, and a source of idle chatter. But its other uses soon put a stop to that. The telephone network became the gateway to a personal universe made out of the calls that any individual wished to make to, or receive from, others (de Solla Pool, 1977). Sociologists like Pinaud (1988) have rightly stressed the importance of automatic routing in enabling people to contact each other directly, without having to go through an operator. All one needs to do to have a particular person on the line, as a rule, is to dial a number. So it is the user that has direct control over the interfacing, with each and every call further confirming the network's immediacy.

This immediacy has been inherent to the telephone since the day that Alexander Graham Bell's assistant heard the words "Mr. Watson, come here, I want to see you", and imagined he was hearing them at the exact same moment as they were being uttered. Even though the quality of phone communications long remained mediocre, it never affected that sense of instantaneousness. Digital technology may have revolutionized the network's *modi operandi*, but it has not rendered transmission, as far the user is concerned, any more or less instantaneous. And while perceptions of distance may be affected at times by communication failures, the differences today are insignificant; and other perceptions have replaced that of 'technical distance'.

*   Previously published as « La Portée Sociale des Réseaux». In: Dupuy, G., 1991, *L'Urbanisme des Réseaux: Théories et Méthodes*. Paris: Armand-Colin, pp. 45-59. Included with permission.

Analysts agree that the current telephone network, which any person can access wherever they are for an instant and direct relationship – in one direction, at least – with whomsoever they choose, is charged with unique meaning. It has opened up a space in which to assert the symbolic empowerment of access to the world. The home or mobile phone is a focal or pivotal point enabling people to develop their own new territory where they can exert their power through opportunities to order, manage, obtain or transmit information, as well as to bring interlocutors into play or to forge emotional bonds, and so on. Anthropological research highlights a discontinuity, a partitioning effect, over and above that focal point (Lauraire, 1987). Further afield there are other points whose topological distance generates a blend of spatial representations, emotional considerations and price restrictions.

Notwithstanding the network's characteristic discontinuities and 'nodalities', the telephone really does seem to have created a new, intangible, territorial structure giving consistency to spaces formerly regarded as so fragmented as to suggest that the network was shaping a 'new personal, inhabited, geography; a new form of urban planning' (Bornot & Cordesse, 1981). This new territory already has its rules of law. The telephone network is a territorial space regarded as ever more vital by the collective psyche. How can anyone live without a phone? And what would happen in the event of a repeat of those rare incidents where entire neighbourhoods, towns and even regions have been deprived of access to the network?

Almost from the outset, the French government reached a landmark consensus over the need to guarantee such access for vulnerable members of society – the elderly, the handicapped and others – and even to exempt them from a share of the charges. And in the United States, the issue came before the highest authorities in the striking form of a genuine right of access for all. Deregulation of the American telecommunications sector, however, saw the network operators raising subscription fees and local call rates. Underprivileged sections of society, unable to pay their bills, automatically had their subscriptions cancelled.

The question then arose as to whether life in an American city was possible without access to a telephone, not least because it was the only way to reach a doctor or the emergency services, for example. Advocacy groups successfully lobbied politicians to pass laws that would provide a lifeline, i.e. guaranteed minimum local access for all to the network, even in the event of a cancelled subscription. And when the Californian state power sector was deregulated, consumer groups managed to have that lifeline extended to the electricity network (Anderson, 1981). Basically, the law had recognized *a posteriori*, as is so often the case, the territorial reality of a network from which none can be excluded. *Jus soli* had made way for the right to a connection.

If the telephone network really has become so significant, it is argued, what about the infrastructure networks carrying physical flows? Where does the water supply network, whose one and only role for over a century has been to meet a basic need, stand in relation to the communicational symbolism of the modern telephone network?

Sansot (1984) answers these questions from an ethnological rather than a sociological point of view by contrasting the shower with the bathtub. Taking a bath – a slow process of cleansing the body through fusion with water – is seen these days as a symbol of cosy intimacy. The fact is that the bath can be used independently: a person can bathe in a tub after having previously filled it with water, i.e. without needing to be connected to the network at the time. Taking a shower, on the other hand, requires an immediate connection in order to have the adequate pressure. Hence, "we are the stakeholders, the end points of a network of which we seem to be the users but which, in actual fact, has turned us into one of its various segments". The shower, in the collective psyche, conveys the image of a network where access is ubiquitous (everybody knows they are all connected), instantaneous (or at least fast, as reflected in the somewhat aggressive jet of the shower) and immediate (anybody can turn on the tap whenever they want to have a direct connection to the network).

So the infrastructure network delivering pressurized water to the home gives the water board subscriber the chance to enter into contact with what Sansot describes as a 'new topological space of network stakeholders'. Sansot's rather intuitive parallel with the telephone may appear well founded, but it still needs verifying. Confirmation can be found in a survey carried out in the Moroccan capital, Rabat, where many people at the time were still waiting to be connected to the water system: "the materiality of access to drinking water – i.e. to the network – acts not only as a physical link between all those connected, but also as the symbolic link of belonging to a single community, a single organized territory: the 'service city', the 'official city', the 'legal city'" (Lacoste, 1991).

A similar case can be made with respect to the mains drainage system. Toulouse city services, unable to extend the system to every part of the city, provided unconnected neighbourhoods with individual, fully maintained, sanitation facilities. Users in those neighbourhoods enjoyed exactly the same services as in the rest of the city. But they regarded it as a mere stopgap measure, and continued pressing for a proper connection (Beyeler, 1991). One cannot hope to partake in the new urban lifestyle without being a stakeholder in the water mains system.

The same can be said for the electricity network, which is present in every area of everyday life and represents more than just a collection of wires and machines for generating or, as electricity company bills seem to suggest, delivering kilowatt-hours (Stiegler, 1994). In the light of the manifold uses it makes possible through a variety of possible sources – thermal, hydraulic, nuclear, to name but three – and interconnectivity techniques, across ever-wider geographical scales, subscribers also tend to see it as a kind of territory in which they share with fellow stakeholders the right to an instant and direct connection to electric power at any given time, wherever they may be. The fact is that a look at the technical side of running the network happens to reveal frequent – daily and occasionally real-time – changes from one fuel source to another through despatching. Meanwhile, the switch represents a commonplace yet pivotal key to territorial power, to the door of the network-cum-territory.

Further confirmation of the new meaning attached to the networks can be seen in a range of research findings pertaining to the field of transport. Dekindt (1986), in a study of the Parisian metro system, describes the network as a "combination of tangible or intangible lines [that] are not so much dividing up territories as actually forming a territory *per se*". He shows how it was originally the infrastructure network, characterized by mechanical and electrical machinery, that set the rules and benchmarks for the 'grid' and the 'profession'. But the role of reticulation has changed considerably in our societies over the past century.

Networks are no longer seen as a means of organizing external space so as to provide a city with transport, for instance, but as networks in their own right. Consequently, the new meaning of the protocols and rites governing entry into a network that has actually become a territory – a network-territory – together with the underlying symbolism of the node or junctions where a rule that each individual interprets in his or her own way serves to 'divide, distribute, systematize [and] underpin (…) a unit: the network'. This would seem to suggest that the metro system, like Sansot's water supply network, has its urban stakeholders; which corresponds with the observations of Serres (1972) on what the interchange means to the road network.

Senett (1979), incidentally, noted with some dismay the inescapability of the transport network as exemplified by the traffic on the roads. What he called 'unlimited motility' had come to be regarded as an inalienable personal right. Everybody must be able to travel, not for taking a sight-seeing tour around town like tourists or gallivanting teenagers, but for going from A to B or C or D, i.e. for weaving themselves a network with other points than their own. No points must be barred. The least restriction, hold-up or need to switch to another means of transport would cause anxiety, annoyance and anger. People must at all times be offered wide-ranging, instant and direct links in their travel choices, the motor car being the 'logical tool for enabling us to exercise such a right' (Sennett, 1979). The road network must submit to the rule and, hence, take on a higher social and territorial meaning. This, as confirmed by bus passenger surveys carried out in the suburbs of Paris in the late 1980s, also applied to public transport (Dupuy, 1987b).

The non-functional significance of travel networks was also highlighted, after many years of historical and sociological research, by the *Centre de Sociologie Économique et Politique* (Centre of Economic and Political Sociology). Reggazola and Desgoutte (1979) criticized the conventional position of transport experts depicting cities as uniform, collective spaces separated from the countryside by boundaries, with urbanites making their various journeys by one form of transport or another. Those uniform spaces, those territories and local systems, have not existed since the late eighteenth century, when they were broken up by industrialization. They had become 'insignificant in and of themselves' (Reggaloza & Desgoutte, 1979). Places would only gradually recover their meaning through relationships forged with other places, with other points.

In the course of the twentieth century, a framework of interrelationships established in the previous century came to construct a unique new territory that was altogether different from its predecessors. A daily journey, for instance, "is not a journey within a uniform space, but a dual spatial and temporal journey of symbolic significance" (Reggaloza & Desgoutte, 1979). The infrastructure network providing for such journeys plays two distinct roles: representing memory of the past – materializing and channelling flows – and acting as the current, collective means of a general exodus whose goals are not necessarily known or intended. It amounts to something of a revolutionary appropriation of a new network-territory no longer confined to city limits and depicted by Reggazola and Desgoutte (1979) as incorporating "parts of the N7 trunk road, motorway service stations, the major winter sports resorts, marinas and so on, bearing in mind that the network endpoints subdivide into finer branches extending as far as the dirt tracks open to high clearance tractors in mechanized intensive viticulture".

Once again, this acceptation of transport – which favours an albeit mental picture of spatio-temporal relations, destination choices and the exodus to possibly far-off places that nevertheless still belong to the same overall territory – features the strong signifiers attached to network access: almost totally ubiquitous, even though most of the migratory flows amount to commuting back and forth; direct, providing individual urbanites with at least a potential opportunity to become actors and to make choices at the network nodes; and as instant as possible given how the speeds are ever-increasing yet never quite fast enough.

Anyone able to read the signs can detect this perception of the transport network as a new and abstract territory in patterns of daily behaviour; and the views of Reggazola and Desgoutte in the late 1970s were confirmed a few years later in the findings of studies on long-distance daily commuting and mobility carried out by INRETS, the French institute of research on transport and transport safety (INRETS, 1983; INRETS, 1989). The question is raised as to why the real outcasts of the rapid transit metro system are those that are not moving, that have chosen to live on the station platforms they have territorialized, and that sit watching the trains and the people on the move – a contemporary reflection of the normality of networks, even of normality in general – as they pass them by.

Furthermore, Beauchard (1988a & 1988b), in response to those who see nothing but a chaotic crowd in a hypermarket on a Saturday, has revealed the subtle patterns of networking of shoppers as they move from one counter to another following the information contained in a list held on their trolley handle or in an advertisement for an especially appealing item that has to go together with another product found at another counter; or when a familiar guide or a friend met by chance points to a special offer that warrants a detour before they finally move on to pay at the cash desk. Looking at how our society has been reduced to menus such as these – posted at airports, on escalators or on roadside billboards and on public squares, for instance – Beauchard stresses the need for a fresh perception of urban space making room for the network nodes and "the rituals of access to traffic that now play the role of the gates in the old city walls".

Sociologists rightly point out that it is the local level that is jeopardized by the new meaning attached to the networks. While the traditional concept of localness hinged on the idea of self-contained and self-reliant communities, the modern version sees it as a sort of unit of correlation, an 'open network' of interrelations forged via whatever connections and disconnections occur whenever the opportunities arise, and featuring a blend of local and remote relationships. But this paradigm of a new sociology of sociability – which is quite close to the network analysis of American researchers such as Barth (1978) and Boissevain (1979) – needs supplementing in order to embrace the constant nature of the relations offered by the infrastructure networks.

Claval (1973) recalls how the structuring of some older trading networks "remains as solid today as in the traditional world; it is the place granted to the infrastructure networks that has changed". It is the existence of infrastructure and network operators – in the telecommunications, electricity or transport sectors – that has made urbanites feel they really are stakeholders and has made it possible for the networks to be territorialized – through various behaviour patterns and mental perceptions. The territory conveys a sense of durability. Social networks are formed because the individual attaches importance not just to the price but also to the opportunity to strike up relationships, and to the fact that those relationships can change. Yet each of these factors is crucial to the existence of territoriality – hence the importance of the 'right to a network' and what Sansot (1984) calls 'stakeholder status', both of which help ensure its sustainability.

Territorial and economic aspects of urban networks

Even though the networks are now associated with the realm of commonality, the fact that they are all underpinned by the infrastructure network and a functional service gives the impression that each still has its own particular meaning. What is it that actually serves to bring together and combine the networks in a single, possibly imagined, interpretation of territoriality? Bakis (1989) suggests an interesting line of inquiry. Each city dweller reconstructs a network-territory with him/herself at the centre, as seen earlier in the case of telephonic space. Yet it is a single network drawing on every potential relationship made possible by the transport, communications and transfer networks. As such, this network-territory could combine the provision of services essential to urban life with social relationships and linkages with recreational sites or personal centres of interest. It would be 'more fleeting and more versatile' than other territories in that it incorporates, in addition to the potentialities inherent to each network, the opportunities for individuals to vary the combinations and restructuring they implement according to the changes occurring in their own lives.

The emergence of these broad-based, individual, networks has given rise to some daunting procedural problems. At the same time, though, it represents an intriguing working hypothesis akin to what Moles (1987) describes as a 'dynamic myth'. In building their own network-territory – a sort of city of networks revolving around their own personal life plans – urbanites would appear to be developing a new model of society. Moles calls this the networked city. Although a communications expert, he is well aware that the urbanite's territorial plans involve not just the networks pushed to the fore by the ICT revolution, but also those of a more traditional nature. Furthermore, the list is not closed and is even subject to an 'overwhelming diversity' concerning as yet unsuspected aspects of urban life. He goes further than Bakis (1989) in suggesting that the territorial reconstruction of a networked city made up of the various kinds of networks, might be the individual's response to economic priorities. In addition to being the developer, he or she could also be the network-territory's manager, acting within the framework of a 'wider economy' whose rules, of course, have yet to be specified.

In any event, the change in the outlook is, in the light of the history of urban network development, striking to say the least: "what once appeared to be a matter of convenience – supplying the home with goods and services, the easiest to convey being fluids – is now turning into a system of connections linking social units to all manner of network sources with a view to cutting the overall cost of access to those services" (Moles, 1987). So the driving force of that change would appear to be the increase in the overall costs of interactivity within a fragmented space and across an ever-more extensive area – with the efforts to find a suitable means of managing the various connections in time and space leading to the emergence of a territory structured in such a way as to secure a sound living environment and life plan.

A number of surveys and analyses – whose focus, unfortunately, remains far too narrow – seem to confirm the validity of these scenarios. Jaillet (1981), in a sociological study of the Toulouse area, found that the migrants moving out of the city centre and settling in rural housing estates dozens of kilometres away did not feel as though they had actually left the city. Being within easy reach of Toulouse by car, and having a telephone and the amenities provided on estates fully equipped with 'urban' networks, residents felt they were playing as much of a role in urban life as ever, despite having had to change their habits, i.e. to reconstitute their own territory, so to speak, their own city. This, in turn, is confirmed by the *Centre Scientifique et Technique du Bâtiment* (Centre for Scientific and Technical Research on the Building Industry) in its research on how residents perceive space in the light of their past experience as migrants, the only difference here being that the focal point of the territorial reconstitution is not always the home (see illustration 3.1), a fact borne out by the findings of the *Centre de Recherche sur l'Habitat* (Centre for Research on Housing) on the place of the home in the forming of territories and mobility systems (Haumont & Wintersdorff, 1990).

According to Moles, attention should be paid not just to individual urbanites in their residential units and other basic social units, but also to the economic actors, i.e. businesses. In the late 1980s, many companies began to restructure in keeping with the infrastructure networks and, moreover, the availability of ICT networks. In place of trying to introduce faster means of transport and communication into existing structures, they had to completely rethink their means of production and distribution accordingly (Claval, 1973). This led to the proliferation of new relationships with suppliers and subcontractors, the expansion of logistics systems, a tendency towards real-time or just-in-time production – i.e. without stocks – and an emphasis on coming up with sound techniques for the management of economic and, above all, financial transactions. Two common strategies came to the fore, either separately or in tandem: downsizing and branching out. The former entails companies shedding their fixed assets and concentrating on managing a whole range of relationships. Gille (1989) cites the case of a taxi firm that used to run its own fleet of cabs, having to keep the vehicles in good working order and to make sure there were enough people available to drive them. The firm then decided to offload its assets – its fleet – on the drivers, and was reduced to operating a radiotelephone exchange, offering a just-in-time transport service putting prospective customers in touch with freelance drivers who owned their own vehicles and had become partners of its network.

Branching-out results in companies extending their 'in-house' information networks – involving data on their market, their demand, their suppliers, and so on – as far as possible into outside activities where they may have a strategic impact. Bakis (1989), among others, highlights the case of airline companies creating sophisticated computer booking systems, realizing that they could be extended to other companies, travel agencies, various ticket sales outlets and so on, and then finding that profits from the sale of 'just-in-time' booking services could sometimes exceed those made from traditional carrier activities. Furthermore, this approach can understandably lead to an associated policy of downsizing.

These examples from the economic sector of transport offer especially telling insight into how the fostering of spatio-temporal relations between several production and processing sites, for instance, can also help promote in-depth changes in traditional industrial sectors such as the car industry or manufactured goods (Besson, Savy, Valeyre & Veltz, 1989; Savy & Veltz, 1989), and among small-scale producers like the Singaporean company making dentures for a dentist in Frankfurt thanks to the use of ICT and air transport networks (Paché, 1989). The networks therefore offer economic actors much

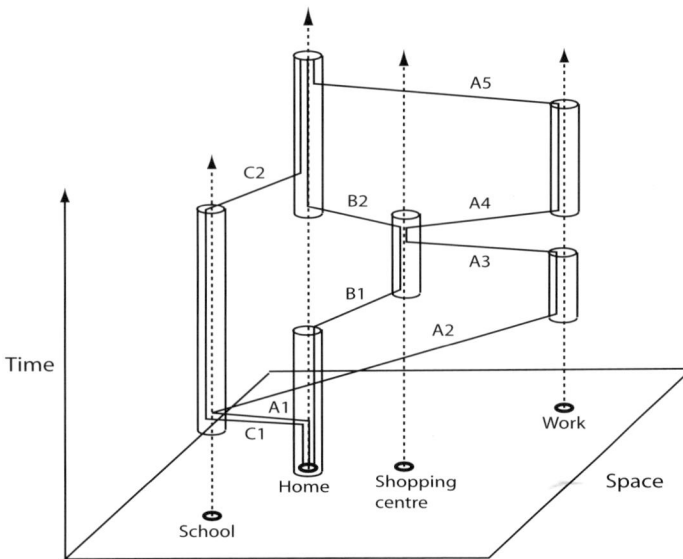

Illustration 3.1   **'Family mobility in the new territoriality. "The husband drives the children to school, then goes to work; he meets his wife for lunch at a restaurant in the mall where she is doing her shopping; the children make their own way home in the evening; and the family is reunited at the end of the day." This is still a quite simplistic picture, however, as it focuses solely on daily movements via the transport networks…'**
Source: after Walford (1981), cited and commented upon by Guermond (1994)

the same as in the case of city dwellers: ubiquitous, instant and direct relationships, whenever and wherever they choose. The difference is that the new models of corporate behaviour have been far more clear-cut than the multifarious behaviour patterns stemming from the non-economic considerations of the individual (Castells, 1989).

In any event, the sheer scale of the changes drove economists to recommend fresh conceptualization for analysing what they called 'the network economy' (Frybourg, 1990). Noting how value creation now hinged on the management of company, customer, supplier and subcontractor relationships – and how crucial it was to have knowledge of those relationships, especially when the various parties were geographically remote from, rather than in close proximity to, each other – they highlighted the need to build new statistical and analysis tools. Society's intuitive grasp of economics was, in their view, based on models no longer relevant to the current circumstances. Citing, among others, the paradigm of the 'factory' and the 'market' (Bressand, Distler & Nicolaidis, 1989) and territorial concepts commonly used in the field of statistics such as the 'region', 'urban unit' and 'labour market area' (Terrier, 1989), they suggested that these be replaced with a network-based concept more suited to handling the economic behaviour of firms and households. Bressand, Distler and Nicolaidis came up with a network comprising a communications infrastructure and an *infostructure* with rules, standards and rights that promoted the actors' expectations and allowed those with access to the network to "forge specific, value-generating, interrelationships. The network needs to give each member the latitude to forge specific relationships with other members in line with configurations capable of evolving over time and according to the applications". Terrier, for his part, suggested that a new statistical framework would better highlight the constituent parts of a new territoriality at a time when the trends in question no longer had the customary spatial consistency associated with geographical proximity. This squares with the findings of Emanuel (1989), whose highly detailed work revealed a reticular arrangement in the hierarchy of services in a number of Italian cities as opposed to the pyramid-type structure depicted by conventional theorists.

The parallels between what the networks mean to economic actors and to ordinary urbanites are hard to miss. In both cases, the nature of the network-territory is the same: placing a premium on the choice of relationships irrespective of distance, i.e. not confined to the neighbourhood or locality; stressing that the relationships depend on the existence of an infrastructure ensuring they are possible at all times; underscoring the importance of rules of law common to all network stakeholders; and allowing the relational architectures that the actors on the network have actually established to change over time. So the network had become a relevant basis upon which to build a model of behaviour patterns and, hence, a suitable replacement for the conventional territorial frameworks in the field of socio-economic analysis.

At this stage it is worth stepping back and taking an objective view of the potential network territoriality. A network, according to the masterly work of Raffestin (1980), is a means by which an actor produces a territory. Raffestin juxtaposes it with two other means: points and bounded spaces. A point is a 'territorial nodosity' whose position in a particular space is determined by that of the actor; it is the 'manifestation of any individual or collective ego'. Indeed, it so happens that the actors are indeed located at 'territorializing' points: the home for city dwellers, the head office or production unit for companies, or the communication node for the taxi firm mentioned earlier, for instance. Their relational plans target other such points as a workplace, a subcontractor's workshop or another communication node – a public transport terminal such as a railway station or airport, for example.

As for bounded spaces, on the other hand, the contemporary meaning attached to the networks has rendered these obsolete as a means of territorialization. The fact is that they involve the dividing up and delimiting of spaces to represent areas of jurisdiction, which is where the problem lies as far as the network is concerned. Geography teaches us about the processes affecting entire spaces: wind erosion in physical geography, for instance, and field theories in human geography. So spaces end up being identified by the area or areas affected by those processes. This has led to talk about 'areolar' space. Areolar space contrasts with localized space in view of the fact that an area, i.e. continuous space, is something other than a collection of points. More importantly, however, it contrasts with linear space, which is formed by "identifying a number of points of reference and interlinking those points in a network. (…) An areolar space, on the other hand, is formed without any prior identification, each place in its own context being its own *raison d'être*. Linear space would be more extrinsic and areolar space more intrinsic" (Berque, 1982).

In producing areolar spaces, the use of bounded spaces clashes with Raffestin's third means of territorialization: the ever shifting, protean, network, which adapts easily to spatio-temporal variations. What matters most in a network is how it represents the various paths between points, as this is what the actors use to develop their strategies and their power over the space in question. Yet the integration of contemporary urban systems evidently places a premium on the network as a means of territorialization (Raffestin, 1987; Di Meo & Piolle, 1989) (see Part 2).

So the rift between urban circumstances increasingly rooted in a reticular territoriality and a school of urban planning historically marked by an areolar conception of urban space could only continue to widen (Dupuy, 1991a: 25-43). The social significance of the network would therefore appear to stem from their role in forming a new and quite unique urban territoriality. Reticular territoriality of this kind is complex in that it involves a host of actors united by the infrastructure networks and endowed with the status of stakeholders through belonging to network-based relational management systems – which is not to say that it is devoid of the power and control-related characteristics usually associated with a territory. The meaning of the networks is clear to see in this aspect of territoriality.

On the other hand, the matter of meaning *within* the network remains something of an open question. For economic actors – i.e. companies – the network is a means of territorialization geared to generating (economic) value. But what about for individual urbanites and households? Does the answer lie in Moles' assertion that they are striving to secure the 'least possible overall cost' for carrying out urban interactivities (Moles 1987)? Or in the ethno-poetic writings of Sansot (1990), which use the myths of Diana and Narcissus to inject a sense of meaning and pleasure into the routes people follow in the water supply or public transport systems? Must they replace one myth with another – an old for a new – and hope that using the networks will help realize the dream of participating in some marvellous deconstruction of reality, some miraculous fusion of time and space (Virilio, 1984)?

Clearly, though, human territoriality cannot, as Raffestin (1987) recalls, do without the signs that give it a sense of meaning. Reticular territoriality too must come up with its own signs. Network semiologists have to help the user know which link to establish and when, and to what end – positive or negative. Areolar territories have boundaries to use as a means of organization, containment and regulation. But what about the network? Cauquelin (1979 & 1987) provides some pointers in highlighting how traditional urban boundaries have been replaced by a proliferation of 'small gates' – barriers, automatic car-park and garage doors, interphones, and so on – and a networked city-specific writing system: signposts, street names and so on.

Signs represent a real challenge for urban planners. In the past they sought to produce the appropriate signs to develop a specific kind of territoriality. But in the light of the rise of the networks and their new-found territorial significance, they must take a fresh look at the matter, which is not going to be easy.

Right now, though, it is time to qualify some of the somewhat forceful assertions made earlier. In all likelihood, the sheer scale of the rise of the networks, and the extraordinary way in which ICTs have injected a new sense of meaning into the older infrastructure networks, have fostered a new, rapidly spreading, genre of urban territoriality. But that does not mean that every other form of territoriality has vanished as a result. Raffestin's points and bounded spaces and Berque's areolar spaces have not been rendered entirely irrelevant. Social and economic actors are still using them to produce territories over which they exert their control, where they are 'at home'. Subtle combinations of the various territorializing techniques have led to the emergence of territorial systems as complex as the city itself (Roncayolo, 1990).

So the network is by no means the only remaining form of territory. Homes and housing represent a unit that, with their means of access, their limits and boundaries, cannot be reduced to a reticular territoriality. The home may well have become a focal point for network terminals – on top of its conventional role, with its garage, bathroom, kitchen and utility rooms, and so on. But Daunton (1981) shows how the introduction of gas, water-supply and drainage systems helped refocus social life on the home and the family in the cities of Victorian England (Daunton, 1981 & 1983). The neighbourhood has not disappeared as a territory as far as all of its residents and local businesses are concerned. Social development surveys show how neighbourhoods have a captive population – immigrants, non-car owners, and so on – for whom the local mall and its surrounding area represent their only real territory outside of the home (Merdrignac, 1989). Urban planning, among others, offers a reminder of how important the local authorities' perfectly areolar territory is for governing a city on behalf of its residents. And Frémont (1988) shows how France is more than a mass of hypermarkets, motorways, and telecommunications and broadcasting networks: its villages, towns and departments still have a place in the country's geography because they have managed to keep their sense of meaning.

In a nutshell, this book is not trying to make out that there is nothing left but the network. It is just trying to demonstrate how it has introduced into our societies a new, predominant, form of territoriality that urban planning has, as a rule, failed to acknowledge.

4   Network Visualization Tools for Urban Planners*

"Nowadays, we are no longer living in cities governed by principles of axiality formed from a hierarchy of clearly defined spaces – avenues, squares, streets, and so on – but in a graph. We are moving around in a map [and] big cities can only be designed, planned, developed and equipped through an abstract approach" (Teyssot, 1988). What means of representation do urban planners have, to make allowance for the exact status of the various connections inherent to the network city?

First there is the map. Networks have long figured in maps, which provide an adequate visualization tool for certain uses in certain conditions (Steinberg & Husser, 1988). Nothing has really replaced the road map in the eyes of a driver embarking on a long journey into unfamiliar territory. André Michelin, the man who championed and pioneered motor car use of the road network in France, codified the appropriate representation (Ribeill, 1992). Its two-dimensional representation gives a now familiar means of picturing that network's topology, conveying the potential kinetics it allows by means of the thickness and colour of the lines. Only its adaptability remains poorly represented. Which is precisely the problem. Road maps adequately represent the operator's command over geometry, homogeneity and so on. But they do not purport to represent how the road system can, according to Fishman (1990), provide urbanites with opportunities to build the architecture of their own networks. Teyssot (1988) hints at the nature of the problem: "in New York, we are given no more than a split second to choose between a 'Van Wyck Expwy' and an 'Interboro Pkwy' before the interchange sucks us onto a one-way road to an unknown or unwanted destination".

Maps are bound to give a fixed, geometrical picture of the network. They have great trouble representing the density of multiple networks, the importance of connector nodes and, more broadly, all of the various features likely to adapt the networks to the uses of the many different operators. While the road map, for instance, may be ideal for depicting major road routes it struggles or gives up trying to represent the urban road network. It is a matter not just of the scale but also of the nature of the information. The network's various uses in the city cannot be represented by means of fixed geometry or even topology. Parking places, traffic lights, and more or less temporary traffic restrictions are critical factors, but they are changing all the time. Combined with the ever-changing nature of city-dwellers' transactional networks (see Chapter 2), that makes it an impossible task for conventional map-making. Academic studies have shown clearly the kinds of limitations placed on the operators at the various network levels described in Chapter 2 and, hence, on urban planners (Akierman, 1988; Offner, 1990).

Technical network operators have sought to come up with their own solutions by developing dedicated representations tailored to specific design or operations-related tasks. By and large, they give up trying to depict the whole network, with all of its characteristic features, and concentrate solely on the part needed to perform a given task. So they are found to design their networks with the help of a simplified functional diagram that looks nothing like a map or even a graph, leaving its territorial role unstated (see illustration 4.1).

---

*   Previously published as « Représentation des Réseaux ». In: Dupuy, G., 1991, *L'Urbanisme des Réseaux: Théories et Méthodes*. Paris: Armand-Colin, pp. 133-143. Included with permission.

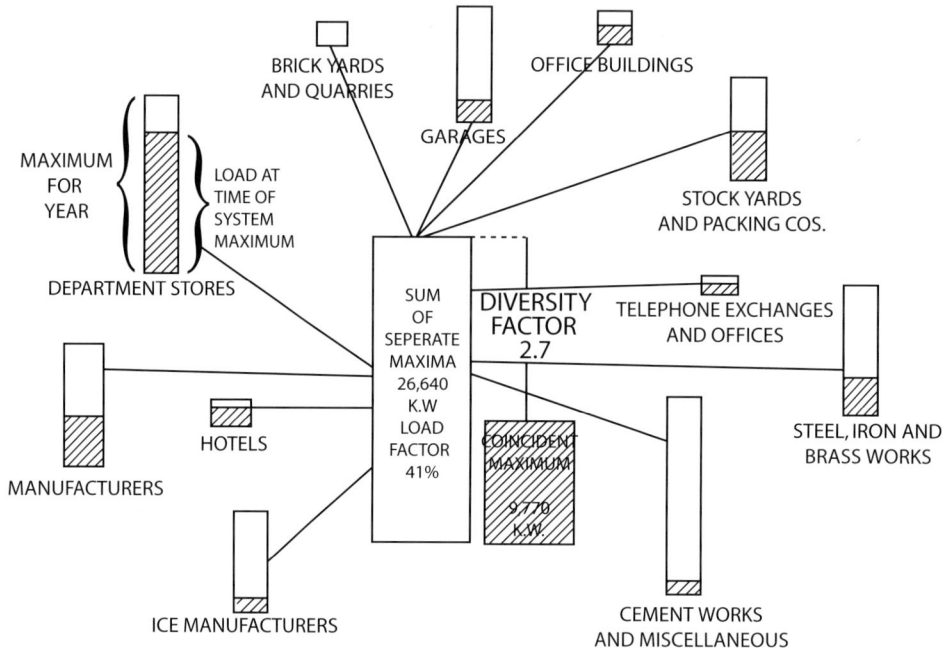

BRICK YARDS AND QUARRIES

OFFICE BUILDINGS

GARAGES

MAXIMUM FOR YEAR

LOAD AT TIME OF SYSTEM MAXIMUM

STOCK YARDS AND PACKING COS.

DEPARTMENT STORES

SUM OF SEPERATE MAXIMA 26,640 K.W LOAD FACTOR 41%

DIVERSITY FACTOR 2.7

TELEPHONE EXCHANGES AND OFFICES

HOTELS

COINCIDENT MAXIMUM 9,770 K.W

STEEL, IRON AND BRASS WORKS

MANUFACTURERS

ICE MANUFACTURERS

CEMENT WORKS AND MISCELLANEOUS

Illustration 4.1   **Samuel Insull's representation of the Chicago electricity network, where the main aim was to show the full range of needs of the consumers connected to the network.**
Source: Hughes (1983)

When work is to be done on the physical network, plans will be needed to pinpoint the networks' various constituent parts together with their simplified characteristic features: a certain diameter cable, a certain type of valve, a power line of a particular voltage, a particular kind of transformer … in a particular place, at a particular depth beneath the road and so on. Those plans used to be hand-drawn, which made them especially painstaking to update. Nowadays, this is the quintessential realm of the geographic information systems that are thriving in the market thanks to advances in the field of information technology (see illustrations 4.2 and 4.3).

These computer-generated models lend themselves well to the changes in scale needed to reflect the network topology. However, they exclude most of the kinetic and adaptive features the operator needs just to manage network operations. The management centres have a block diagram displaying the network's key points and linkages designed to provide a rapid grasp of an emergency situation. But representations such as these are clearly inadequate on their own, and need supplementing with partial schematizations (position of a signal, an open or closed valve, and so on), figures or even still or moving images (state of a crossroads in regard to road traffic, for instance) presented on demand, in real time, on computer screens. Finally, highly schematized maps – often based on the more static than dynamic model of the road map – are proposed for communication with the user, which usually tends to be limited (illustrations 4.4 and 4.5).

When it comes to visualizing not the network itself but the effects of its topology, kinetics and adaptability on the user, it emerges that they can be displayed clearly on a map highlighting the major effects of network connectedness, connectivity and homogeneity: areas well-served by one or more

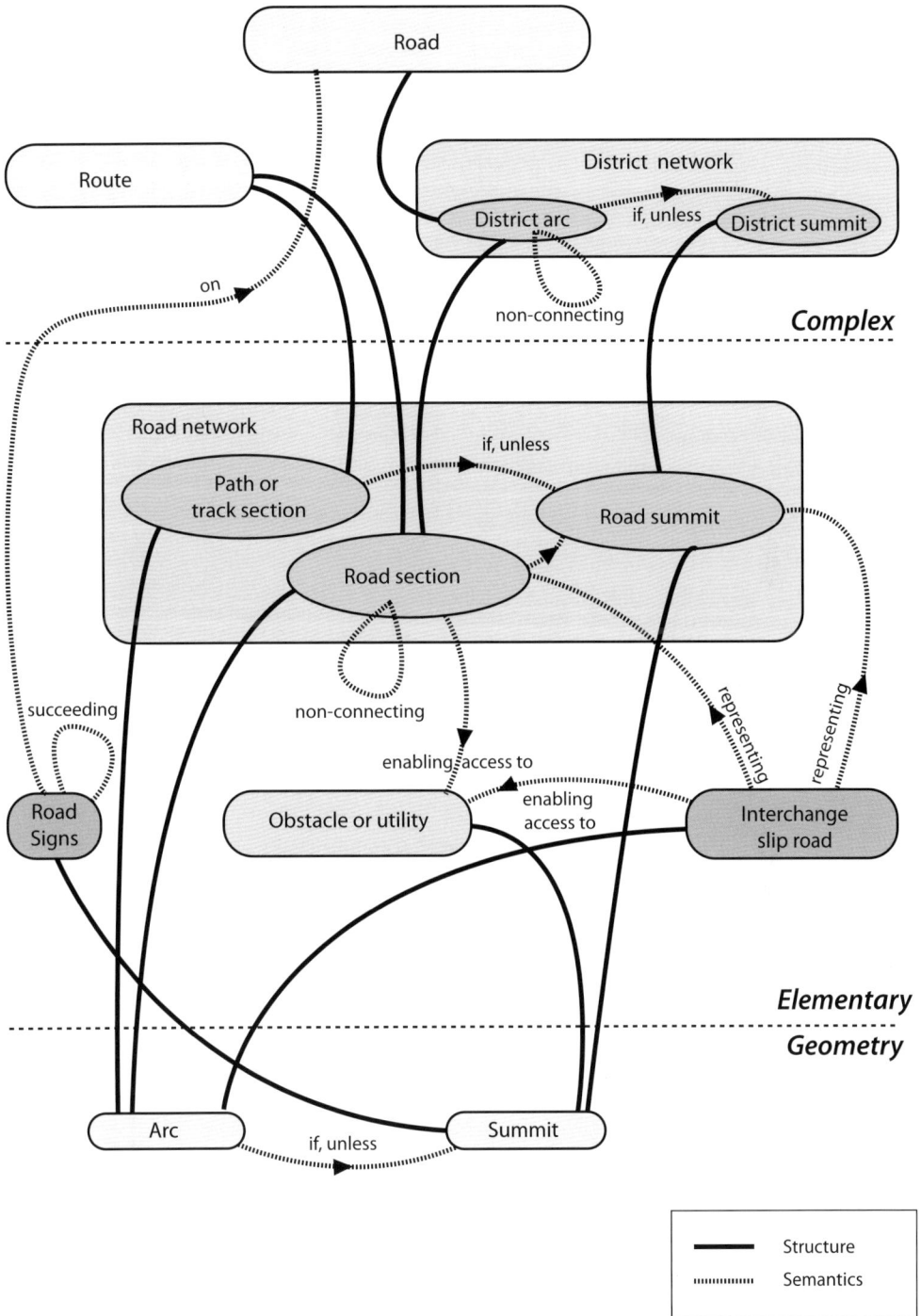

Illustration 4.2   Generative logic-based representation of a road network used by the French *Institut Géographique National* to build a geographic information system.
Source: Salgé & Sclafer (1989)

Illustration 4.3   **Network plan produced by a localized GIS showing the wealth of detailed graphic information supplied just to depict the networks' morphology.**
Source: ARCINFO MAPS, ESPI Redlands, California (1988)

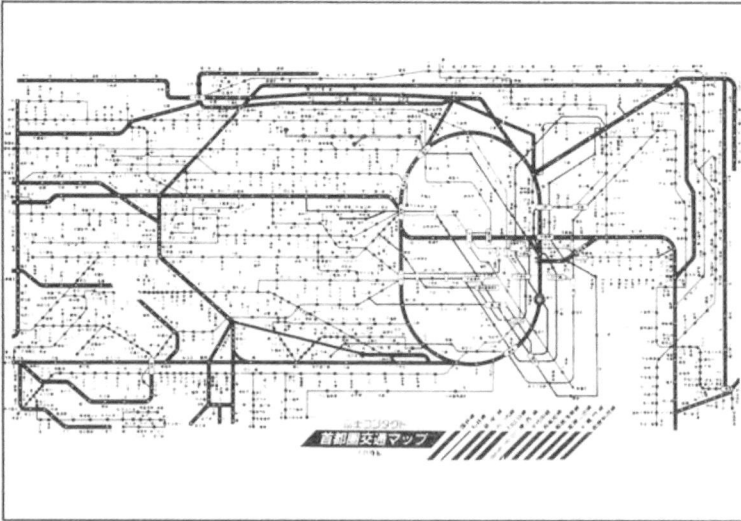

Illustration 4.4   **The Tokyo subway and suburban rail networks made 'simple'**
Source: Supplement of Bulletin d'Informations Architecturales n° 133 (October 1989)

Urban Networks – Network Urbanism

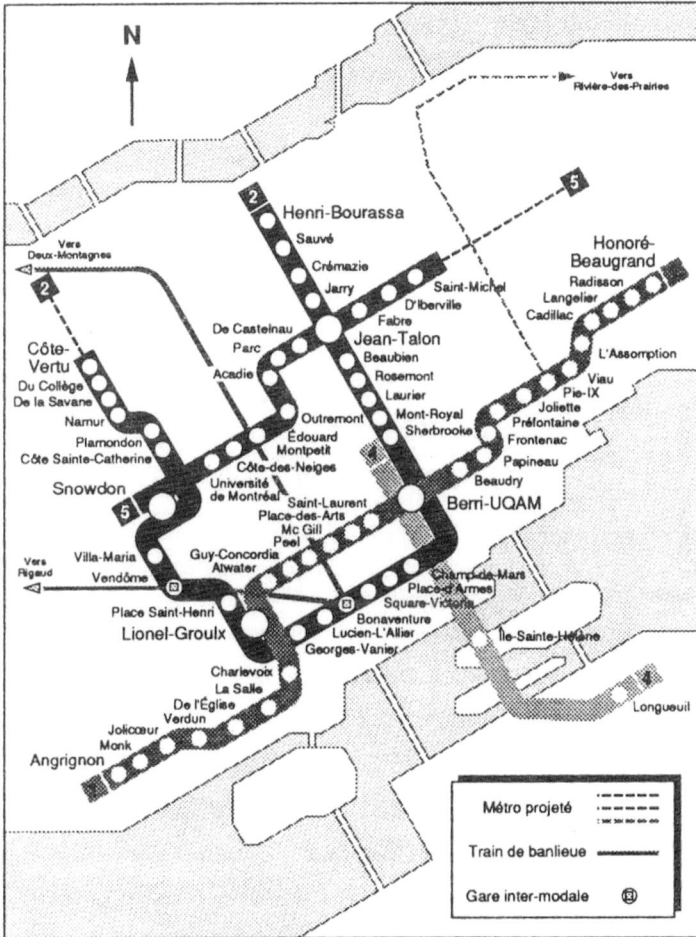

Illustration 4.5   Montreal subway network (circa 1990)

networks, grey areas, isoaccessibility curves and so on (Steinberg & Husser, 1988). But this is a tricky form of representation to handle as it means having to focus on a particular aspect of those effects, e.g. service quality or speed of access; and the fact is that this selectivity is hard to reconcile with the network's wide variety of uses. Indeed, it is bound to draw attention to spaces benefiting more than others according to the aspect selected, thus generating feelings of unfairness that hardly conduce to dispassionate communication with the users. So this type of representation tends to be confined to network design and evaluation procedures (see Dupuy, 1991a).

Does the urban planner find in this panoply of representation models the right tools to carry out his or her work? Clearly, while it may be useful at times to refer to the representations used by the operators, urban planners need tools better suited to their assigned task. The fact is that they cannot do without even a simplified means of visualizing the network's relevant features and how its coverage area interrelates with others – entry/exit points, terminals, nodes, its relationships with other networks, and so on – together with the most comparable representations possible of all the various networks. Research in this field, although not always entirely scientific, has led to the emergence of the 'polar network' concept (Amar & Stathopoulos, 1987).

The polar network is a representation tool devised chiefly for the network design stages, meaning that it can be useful to operators and to urban planners alike. A simplified model is produced by boiling the network down to a diagram depicting an intermediate state between the virtual and real network. It shows a series of points representing either key nodes within the network – vis-à-vis flows, how the network is used and so on – or poles located partially or entirely outside, and illustrating its relationship with other geographical areas. The points can be joined up with linking arcs that, when interlinked, form paths.

The points and arcs are given attributes. There is, for instance, a hierarchy of points – key points and the rest, to put it simply – and several relatively precise attributes for the arcs, or paths, including a Boolean attribute indicating, as in a regular graph, the presence or absence of a link between two points. In most cases, however, other attributes are added to denote the network's kinetics or adaptibility. Depending on the attributes selected, the polar network can come in a variety of forms to arrive at an intermediate state between the virtual and real networks. What is interesting about this kind of representation is that the graphics remain simple, supplemented with more or less extensive files of attributes. It facilitates the work of producing variations to help design infrastructure networks that will be better coordinated with virtual networks, and first-level networks that are better coordinated with second and third-level networks (see illustration 2.4); or strike a balance between networks and areolar coverage areas.

Stathopoulos (1990) describes a full-scale study carried out to test this concept on the Paris area bus network. The representation here is confined to around twenty points, or poles, selected in the light of their importance to the urban fabric of the suburbs, to the bus network itself, or to its links with other such networks as the RER suburban rail service. Connecting arcs, incorporated in order to form paths, are given a frequency attribute represented visually by the thickness of the line, and diversified by means of a file highlighting each line's frequency during five periods of the day: morning peak, morning off-peak, afternoon off-peak, evening peak, and evening off-peak (illustration 4.6).

Illustration 4.6   **Representation of a public transport system based on the polar network concept.**
Source: Stathopoulos (1990)

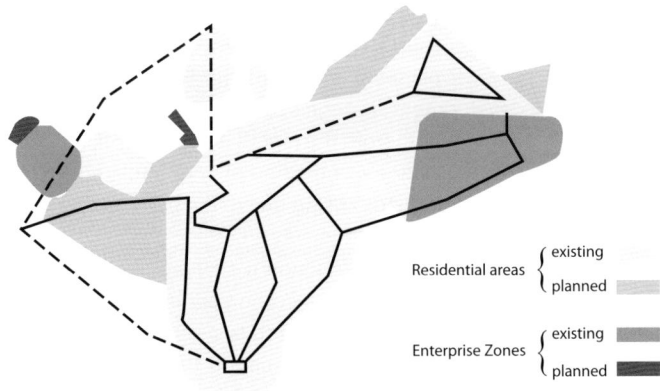

Residential areas { existing / planned

Enterprise Zones { existing / planned

A. PRAO demand forecast scenarios

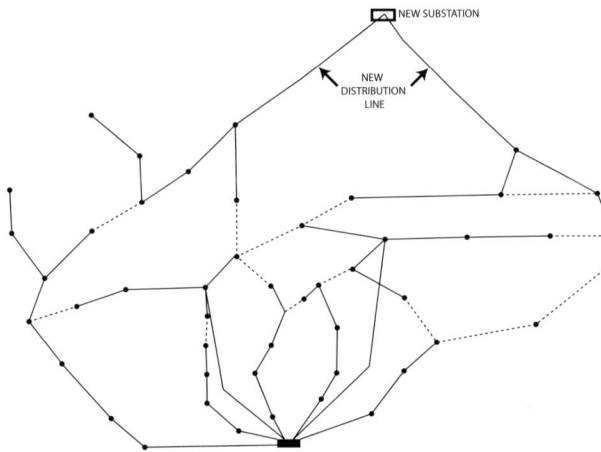

NEW SUBSTATION

NEW DISTRIBUTION LINE

B. PRAO – Strategy 1 – Utilization plan – Year 3

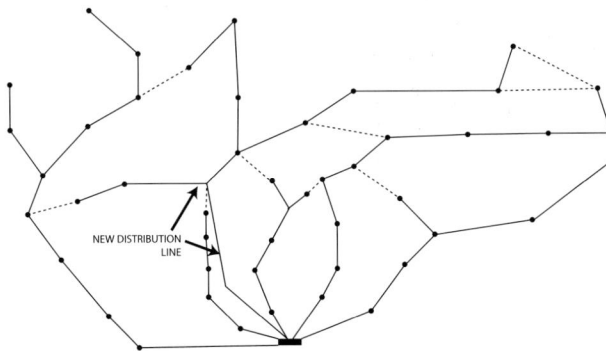

NEW DISTRIBUTION LINE

C. PRAO – Strategy 2 – Utilization plan – Year 3

Illustration 4.7   **Polar network representation in the PRAO model.** Source: Michon (1989)

The polar network concept can also be used to produce a visual representation of cable, water, drainage, postal delivery or electric power supply networks, for instance. Let us take the case of the latter. The PRAO computer-aided network planning model of the French national electricity company, EDF, enables various network development strategies to be compared on the basis of the operator's capital costs and the energy losses stemming from the fact that the network is relatively undersized (Michon, 1989) (see illustration 4.7). At each stage – at the end of one simulated year – the computer redesigns the network in the light of the new needs arising due to increased consumption, further urbanization, enterprise start-ups and so on. It also detects newly emerging constraints likely to hinder the network's performance. A multicriteria optimization function is then applied to the network utilization plan in an attempt to remove the drawbacks without incurring additional capital costs. If that does not work, investments must be proposed. These are subjected to a series of iterations over a given time period geared to testing the various strategies and comparing the associated costs. Illustration 4.7 shows the original network with an initial representation of the demand forecast scenarios, followed by a comparison of two strategies after a period of three years.

The representation displayed in the two utilization plans, which corresponds perfectly to the polar network-type model devised by Amar and Stathopoulos (1987), is what serves to underpin strategic decision-making in the network study. It highlights the network supply stations together with the connection points (residential areas, enterprise zones, and so on). These points and the arcs representing the electricity lines feature the kinds of attributes comparable to the ones that the computer uses to assist in the work of the network developer.

Progress in the field of information technology has provided a fast and effective means of producing full-colour, 3D and dynamic representations that are so conducive to interactivity that on-screen displays are often the preferred option in place of printed maps and plans. Although the technology only does what it is asked to do, network designers now have access to a highly useful range of visualization tools; and planners will soon be able to use maps showing the territorial impacts of one or more networks, e.g. train plus transport from stations: bus, metro, taxi and so on.

But there is still the problem of network representations for the user, i.e. for ordinary citizens. Technology can help. One such example is the in-car satellite navigation system allowing the driver to see a real-time visualization of the part of the road network he or she is using. Is this blend of interactivity and realism the right route to follow, or would it be better to stick with simple, sound tools – easy-to-read maps and plans – that clearly remain as popular as ever? Or else, instead of trying to produce new representations for network users, should they be left to build their own representations from the appropriate information? Such is the approach now made possible by the Internet or, at an even simpler level, mobile telephony. Regarding the latter, the part of the network that is useful to mobile phone users boils down to the personal directories containing all of the numbers they are in the habit of calling, i.e. the potential links they can activate whenever and wherever the need may arise. Above and beyond the mobile phone itself, is this not a highly promising avenue of research as far as network visualization is concerned?

Part II

Network Territoriality: Golden Age and Crises in Cities Around the World

5 Infrastructure Networks and Territoriality in the Outer Suburbs of Paris*

Most research on the history of public utility networks to date has focused specifically on individual sectors. This is understandable, given how water supply, transport or electricity systems, for instance, have each developed according to different trajectories, under the influence of different decision-makers; and given that the researchers have had to base their work on disparate documentary sources. But this has not helped grasp the wider territorial and social impact of network development. While any single network may have a particular influence on urban development, it is the combined effects of all the networks as a whole that gives rise to new forms of spatial organization, new territorialities and, hence, overall social change.

Andrésy, a small town 30 kilometres north-west of Paris, seemed an especially relevant case to study from this point of view because its water, gas and electricity networks were for decades all built, run, maintained and then gradually extended to other towns in the district by a single operator.

Notwithstanding the complicating factors involved in covering not only a region divided into several administrative districts but also a period far enough back in the past to deny us the chance of gleaning first-hand accounts through interviews, we still managed – thanks to the assistance of Philippe Mustar of the *Institut d'Urbanisme* in Paris and the quite substantial material available in the Andrésy archives – to gain valuable and hitherto rare insight into the territorial ramifications of early French network urbanism[1].

The changing face of Andrésy (1850-1912)

In 1850, Andrésy was a tiny, isolated rural town inhabited by under a thousand people and cut off from Paris by the meanderings of the River Seine. The most common means of reaching the capital was a long journey in a horse-drawn boat. After a canal-building programme launched that year and, crucially, the appearance of the first steamboats in 1880, however, it evolved into a bustling inland port – an advance staging post for cargo shipped into Paris and a stopping point for traffic heading the other way, out to northern France and Europe. With activities booming in a variety of sectors ranging from boat-building and repairs to general supplies and administrative affairs, the area attracted a growing community of people working and living on and off the river.

In 1892, Andrésy became connected to the railway network. When the Paris-Conflans-Mantes line reached Andrésy via the bridge over the River Oise built two years earlier by Gustave Eiffel, it forged new relations with the capital in two main ways. On the one hand, it provided a faster, more direct

---

*   This Chapter is an adapted version of an article previously published as "Utility Networks and Territory in the Paris Region: The case of Andresy". In: Tarr J.A., Dupuy G, eds, 1988, *Technology and the Rise of the Networked City in Europe and America*. Philadelphia: Temple University Press: pp. 295-306. Included with permission.

means of transporting fresh fruit and vegetables from the fertile farmlands of the Oise valley to Parisian dining tables. The night train also carried composted urban waste back from Paris, to be used as fertilizer on the fields, thereby furthering the development of cash crop production. On the other hand, it was instrumental in the emergence of a thriving local tourism trade, as the Seine and Oise riverbanks became a popular destination for Parisian holidaymakers and day-trippers, with a proliferation of restaurants, hotels and boarding houses being opened to cater for the masses, and a scattering of country homes being built for the wealthy (Green, 1963). In the meantime, Paris had forged another link with the region in the shape of an underground pipeline built in 1890 to remove its sewage and discharge it on the alluvial plain of Carrières. Although useful as a fertilizer for local crop farming, the raw sewage ended up contaminating the groundwater and making it hazardous for people to continue using the wells that had supplied them with drinking water for centuries.

In this way Andrésy saw its identity as a self-sufficient rural community fade as it became absorbed into Paris' expanding sphere of influence. In addition to the taste of the prosperity to be had in such a relationship, on the downside it found itself confronting problems of a distinctly more urban nature: the need to secure clean sources of drinking water in the face of environmental pollution; a mixed resident population of farming and riverbank communities dependent on trading relations with the capital; and a seasonal influx of tourists not only seeking to relax in the countryside but also expecting to enjoy the comforts to which they were accustomed at home.

Andrésy was not, of course, the only town in the region experiencing such changes, especially after the turn of the twentieth century with the improvements to the road network; the installation of a new telephone cable via Saint-Germain-en-Laye, completed in 1900; and the construction in 1912 of a new railway line running directly from the banks of the Seine and Oise to *Les Halles* – the central marketplace of Paris – and once again carrying fresh fruit and vegetables one way and urban waste the other (Dupuy, 1977). But what made it a good case study for our area of interest was the fact that its various utility networks had, we repeat, all been developed and operated by the same actor.

Public utilities

In 1894, the Andrésy town council decided to grant the sole right to set up, run and maintain the conduits necessary for a water provision network on all roads of the municipality for a period of sixty years to the Mallet Corporation, a family firm first set up in the mid-1800s by the chemist Alfred Mallet to commercialize a natural gas purification process he had invented for the purpose of public lighting. In so doing, the councillors were entrusting the town's utilities to what had become a major French gas and chemicals operator, with a raft of plants and distribution networks throughout the land to its name, currently headed by its founder's son, Paul Mallet.

The company began by building a pumping plant on the Oise riverbank to supply drinking water to homes in Andrésy and, in 1896, to the neighbouring town of Conflans-Sainte-Honorine. In 1897, it acceded to a further request from the council to upgrade the public lighting system, and developed a new system replacing the old oil lamps with gaslights. The water and gas networks were mutually complementary: some of the coal gas was distributed via the gas network while the rest was used to operate the river pumps that fed the water network. Once they were up and running smoothly Mallet secured the council's permission to extend the networks to other municipalities in the district, and later diversified into supplying gas for domestic lighting and cooking (see illustration 5.1).

In 1924, the local authorities decided to bring electricity to Andrésy and the Mallet Corporation – now in the capable hands of Marcel Mallet, following his father's demise the previous year (Vaudoyer, 1946) – negotiated and won a contract to set up a major new network linked to the Parisian operator Nord-Lumière.

Meanwhile, the quality of water drawn from the Oise continued to deteriorate. By 1932 it had grown so poor that the treatment processes no longer had any effect, and Mallet offered to provide the town – and, yet again, many of its neighbours – with a new source: artesian wells drilled 500 metres deep into the ground.

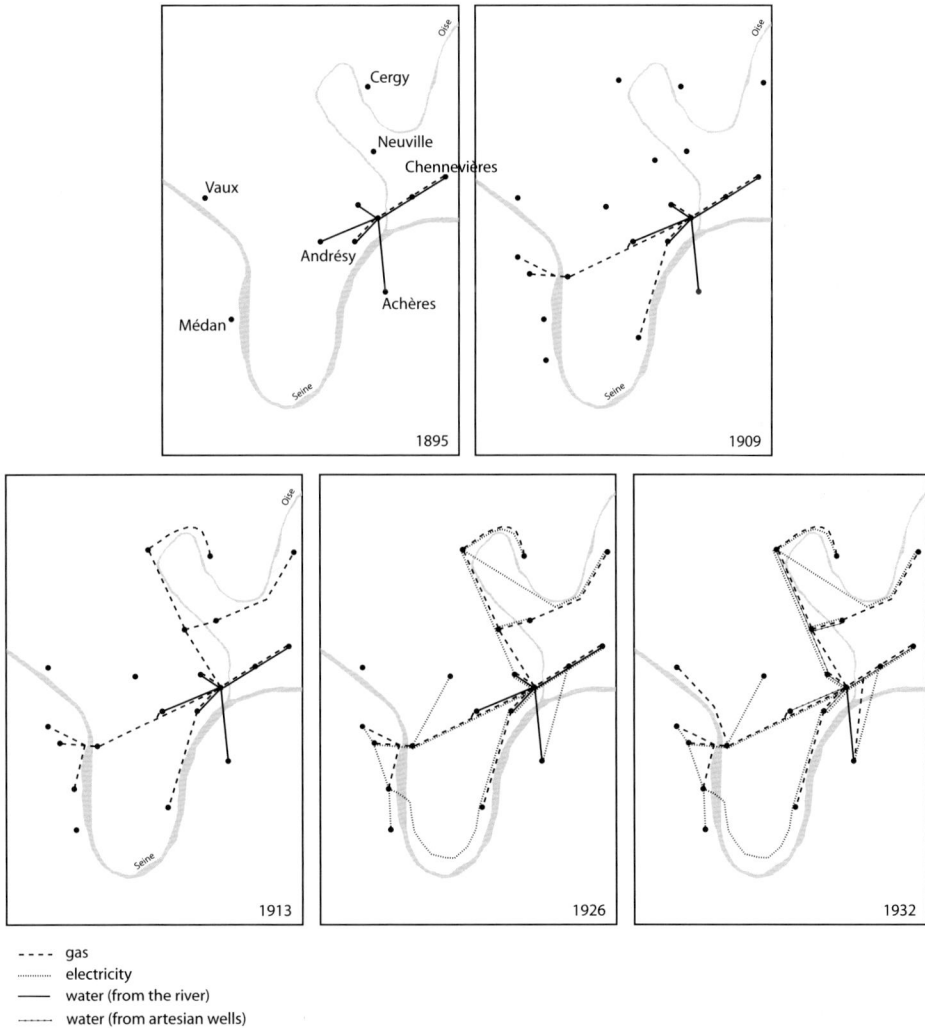

- - - - gas
.... electricity
———— water (from the river)
------ water (from artesian wells)

Illustration 5.1   Expansion of the Mallet water, gas and electricity supply networks (1895-1932)

Within the space of just under forty years, Andrésy and its surrounding region had been equipped with networks supplying gas for streetlights and homes, water from the river and later from artesian wells, and electricity for public lighting and industrial and domestic uses. The fate of those networks had remained for more than half a century in the hands of a family firm that grew into a service provider to tens of thousands of homes in as many as sixteen towns and villages in the Seine and Oise valleys.

A springboard for regional development

In the light of the above we can see how the 60-year concession gave a sense of focus and continuity to infrastructure network development in Andrésy and beyond under the stewardship of a sound local and regional operator.

Less than a decade after securing that concession, Paul Mallet, keen to fulfil his company's basic commitments to providing *Andrésiens* with quality public utilities, had spotted its potential to pioneer wider regional development and to pave the way for the Seine and Oise to become part of the expanding Paris region. What is more, he was fully prepared to invest his own money in capitalizing on that potential. The first step would be to extend the Andrésy gas pipelines to neighbouring towns. But that would amount to a violation of the terms of the original contract. So Mallet embarked on a series of talks with the authorities, and eventually managed to negotiate a positive outcome by promising to equip the town with electricity as soon as he possibly could – a pledge that would not be honoured until after his death, some twenty years later.

Documentary evidence shows that the relationship between the Mallet Corporation and Andrésy council was somewhat less than smooth, and the same was probably true in the other towns too. The minutes of council meetings attest to frequent wrangling over the price of gas, water and lighting and complaints about the quality of services in one neighbourhood or another. Yet the councillors' firm official stance always seemed to stop short of calls for the relationship to be terminated. Ultimately, they appear to have had a deep respect for the company's technical and economic standing and, indeed, for its owner, a man described in the minutes of a meeting on 13 January 1898 as "a hardworking person in whom one can place the greatest confidence and whose enterprise embodies every possible assurance of stability and high performance".

The fact is that the authorities usually ended up delegating the right to build, run and charge users for public utility services because they lacked anywhere near the necessary technical expertise and financial resources to do so themselves. Mallet, on the other hand, had accumulated a wealth of experience in the field and, at the end of the day, was a fully self-financing operation. Indeed, the Mallets wrote on a number of occasions to the mayor of Andrésy to remind him of the public works their company had done at its own expense, incurring costs that should by rights have been covered by the municipal budget, e.g. the construction of an emergency telephone line to warn the Andrésy pumping plant of impending disruptions in the electricity supply after the Nord-Lumière network transformer at Puiseux had been hit by lightning. Furthermore, the Mallet Corporation was especially adept at coming up with tailor-made solutions to meet local demand, developing and perfecting techniques that would not only earn it a tidy profit but also, and perhaps more importantly, secure customer loyalty on the part of the users and boost its prestige in the eyes of the profession. So successful was it in achieving its goals that it soon earned a reputation as a pioneering innovator through such technological breakthroughs as:

- The installation at the Andrésy plant of prototype gas-powered engines powerful enough to pump water to homes located at an unprecedented altitude above the river;

- The exploitation of by-products from the plant's patented coal distillation and natural gas treatment processes – coke, benzol and a variety of substances for use in road surfacing and so on – all of which helped balance its books and, at the same time, promote its diversification as a petrochemicals supplier;

- The development of high-pressure gas piping systems, one as much as seven kilometres in length, which enabled the network's expansion into the Seine and Oise valleys;

- The 500-metre deep artesian wells, regarded as a technological feat at the time, which gave fresh impetus to the Mallet water supply network.

These were just a few of the examples that turned the Mallet Corporation into an economic powerhouse and something of a local institution, which is why the relatively powerless authorities were so reluctant to take the plunge and terminate the concession.

New network territoriality

As the Andrésy-based infrastructure networks spread to neighbouring towns and villages, they cut through administrative boundaries and, in so doing, gradually ended up creating new territorialities. Local communities that had previously had little in common with each other found themselves drawn into new interrelationships where they were all drinking the same water (from 1895), lighting their homes and cooking with gas from the same refinery (from 1909), and walking streets lit by an electricity network equipped with public funds raised by a special inter-municipal body (from the 1930s). In return, they all played their part in maintaining the Mallet Corporation in financial equilibrium while their elected representatives, acting within the framework of the inter-municipal body, served to underpin its territorializing power (Raffestin, 1980).

But what does it actually mean to talk about 'local populations'? Who were those public utility users occupying the new infrastructure network-territory?

Taken together, the various networks had helped bring about the spatial and social transformation of Andrésy and, no doubt, its neighbouring towns. As early as 1898, the town council had recognized that granting Mallet an "exclusive territorial monopoly for the installation of gas for lighting and water supply would boost the town's future prosperity; increase the well-being of its inhabitants; and attract a good many people coming in search of a pleasant and comfortable place to spend their holidays". As a matter of fact, much of the subsequent urban development work in and around Andrésy would be geared not so much to providing public utilities for the locals, as to catering for the Parisians that were, in a sense, invading and 'annexing' the area to the capital: on the one hand, entertaining the recreation-hungry tourists crowding the dance halls and literally swarming onto the river in rented rowboats; on the other hand, ensuring that the villas of the wealthy, built on the banks of the Seine and the slopes of Hautil hill on plots of land purchased from local farmers and winegrowers, enjoyed access to the kinds of amenities already available in Paris: running water, gas and electricity.

Ultimately municipal zoning maps could not stand in the way of such overwhelming demand, and the administrative and social landscape changed out of all recognition. Whereas historically Andrésy had maintained fairly close relations with Poissy and Saint-Germain-en-Laye to the south, the new network territorialities forged links not just with Paris but also with the other real estate-rich riverside communities of the Seine and Oise to the west and north; all underpinned, of course, by the expansionist ambitions of the Mallet Corporation.

However, the company would not figure among the leading players in the next phase of network-territorial change that came with the post-war nationalization of the French energy sectors, soon after Marcel Mallet's death in an accident in 1944. Since the ensuing improvements to the road and rail systems, the industrial development of the Seine valley and the massive suburban housing development programmes – including the construction of Cergy-Pontoise new town – a number of local communities around Andrésy have been converted into dormitory towns for Paris' nascent commuter belt. While the Mallet networks may still exist physically, their territorializing role is very much a thing of the past.

Conclusion

What does this case study tell us about infrastructure development as a whole? First and foremost that it is just that: holistic. Not one of the Mallet Corporation networks can be considered as a single, self-contained unit. Aside from the various technological factors, there appear to have been two overriding reasons for this:

- First economic: Mallet sought to spread its investments across several networks at once in order to expand not just the actual infrastructure but also its customer base so as to be able to cover the basic equipment costs. Networks already up and running served as 'bargaining chips' for securing new construction or expansion contracts – the water-supply system helping it branch into gas and then electricity, for instance, or a contract with one particular town paving the way for another with one or more of its neighbours;

- And second social: as Andrésy and its surrounding area were drawn increasingly into the Paris region, it created the need to provide sanitation and other urban services that were normally the responsibility of the local authorities.

By and large, it was the overlapping of the strategic goals of the entrepreneur with the social objectives of the authorities that led to the emergence of a new network-territory underpinned by the Mallet plants and processes, capital and consumers. But another instrumental factor was the opportunity for whole towns to make a living from tourism and the property market, i.e. from contributing to their annexation by Paris.

Notes

Note 1   All unreferenced quotations in this Chapter come from documents contained in the archives of Andrésy town council.

"In the period of consolidation of the unitary State, in the middle of the consolidation of its executive power (1880-1910), the policies of the networked technical services constituted instruments of maximum importance for the government of Italian cities, both on the part of the State and on the part of the local governmental bodies. Those instruments, not normally considered straight 'urban instruments', still have non-marginal effects on the organization of the city: in a phase that urban history defines as the 'radial-centric city', the basic service networks (public transport, water pipes, gas, electricity, sanitation) confirm and ratify this model of growth and at the same time constitute a way to manage the urban expansion. Municipal activities and decision-making regarding the infrastructures and services shape the elaboration and performance of the ordinary urban instrument, when one exists; but more often – especially in this phase – they replace the instrument aimed at achieving the same goal of territorial configuration: that of the radial-centric city."

From: I servizi tecnici a rete et la questione della municipalizzione nelle città italiane (1880-1910) *by Donatella Calabi; in Morachilllo, P., et al., Le Machine imperfette: architettura, programma, istituzioni, nel XIX secolo, Officina Edizioni, 1979*

6   Adapting French Cities to Car Traffic during the Post-war Years: Uncle Sam's Math Lesson[*]

In the aftermath of World War II, America greatly contributed to the economic reconstruction and development of Europe. Thanks to the Marshall Plan, Europe was able to rebuild much of what had been destroyed during the war. However, the transfers from America to Europe were not only economic and technological. Indeed, in some fields, in particular roadworks and car traffic, European engineers continued to draw inspiration from American methods, as they had been doing since long before the war.

The influence of American technology on European engineers concerned not only the fields of roadworks and regulatory road signs, but also that of traffic forecasting. Though forecasting traffic flows between cities is not too difficult, within cities it becomes a complex task, requiring sophisticated techniques. Since cars were popular in America long before they became so in Europe, American engineers were already experienced in solving the problems now facing their European counterparts. The latter were thus strongly tempted to borrow American methods through a transfer of 'intellectual technology'.

The way this happened in France is particularly interesting, since the transfer process was not taken over by consulting firms, as was the case in other countries, but was kept under state control. Indeed, the state was responsible for building roads and conducting the necessary surveys, and also, at the time, for urban development and city planning. Our study spans the years 1950 to 1975. After 1975, during the political and administrative decentralization process, these forecasting methods continued to be used. At the same time, public opinion was becoming increasingly aware of environmental issues, such as landscape preservation and quality of life. Today, environmental activists are blocking the construction of new urban freeways. Will the American methods transferred to France to adapt cities to car traffic fail because of their inability to take account of environmental issues? A study of how the situation evolved in France from 1975 till now should enable us to answer this question.

The first traffic forecasts

First and foremost, let us take a closer look at the history of traffic forecasting. Various counting methods were used very early on to measure traffic flows. In Europe and in America, counting urban car traffic was considered a means to evaluate how wide roads should be built (Danger, 1935; Swan, 1922). 'Origin-destination' surveys were developed in the United States before World War II. Their aim was to determine where to build road bridges (to cross rivers or railroad tracks), on the basis of motorists' itineraries (Clark & Peters, 1965). These surveys revealed 'desire lines' which differed from actual routes. In order to forecast future traffic flows, American forecasters simply extrapolated on the basis of traffic 'growth factors' such as the increase in car ownership rates (Patterson, 1966; Stopher, 1971).

---

[*]   Previously published as « Adapter les villes françaises à l'automobile dans les décennies d'après-guerre : la leçon de calcul de l'oncle Sam ». In: Kaspi, A. (2000, ed.) Les relations franco-américaines dans le domaine de la technologie. Proceedings of a colloquium organised at La Fondation Singer-Polignac, 26 November 1998. Abbeville: F. Paillart. Included with permission.

In the early forties, a traffic forecasting method which could be applied to an entire urban area (both existing and projected) was developed in Detroit (Dutton & Starbuck, 1974). This technique was much more ambitious than the previous ones, and rather specific circumstances explain its invention. The automobile and road industries were pressuring the government to allocate more funds to the construction of roads, especially in urban areas. These demands were met thanks to the 1946 Federal Highway Act. However, given the nature of these funds (a special fund financed by fuel taxes), the Bureau of Public Roads demanded that investments be justified by strict methods. Advances in computer technology made it possible to perform calculations which so far had been impossibly difficult. In this context, Voorhees (1956), using both theoretical analysis and practical experience, developed a statistical-mathematical model based on a 'general theory of traffic movements'. Thanks to this model, he was able to meet both the automobile lobby's and the American administration's demands by drawing up guidelines to promote investments for the construction of roads, to increase car traffic and boost the automobile market, all this at minor cost (illustration 6.1). After Detroit, these new methods were extended to Chicago and Pittsburgh and gradually, to other cities all over the U.S.

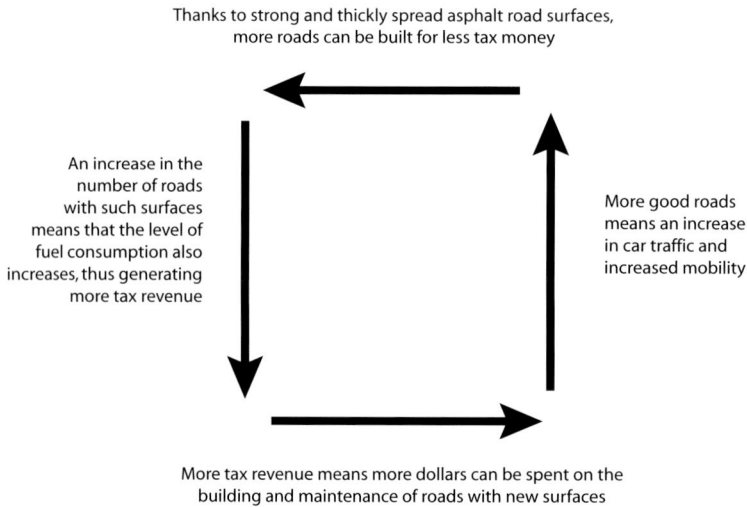

Thanks to strong and thickly spread asphalt road surfaces, more roads can be built for less tax money

An increase in the number of roads with such surfaces means that the level of fuel consumption also increases, thus generating more tax revenue

More good roads means an increase in car traffic and increased mobility

More tax revenue means more dollars can be spent on the building and maintenance of roads with new surfaces

Illustration 6.1   **The magical Circle of Asphalt.** (Asphalt Insitute, 1966)

The transfer: its historical context and conditions

The method reached France in the early 1960s and was finally adopted ten years later. True, the U.S. and France differed in many respects: institutions, forms of urbanization, transportation systems, lifestyles, and so on. Why was it possible for this imported, American, planning tool to be so quickly and painlessly transplanted into a European, and more specifically, a French context?

The first reason is that the automobile production and road construction industries were at the time quite ready for such a transfer. Indeed, despite the destructions wrought by the war, France, England and Germany had a dynamic automobile industry. The domestic market was going through a boom. By 1966, half of French households owned a car. However, beyond exports, the future growth of the automobile sector depended on the increase in the distances covered by cars: as distances grew, the frequency of replacement of cars, the consumption of fuel, lubricants, tires, spare parts also increased. In the early 1960s, however, French motorists still drove very little compared to their American counterparts, and the number of kilometres they covered each year was half that covered by German motorists (Faure, 1959).

To encourage people to drive meant developing road networks. Unfortunately, the existing road system in France, though dense, was not adapted to modern driving habits, especially in urban areas. The French budget for roadworks was almost as high as the American budget. On the other hand, France invested five times less in the construction of new roads. As is customary in Europe, the automobile and road lobbies remained in the background. However, the *Plan français*, a government institution in charge of coordinating public policies and private decisions, emphasized the need to support the automobile industry by investing more in the construction of roads. After the war, following the American example, France created a 'Special Investment Fund for Road Construction' (*Fonds Special d'Investissement Routier – FSIR*), financed at first by taxes on fuel. At the time, road construction policies were both insufficient and inefficient: funds were spread thinly over the many municipalities and various local administrations, and the network as a whole remained inefficient.

Investments thus had to be increased and more efficiently distributed. Highways were needed to satisfy people's love of speed, and as a result, the distances travelled by car also increased. Population migrations towards large cities underscored the necessity of developing urban road networks that, in their actual state, were ill adapted to car traffic. Urban growth and the implantation of new economic activities also entailed building new roads.

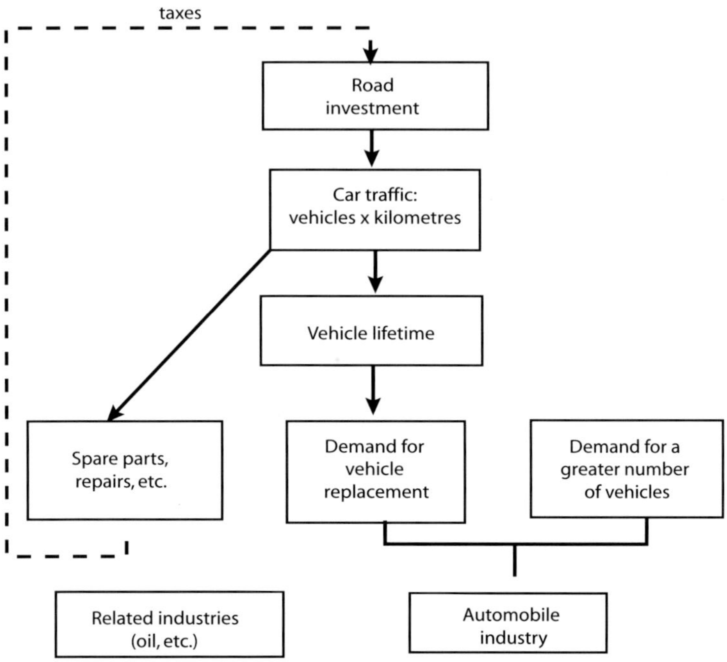

Illustration 6.2   From road investment to automobile industry

The oil and automobile industries believed that automobile-related state taxes should be used to build roads (particularly through the FSIR), and that accordingly, the state's choices in terms of investments in infrastructure should be made on a rational basis. Thus, during the 1960s, it became clear to the French institutions in charge of road infrastructures that the road networks had to be coherently and rationally adapted to car traffic. Even though, officially, the aim of government policies was to solve transportation rather than traffic problems; even though city-dwellers still mainly rode bicycles or used public transportation (or simply walked); even though European cities had a very vulnerable and delicate urban fabric in terms of architecture, historical heritage, and what would later be called 'the living environment'; the French administration's new urban policy, nevertheless, focused on motorists' needs. This policy was to a large extent supported by the new traffic forecasting technologies imported from America.

The influence of American traffic forecasting models in France

Documents obtained from American professional associations were brought back to France and translated into French. For example, the *Technical Manual for Highway Traffic* was translated into French as early as 1953. In 1954, a government institution called the Bureau of Surveys and Research on Traffic (*Service d'Etudes et de Recherche sur la Circulation – SERC*) was created. The SERC imported American methods: origin-destination surveys, traffic-increase factors. The SERC's aim was first and foremost to obtain quantitative information on traffic flows, and to determine how much time could be saved for drivers by improving road networks and infrastructures.

The surveys (SERC, 1962) showed that American methods could perfectly well be transplanted into the French context. Although there were many differences between the two countries – in France, for instance, the use of two-wheeled vehicles and public transportation was still very popular – they seemed to be disappearing fast.

In 1965, after having conducted several surveys in large French cities, the SERC presented authorities with what was then called 'coherence tests'. The aim of these tests was to evaluate, with the help of traffic forecasting methods, whether the road construction projects were in agreement with future urbanization prospects. The models used were directly inspired by the American theories developed ten years before. These tests were gradually implemented in several big cities of France. In the larger cities, where city planners planned future urban development, these urbanization prospects represented the main input for traffic forecasting models.

Consultants then tried to take over the market for these models by adapting American techniques to the French context. However, the SERC stood guard and tried to preserve the government's dominant, and even exclusive position in the field. In 1967, the SERC elaborated its own model (DAVIS), soon followed and completed by another (FABER). These models borrowed the American models' classical UTMS-structure (Urban Transport Modelling Systems) while making the input and output data more accessible to French technicians. In 1971, twelve large cities in France were using traffic forecasting methods. At that time, American traffic models were at the height of their popularity. Paris received special treatment. A specific study was needed, because the city had been having serious traffic problems since the late 1950s. Its transportation system, although well developed, was unable to catch up with the pace of urbanization. Two major tendencies emerged. On the one hand, the 'pro-car' tendency of the SERC, which was in favour of carrying out an extensive, 'heavy duty' study of the Chicago type, which consisted in applying the traffic forecasting method. On the other hand, the

Institute of City Planning and Urbanism of the Paris Area (*Institut d'Amenagement et d'Urbanisme de la Region Parisienne – IAURP* [1]), which the government had entrusted with the task of planning the *villes nouvelles* (new cities) of the Paris area, was in favour of conducting a smaller, lighter study, complete with detailed surveys among public transportation users and sophisticated theoretical analyses.

These studies would enable public authorities to develop a new model which would be better adapted to the local context and in particular, according to the IAURP, would allow public transportation to continue playing a significant role in the Paris area. A compromise was thus found: the specific characteristics of the Paris area would be taken into account, and the collection of the data needed to construct an American-type model would be made possible. Thus, French public authorities increasingly favoured the 'all-car' approach, although Paris, thanks to its public transportation system, received special treatment.

Towards decentralization

In the early seventies, due to widespread criticism, the inflow of new methods from America slackened. The year 1968 represented a turning point for French society. In the general atmosphere of rebellion and protest, all the government's previous policies, including urban transportation policies, found themselves under scrutiny. At first, there was no question of actually condemning them. What critics mainly focused on was the discrepancy between the long-term policy of adapting the city to car traffic, and the everyday needs of city dwellers (Fichelet, Fichelet & May, 1970). Local authorities complained of traffic jams, parking problems, and demanded that solutions be found immediately. Public transportation advocates were concerned about the decreasing quality of service and the deepening financial losses of public transportation companies. Although these issues were at the centre of a public debate, the existing system, based on traffic forecasting models, was not called into question. The only resulting change was that short-term measures were taken and added to the existing long-term plan for urban road networks. With the support of the state, municipalities would now be able to plan and implement traffic routes in order to improve quickly and locally the traffic situation (one-way streets, parking regulations, road signs).

Interestingly enough, traffic forecasting models were thus made to serve a different purpose, since they were now used as a support to establish such traffic routes. However, during that period, the central government continued to encourage, by means of financial incentives, the widespread and systematic use of these models for long-term studies.

Technically speaking, the models themselves did not change over the decade, except that they were adapted to the improved capacities of modern computers. What did change, on the other hand, was the environment in which the models were applied. In the past, government-paid engineers would carry out coherence tests for urban master plans but would not share their methods – nor even sometimes their results – with local elected representatives or public works departments. This was no longer possible. Nor could such issues as parking problems, public transportation, the integration of the road network into the urban fabric be 'ignored' any longer. The models were now seen as a simple tool, a technically necessary element to be used in the framework of a more global approach bringing together all concerned local representatives while taking into account all possible obstacles to investments in road building. In France, demand for greater decentralization was growing and the American example, with people's violent reaction of protest against urban highways, seemed to have impressed public authorities.

Within this ten-year span during the 1950s and 1960s, not only were theories transferred to France from the United States, but so was their practical application in the field of urban road planning. To what extent did this transfer help France solve its urban transportation problems?

Urban transportation and car traffic: how French cities adjusted

In 1962, a French commentator wrote, with quite a bit of insight: "[for car traffic models], the localization of population groups and of future jobs is considered as data, and not as a parameter. Public transportation, parking regulations, traffic jams in the city centre are only summarily taken into consideration as mere inconveniencies, and are never treated as they should be, that is to say as factors which play a role in the overall equilibrium of human movements within a city, and as possible tools to be used in the implementation of a transportation policy" (SERC, 1962). This analysis referred to American traffic models, which were adopted in France for the very reasons mentioned: the aim was not to elaborate a transportation policy but to adapt roads to car traffic.

Although the model was never used, either in France or in the United States, as a basis to draw up a real urban transportation policy, it nevertheless did address transportation problems. It was designed and built to foresee increases in traffic flows in terms of the total distance covered by cars (and even to ensure such an increase by determining the necessary width of roads). This 'self-fulfilling prophecy' effect appears clearly after a detailed analysis of the model's mathematical and statistical formulation (Dupuy 1975). However, urban transportation issues, in other words issues concerning movements which are necessary to an urban system, could not be completely ignored. Simply, owing to the increasing popularity of cars, the nature of these issues was modified and seen in another light. Thus, unlike their American counterparts, French forecasting models could not be applied regardless of municipal limits. Indeed, local financing systems (which are increasingly burdened), and urban planning projects, without which the models could not be efficiently used, are organized according to administrative municipal divisions within the urban area.

Finally, traffic models, both in France and in the United States, served as a basis for research aiming at rationalizing and bringing more coherence to investment decisions in road construction matters. The role of the FSIR in France and of the Highway Trust Fund in the United States, of the Road Department in France and of the Highway State Department and Bureau of Public Roads in the U.S. was not limited to building more roads in order to encourage motorists to drive more. They had to ensure that investments were globally rational. If the coherence of road projects could not be proven, the necessary funding was difficult to obtain. The traffic forecasting models thus had to take into account urban planning concerns.

The traffic forecasts calculated by these models soon turned out to be wrong. This was to be expected, given the hypotheses on which they were based (Bonnafous & Plassard, 1974). Furthermore, judging by the above-mentioned orientations in matters of car traffic regulation, the aim of these models was not to provide an accurate forecast of traffic flows, but mainly to ensure the coherence of road construction policies promoting the use of cars. These obvious forecasting errors did not destroy the scientific reputation of these models which had been so highly praised by experts such as Voorhees. The amount of data used and the extreme complexity of the processing system made the mechanisms at work in these models quite unfathomable. France and the U.S. both took advantage of this 'mysterious' aspect

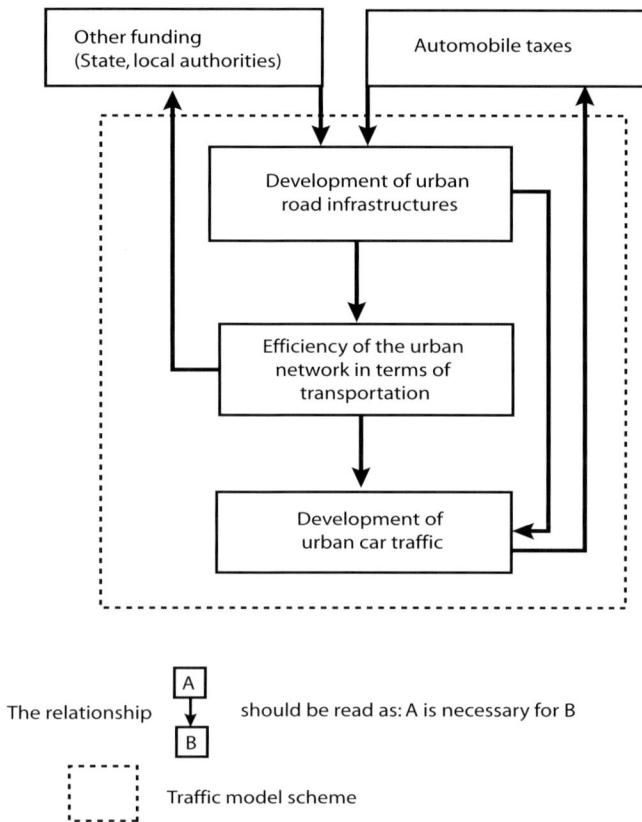

Illustration 6.3   Traffic model scheme

to render their ambiguous approach more acceptable: under the pretext of urban and transportation planning, the aim was to encourage driving. How else in the sixties could one defend such a massive and infinite increase in the volume of car traffic, a phenomenon which meant that urban space had to be entirely reorganized? The state could not openly announce to mayors and city-dwellers that their cities were going to be 'Americanized' without fail. Behind the mask of complex statistics, incomprehensible mechanisms and sophisticated algorithms, the car traffic models mysteriously played their part, away from the public eye.

This transfer of 'intellectual technology' between the United States and France brought about another 'transfer' of a more strictly urban nature. Those who doubted its reality or who could not see it in 1975 could not but acknowledge it twenty years later, whether they are happy about it or not. As the General Delegate of the French Federation of City-Planning Agencies declared at the Annual Meeting of the Federation of City-Planning Agencies in March 1996: "Urban sprawl was caused by cars, maybe because driving was excessively encouraged and because road networks were improved to such an extent that people were able to travel ever greater distances." Uncle Sam's models were much more than math lessons, aimed at teaching us how to forecast traffic flows. They opened the way for deep transformations in the fabric of European cities, causing them to become increasingly 'Americanized'.

The environmental issue

Today, several highway or urban freeway projects in France, in Germany, the Netherlands, Belgium, and in Great Britain have been halted for environmental reasons. Environmental protest movements were born in the mid-1970s. Up until then, activists had been demanding that the transportation system for the working population be improved. Gradually, this protest movement targeted its complaints, which were just as virulent, though less organized, towards the preservation of landscapes and residential quietude. The middle classes joined the battle to protect the quality of life they had worked so hard to earn. Criticism was mainly levelled at the transportation infrastructure. Indeed, in this field, it is usually the state, whose role it should be to protect public well-being, which initiates the large-scale projects perceived as harmful. Furthermore, the purpose of a new highway is not as immediately understood and evident as that of a new school or a hospital.

The state's response to these protests was ambiguous. At first, during the 1970s, opposition remained low-key and the government did not represent a united, hostile front against environmental activism. On the contrary, environmental conservation, safeguarding the national heritage, protecting the quality of life were considered important issues in the higher spheres of the Administration and in some political circles. Thus were created the *Délégation à la Qualité de la Vie* (Delegation for the Quality of Life) and in 1971 the Ministry of the Environment.

As criticism against road infrastructures grew in intensity and precision, the authorities attempted some improvements. The integration of road construction projects into the local environment received greater attention. An impact-study methodology was used for large-scale projects from 1976 onwards. Since 1983, new infrastructure projects cannot be implemented without a preliminary survey. Thanks to these measures, protests abated but did not altogether die out. They remained most virulent in places where environmental activism was supported by powerful local interests: in Paris, the expressway project on the left bank of the Seine and a North-South expressway project ('Vercingétorix') were abandoned. Local residents pressured the government into halting the A86 highway project, which was supposed to cross a forest in the western suburbs of Paris, a well-to-do area.

During the 1980s, several obstacles came into the way of those who favoured the development of road networks. The first was decentralization and the delegation of power to local authorities, in 1982. Indeed, this process endangered the coherence of the road network, for which the state was responsible (in particular through urban planning): in matters concerning road infrastructures, power was shared between central and local authorities; municipalities were in charge of urban planning. Environmental activists thus took advantage of these weak spots in the decision-making system to pursue their goals.

The government was also coping with an economic crisis and trying to avoid spending on expensive projects. Due to environmental measures, urban road infrastructures were increasingly costly (up to 1 billion French francs per km for an urban freeway). Urban roads had to be either built underground or covered; they had to be invisible, odourless, and aesthetically pleasing; the trees pulled out in the process had to be replanted, and so on.

A private financing system of urban roads (through concessions and tolls) emerged at the end of the 1980s, matching that of the interurban highway system (generally toll highways). New urban toll freeway projects, fostered by recent technological advances in the field (tunnel-diggers for underground highways, automatic toll collectors), cropped up everywhere, in Paris and the Paris area, in Lyons, and in the large cities in the south of France. These projects were criticized not for their environmental impact, but because they required the payment of a toll: this was considered unacceptable (the unit price for using an urban highway is about ten times that of an interurban highway). When the first urban toll highways opened in 1995, critics continued to loudly voice their opposition, in Lyons and Toulouse for instance. In some cases, construction projects were blocked (A104 In the Paris area, A8bis in Nice, and so on). The A14 toll highway managed to open in 1996 only because it was a (very expensive) model of environmental preservation.

In the new context of rising environmental activism – practically non-existent in the 1960s – could the American traffic-forecasting models, which had been so useful to French road engineers in the 1970s, continue to serve their purpose?

Uncle Sam's math lesson: is it still relevant?

American traffic models made it possible to anticipate needs and thus justify the construction of new roads. Towards the end of the 1970s, they were applied to a slightly different purpose – that of traffic management. In other words, they were used to manage traffic flows thanks to minor arrangements inside the city. Thirty years later, and fifty years after these models were developed in the United States, what can be said about them? Were they able to take account of the growing demand for environmental preservation? Why haven't they been able to convince the public that this or that new highway was necessary despite environmental side-effects?

First of all, American traffic forecasting models are still very popular in Europe, and especially in France. DAVIS, which was developed in 1967, is still actively used today. 95 Percent of French transportation surveys are based on the Urban Transport Modelling Surveys imported in the 1960s.

However, the development of computer and software technology, as well as the transformation of the problems themselves, has led to numerous changes. Computations have been broken up into smaller parts, to take into account the behaviour of smaller, more homogeneous, groups of transportation users; traffic forecasting models are applied to cases where people use several means of transportation; the factors causing traffic increases have been isolated (time saving or other service improvements). Furthermore, when private consulting firms began to market very efficient new traffic models, the state lost its monopoly in the field of traffic models. As a result, models are now used in new and varied ways: to forecast the effect of changing the direction of automobile traffic, to study the impact on traffic of the construction of a new shopping mall, or the possibility of building a new public transportation connection. The models are even used to assess the profitability of urban toll highways, even though it is rather difficult to predict the potential users' willingness to pay.

Nevertheless, though these models have remained highly popular, they are far from adapted to the problems facing road administrations today, particularly the environmental issue. The environmental questions mentioned in the preceding paragraph can be efficiently accounted for only if road networks and urban planning are organized in a coherent manner. The original American models did so, and the French methodology of the 1970s formalized this approach. The aim of traffic forecasting was to test the capacity of the entire road network to absorb the traffic flows predicted by urbanization forecasts. Long-term urban planning projects saw the city as divided into separate sections: a residential district, a business district, a green area, a traffic network, with strict zoning regulations to avoid disturbances.

The location of future transportation infrastructures was marked off a long time in advance to prevent urban development in the immediate surroundings. However, due to the lesser part played by the state in urban planning questions from the 1980s on, coherence has now become problematic.

Models are of no help to anyone if future urban projects are not integrated into a global model accepted by all. In theory, what would be needed are models forecasting both traffic and future urbanization. Such models were attempted in the United States around 1960, with no significant results. Recently, since this problem concerns many countries, an international study group has been created to find a solution (International Study Group on Land Use and Transport Interaction[2]). As yet, however, theoretical research and technological progress have not been able to produce an operational model. Thus, one cannot simulate the long-term environmental impact of road construction.

The 'multicriteria' approach (Mellet, 1971), suggested for the first time in France in the 1960s and codified in 1986 by the *Direction des Routes* (Road Administration) did not provide a satisfying solution either. This approach consisted in comparing several possible variants of a single project, and assessing their quality according to several criteria, particularly the environment. But according to this method, the projects compared are equivalent in terms of traffic since they are based on the same forecasting model. Thus, those who criticize the project will necessarily refuse all its variants, since they disagree with the forecasting method in the first place. Nevertheless, two of the French engineers who had participated in the adaptation of the American models to the French context in the early 1970s have tried to adapt them once again to the new environment-friendly context (Dupuy, 1975). Their approach includes an assessment in monetary terms of the cost of environmental protection (which is low compared to the value of the time saved thanks to the new infrastructures). More specifically, this approach considers the fact that highways provide greater accessibility for those who are interested in open, 'green' areas, in a less dense, less polluted environment. Highways and corresponding traffic are thus given a new, pro-environment justification. The mathematical aspect of this approach makes it a direct descendant of the models imported from the United States in the 1960s. In this case, 'Uncle Sam's math lesson' has clearly been well learned. This method is applied nowadays in the Paris area, even though the groups concerned aren't all satisfied with it, nor are all the road engineers. The state, however, supports its implementation.

Thus, none of the traffic forecasting models imported from America are entirely proof against the attacks of environmental protesters. In some cases, the activists themselves have acquired the expertise enabling them to call into question the implicit function of a traffic forecasting model. Opponents of the A8bis or A104 projects, for example, criticize the model's underlying hypotheses, such as the distribution between local and transit traffic, the induction of traffic, the impact of increased accessibility on urbanization, and so on. The black box is more than just half-opened!

However, it would be wrong to speak of failure. The 'hard-line' opposition, acting through the counter-expertise of assessment methods, has concentrated on several symbolically chosen large-scale projects. But collusion between radical anti-automobile activism (which may originate in the fear of the greenhouse effect) and powerful local interest seems quite unlikely. In the meantime, the network is being gradually but systematically modernized and extended, thanks to 'classical' traffic forecasting models. As opposed to the 1965-1975 period, methodological questions are no longer considered crucial. The state keeps a low profile in urban planning matters. Municipal land use plans (*plan d'occupation des sols* and *plan local d'urbanisme*) have replaced the more far-reaching *Schémas Directeurs d'Aménagement* (Master Plans). Road construction projects are no longer suggested by the central administration but by the *Conseils généraux des departments* (French departmental councils).

Despite the importance of environmental aspects, French cities are still being 'Americanized' with traffic models developed in the United States almost fifty years ago. The figures speak for themselves: urban density in France has been reduced by half within 35 years. Traffic on French road networks increased by almost 40 percent in 12 years (1982-1994); at the time when environmental opposition was at its fiercest. Still, notwithstanding the pressure, 'Uncle Sam' is still teaching the French how to adapt the city road network to car traffic.

Notes

Note 1   IAURP was created in 1960. In 1976 it changed its name to IAURIF – *Institut d'Aménagement et d'Urbanisme de la Région d'Ile-de-France*, currently still in operation as the regional authority on spatial planning in the greater Paris region.

Note 2   The ISGLUTI (International Study Group on Land Use and Transport Interaction) programme dates from the 1980s (Webster and Paulley, 1990).

"Technology is critical to the city-building process and the operation of cities, but historians have not paid serious attention to its vital role in shaping the urban environment until the last decade or so. Although technology and cities have always been interdependent, only since the advent of industrialism in the nineteenth century have urban technological networks evolved. Today, what we call the urban infrastructure provides the technological 'sinews of the modern metropolitan area: its road, bridge, and transit networks; its water and sewer lines and waste-disposal facilities; and its power and communication systems.

These 'sinews' guide and facilitate urban functioning and urban life in a multitude of ways, some positive and others negative, some visible and others invisible. The infrastructure includes not only networks but also structures and machines, and it is located both above and below the ground. It is both publicly and privately constructed and operated, with variations not only from country to country but also from time period to time period within nations. Technological infrastructure makes possible the existence of the modern city and provides the means for its continuing operation, but it also increases the city's vulnerability to catastrophic events such as war or natural disaster. While technology may enhance the urban quality of life, it may also be a force for deterioration and destruction of neighborhoods, as well as a hindrance to humane and rational planning."

From: Technology and the Rise of the Networked City in Europe and America *by Joel Tarr; in Tarr, J.A. & Dupuy, G., Temple University Press, Philadelphia, 1988*

7   Crisis in the Urban Infrastructure Networks: The Case of Buenos Aires[*]

Background

Urban infrastructure networks

"A complex arrangement of the lines, communication channels, electrical conductors, piping, and so on, serving the same geographic unit and administered by the same company"… that, in a nutshell, is how the dictionary defines the networks providing the modern city with its basic facilities (Petit Robert, 2007 edition). Their incredible development has left a lasting impression on the contemporary history of the urban condition in Western societies. Rural-urban migration in the nineteenth century created new needs in terms of drinking water supply, waste water drainage, lighting, transporting people and goods, road traffic, communication and so on. In order to keep liquid flows, gas behaviour, electricity and so on under technical and scientific control, and to have the capacity to work with cast iron, steel, cement, concrete and other such materials, specific solutions had to be found based on the sustainable construction of installations capable of conveying, storing, treating and distributing water and various forms of power widely throughout the urban area.

People themselves would be carried along lines more or less directly bridging the ever-wider divide separating the home and the workplace. City, regional and national governments would seek a role in the provision and administration of services. Private economic operators would discover new investment sectors with unique conditions in terms of monopolies, economies of scale and increasing returns. Partnerships involving private companies under public control – in combinations that varied from one country or even city to the next – led to the establishment of infrastructure frameworks that would both underpin and steer urban growth. Despite being a crucial aspect of the modern city, the resulting body of networks received virtually no serious attention until 1983 when Paris hosted Europe's first international seminar on the contemporary history of urban infrastructure networks (Dupuy & Tarr, 1984). In addition to highlighting the variety of network-building processes over the previous two hundred years, the seminar revealed the underlying similarities of this facet of urban development in cities across the globe.

An emergent crisis

By the mid-1980s, however, infrastructure networks almost everywhere were already showing signs of weakness. The problems in developing countries stemmed from the fact that their existing facilities were struggling to cope with a burgeoning population. Entire neighbourhoods lacked access to basic minimum services – water, sanitation, transport, and electricity – and the resulting divide raised doubts

---

[*]   Previously published as two Chapters in Dupuy, G., 1987, *La Crise des Réseaux d'Infrastructure: le Cas de Buenos Aires*. Paris, LATTS, pp. 11-24 & 251-270. Chapters : « Recherche sur Buenos Aires: La Ville et ses Réseaux » & « Les Réseaux d'Infrastructures et la Ville ». Included with permission

as to whether some shanty towns or other such examples of spontaneous or 'anarchic' urbanization could every really become part of the city *per se* (Coing, 1980).

But the situation in some developed countries was critical too, with the water, sanitation, public transport and road systems suffering from a complex mix of factors including an ageing infrastructure, scarce fiscal resources, and a lack of maintenance. Nowhere near enough funding could be raised to cover the costs of renovation and rehabilitation, and to reverse the cumulative processes driving some networks to the brink of collapse. Hard-hitting reports were produced in the United States and Great Britain. While the situation in other countries may, on the face of it, have seemed less serious, the prospects for the future of their urban networks were, in fact, no less alarming (Tarr, 1984; Gakenheimer, 1986; Triantafillou, 1987; Dupuy, 1988b). Aside from the technical and economic picture, the crisis could be seen to reflect an erosion of the urban bonds that had, in the past, enabled the provision of basic utilities for all city dwellers. The economic crisis was making matters worse. When money is scarce, the haves are less inclined to pay for the have-nots and the centre stops subsidizing the outskirts, or vice versa. The upshot, for an urban culture where connections to the distribution and transport networks have become a social norm, is worrying to say the least.

Illustration 7.1   **Imported technology played a key role in urban infrastructure networks development**

The case of Buenos Aires

In the mid-1980s, Buenos Aires could not be pigeonholed in either of the above two categories. As a matter of fact, it fell into both. Walking through the streets of the Argentinean capital, one did not have as deep a sense as in other developing countries of the dichotomy both dividing and uniting districts with access to the full range of public services and those with none whatsoever. At the same time, however, the situation in a city whose former prosperity had, over the years, drawn vast numbers of people from Europe, from other parts of Argentina and from its neighbouring countries, could not be compared to that of the cities of the north-eastern United States, for instance, whose populations had deserted them for the sunbelt states.

The reason for choosing to study the urban infrastructure networks of Buenos Aires was that the 1983 seminar in Paris had established the need to complete the picture of network development in European and North American cities with comparative analysis of a capital city more recent than those of Europe and less marked by industrial urbanization than Chicago or Pittsburgh. Furthermore, the seminar had suggested that international transfers of technology and technical models had played a key role in the history of urban network development (see illustration 7.1). As isolating that role clearly enough to be able to pinpoint its effects was impossible in the case of European and North American cities, a representative example of the impact of foreign influences would have to be found elsewhere. Buenos Aires was chosen for practical reasons, after a number of other candidates had been eliminated. It meant studying a city whose infrastructures were not entirely unrelated to those of cities in the developed world, but whose urbanization and dependency on foreign assistance was more akin to the capitals of the South.

The research

The approach

Previous research had shown how the current predicament of the infrastructure networks could only be grasped by regarding them as the end product of long-term developments that must be analysed before embarking upon any assessment of the predicament itself (Dupuy, 1984; Tarr, 1979; Dupuy & Tarr, 1984). Therefore, we decided to opt for a diachronic approach.

Ideally, from the point of view of the papers delivered at the 1983 seminar, this project would have called for methodical research on the history, development and current state of Buenos Aires' infrastructure networks on top of pinpoint analysis of its urbanization, and a detailed examination of the networks' morphology set against their relationship with the urban area (Dupuy, 1986). However, we did not have the necessary means for such work. Buenos Aires was, as mentioned earlier, located in a country that could be classed neither as highly developed nor very poor. This may have worked against us in that it denied our project access to the conventional research funding channels usually associated with one of those two categories, seldom with both. So we had a choice between dropping the project altogether or working with whatever opportunities presented themselves, with partial contributions and with the findings of previous research done within a variety of other frameworks. It meant that we could never hope to have the overall unity of a coherent research project, but the same basic threads were ultimately found to run through the constituent sector-specific studies. Our limited means had compelled us to narrow our focus to just three sectors: water, sanitation and transport. But given their role as basic infrastructure sectors, the nature of the needs they were designed to meet and the sheer cost of the equipment, they were representative enough to suggest that studies on the electricity, gas, telephone, public lighting or roads networks would have revealed if not the same historical background, then at least the same development trends.

A city, a capital, an urban area...

From the administrative point of view, the situation in Buenos Aires when we began our research in the mid-1980s was fairly complex. As the federal capital, the city came under the jurisdiction of the Argentine government, while its surrounding suburban municipalities or *partidos* were governed by the Buenos Aires provincial authorities. Together they were commonly known as Greater Buenos Aires, and although that is the title we shall be using for the extended urban area in the course of this Chapter, it officially referred strictly to the suburban belt plus an additional 19 *partidos* (illustration 7.2). Furthermore, since being federalized in 1880, the city no longer belonged to the enormous Buenos Aires Province extending across the vast, flat *pampas* (plains), which had its capital in La Plata.

The city of Buenos Aires stands on the site of the first permanent settlement established in 1580 on the southern bank of the Rio de la Plata or River Plate, which runs the length of the present-day urban area in a north-west/south-east orientation. Once levees had been built to protect the town against flooding, the river ceased being a threat and became the key to its future role as a commercial port. With an extensive railway network bringing in supplies, Buenos Aires developed into a major trading centre through the distribution of the abundance of meat and grain farmed on the *pampas* to the rest of Argentina, to neighbouring countries and to Europe.

Buenos Aires' growing prosperity and its reputation for hospitality naturally made it a magnet for European migrants. By 1930, more than five million people had moved there. Although the rate of rural-urban migration subsequently declined, a further 1.5 million arrived between 1930 and 1960, this time from a wider variety of places. By the mid-1980s, there were close to 10 million people living in the 2,800 km^2 Buenos Aires urban area. Interestingly, though, only half of them had actually been born there: 37.5 percent came from other provinces, and 11.5 percent from abroad. What is more, population growth centred solely on the suburbs, leaving the federal capital, which was losing a share of its inhabitants, populated by just three million.

As far as economic activities were concerned, the situation in Buenos Aires had long remained fairly balanced between the secondary and tertiary sectors – the former was still employing 45 percent of the working population in 1984 – with a highly mixed variety of activities in both. Spatially, though, the picture was somewhat less balanced: two-thirds of service-sector activities were based in the federal capital and two-thirds of industrial activities in the suburbs, which did not prevent small-scale manufacturing companies from continuing to operate in, and pollute, the city centre.

Buenos Aires' past history had also produced a variety of different forms of urban development. The federal capital was the work of urban planners – equipped since the early nineteenth century with the necessary infrastructure and services to cater for a large population, and even for the prospects of further growth due to rural-urban migration – but the sprawling suburbs had developed without any genuine planning control, in line with a long succession of rationales. The advent of the tramway at the turn of the twentieth century had led to the emergence of a first band of villages on the fringes of the city; the use of suburban railway stations had served to further the urbanization of more outlying areas;

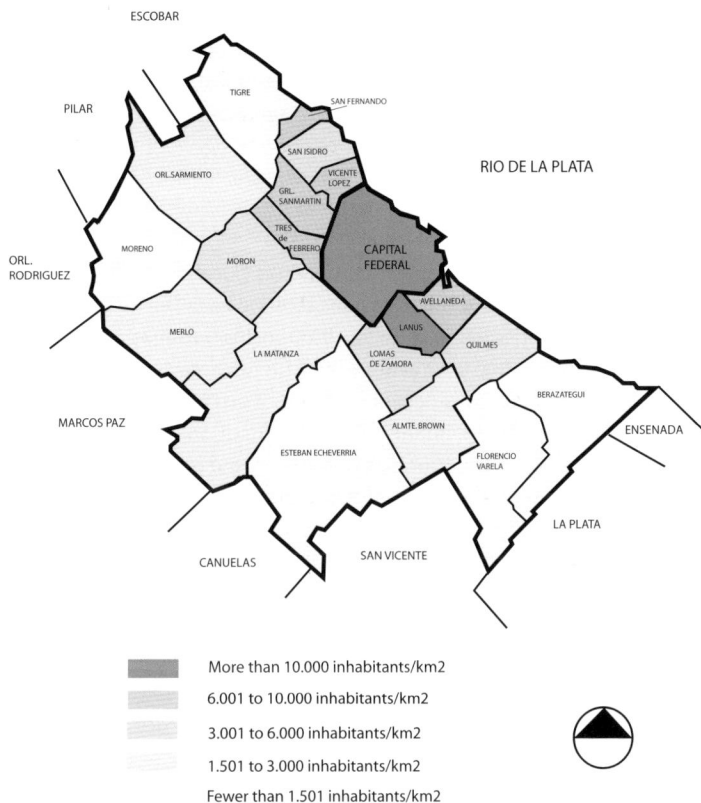

Illustration 7.2   **Population density in the Greater Buenos Aires *partidos* in the early 1980s.**
Source: El Transporte de Personas en el Gran Buenos Aires, a CEAP-CTAPBA report on
public transport in the Greater Buenos Aires area (September 1984)

and the road and bus networks had done the most to help foster the urban sprawl pushing out from the
capital – virtually unnoticed due to the lack of high-rise buildings – along lines determined by existing
village cores and the need to avoid the risk of flooding. The lack of overall planning could be seen in
the scattered infrastructure and the absence of genuine secondary urban centres. In social terms, the
suburban *partidos* may have retained a strong sense of identity, but the geographical distribution of
jobs and services resulted in significant flows of people, with more than a million entering the federal
capital every day, for instance, and over three million travelling between suburbs.

One observation and a couple of questions

Our first impression of the Buenos Aires infrastructure networks was that they were in a state of physical
and functional decline. Just 63 percent of the urban area's 10 million inhabitants had running water,
and fewer than half were connected to the sewerage system. Service standards had deteriorated
on the rapid transit system and it had been losing customers for years. Suburban trains were slow,
uncomfortable and often jam-packed. Access to the telephone network was extremely scarce; highway
maintenance had barely changed in half a century, pavements were cracked and roads in the suburbs
unsurfaced; and there were problems with storm-water runoff, short circuits, and serious pollution
of the river and its tributaries. In short, the situation in Buenos Aires was increasingly redolent of the
infrastructure network crises in developing and developed countries alike.

Two questions sprang to mind. In the 1920s, Buenos Aires had been one of the best-equipped cities in the world: its water and sanitation systems were outstanding, even monumental; it was a world leader in electrical power, which had been critical for the meat industry's cold stores; it had an admirably designed road network, an extremely dense and extensive system of tramway lines, and the first metro in Latin America, just 13 years after Paris; and its telephone network had been enhanced with new technologies since before the turn of the twentieth century. So how come every network was now beset by failures, breakdowns and all types of problems?

The second question arose in observing not the networks but the city itself. While the networks did indeed seem to be in serious trouble, Buenos Aires did not have the air of a city in crisis. It was not about to be abandoned, as reflected in the strong opposition to President Raúl Alfonsín's plans to move the federal capital some 1,500 km down the coast to Viedma. Nor was it strictly speaking a two-tier city, with the many excluded from a decent standard of urban life in favour of the wealthy few, the 'true' urbanites. It could be described, on the whole, as a functioning city that worked and consumed and agglomerated a good share of the country's population and power. The urban system was holding up in a challenging environment: the water network did not serve the entire urban area, but there was no actual shortage of water; poor sanitation was a suspected cause of ill-health, but Buenos Aries had not suffered an epidemic since yellow fever claimed some 20,000 lives back in 1871; the rapid transit system was run-down, but millions were still travelling around the area every day. So how could a metropolis of 10 million inhabitants manage to survive in spite of the countless deficiencies of its networks?

The Buenos Aires infrastructure network crisis

In order to fathom this apparent paradox, and to come up with possible pointers for further research, we decided to focus on the following four areas: technical, economic and policy-related aspects; the political/administrative system; urban development; and grass-roots solutions for adapting to and coping with the crisis.

Technical, economic and policy-related aspects

As the problems affecting the infrastructure networks of Buenos Aires were commonly believed to be rooted in their technological obsolescence, we chose to begin with an analysis of the technical history of the water, sanitation and metro rapid transit systems. It soon became clear that the crisis had nothing to do with technological determinism. The networks had been designed, adapted and expanded with the most efficient techniques of the day. What is more, evidence of the excellence of Argentine technicians and engineers and the fact that they followed the latest developments in their field could be seen in the sectors of, among others, drinking water supply, with an outstanding system of reservoirs, underground conduits and modern filtering units; drainage, with the implementation of some highly elaborate flood-proofing projects; and public transport, with the ultra-modern equipping of the railways and pre-metro light transit system. Argentina could not be described as having been excluded from technical advances in urban engineering. The example of the Palermo water filtration plant using well maintained older pumps more than the recently installed models refuted the theory that the problems stemmed from the natural obsolescence of facilities at the end of their service life; and the fact that the Parisian metro had only just replaced the especially resilient, yet aesthetically somewhat outdated, trains in service since the 1930s meant that the shortcomings of the Buenos Aires rapid transit system could not be ascribed to the age of the rolling stock.

Having noted that technical aspects were not the chief cause of the infrastructure network crisis, our attention turned to the realms of policy-making and economics. Argentina had obviously been in a situation of economic dependency for quite some time. Foreign capital began being invested in urban service supply during the boom in the Buenos Aires economy at the turn of the twentieth century. European companies, be they suppliers or concessionaries, reaped the benefits of the country's prosperity (see illustration 7.3 and 7.4). But even though a number of foreign firms continued – in spite of the difficulties linked to local circumstances and increasing globalization – to maintain a more or less active presence through to the mid-1980s, developments at home and abroad during the 1930s had led to a massive withdrawal of foreign capital. With domestic investors failing to fill the breach and even being driven by political instability and prohibitive rates of inflation to expatriate their capital, the networks in the low to medium revenue generating public-service sectors suffered considerably.

This explanation, although relevant for the railway, tramway and rapid transit systems, was somewhat less convincing in regard to water and sanitation. The Buenos Aires city authorities had been very quick to take control of operations in those sectors. But given the scarcity of public funds and the high cost of private capital, the problem had more to do with policy priorities. In the mid-1980s, the *Obras Sanitarias de la Nación* (OSN) public sanitation services were as reliant on state funding as any other national urban network operators. Yet the provision of urban services in Buenos Aires was clearly not considered a national priority. It was not that the authorities were doing nothing, just that their action was sporadic and limited in scope. They had moved swiftly to honour their election campaign promises to complete an extension to the metro E line and to start work on a pre-metro light transit system, for example. But there was no overarching policy to restructure the metro and to link it up with the bus and railway networks; nor any solution to the urban level-crossing issue which was causing both bottlenecks – for road traffic and suburban trains alike – and frequent, serious accidents.

Illustration 7.3   **Dependency of the Argentine economy and public service networks on European capital in the early 20th century**

Illustration 7.4   When Argentina was a prime market for French companies (early 20th century)

Furthermore, the former military junta's pledge to create a metropolitan green belt or *Cinturón Ecológico del Área Metropolitana* (CEAMSE) as an overall means of managing the collection and treatment of domestic waste relied on a self-financing scenario that had proved hard to implement after the country's return to democratic rule. The PROAGUA water resource management programme set out to tackle the most glaring shortcomings of the drinking water supply system without seeking to address the broader issue of the urban area's water network as a whole.

Why did the authorities fail to take a front-line role *vis-à-vis* services deemed crucial to the functioning of the city and its plainly run-down networks? There were three possible reasons: the problem of the federal capital's political/administrative system; a structural crisis linked to urban development strategies; and the emergence of a host of stopgaps designed to adjust to and cope with the failing infrastructure.

Urban Networks – Network Urbanism

The Buenos Aires political-administrative system

In addition to the administrative division between the federal capital and the suburban *partidos*, reflected in the state of their respective infrastructure networks, we also found a tendency towards urban spatial segregation among the various *partidos* and within the capital itself – in the La Boca district, for example. As a matter of fact, no single political authority had asserted itself throughout the Greater Buenos Aires area. The Buenos Aires provincial government, which carried great weight in the federal system, granted the *partidos* under its jurisdiction genuine freedom from interference, thus allowing for the forceful expression of views of every political complexion – radicalism, Peronism and others. So the federal capital remained something of an enclave, governed by a sound yet territorially limited administration.

Policy-makers and technicians alike were well aware of the need to address the public service and, moreover, network management problems at the level of the whole of Greater Buenos Aires. In the field of sanitation, the OSN was responsible for taking action across the bulk of the urban area; and CEAMSE brought the federal capital and *partidos* together in a major development project geared to the collection and disposal of domestic waste (Collin-Delavaud, 1984; Dascal, 1986). But apart from the fact that their respective initiatives were sector-specific, the misgivings and objections they encountered in implementing pan-urban area policies tended, more often than not, to bring those policies to a standstill. In urban transport, while the clear-cut need for overall Greater Buenos Aires policy-making had resulted in studies and reports on the matter, implementation was hampered by a host of idiosyncrasies, not least on the part of the provincial government. The struggle to combat flooding had exposed the antagonism between the federal capital and the Province of Buenos Aires on the one hand, and among the various *partidos* on the other (Albini & Costa, 1987). The suburban municipalities directly threatened by rising river levels in November 1986, for example, erected flood barriers to ensure their own protection, without considering the serious damage that might be caused to towns and villages further upstream.

Meanwhile, President Alfonsín's plans to move the federal capital to Viedma and to create a new province of Rio de la Plata incorporating Buenos Aires and its suburbs merely reflected the powerlessness of the government to resolve the city's problems and to manage its infrastructure networks properly within the framework of the current political-administrative system.

Urban development

In the case of the water supply and sewerage systems, the OSN was not lacking foresight. Not only had the oversizing of the Buenos Aires infrastructure been due to rural-urban migration forecasts, but the network planning had also included a clear picture of future urban development beyond the city limits. OSN decision-makers originally opted for a ribbon development-type blueprint, with the main collectors and pipelines following the railway and tramway arteries – the only real links to the capital. Although urban development did indeed stick to those arteries, the water and sewerage networks could, in all likelihood, have been expanded in line with the demand for services, which would have helped avoid the current predicament.

The end result – a more sprawling form of urban development – rendered the OSN's infrastructure-building efforts almost futile (Bodard, 1987). The gradual piecing together of an albeit far from ideal road network made it possible to develop the land between the original arteries, but the uncontrolled parcelling-out and self-built housing culminated in a critical situation as the gap gradually widened between network supply and service demand.

Similarly, one of the reasons for the crisis in the metro rapid transit system was its inability to cope with emergent passenger traffic trends. Originally designed to serve the federal capital and to connect the workplace to the home, the system struggled to come to terms with the changing spatial distribution of jobs and housing. Lozada (1987) shows how the urban core had shifted and how industrial activities had been established in the suburbs, with many residents moving out of the capital and passenger traffic switching to a suburban railway system that lacked adequate link-ups to metro stations. The railway-metro tandem found itself hard pressed to compete with the *colectivo* bus lines officially assigned to connect the suburbs to the centre. Any chance of restructuring and expanding the metro system therefore went by the board. Ultimately, what led to the system's unsuitable design and stagnating traffic was the fact that it was out of touch with urban development.

Urban change in Buenos Aires city, therefore, appears to have stemmed from decisions that led to maximum land-use intensity facilitated by the road network, bus lines and private transport, i.e. the motor car. Urban development of that kind should have been accompanied by extensive development of the fixed water, sewerage and rapid transit infrastructure networks, which was completely unaffordable. The networks could not serve the urban area effectively, and were sucked into a vicious circle of service restrictions, recourse to alternative solutions, disillusionment, scarce means and a lack of political will, and so on and so forth.

Adapting to the crisis: substitutes and alternatives

The worst is not always inevitable. Crises do not necessarily end in chaos. One must not be fooled into believing otherwise by the apparently indispensable nature of the water, power and transport networks. In Buenos Aires, perhaps more than anywhere else, the shortcomings of the public service networks had led to the emergence of a host of stopgap measures. Not for the first time. The Argentine capital had been living on a stock of outstanding yet inadequate infrastructure ill-suited to future urban changes since the 1930s. A whole industry and economy seems to have sprung up around the management and use of alternative techniques aimed at adapting the networks, as far as possible, to the changes. A varied range of substitute or supplementary mechanisms were brought into play at various levels in order to manage service supply in the face of such factors as population growth, anarchic urban development, political instability, scarce financial resources, and an outdated administrative system.

The situation in Buenos Aries was, in many respects, quite unlike any other city in the South. When a city's population growth has been due chiefly to migration from rural areas, one often finds the migrants compensating for a lack of urban services by falling back on their rural roots and traditions. In the case of Buenos Aires – an urban area boosted in size by an influx of international migrants with a wealth and diversity of technical qualifications – the many alternative solutions adopted have been of a resolutely technical nature, stemming from a sense of individualism rather than from tribal or extended family-type structures. What is more, those solutions have been of a micro-capitalistic nature, with personal savings mobilized to make up for a lack of public or private funding, and to enable individuals and small-scale companies gradually to produce their own basic installations, which they have managed as adaptive personal assets. A perfect illustration of these two, undoubtedly correlated, aspects could be seen outside the realm of networks in the practice of self-built housing – the predominant form of urban development in Buenos Aires at the time of our research in the mid-1980s.

In the light of these distinctive features, and the fact that the network crisis had already been ongoing for some time, the solutions adopted in Buenos Aires were quite different from those of other developing-country capital cities, which have been so unsafe as to have made immediate standard-setting work a must. They were often extremely sound in every sense of the term. Technically acceptable in terms of design and maintenance, and economical – managed by individuals on years' worth of personal savings – they have been known to compare favourably with official network development projects. So much so that international organizations have had no hesitation in presenting the *colectivos* bus routes in Buenos Aires, for example, as an alternative model to the proposals put forward for rapid transit networks (Hibbs, 1983).

One must bear in mind, of course, that those solutions were still mere stopgaps, implemented to cope with the lack of networked public services and so on. But it is not hard to see how their resilience, their widespread application and, indeed, their very existence helped make what has rightly been described as a network crisis more bearable; how that crisis, in spite of its far-reaching ramifications, did not lead to chaos or bring the city to a standstill; and why the public authorities were able both to recognize the seriousness of the problems affecting the networks in their charge and, at the same time, to refrain from making their rehabilitation a genuine policy priority.

There are many examples of compensatory or adaptive mechanisms in every sector. We could talk about the private mini-exchanges and point-to-point overhead lines used to make up for the failings in the Buenos Aires telephone network; or how individuals and local craftsmen were doing the work of the city engineering departments in repairing pavements, manhole covers and so on, to name but a few. But let us stick to those sectors forming the focus of our research.

In regard to the drinking water supply system, for instance, there were two main courses of action: on the one hand customizing the network, and on the other tapping into other sources. As far as the former was concerned, we found a proliferation of individual cisterns providing practically every building with what had come to represent the normal means of micro-managing the network. Like most of its European counterparts, the Buenos Aires network had been designed to supply buildings from large, central, pump-filled reservoirs located at high points around the city. But the need to supply some very tall buildings from lower-level reservoirs meant having to depart from the network's basic design principles; and the building cistern soon came to be regarded as a safeguard against the various vagaries of the network – drops in pressure, power cuts stopping the booster pumps needed to supply upper floors, and so on – even for Buenos Aires' many low-rise buildings. Cisterns were now crucial to urban life and, at the same time, a distinctive feature of the Buenos Aires cityscape.

As for resorting to other sources, the lack of a network made the water pump (*bombeador*) a must. Despite the subsequent restrictions imposed by the pollution of first and even second-level groundwater, the system undeniably had its merits. It gave people who were building their own houses, and unlikely ever to be connected to the network, access to a variety of technologies ranging from the most basic hand pumps to the most sophisticated deep well pumps. The availability of those technologies, together with a combination of skilled well-diggers and pump-manufacturers and a market in second-hand pumps, gave them the chance to enhance their installations as far as their personal savings would allow. The several hundred thousand, maybe even a million, *bombeadores* in Buenos Aires may well have made the network crisis more bearable. But that significant stock of personal equipment systems also served to undermine or inhibit network development. *Bombeador* owners were hardly going to want to pay for the network to be installed or for cubic metres of water that they could tap, free-of-charge, from underground resources. Furthermore, in spite of the OSN's proposals to expand the network at some unspecified point in the future, policy-makers at the local and federal government levels had other, more pressing, issues on their minds.

Meanwhile, alternative solutions were also devised in order to cope with flooding and sanitation: landlords in the La Boca district of Buenos Aires seeking to offset the impacts of a failing storm-water drainage system by raising the ground floor of their buildings, sometimes several times for a single building; ingenious devices installed to protect private property against rising storm and, above all, waste water; the decision by the *Servicios Eléctricos del Gran Buenos Aires S.A.* (SEGBA) electricity company to protect cables and transformers by reverting to overhead electricity lines, and so on (Parrod in Dupuy, 1987a). At the Greater Buenos Aires level, the problems caused were of an altogether different scale, calling for effective flood-control mechanisms deployed across the entire area and community-wide solutions that the government was slow to implement. But it was striking to see here and there the grass-roots efforts to stave off a disaster of enormous proportions – makeshift dams or dykes and extra storeys added to buildings. The overall effectiveness of the measures may be debatable, yet each represented an alternative to an inadequate drainage system.

In the transport sector, while the data on the metro system stressed how run-down, technically obsolescent and even unsafe it had become, the actual situation was not quite as bad as it seemed. Buoyed by extensive long-standing expertise, in-depth knowledge of the equipment and relatively unsophisticated yet efficient public information procedures, the system had managed to provide passengers with what amounted to an almost decent service. Some of the stopgaps would probably have been at odds with modern operating standards, and hard-pressed to contend with any major increase in the volume of passenger traffic. But a detailed comparison with other run-down systems such as the New York subway (Bouvier, 1986) would confirm the key role of the regulatory mechanisms arising out of the crisis in Buenos Aires.

That said, the real alternative to the rapid transit system came, as mentioned earlier, in the shape of the *colectivos* bus lines. Privately funded and managed, and operated by a host of small contractors, the *colectivos* could hardly be expected to serve as a single, all-embracing solution to a big city's public transport problems. But they had long played a key role in Buenos Aires, partly replacing and partly supplementing the railways and the metro. With their flexibility in terms of creating or rerouting bus lines – and, to some extent, of the volume of passenger traffic they could handle – they managed to keep up with the Argentine capital's unique form of urban development. The government acknowledged their role by establishing a versatile operating environment for this mode of transport. In addition to taking the sting out of the metro crisis, however, the *colectivos* most probably also tended to compound it.

Adapting the urban system: towards a new hierarchy of networks

So the image of Buenos Aires in the mid-1980s amounted to a surprising mix of a city whose infrastructure networks were in crisis but whose history had seen the emergence of a host of alternative solutions that prevented that crisis from evolving into full-blown urban blight. The status of those stopgaps – the fruit of human ingenuity and expertise, devised in response to the need to cope with deteriorating conditions, and based on a solid core of existing facilities – was unclear. They meant that there was no comparison between Buenos Aires and cities such as Paris whose urban development had been shaped by its public service networks. Yet they also made it necessary to challenge the view that the network crisis stemmed from the physical state of the infrastructure. A holistic approach helps provide clearer insight into how unbridled changes in the economic, demographic and urban environment can, to a large extent, be regulated by adjusting service supply and the inner workings of the urban system in such a way as to give people the latitude to adapt the networks, to micro-manage their services, and to develop their own independent solutions.

This cannot happen anywhere. It calls for effective synergy and complementary relations between different networks. Analysts have been in the habit of studying those separately on account of the fact that they involve different flows – drinking water, waste water, electricity, passengers, and so on – and different forms of organization. In the long run, however, the various networks do not evolve independently of each other. We noted many examples of interrelationships between different kinds of networks in Buenos Aires. In some cases, they had tended to make the crisis worse: the deteriorating suburban railways affecting the metro rapid system; the drainage system's failure to deal with storm water having a negative impact on the electricity network, not least in La Boca; and flooding in the federal capital causing power failures, breakdowns on the metro and traffic jams on the roads.

But the positive effects were more numerous, more lasting and ultimately more important. Some networks were crucial to the deployment of the above-mentioned substitutes and alternatives: the *colectivos*, of course, would never have come into being and extended their services had it not been for a road system that, despite its mediocre quality in the outskirts, gave the overall urban area a strong degree of connectivity; and better interlinkages with the trains and the metro would obviously contribute to their further development.

The electricity network played an especially crucial role in providing the power to operate the pumps needed to fill the individual cisterns used to micro-manage water supply; the electric motors conveying water from the *bombeador* to the storage tank, without which it would never have become such a popular alternative to the water-pressure system; and the storm and waste-water removal pumps used for sanitation in La Boca. Other examples show how the telephone network, for instance, in spite of its flaws, had helped compensate for the failings of the metro signalling or early flood warning systems, among others.

Which brings us back to the network hierarchy we adopted at the outset of our research project. Water and sanitation systems, roads and public transport infrastructure – the most costly components of contemporary urban development – may well appear to perform vital urban functions, but this is not necessarily the most relevant aspect from the point of view of a rapidly changing and, necessarily, ever-adaptive urban system. The multifunctional nature of the flows carried on the road networks, power networks – especially electricity – and information networks definitely does seem to make them a must. The development and expansion of the latter two networks, which will not necessarily call for significant means, can help pave the way for adaptive mechanisms of the kind described above. Studying the case of Buenos Aires has served to open up new prospects for network planning. The urban stakes are so high that this is an area worth exploring further and in greater depth.

8   Networks versus Territorial Sovereignties: A Comparative Study of Eurovision[*]

In 1954, the EBU union of European broadcasting organizations – going beyond the rather corporatist goals of defending the interests of broadcasters, promoting and coordinating the study of all broadcasting-related issues and fostering exchanges of information on all matters of mutual interest – set up a vast radio and television broadcasting network spanning Western Europe and even extending into North Africa. Television viewers would subsequently become familiar with the Eurovision network thanks to the logo appearing on their TV screens when their national broadcasters were putting on programmes being shown across the network (see illustration 8.1).

Illustration 8.1   The original logo of Eurovision in the 1960s

Eurovision set an example as a network striving to harness the most modern telecommunications and broadcasting technologies in an apparent endeavour to provide the most extensive, frequent and rapid transmissions possible, unfettered by national boundaries. Would it emerge as the epitome of the kind of transnational network that many had predicted would do away with those boundaries and break up traditional territorialities? Or was it, in spite of appearances, organized in such a way as to comply with – and remain subject to – the political map of national territories? We shall seek to answer these questions by comparing Eurovision with other types of networks of differing geographic scales.

Networks as a means of *deterritorialization*

Communication, transport or energy networks, given their natural disregard for boundaries, almost obviously play a negative role from the point of view of the territory, in the conventional sense of the term. Sociologically speaking, a territory hinges first and foremost on an 'us versus them' mentality; it is a space from which we can not only exclude but also seek to wield power over others (Raffestin, 1980). Furthermore, it is the hub of its population's entire social and working life. Historically, the law has turned territories into jurisdictions over which a particular authority exercises control over – and, theoretically, for the benefit of – the local community.

---

[*]   This Chapter is an adapted version of an article previously published as « Le Réseau Eurovision ou le Conflit du Réseau et des Territoires ». *NETCOM*, 1 (1), 1987, pp. 191-202. Montpellier: UGI. Included with permission.

Established, inherited territorial boundaries, however, seem vulnerable to the challenge of any network that is efficient, dynamic and adaptive enough to expand and interlink whoever wants it as soon as they want it, i.e. to the apparently inevitable threat of being breached, undermined and abolished. There are many examples. The *commune* – France's smallest administrative division and a territory whose roots stretch back to the parishes of the *ancien regime* – may continue to represent a particularly resilient mesh of interlinkages in rural areas. But the development of inter-*commune* tram, road, water and gas networks has rendered it almost meaningless in the city, whose residents look instead to the authorities to take care of everyday matters, the running of utilities and so on. Territory is now seen in intercommunal rather than municipal terms. A similar trend could be seen in the countryside as rural areas became increasingly equipped with roads, electricity and water supply, domestic waste removal services and so on. The most visible sign of this was the emergence of a proliferation of intercommunal unions; although it merely reflected the fact that something of a process was under way, to the detriment of communal boundaries.

At another geographic scale, the railway, telephone, electricity, road and television companies have breached territorial boundaries in expanding their networks across vast areas, interconnecting remote points and forging ties between places that formerly used to ignore each other. Limousin district farms are no longer really cut off from the outside world insofar as the networks now provide them with all of the links needed for a near-urban lifestyle. While manifestations of urbanization have spread throughout the countryside, however, urban territory, even in the broader sense of the term outlined earlier, has been losing its identity.

The Paris area public transport system and its *carte orange* travel card scheme provide an eloquent example of this. Commuting in the Ile-de-France district has profoundly undermined the existence of a Parisian urban territory, even one extending as far as its outlying communes. Indeed, the RER rapid transit train service between Paris and its suburbs and the suburban lines of the SNCF French national railway company have enabled significant flows of commuters to pass through what had once been regarded as impenetrable boundaries.

For a while it looked as though the worker's ticket system would constitute a lasting barrier. But the momentum created by the *carte orange* was such that the regional boundaries of Ile-de-France were unable to prevent the SNCF railway network from forcing its way outside the region. By the late 1980s, a huge suburban network stretching way beyond the existing regional boundaries had become a genuine prospect for the thousands of people working in Paris and living more than 100km away in cities like Orleans, Rouen or Reims. In this way the railways and other networks, with their well-known qualities of connectedness, connectivity, homogeneity and isotropy, were contributing to the *deterritorialization* process challenging the borders of long-established territories.

The Eurovision network took that trend to the international level, spinning its web across the borders of European nations from Finland to Italy and from Portugal to Austria to the former Yugoslavia, Turkey, Morocco, Algeria, Tunisia and even Libya (illustration 8.2). EBU sought to ensure the exchanges of television broadcasts among member countries by equipping that network with substantial technical means. As a matter of fact, it created four separate networks to help sustain those exchanges: two of them permanent – one for pictures and the other for sound (see illustration 8.3 and 8.4); and two occasional – one for contributions, to enable a particular programme to be broadcast from each country, and the other for distribution, i.e. for pictures to be broadcasted in any country requesting them (illustration 8.5). This called not only for high-capacity broadcasting infrastructure, but also for production departments, monitoring systems and, later on, satellite reception stations.

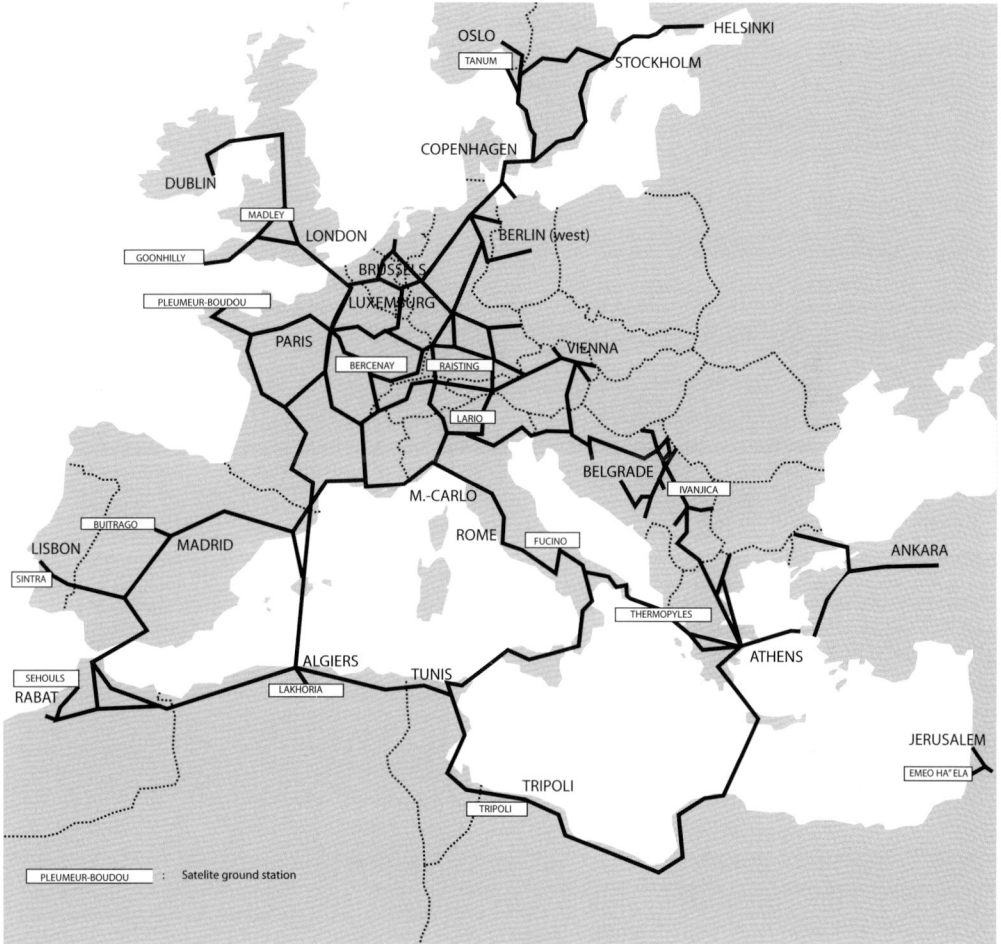

Illustration 8.2   Eurovision network (31 December 1981)

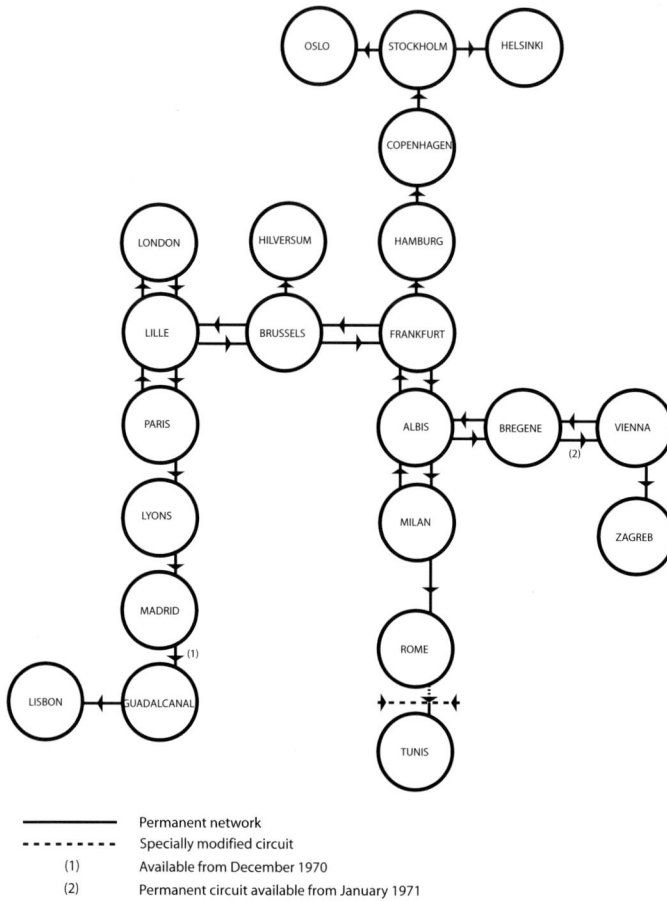

OSLO STOCKHOLM HELSINKI

COPENHAGEN

LONDON HILVERSUM HAMBURG

LILLE BRUSSELS FRANKFURT

PARIS ALBIS BREGENE VIENNA
(2)

LYONS MILAN ZAGREB

MADRID ROME
(1)

LISBON GUADALCANAL TUNIS

```
————————   Permanent network
- - - - - - - -   Specially modified circuit
(1)        Available from December 1970
(2)        Permanent circuit available from January 1971
```

Illustration 8.3   Permanent Eurovision network (pictures)

At first sight, Eurovision appeared to be a model deterritorializing network, using the most modern telecommunications technologies to broadcast messages across national borders. But did it necessarily mean an end to all forms of territoriality?

Network territorialities

In the 1960s, futurologists and forecasters contemplating future progress in the transport and telecommunications industries were predicting the advent of a uniform, homogeneous space (Libby, 1969; Wise, 1971; Gottman, 1972). It would soon cease to matter either to businesses or individuals where they were based. Travelling would be so easy that the advantages of an urban site would scarcely outweigh those of a rural site. Better still, the new telecommunications would remove the constraints of geographic distance for one and all, realizing the dream of total aterritoriality.

OSLO   STOCKHOLM   HELSINKI

DUBLIN

HILVERSUM

HAMBURG

LONDON   COPENHAGEN

BRUSSELS
EBU   COLOGNE

PARIS

FRANKFURT

RTB / BRT   WIESBADEN

VIENNA

MADRID   ZURICH

GENEVA
EBU
(1)

ALBIS   ZAGREB

(2)

LISBON

MILAN

ROME

TUNIS

_____ Programme circuit
- - - - - - - - 4-line control circuit
(1)   Voice quality (for talk-back circuits)
(2)   Permanent circuit available from January 1971

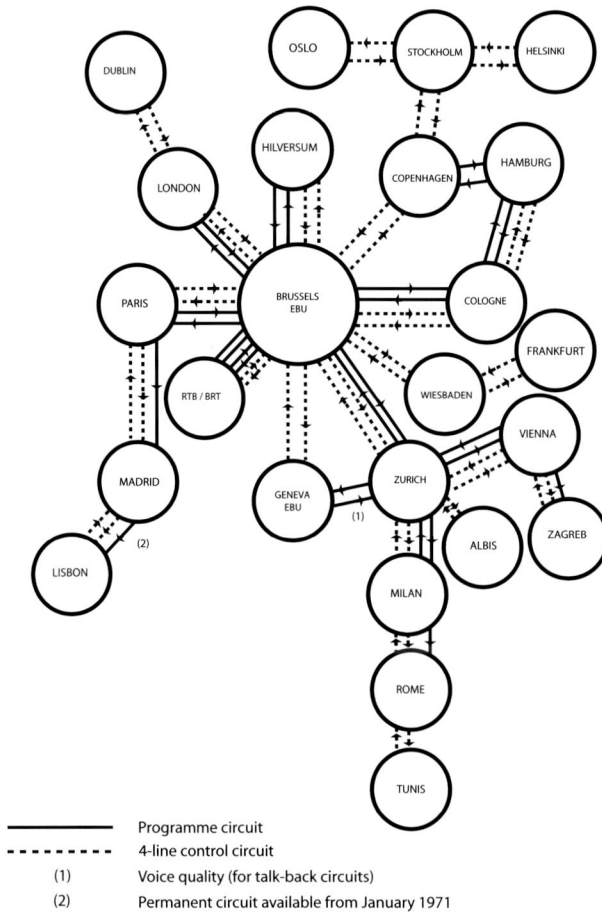

Illustration 8.4   Permanent Eurovision network (sound)

Clearly, though, not all of the predictions – which, incidentally, merely echoed those made by Henry Ford and others in the 1920s with respect to prospective electricity networks (see Chapter 1) – did in fact come true. The development and expansion of networks did not culminate in widespread aterritoriality. Although they caused the crumbling of old territories, they then ended up creating new ones. In the nineteenth-century, the tram network in many countries created the extended urban territory whose layout was typical of the fruits of ribbon development. Later, other forms of *reterritorialization* emerged in France with the new urban perimeters devised to meet public transport management needs; the new territory for Paris-region suburbanites which gradually took shape as a result of the five-zone *carte orange* travel card scheme; and the seemingly new territory created by the provincial railways cutting through legally defined, yet not always highly consistent, regional administrative borders. At the same time, the water supply and sewerage systems opened up a new urban-rural divide between well equipped urban – albeit in many respects rural-looking – areas and a poorly equipped countryside. And the construction of cable networks has called for the defining of new territories amounting to an odd fusion of *communes* of disparate demographic, technical and political characteristics.

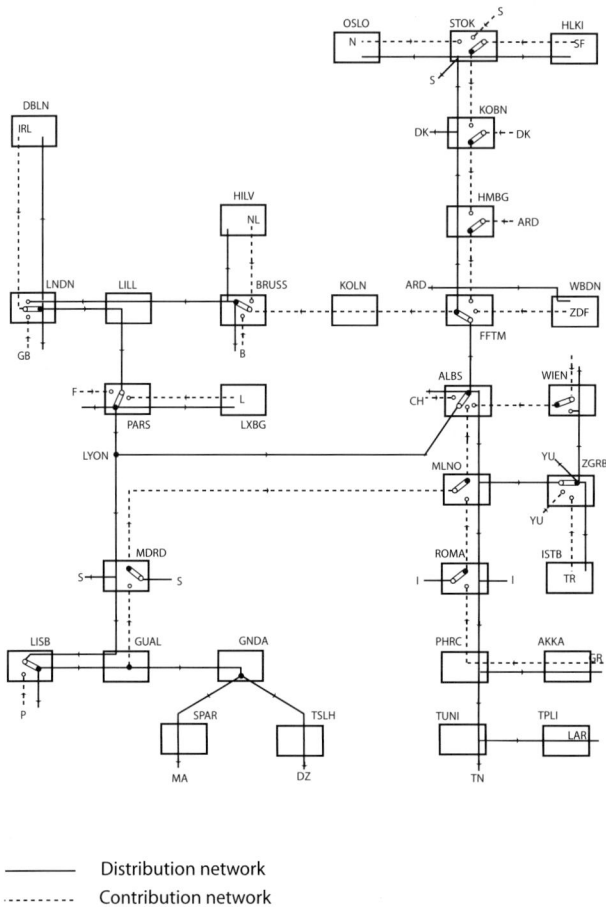

Illustration 8.5   Eurovision input and broadcasting networks

—————— Distribution network

---------- Contribution network

The new network-generated territories have not, of course, been built on the same bases as their predecessors: their actors' influence, their power structures and their spatial layout are all different.

A look at the nature and functioning of Eurovision shows that EBU had in fact set in place a new European territory of communications revolving around a strong north-south axis with branches to the east and west serving every Member State of the European Union, and looser peripheral links to countries formerly under the control of some of those States. The capitals of that new territory were Brussels, a sort of technical hub, and Geneva, the administrative centre. The boundaries between EBU member countries may have vanished from the network charts, but new ones had appeared separating them from the countries of the east. Some areas were clearly marginalized. In short, everything appeared to point to the emergence of a new territoriality. But then again, not everything is always as it seems.

Resilience of national borders

Far from running their course, as a matter of course, *deterritorialization-reterritorialization* processes of the kind outlined above with respect to Eurovision come up against some seriously obstructive obstacles, not least national borders (see Chapter 14).

Although the motorway network definitely has, on the face of it, formed a new international territory for road traffic, the same cannot be said for the railway network, for example. The well-know difficulties encountered by the TGV high-speed train and Channel Tunnel projects – together with the other, less well-known, problems affecting rail freight – have shown clearly that national borders still exist and that networks are still compelled to abide by the various rules prevailing over the various territories.

Eurovision is an even more telling example. It was a thoroughly modern network held back neither by the inertia of a technical heritage from a bygone age nor – given the immediacy of broadcasting – by the limitations of distance constraining the physical networks, not least in the field of transport. It was designed and managed in a manner geared more to preserving and protecting national sovereignties than to acting as a medium for creating a new European territory of communications.

Compared with the other territorial networks mentioned above, Eurovision was:

- lacking in connectivity, with scarcely any alternative paths or direct links for broadcasts, and a Brussels-based tree-network structure providing each state with monitoring and distribution services;

- highly heterogeneous, with some links facilitated by high-performance equipment and others with limited possibilities, thus gradually opening up a gap between northern Europe and the rest of the network;

- anisotropic, as reflected in the network's north-south axis.

Examples of how the states apparently managed to secure unconditional respect for their national borders in the running of the network could be seen in its exceedingly heavy decision-making procedures, including for news broadcasts; the prohibitive pricing policy applied to what some states deemed to be undesirable linkups; the almost systematic elimination of internationalist partners – private TV channels, picture agencies and so on; and an overcautious approach to the development of satellites, which were regarded in technical terms, as a means of transmission, rather than as potential nodes in a new network and a new international territory of communications (illustration 8.6).

At the time of writing this article back in the late 1980s, it was hard to tell whether this amounted to a phase of transition or a rearguard action on the part of the old territorial authorities in a last-ditch effort to defend a territory being distorted by new networks – in which case, the TGV and European electricity networks were just a few years away from creating new European territories for transport and power; and national borders were on the verge of succumbing to satellite transmissions, and so on; or whether those borders represented the political and symbolical boundaries of indomitable territories? Did national territorialities have a bona fide bastion against the threat of *deterritorialization*, a bastion around which European states could 'rally' and harness the development and expansion of technical networks?

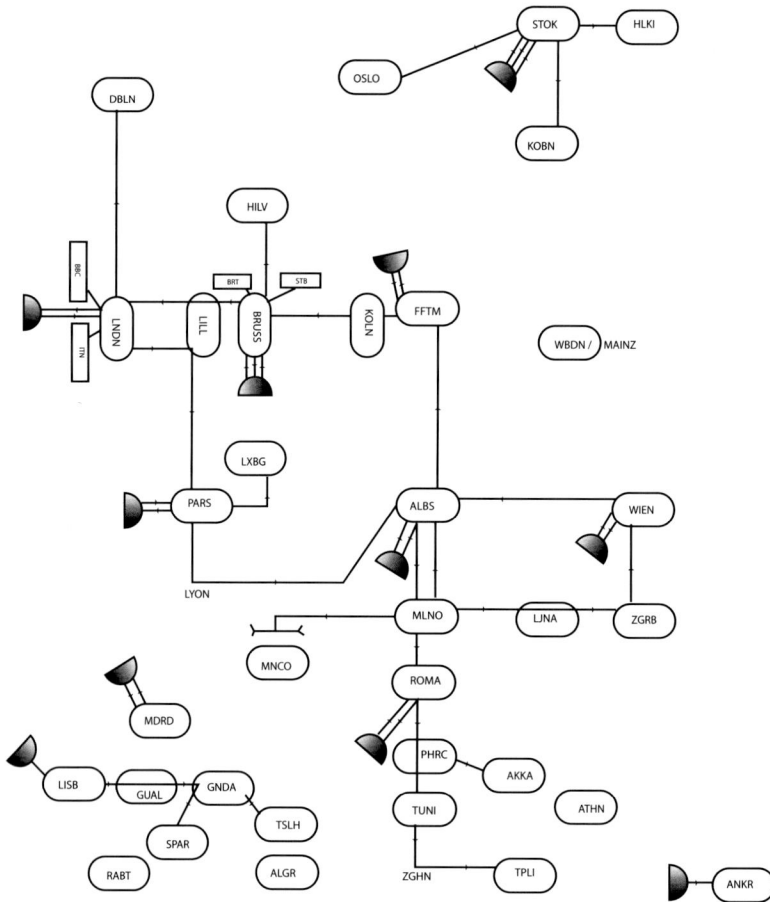

Illustration 8.6 **New layout of the permanent network using satellite reception dishes**

The answers to those questions lay not in the technical, i.e. functional, nature of the networks but in the often profound meaning attached to them by grass-roots actors. Sansot (1984), for example, draws the not entirely functional distinction between a shower and a bathtub: the shower brings the pressure and flow of a network into the home in real time, 'plugging' the user, so to speak, into the world of the here-and-now, the present-day world of running water; whereas the bathtub harks back to another time, to another, staunchly intimate and domestic, territory (see Chapter 3). Clearly, this apparently simplistic example of water could not hope to capture all of the complexities of the case of television broadcasting. But it did provide pointers for more in-depth thinking on the social value of technical networks and how it affected the evolution of territories.

Part III

Motor Cars: System, Network and Dependency

9   The Automobile System: A Territorial Adapter*

It is simple to buy a device commercially known as a *universal adapter*. This is an assortment of more or less sophisticated electrical plugs of various sizes, with transformers for different types of current; sometimes it includes AC/DC transformers or rectifiers. This device makes it possible to obtain electricity for any type of appliance, from any network supplying electrical current of any kind. The apparatus is small and lightweight and forms part of the necessary travel equipment for the experienced international traveller as there are still many different national electrical standards (Bunn & David, 1991). How else could one use a portable computer, electric razor, or electrical travel iron on a trip abroad, when neither the wattage, the tension, nor the shape of the plug corresponds to what is found at home? The universal adapter is a long-term insurance for the traveller, a general guarantee that under all circumstances he or she will have access to the indispensable element which electricity has become, a 'comfort zone' of which the boundaries are designated by the possibility of being able to plug into a network.

In this Chapter (which borrows from two other works by the author) (see Dupuy, 1995a, 1995b), I shall demonstrate that the automobile plays a role identical to that of the universal adapter in the service of the 'travellers' we have become in a world undergoing enormous transformations. This is not to say that we are permanent globe-trotters. Rather, the multiple changes being produced in human society as a result of economic and social evolutions, would cause us to loose control of the space around us, lessening our potential for territorial appropriation, were we not an increasingly expanding group of people owning cars that have truly become a type of universal territorial adapter. It is this role that explains, in my opinion, the incredible advance of the automobile throughout the world.

I shall begin by tracing the history of this phenomenal advance of the automobile, recalling here for the record the dire forecasts of the 1970s that predicted quite another story. I shall then demonstrate how cars have found a place today in a comprehensive, more and more fully integrated system. This leads to questioning the public-private mixed economics of this system, which in the eyes of many has conferred absolute advantages on the automobile in terms of ensuring its long-term territorial dominion. I shall closely examine two historic examples of the automobile in its role of adapter: American suburbanization and French rural urbanization – or 'rurbanization'. Other examples will show the extent to which the automobile is likely to play out its technical role of territorial adapter, thus proving that the term universal adapter is not unfounded. I shall then conclude with a brief survey of trends to come.

Catastrophic forecasts and the automobile boom

In Europe, as in the United States, automobiles came into general use only after World War II. They advanced quite rapidly from then on, the individual growth rate differing by country. In France, half of all households owned a car by 1966; in Germany this occurred in 1970, and in Great Britain in 1971.

---

*   This Chapter is an adapted version of an article previously published in *Flux, International Scientific Quarterly on Networks and Territories*, 21, 1995, pp. 21-36. Included with permission.

As early as the beginning of the 1960s, the American Lewis Mumford had already warned Europeans that the automobile would engulf European cities the way it had American cities. Respect for Europe's thousand-year-old history alone seemed to indicate that something had to be done. According to Mumford, there was still time to take action. Visiting the large European cities at the beginning of the 1960s, the well-known urban historian thought he saw the signs that Europeans were coming to their senses. Here, at least, they were in the process of reconciling the irreconcilable, by adapting the car to the city. He congratulated them for having invented minuscule vehicles like the Goggomobile or the Isetta, "that fit admirably into a tight urban pattern. The cars are sized to the human frame, not to the human ego" (Mumford, 1964).

Illustration 9.1   **'Ghost Parking Lot', catastrophist sculpture from the end of the 1970s. The automobile has not, however, disappeared .... (Hamden, Connecticut: the Hamden Plaza Shopping Center, 1978).** Photo courtesy of Unipix

Meanwhile in France, voices had already been heard in an effort to halt the momentum of the growth in car ownership. Alfred Sauvy wrote his truly anti-automobile pamphlet *Les quatre roues de la fortune* (The Four Wheels of Fortune) in 1968. He prophesized that either the city would be destroyed or that cars would disappear. His predictions were based on the impossibility of the finite container (the city) to hold continuously increasing contents (the fleet of cars). Sauvy used the city of Paris as an example. Seven million m^2 were required for 100,000 cars to drive in the streets; an additional five million m^2 were needed to park an additional 250,000 cars, for a total of twelve million m^2. But the total available street surface in Paris at the time equalled only ten million m^2. And if the 1.7 million cars registered in the greater metropolitan Paris area were included, the entire surface of the city of Paris would obviously be submerged! "The car manufacturers continue to build square meter after square meter of mobile surface; when will they realize that the square meters of fixed surface have run out?" (Sauvy, 1968).

Some time later, other voices were raised against the capitalistic nature of the automobile. The cost of buying a car was relatively painless for the affluent, but not for other members of society. For this investment a great number of man-hours were needed, which should be taken into account in any general economic assessment made over a given period of time. In this way, a speed equivalent for each type of transportation could be calculated: the comparison leaned not in favour of the automobile, but, paradoxically, of ... the bicycle! (Dupuy & Robert, 1976; Illitch, 1974).

During the 1970s, the successive rises in oil prices resulted in more dire forecasts, both in Europe and in the United States. The automobile, dependent on petrol, would eventually fall victim to the implacable pressure of the OPEC, if not to the scarcity of oil as a planetary natural resource in the very long run. Problems caused by cars, along with accidents and pollution, were often cited during this period. It was thought that acid rain and the hole in the ozone layer would thus eventually bring about a drastic reduction in the numbers of cars (see illustration 9.1).

Illustration 9.2   **The 'Gol' developed by Volkswagen for the Brazilian market.**
Twenty years ago the automobile expansion was still worldwide.
Source: Georgano (1990: 208)

These warnings were not all in vain. 'Cleaner', safer cars with better petrol mileage resulted directly from this clamour (Lamure, 1995). The highway system itself gradually improved so as to ensure better driving conditions (McShane, 1994). Nonetheless, it can be said that the oracles that predicted the disappearance, or even just the lessening in numbers, of the automobile by the end of the century were clearly misguided. In the industrialized countries the fleet of cars has sharply increased, and in the developing countries, in spite of low mean incomes, the number of cars has also increased. The increase in the amount of cars in these countries (not counting China) exceeded 60 million vehicles between 1990 and 2000 (predicted by Altshuler, Anderson, Jones, Roos & Womack, 1984). Argentina issued license plates to 342,000 additional cars in 1993.

The phenomenon of buying cars, in countries where socio-economic and political conditions permit this, has become a trend (illustration 9.2). The boom in both car buying and traffic in the French overseas territories is quite revealing, as well as the growth of car fleets in Turkey, China and countries in Eastern Europe. In France, as in other European countries, growth perspectives are not enormous (Madre & Armoogun, 1994). But analysts no longer risk forecasting a saturation level of the automobile market. In the United States, for example, it had been thought that a 'natural' level of saturation would be reached at one car per worker. Growth largely exceeded this limit, and the forecast was proven wrong. Then a limit of one car per household was predicted; this too fell short of the real number of cars. Finally it was thought that saturation would be reached at one car per adult. It has been demonstrated that even this will not always constitute an absolute limit (Korver, Klooser & Jansen, 1993).

In France, there were just over 40,000 cars in 1907. In 1995 there were more than 24 million vehicles, or 425 cars per thousand inhabitants. At the turn of the 19th century there were practically no cars; in 1990 there were half a billion cars driving around the planet! How are we to explain the incredible automobile boom? How should we interpret the erroneous predictions of the 1970s and 1980s? To begin with, it is important to understand that the question here is not the multiplication of the number of automobiles over a given historical period, but rather the progressive build-up of a progressively more integrated entity which we shall call, using Peter Hall's term, the 'automobile system' (Hall, 1988).

The automobile system

In 1923, as Wolfgang Sachs has pointed out, it was predicted that in a very near future houses would come equipped not only with water, gas, electricity, bathrooms and central heating, but also with a car in the garage (Sachs, 1992). The car in the garage, much like a computer terminal providing the access to a network (Fishman, 1990)? But which network? Not the network of streets which cities had inherited from the past, built for pedestrians inside city limits and for a small number of carriages and carts outside these limits; but rather a network connected with main roads and highways leading to resorts, through country roads linking up farms and villages, finally ending at the national borders. "The road itself is a network, a ribbon from which it is impossible to escape, except to drive into a garage" (Sauvy, 1968). The road reaches out to other roads that originate from the garages of other houses or from the parking lots of apartment blocks. The road is the medium that supports a genuine automobile system. It is no longer the system which created mass-produced standard cars, the Model T Ford "driven by mostly inexperienced drivers, over primitive roads ending at the city limits" (Hall, 1988). It is now a fully integrated system, thanks to the road network that crosses the borders of the numerous administrative component parts (Menerault, 1994). The system includes, first of all, a particularly economical process of mass production and consumption. We shall return to this point. Sufficient standardization is presumed to allow access to service centres. Uniform traffic rules are necessary, which must in the first place define within the category 'vehicles' what is meant by 'automobile' – and the task is not easy – in order to set down a minimum number of socially acceptable rules (Fridenson, 1991).

Sub-systems of information and communication (e.g. car radio, mobile telephones) are accumulated and added to the system. Standardization becomes more and more widespread. A number of rules and traffic signals that originated at the beginning of the century in American cities or counties (more rarely elsewhere), are today recognized all over the globe. First used in Detroit in 1914, the 'stop' sign is "a red, octagonal sign, signifying the same thing in Libreville and in Lusaka, in Bagdad and Washington, Barcelona and Madrid" (McShane, 1993). William Phelps Eno, one of the first international experts in highway engineering, has gathered widespread following. The French motorist drives his car across French borders, knowing that there will be no surprises on the roads of other countries. When business or travel takes him across the Atlantic, he can rent a car at the airport, and will probably find the city more foreign looking than the automobile system itself.

Everywhere service stations, motels (illustration 9.3), fast-food restaurants, shopping centres and malls complete the integrated system, with huge parking lots, and with a car in the garage that "invites one to look for a job in the neighbouring county rather than close to home", or to prefer "frequenting a downtown club rather than the local bar", to look for one's friends elsewhere rather than next door (Sachs, 1992; Wiel, 1993; Piveteau, 1990), and, finally, to become 'outwards oriented' (Raux, 1993).

Illustration 9.3   'Western Motel'. The motel as an integral part of the automobile system, seen by Edward Hopper, an American painter particularly sensitive to the new landscapes generated by the automobile. Courtesy of Yale University Art Gallery

This system influences where people will settle in relation to each other as well as how they will spend their time. The 'radical monopoly' of the automobile in an abstract way denounced by Ivan Illitch, finds a practical application here (Illitch, 1974). As Wolfgang Sachs observed with regard to Germany: "Everyone imagines that everyone else has a car, implicitly assuming that everyone moves around by car: remedial classes at school are held in the afternoon because the teachers can easily return to school. The doctor decides to live in a pleasant spot outside the town, because all his patients own cars anyway; and the factory can require the workers to be on time early in the morning because they can drive to work by car" (Sachs 1992).

For the huge majority of people, the network underpinning this system links each node to every other one throughout the territory: "Roads are infinite and offer an infinite number of combinations" (Sauvy, 1968). But this infinite number of connections, this extraordinary number of possible combinations at the same time means system dependency: "with the development of mass motorization, cars have become dependent on the highway system, in the same way that the numerous individual appliances now depend on electrical supply: it is the independence within dependence of this supply that connects us" (Sachs, 1992).

This system, along with its technical, social and aesthetic aspects, possesses a fundamental economic dimension. This particular economic aspect has indeed allowed the greatest number of people to cover large areas quickly to get to a multitude of places.

A system of mixed private-public economics

The economics of the automobile involves, first and foremost, a good that is bought and sold; next, there are the services provided to users; and finally, the nuisances that society has to deal with. It should be noted at the outset that economic theory has already taken into account the automobile market. We are now just beginning to know how to evaluate economically the nuisances and risks of cars. In contrast, economists are more cautious about the convenience of using cars to the extent that the question of the choice between private car and public transport, so vital in urban planning, is still often presented in a truncated fashion, without sufficient reference to the reality of observed behaviour.

How many cars must be sold in order to realize a profit given the billions of euros (or dollars) spent introducing a new model on the market? In a ruthless world of market competition, the exact answer to this question is closely guarded by each automobile manufacturer! Even so, mere extrapolation allows for the calculation that several hundred thousand cars of a particular model must be sold in order to break even. Volkswagen sold more than ten million *Beetles*, and everyone spoke of miracles and fabulous profits. A Japanese car manufacturer decided to launch a specific model on the European market of which only a few thousand cars were sold, at considerable loss (compensated in this case by the success of other models). The law of the market is thus extremely rigid for the manufacturer: simple equilibrium is attained only by the mass production of standard cars. This law can be made to bend through wise policy management of 'top' and 'bottom' line models, which progressively orient the clientele of the standard, economy model at the base towards 'top-of-the-line', more expensive and thus more profitable models. 'Japanese-style' production organization authorizes a certain diversification of options and a lowering of costs. It does not call into question the necessity to build standard models or at least standard base frames.

For the consumer, buying is facilitated through credit and the development of a used-car market. But in particular, the mass production of standard models makes substantial cost reduction possible (Bricnet & Mangolte, 1990; Roos, 1992). It may be estimated as well that the increase in production from 100,000 to 400,000 units reduces the average cost per unit for chassis pressing by 30%. On the long run, these savings are passed on to the buyer by lowering the sales price. The economics of automobile buying is thus characterized by extremely marked economies of scale.

Once purchased, the automobile provides a service while slowly wearing out mechanically with the accumulation of kilometres, and depreciating in value over time. A true estimate of cost per kilometre will take these elements – which are hardly negligible – into consideration. In France, the Fiscal Department estimated this cost in 1995 for professional use between 2 and 3 francs per kilometre for a 7 horse power vehicle. In spite of this, the average motorist in France thinks of his car as a marginal expense, or even just in terms of the cost of petrol only. This leads to a paradoxical state of affairs. In economic terms, without even mentioning external effects, it costs a citizen much less to go to work by means of public transport. However, common opinion considers the difference in cost between public transport and going by car as insignificant due to the difference in convenience, in favour of the automobile. We shall return to this (apparent) contradiction.

Even when evaluated at real cost, the cost of the services provided by the automobile seems quite low. For this there are two basic reasons. The first is that economics does not take into consideration the cost of the task of driving the car. In the first years of the automobile, salaried chauffeurs took care of the vehicle, prepared it for trips, drove their employers, repaired mechanical breakdowns and protected the passengers from nuisances. At today's salaries, maintaining professional chauffeurs would have limited automobile use in a drastic way. History evolved otherwise. With very rare exceptions, there are no longer chauffeurs, and car technology has evolved in the direction of simplicity and reliability. Mr. and Mrs. Average have learned to drive, do not mind spending hours behind the wheel, and in any event do not count the time they spend there (to which might be added the time necessary for learning to drive) in economic terms as work time. In France, the State calculates the profitability of road investments by taking into account the value of the time 'lost' over a given itinerary. This value is calculated with respect to the cost of the amount of work that could have been done by active drivers during the 'lost' period of time. In economic terms, then, a distance of five kilometres would have costed, in 1995, 30 to 40 francs in a city other than Paris, and 7 to 8 francs in rural areas (taxes included). But for the motorist, it seems that the time spend at the wheel (other than during traffic jams) is not considered as 'cost', but rather as 'gained', which completely modifies the basis of the calculation. What explains this evaluation of the driver's activity? Here again, non-economic dimensions of owning a car must be taken into account: there is an element of power over one's immediate environment and over others, a mastery of time and space, and the personal marking out of territory (Ruppert, 1993). Sociologists and psychologists have considered these other dimensions, which are indispensable for properly evaluating the cost of the convenience of using cars.

The other reason for under-estimating the cost of automobile service stems from the fact that car use falls under the heading of 'mixed economics'. The individual pays for the car, upkeep, insurance and fuel. Various public bodies pay for the network of roads and streets that support traffic, for parking, traffic signals, traffic police, and so on. Without paved roads and super-highways, without parking spaces on public streets, without traffic signals, the automobile would be absolutely incapable of providing any service at all. History has shown the importance of the constitution of the infrastructure network, the necessary support for the incredible advance of the automobile. Particularly within the city, a dense network of streets (representing up to 30 percent of the urban surface; in Los Angeles, nearly 40 percent), public parking areas, sophisticated traffic signals, and abundant police services are what make it possible for the automobile to do its job.

The motorist contributes heavily to public budgets through taxes on the car itself as well as on petrol and oil. Nevertheless, it is as if the mixed economy of the automobile system reduced the cost of the infrastructure to the sole amount paid by those who drive cars. Tolls paid in various forms might serve to rectify this situation. But the fare system of infrastructures, and the management of paid parking lots have not, until now, been devised to make motorists pay the real cost of the advantages which they gain from the system. The objective has been to maintain a certain fluidity in traffic and parking within cities, while respecting the rights of the residents living along the streets. More rapid financing for building new super-highways has been a priority. But the economics of automobile system has until now not been profoundly modified in the sense of assigning private charges to the automobile system. In many countries, the public authorities, either national or local, continue to play a role of active accompaniment to the expansion of the automobile sector.

The infrastructure that has been set up over the years in order to benefit the car, in the city as well as elsewhere, has thus led to the constitution of a genuine system. This automobile system has conditioned the access to numerous places, residential buildings, shops and services in terms of motorization and driving a car. The automobile system has more and more in common with a 'natural' monopoly, in the terms of economists, a 'radical' monopoly to use Illitch's term, or a 'universal service'. The system in question covers the entire area on the map well beyond city limits, including recreation areas, other cities, and vacation homes.

This system, which allows for all sorts of relationships, all sorts of networking, is the producer of positive external effects (named 'club effects' or 'network effects' by economists), and obtains considerable advantages for motorized consumers, to the point that one might ask whether tomorrow it will still be possible to live without a car, and if so, where. As we have seen, the economics of the automobile are complex. The economies of scale that regulate the market product have certainly facilitated the popularization of the automobile. But the continuous expansion of the automobile system, including both motorization and increase of mileage travelled by car, which has had a large impact on regional development, cannot be explained only by economies of scale. Beyond economies of scale on the supply side, a widespread, standardized automobile system governs demand at the base of a mixed half-private, half-public economy, economy of services, characterized by marked localized negative external effects (in particular in towns), but also by very positive external effects which concern much larger areas of territory (see next Chapter).

The automobile and territorial adaptation: suburbanization

The external territorial effects have produced and are producing a territorial car technology, in the sense that they allow individuals to adapt their functional territory to the changes in living conditions to which they are more or less subjected. The automobile thus appears as an 'adapter'. For an individual or for a household, owning a car corresponds not so much to a 'tactical' decision, a momentary choice between car or public transport for such and such a trip, as to a truly 'strategic' choice. The acquisition of a car means simultaneously acquiring freedom of movement; having access, under all conditions and circumstances, to a variety of places which are frequently poorly accessed by public transport; maintaining a link with the countryside; transporting small children or the elderly; being able to go off for a week-end; leaving on vacation, carrying skis, pulling a trailer; and so on. One might say that the decision to buy a car comes as a result of all these possibilities, providing a kind of insurance for unforeseen circumstances that might arise in the future. For a woman, this might mean being able to deal with the consequences of a possible divorce (having to move, being given custody of the children, changing jobs). For young people, it means having ready access to a large job market while continuing to take advantage of living at home with one's parents. The importance of potential effects justifies initial investment. Then, as the car is used for this or that errand or trip, cost is evaluated, naturally enough, in terms only of the marginal cost (petrol, tolls, and so on).

The characteristics of the automobile system that we have discussed above signify that the adaptation is not specific to a particular individual in a particular circumstance. It is obvious that the automobile has been playing the role of adapter for a long time for hundreds of thousands of individuals, in different times and in different countries and under many different conditions. This is why one might speak of a 'universal adapter', comparing the automobile to an electrical travel device. A first example of the territorial adaptation made possible by the automobile is suburbanization.

The suburban territory is created by those who, using their automobile advantageously, decide to live a certain distance away from the centre of the city. There they find a less restricted physical environment (the built environment is less dense, there is less traffic; residences are larger, the vegetation is more abundant and nuisances are less concentrated), but in particular they find a more homogeneous and more valorizing social environment (Fischer, 1992) with more advantageous financial conditions (lower property prices). At first, the link with the centre of the city is very strong, because this is where jobs are still found. The car thus guarantees at least the possibility of a daily commute. But this link tends to get less strong when a certain threshold of peripheral urbanization has been attained. Services and facilities begin to appear in suburban areas, contrary to what Lewis Mumford declared, as late as the beginning of the 1960s (Mumford, 1964) (see illustration 9.4). The high density that had been synonymous with good service in the traditional urban fabric is no longer necessary. Even when facilities are dispersed, the automobile makes them accessible under good conditions. The presence of employees (particularly women) attracts jobs. Once again, dispersion is overcome by the possibility of driving; the two-car family becomes a reality. Finally, through governmental initiatives as for the English 'new towns', or else through entirely private developments as for the American 'edge cities', entirely new centres appear (Fishman, 1990).

Historically, in Great Britain the suburb appeared very early. Across the Channel from France there were garden cities and new towns, also suburban in nature. It is clear that the suburban territory needs a good network of inter-city highways or, at least, efficient connections to an excellent system of public transport. The United States illustrates the first case, Great Britain the second. The Paris greater metropolitan area exemplifies the second type as well.

Suburban territory is essentially populated by the affluent middle classes, and the habits and buying power of suburban inhabitants have a strong influence on the types of cars they buy, in the historic case of one-car families as well as in the present state of multi-car families. The suburban model reached its highest development in the United States. More than half of the American population lives

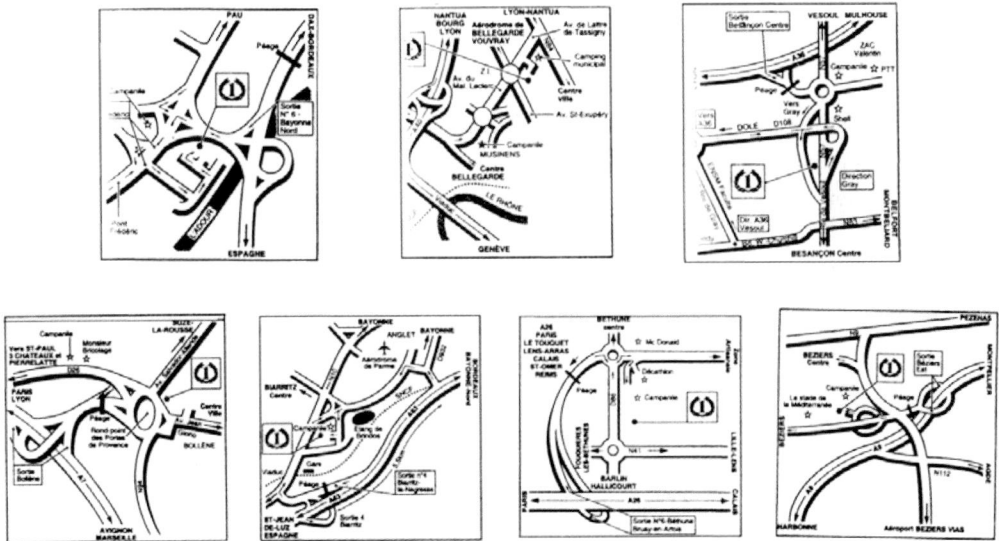

Illustration 9.4 **The localization of 'First Class' hotels as an integral part of the automobile system. A new kind of hotel service adapted to the automobile was developed in France at the nodes of the highway network.** Source: Catalog for France of the 'Premiere classe' hotel chain (1994)

in the suburbs and more than half of the office space is located outside of city centres. From 1940 to 1950 more than any other type of car, the station wagon symbolized the reality of American suburban territory. Originally devised as a kind of taxi to take travellers and their numerous bags to the train station, the station wagon later became the ideal vehicle for housewives to drive husband and children to their multiple activities and jobs located all over the decentralized city (Corn, 1992).

One might indeed say that the automobile, by facilitating large-scale suburbanization, made it possible for numerous inhabitants of English and American cities to put together the territory for a more acceptable urban lifestyle. The automobile thus very early assumed the role of territorial adapter.

The automobile and territorial adaptation: 'rurbanization'

A second example of adaptation is what the French have termed 'rurbanization' (= rural urbanization), and France is the country which best illustrates this phenomenon. The high level of rural activity maintained in France (in 1975 England numbered a farming population of only 3 percent, while France still boasted a population with more than 9 percent farmers), in such close relationship with the towns that farmers share essentially the same attitudes and types of consumer activity as city dwellers. This was observed thirty years ago and related to the advance of the automobile (Bauer & Roux, 1976; Bonnet, 1980). These tendencies have since been confirmed (Benoît & Irrmann, 1989; Frémont, 1988; Cribier, 1994). For example, Cribier (1994) has shown that, regardless of social class, six out of every ten Parisians move to the country at retirement age. She has also noted that France is an exception, since rural migrations are different in the other European countries and in the United States.

There may be historical explanations for this 'tropism' towards the French countryside, in what is an otherwise very urbanized country. Seen from the point of view of the French car industry, the situation is presented in the following terms: "The countryside is the halfway point in the automobile landscape, midway between reconstructed cities and old urban centres, highways and railroads, high density and deserted rural areas, rich and poor societies, and what made it possible for the French car industry to find an identity and give the French car its own specific characteristics" (Filderman, 1992).

In *L'Automobile Impensable* (The Unthinkable Automobile) the sociologist Denis Duclos perceived the originality of the rurban model (Duclos, 1976). Confronted with the situation of an evolving job market in the 1960s and 1970s, the ideal of the workers' city built next to the factory was shown to be completely impracticable. Mobility was the key to finding a job further away, to being able to change quickly from one job to another. The conjugal family became the norm, making limited mobility possible, starting at the neighbourhood unit where it found its place. Rurban space constituted at the same time for employees the first rampart to total mobility, which is what employers were hoping for. Beyond was another line of defence. Employees were also trying to maintain family networks, now often spread out over a much larger territory (an entire region, or even the whole country), which, if confronted with the eventual dysfunctions of the job market, might provide them with symbolic exchanges and material benefits.

As a tool in this double logic, the car could be used to drive to work, but also to maintain the traditional family networks which at the time were still largely to be found in rural areas. "Everyone in the family finds himself in a position to increase the frequency of visits, relationships of contact and reciprocal aid, practically as soon as he begins his professional life." This sociological analysis has been reinforced by geographical studies, in which the degree of importance in the links with the country for French city dwellers has been observed (Lévy, 1994). This will undoubtedly be extended by a careful examination of the constitution and utilization of second homes (a pool of 2.4 million units at the time this article was written).

Thus a type of 'small' French automobile was developed. When it appeared on the work market, it allowed the young household to cover the urban/rural territory of the extended family network. Driven away from home, it transported family members out to the network of the extended family. It goes without saying that it also drove everybody to work. It linked urban to urban and urban to rural, thus strengthening the extended family network. This car was 'small' for three major reasons. Firstly, it had to be inexpensive to buy as well as to operate, in order to be affordable for young couples just starting off. Secondly, it was intended for small families. Finally, it was supposed to be used for 'rurban' trips: "In France, the density of the network, the sinuosity of the roads, the absence of heavy-traffic highways induced the utilization of small cars with extremely reliable, because constantly in use, brake, transmission and steering systems" (Bardou, Chanaron, Fridenson & Laux, 1977).

Thus one sees how the European, and in particular the French automobile played a role as 'territorial adapter' in the 1960s and 1970s, by making the reconstitution of a half-urban, half-rural territory possible for a population recently urbanized and still dependent on its roots in the country.

For the record, the French case is exemplary, but not unique (see illustration 9.5a, b and c). In Italy, Marco Bonatti finds the reasons for what he has called 'the automobile cult' in the fact that the car became an essential condition for the mobility of the masses. The most meaningful image for him is the following: "The parking lot located in front of a factory, at closing whistle on the last Friday of July. A few years ago, one might still observe the families waiting for the husband and/or father. They would be in the parked cars, their bags loaded on the roof. As soon as he had punched out, the worker headed straight for his car, got in behind the wheel, and drove the family off on vacation" (Bonatti, 1992). The car, incidentally, would be a Fiat 500, another 'small' car, derived from the Topolino from before the war, the symbol of the Italian dream of social advancement. This car was used as much for home to work trips as for pleasure rides and Sunday picnics. But in particular, Romano Strizioli tells us, "for the family it was used to drive up and down Italy, full of luggage, from the industrial North down to the South where the parents still lived" (Strizioli, 1990).

In Spain, the Seat 600 played a comparable role (Ciuró, 1970; Leralta, 1991). Chosen by an overwhelming majority of skilled workers and the middle classes, this car provided the means to drive off along the highway during weekends or vacations to reach the 'bit of land' where the whole family was gathered to prepare a *paella* or to grill chops over a fire. This 'bit of land', most often illegal land plots, rarely had water, electricity, or sewers. But – the automobile aiding – it was linked to the highway, via a monumental entrance gate, through a network of paved roads (Goytisolo, 1993).

One thus perceives how this 'rurban' form of territorial appropriation by the automobile differs profoundly from the suburban version. One also understands why European cars are associated with rurbanization (the *Simca Aronde* is a good historical example for France), and are fundamentally different from the American types, influenced less by the size of the country (as has too often been claimed) as by the buying power of the household and its corollary, suburban territory.

Illustration 9.5   Automobile 'rurbanization' in Europe.
a. In Great Britain, at the end of the 1920s. Source: unknown
b. In Italy, at the end of the 1950s. Source: Mende & Diete (1994: 69)
c. (see opposite page) In France, at the beginning of the 1960s. Source: Lauvray & Pascal
(1995: 24)

Urban Networks – Network Urbanism

The automobile: universal territorial adapter

The territorial adaptations discussed above are, in some ways, purely theoretical models. In reality, they may co-exist or be recombined. In the United States, during the first decade of the century, the T-Ford was the car for all jobs, like the 4CV or the 2CV in France during the 1950s; like the French or Italian 'rurban' car, it did not exclude an occasional utilization outside of family networks (Bonatti, 1992; Strizioli, 1990). With two-car, and later multi-car families, territories are transformed and interconnected.

The suburban territory is no longer as dependent on the downtown area as before. Perhaps we are witnessing, in France as in the United States, the birth of 'peri-urban' territory, which will replace the notion of 'suburban'. In France in 1979, more than half of households that had recently moved to individual peri-urban houses already possessed at least two cars (Mayoux, 1979); ten years later, a quarter of all French households possessed at least two cars. It might be concluded that the second car participates in this notion of 'peri-urbanity', with the first car being simply suburban, unless it rather continues to confirm 'rurbanity'. The trend for automobile manufacturers, as seen in the automotive press, would indeed seem to be going in this direction.

There is a distinction made between 'road' cars and 'city' cars. But in fact the 'road' cars may be used equally for suburban territory as well as 'rurban' or 'touring' models, while the so-called 'city' cars are already targeted for a market of multi-car families in the rural and peri-urban areas. The effects are certainly important for the territorial adaptation to the automobile, but statistics are currently lacking.

Whatever the reason, each of these automobile territories signifies the conquering of a residential space different from the purely urban milieu. These territories mark, not a simple evolution, but a rupture with the city and its historically marked identity. These territories are defined in contrast to this city, in contrast to the territory which the city represented and against its limits, in contrast to its relations with the countryside, in contrast to the power structures intended to dominate the totality of these relations.

In the first phase of the construction of automobile territories, reconstitution rather than innovation is observed. The automobile is used to search for one's roots and to renew ancestral ties with entities that are today considered mythical: the wilderness, the hamlet, the village. The common symbolic reference of automobile territories to 'the earth', stressed by Frank Lloyd Wright, has much to teach us in this respect (Bedarida, 1984). In any case, the notions of density, proximity and built-up area with which the city was formerly identified, have been turned upside down by a practically limitless automobile system.

Natural boundaries are pushed back again and again by the extension of the road network or the adaptation of vehicles (for example 4-wheel drive vehicles); artificial boundaries (barriers, toll booths, various restrictions) are vigorously resisted. Centrality is obviously redistributed towards the major nodes of the road network and, on the edges, towards the home of each driver, which becomes the central point for the trips for each member of the family (Moles, 1987; Fishman, 1990). "The rural world (...) is no longer a traditional, closed space" (Bailly, 1994), a photo-negative of the city defined as a place of movement and modernity. The image of the city as it used to be, surrounded by countryside, now seems to belong to a distant past, victim not of the forced automobile implosion feared by Sauvy, but of the suburban explosion, which was a voluntary choice (i.e. rurban). With the extension of networks of electricity, telephone, water and sanitation (Dupuy, 1991a), the automobile and the automobile system have finally played a determining role in numerous territorial adaptations.

This role of adapter has visibly been extended to situations other than those that brought about suburbanization and rurbanization. Without going into an exhaustive analysis, we would here like to review the role played at the present time by the automobile in territorial adaptations necessary for certain categories of the population more subjected to major upheavals than others, such as the elderly. There are more and more old people, and they are forced to redefine their vital territories as the years pass. The limited scope of this Chapter does not make it possible to deal properly with this question here. Instead, we shall limit ourselves to three other equally significant categories: women, young people, and immigrants.

Virginia Scharf has studied the role of the automobile in the life of American women during the period from the beginnings of the automobile to the 1930s. Her conclusion is clear: thanks to the automobile, the sphere of feminine activity was transformed and enlarged; but it did not explode (Scharf, 1991). With the appearance of two-car families, another aspect of women's liberation became apparent. The permanent availability of a car, a professional activity and another income, justified and made possible – to a certain extent – autonomous movements. This made the automobile the instrument of a new way of life, the instrument of an authentic liberation, an emancipation from the 'suffocating' environment of home and neighbourhood (Coutras, 1993) (illustration 9.6).

It must be noted that between 1985 and 1995 in France the proportion of women as primary car drivers has increased by 40 percent; in 1994 85 percent of women 24 years old had a driving license; 35 percent of all car buyers were women. Analyses show, however, that automobile liberation has remained in

Illustration 9.6   The automobile and the redefinition of feminine territories. These new territories of the automobile recombine time and space. Source: Neret & Poulain (1989: 42)

some ways 'conditional'. A woman may use her vehicle to move about alone, more frequently and further away, without having to give a detailed account of her movements. But this new latitude, judged positively by women, is essentially used to resolve the problems that arise due to the multiplication of activities, the spreading out of jobs and the number of locations involved.

A survey carried out simultaneously in the United States, the Netherlands and France mentions the extreme complexity of trip itineraries for working mothers. This complexity is due to the fact that movements are accumulated (work, drop-off/pick-up of children, shopping, bank, and so on), and are combined with the number of activities in which the children are involved, which vary according to the day and the week, and with the unforeseeable nature of certain movements, for example when a child is sick. The Dutch survey shows that, even in a country that provides a high level of public transport (the opposite of the American situation), only a car allows a mother to resolve the complexity of this problem (Rosenbloom, 1992). We might conclude by stating that the automobile has permitted women in modern society to reconcile a role both within the family and within the economy, to adapt their territory with regard to that of women in former generations.

The automobile also means territorial adaptation for young people: the car symbolizes access to adult territory, far from parental control (Barjonet, 1989; Gossiaux & Barjonet, 1989). It has been observed that driver education and obtaining a driving license now starts increasingly earlier. In the United States, depending on the individual state, a license may be obtained at the age of 16, in some states of 15.

Does this precociousness signify the appearance of a new rite of initiation in our advanced societies, as has been suggested? It has been observed in any event that the driving test is taken as early as possible, and that this constitutes an important step for young people. According to a survey carried out in 1993, 70 percent of the students at the University of Paris-Nanterre had a driving license. Car ownership follows the same trend; the only limit to owning a car is the economic capacity of the young person or his family to cope with the financial burden. It is particularly interesting to see that these significant trends are present not only in the university milieu, but also in that of the *lycée*, although nothing until now has been done to encourage them (Dupuy, 1991b; Dupuy & Gerrninet, 1992; Krost-Lapierre, 1993).

For immigrants, the automobile also plays a role in the adaptation of the territory. The car allows one to preserve one's links with the homeland, on vacations; in this way family or tribal links can be maintained in spite of the dispersion of family members. In addition, the car makes integration within the host country somewhat easier. The Portuguese in France, the Turks in Germany, and North Africans in Belgium have used the car – often a used car – in this way, when they were able to afford one. The movement goes on. In certain ghettoes where immigrant populations are concentrated, car ownership is higher than 50 percent. Foreign immigrants have found in the automobile system a place which the host city or country has refused them: "… one finds in these populations [North Africans on the outskirts of Lyons] massive ownership of old, battered cars which are used for shopping, Sunday outings and family visits …" (Chevalier, 1994).

Conclusion

In conclusion, it appears that the automobile has been, and continues to be, a universal territorial adapter. In the face of strong migratory trends, the automobile has sometimes delayed, sometimes completely thwarted the hopes for residential change. On the other hand, the car has sometimes been able to reinforce them, as in the case of suburbanization. In any case, the automobile has contributed significantly to the recomposition of a number of territories.

This role of the automobile deserves to be compared to other processes and regulatory practices that operate along the same lines. The ups and downs of the property market are equally capable of determining a territory, especially in the urban milieu, by increasing value for a few individuals and entirely excluding all those whose financial means do not allow them to buy certain properties or houses. In economic systems with less free enterprise, urban planning and development pursue the goal of assigning allotted territories for the development of certain activities or lifestyles for certain groups of the population. Zoning in all its forms is frequently the tool for these territorial compositions that are supposed to be imposed on individuals.

With respect to these practices, we should consider the automobile, a universal adapter as we have seen, as an alternative, as the super-powerful instrument of a territorial policy, which until now has only been implicit but that is nonetheless real. Three reasons seem to argue in favour of this thesis.

First of all, and as we have seen, the automobile has had considerable effects on territorial adaptation, undoubtedly more powerful than the efforts of planners, and far surpassing in geographical breadth those of the property value market. Secondly, the automobile is not, as is too often repeated, the simple means for individual liberty resulting in unpredictable behaviour patterns and chaotic effects. The modern automobile exists only in the context of an eminently collective automobile system, with its rules and standards, producing in the end coherent territorial compositions such as suburbanization and rurbanization. Thirdly, the role of orientation and regulation by public authorities in the automobile system is considerable, whether for financing, automobile standards, protection or opening of markets, or planning.

There are thus many policies concerning the automobile system and these policies directly affect the role that the automobile can play as territorial adapter. How city vehicles evolve in the future will depend, for example, on the severity of pollution controls decided upon right now. And, likewise, the future of European city centres will no doubt depend on the availability of such cars. In the same way, the policy of certain third world countries regarding the development of the automobile system is already being directed towards territorial development: Brazil and China come to mind as examples. According to the forecasts, the world supply of automobiles will attain 1217 million vehicles by 2020, and will exceed 2,5 billion by 2060 (Lamure, 1995). It is high time for those who think they still have any say in territorial development and planning to recognize the place of the automobile in their plans.

"The automobile-based system (…) consisted in:

- the development of a system of mass production to bring the automobile within the reach of the average household (…);

- the development of a set of servicing centres which, coupled with mass production and standardisation, made it possible to maintain mass car ownership at a high level of performance;

- the development of a set of uniform codes, traffic regulations, driver testing and the like;

- the construction first of a network of paved roads and then of motorways for high-speed access;

- and the development around the latter of a network of facilities in the form of motels, fast-food restaurants and similar facilities specifically catering to the automobile traveller (…) "

From: Impact of New Technologies and Socio-economic Trends on Urban Forms and Functioning *by Peter Hall; in OECD, Urban Development and Impact of Technological Economic and Socio-Demographic Changes, Report of an Expert Meeting, OECD, Paris, June 1988*

10   From the Magic Circle to Automobile Dependence: Measurements and Political Implications*

Introduction

Automobile dependence is becoming an ever greater obstacle to sustainable transport policies. This dependence is due mainly to the fact that the positive effects for drivers of the growth of the automobile system are greater than the negative effects of traffic congestion. The model described in this Chapter is a simple one; it is based on an analogy with telecommunications systems and presents these positive effects in terms of accessibility. On the basis of the model, quantitative measurements of the French situation were made. Results show the importance of positive effects, which make it extremely difficult to reduce automobile dependence. Adopting a *laissez-faire* approach would only lead to very slow changes. Taxing automobiles and automobile use is not enough to offset the above-mentioned effects. Urban densification, beyond its segregative impacts brings little more than local solutions to a problem which is increasingly global. The results presented in this Chapter suggest the implementation of policies which would have a direct impact, within the automobile system, on the processes which generate these positive effects. The aim of these policies would be to diversify vehicles and their ownership, modify road networks (more, but slower, roads), and limit the *capillarity* of these networks. The policies proposed in this Chapter are both effective and realistic, since they aim to reduce automobile dependence, but not the quality of service provided to drivers.

Automobile system, positive effects and dependence

Some forty years ago, American oil industry and road engineers discovered the 'magic circle' of automobile development (Asphalt Institute, 1966; see illustration 6.1). They observed that the increase in automobile traffic led to the expansion of the road network, thus encouraging car owners to drive more, more people to buy cars, resulting in an increase in traffic, which was once again followed by the growth of the network, and so on and so forth (see illustration 6.1). Obviously, such snowballing was a boon to those in the oil and road business. The magic circle has not stopped turning; on the contrary, it has accelerated to such a degree that we now view it with more concern than wonder. In the fifty years that followed WW II, the automobile stock and traffic have more than doubled in the United States and were multiplied by ten in Europe. At the world level, the number of automobiles has grown much faster than the population: there were 14.2 people per car in 1980 and only 12 in 1993.

---

*   Previously published in *Transport Policy*, 6 (1), Dupuy, G., "From the 'Magic Circle' to 'Automobile Dependence': Measurements and Political Implications", pp. 1-17, Copyright Elsevier, 1999. Included with permission.

An article from 1995 raises the issue, formulating the question in its title (Newman, Kenworthy & Vintila, 1995): *Can we overcome automobile dependence?* Given the context of generalized automobile use, the expression 'automobile dependence' means that as individuals, we cannot live without cars, just as a smoker cannot live without cigarettes and a drug addict without drugs. This is what Ivan Illitch denounced two decades ago as the 'radical monopoly' of automobiles (Illitch, 1974); a monopoly which has negative effects even on those who do not own a car. According to Newman and Kenworthy, certain cities, Los Angeles for example, show a collective dependency on cars, whereas others, like Paris, are less automobile-dependent (Newman & Kenworthy, 1991). Finally, from a more global point of view, automobile dependence and the resulting increase in motorization and car traffic cause natural resources – space, oil and fresh air – to become increasingly scarce. In an effort to overcome this dependence, Newman and his colleagues advocate the rehabilitation of physical planning. In their opinion, a strong redensification of cities would diminish automobile dependence.

This opinion has been widely criticized. Some of Newman's detractors believe that automobile dependence is simply a reflection of people's preference for living in less dense areas and travelling faster. Thus, one should take no particular measures and just leave it to the market to reveal such preferences, determine prices and regulate consumption (Gomez-Ibanez, 1991). It is most interesting to note that Melvin Webber, a well-known former physical planning advocate, shared this point of view (Webber, 1992). However, according to other detractors, though a certain number of adjustments may be necessary, the solution is not in physical planning: if the aim is to reduce motorization and automobile use, one must raise the cost of fuel, increase taxes, set up tolls, and so on.

Sensitive government intervention to manage the negative externalities of auto use is increasing all the time. Congestion pricing, parking buy-out, hot lanes, off-site trip generation management are new ways for controlling the trend. But it is always controlling from the periphery, not dealing with the centre of the matter.

In 1995, Phil Goodwin published a report on car dependence in the United Kingdom. In the introduction, Goodwin speaks of the necessity of reaching a political consensus in order to reduce automobile-related costs. But "all serious statements", he writes, "now refer to the difficulties such policies face, imposed by 'car dependence'. In part, this is simply a recognition of the obvious observation that car use is very widespread, and deeply connected with the patterns of everyday life. Improving our understanding of the sources and consequences of the role of the car in modern societies should help us understand which policies will work and which will not, and how to achieve desirable economic and environmental objectives with the minimum of harmful, or destructive side effects" (RACS, 1995).

This corresponds precisely to our point of view on the question. Goodwin's both sensitive and comprehensive approach reveals the possibilities and limits of traditional methodology for the analysis of car dependence. Our aim is thus to present an original explanatory model. Given the controversy raised by Newman's work, it is necessary to carry out measurements and assess the policies (especially as concerns land use planning) proposed to reduce car dependence. We will thus make policy-making suggestions, based on the measurements provided by our model.

In this Chapter, we will first provide a simple model which explains the true nature of automobile dependence and what its actual components are. From there on, we will suggest a few policies, which are more efficient than Newman's, to reduce this dependence.

For Peter Hall, the automobile-based system is based on mass production, service centres for all, high-level performance of automobiles, a set of traffic rules and regulations, a network of roads and highways, a network of facilities which are necessary to road travel (motels, fast food restaurants, and so on) (Hall, 1988).

Mirroring part of Hall's criteria, our model for the analysis of automobile dependence is built on the measurement of the positive effects produced by the automobile-based system. It is based on the concepts of club and network effects, usually applied to telecommunications but adapted in this case to the automobile sector (Hayashi, 1992; Capello, 1994; Economides, 1996; Curien & Dupuy, 1996). The basic idea is the following: what a person gains by joining a club (or a network) depends on all its present members (those already in the network). In the literature, the terms of club or network positive effects (or externalities) are used interchangeably although in fact they are dealing with stock effects (or externalities) (cf. bibliography of Capello, 1994). This is owing to the fact that in the telecommunications network, such a distinction is not always necessary, which is not the case for the automobile system.

According to our model, access to the automobile system occurs in three stages:
- a.   obtaining a driver's licence
- b.   acquiring a car
- c.   travelling on the road network.

At each stage, there occurs a specific positive effect caused by the presence of other members who have already passed this stage. For stage (a), it is in the full sense of the term a club effect, created by the number of people who already possess a driver's licence. The proportion of drivers in the overall population increases the gap between the maximum speed allowed to those who have a licence and to those who do not. For stage (b), one should rather speak of a fleet effect, linking services for drivers to the size of the automobile fleet. For stage (c), the term network effect is most appropriate, as the effect depends on the distribution of car traffic on the road network.

These three positive effects interact cumulatively, and as a result there is considerable pressure to enter the automobile system. Despite negative effects (congestion) in very dense urban areas, dependence is thus very strong and extremely difficult to overcome.

Remarks concerning methodology

In accordance with our definition of the automobile-based system, we will study not only the behaviour of the individual driver, but also the road network he or she uses and the services offered to him or her. As to the variations in the automobile-based system, these can only be shown by comparing different periods of time or different countries. This creates several methodological difficulties: in such comparisons, variables external to the automobile system *per se*, such as demography, income, fuel prices, also differ and must also be taken into account. For this reason, the available data do not allow us to carry out very precise analyses. The study carried out by the RAC Foundation for Motoring and Environment does not refer to a strict definition of the automobile system or of car dependence and in this respect it was able to provide relatively precise analyses based on available data, pertaining to specific contexts (RAC, 1955).

Previously published analyses (see Chapter 9), though often quite informative, have two main drawbacks. In the first place, they are qualitative (Sachs, 1992). Secondly, they do not isolate the specific impact of automobiles in relationship to other changes (Kunstler, 1993). In light of these drawbacks and taking the limitations of the data into consideration, the information we have is significant enough to have an impact on actual knowledge in the field as well as on potential policy-making.

We limited our analysis to a calculation of *elasticities*. These elasticities express the effect of a variation in the composition of the club, fleet or network on the personal benefit to an individual of the automobile system. This limitation was necessary because of the lack of available data. Thus, it was impossible for us to adjust the functions representing the benefits gained for any given composition of the club, fleet or network. But formulating the issue in terms of elasticities nevertheless has one advantage, which is that most analyses explaining motorization and road traffic on the basis of variables such as income, price and existing road infrastructures are usually formulated in terms of elasticities. This has made it possible for us to compare our results with these analyses, as will be seen later.

The model is strictly limited to the benefits provided to the car driver by the automobile sector, in other words to the *positive sectorial effects*. The negative externalities of the automobile system (traffic congestion, pollution) have already been widely studied and are relatively well known as compared to the positive effects and for this reason, these issues will not be dealt with here, except when they interact with the positive effects we are trying to measure (see later in this Chapter). Next, the model is only concerned with the positive effects which can be expressed in terms of benefits within the automobile system. Thus, the analysis does not look into the effects which may be important but are of a more sociological nature. For instance, the positive effect that having a driver's licence or owning a car can have on a person's social status are not included in this study. It is true that this played a crucial role in the past, in the popularization of automobiles (Boltanski, 1975). However, this effect is no longer as strong as it used to be, except in countries which are only beginning to become motorized. An interesting review of the literature, covering both sociological and psychological aspects of car dependence, can be found in (RACS, 1995). We will come back to this point at the end of the Chapter.

The benefits of the system for the (present or potential) automobile driver are measured in terms of speed or access to services. We will refer to the common notion of accessibility. Accessibility indicates both the possibility of reaching a place or specific service within a given amount of time and the choice of available destinations from a given point within a given travel-time (Taylor, Young & Bonsall, 1996). If d represents the density of available services (number of services per surface unit) and s the speed of travel in the network (number of km which can be travelled within one hour in any direction from a given point), accessibility a is proportional to d and s^2. From then on, the relative variations of a, s, and d are linked by

$$\Delta a/a = 2(\Delta s/s) + \Delta d/d$$

According to whether the composition of the club, fleet or network affects the individual benefits gained from the automobile system thanks to the density of services only or to speed only, the corresponding variations of accessibility will be measured either from

$$\Delta d/d$$

or from

$$2 \ \Delta s/s$$

Accessibility, as studied here, concerns only automobile-related services, in other words, services provided within the automobile sector, a more limited framework than the automobile system. Positive effects also play a role in the supply of services related to the automobile system and provided by other sectors (the business or health sectors, for example). However, it was impossible for us to evaluate all these effects together, because of which we chose to limit our investigation to services provided by the automobile sector itself (sales, repairs, and so on).

For this study we used French data (see Orfeuil (1993) for a synthetic and comparative description of the principal French data concerning automobile use and ownership). To illustrate the results of positive effects, we chose to study them in the context of an 'average' French region: the Auvergne region. However, on the whole, the results can be generalized to other French regions and even to other countries.

Now that the framework has been established, we will successively analyse three effects: the club, the fleet and the network, and observe how the three combine in a cumulative process. This will lead us to some measurements (some of them comparable to Phil Godwin's results) and to their political implications, particularly in relationship to Newman's position on the subject.

Club effects: the driver's licence

Obtaining a driver's licence is the first step necessary to enter into the automobile system. In France, a driver's licence is often considered the same as an identity card. It is required for certain jobs. Young people consider it a symbol of adulthood. It is a sign that one belongs to a club of licensed drivers, a club which provides benefits to its members. Among these benefits is the right to drive a car according to the highway code, and to drive fast: in France, the speed limits are 90 km/h on an ordinary road and 130 km/h on highways, with small variations according to the type of infrastructure such as 50 km/h in very dense urban areas, 110 km/h on some suburban roads, and so on.

The benefits of entering the club can be measured by comparing the situation of those who do not have a driver's licence but are allowed, according to French law, to drive small cars – *voiturettes* – which cannot go faster than 45 km/h. Other comparisons, with public transport users or cyclists, are also possible. The point of comparing with *voiturette* drivers is that they are technologically similar: the *voiturette* is a small car whose motor has been bridled by the manufacturer to make its speed compatible with legislation. The door-to-door difference in speed between a regular car and a *voiturette* corresponds, on an average, to the difference of speed between a car and public transportation. With a *voiturette*, one can cover longer distances, using less effort, than with a bicycle. Further, with a *voiturette*, one

Points accessible in 1 hour by 'voiturette' from Gannat

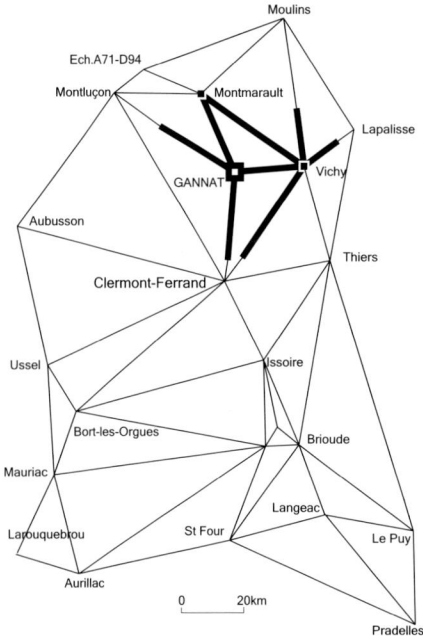

Points accessible in 1 hour by car from Gannat

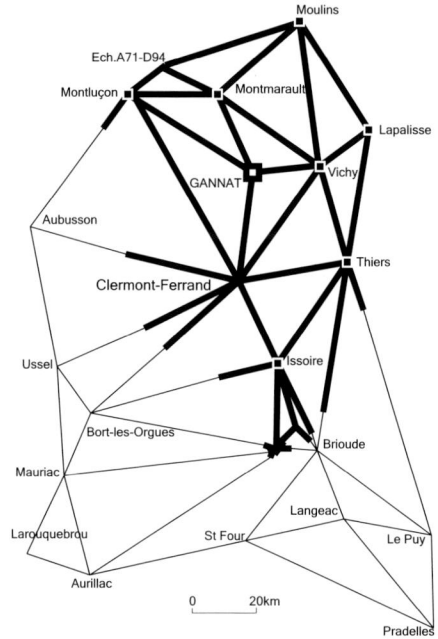

The bold lines show the distances that can be travelled in one hour departing from Gannat on each of the possible itineraries

Illustration 10.1   **The club effect. Accessibility gain owing to the speed allowed to the club members (driver's licence holders) as compared to non-members: driver's licence not required / driver's licence required**

can carry the shopping home, which is not so easy to do on a bicycle, a motorcycle or using public transportation. Thus, in terms of the Goodwin report (RACS, 1995), it is more relevant to compare car driving to *voiturette* driving than to bicycle riding or public transportation.

Illustration 10.1 shows the advantage of having a driver's licence over not having one. Taking a small French town, Gannat (population ca. 6000, Auvergne region, central France), we calculated the distances a licensed driver (member of the club) can travel in one hour as compared to those travelled by a non-licensed driver (not a member of the club) using the same road network.

The club effect is modelled as follows. The benefits obtained through being a member of the club are measured by the increase in accessibility as shown in the difference between the maximum speed authorized to licensed drivers and that authorized to non-licensed drivers driving *voiturettes*. This advantage supposedly depends on the proportion l of licensed drivers in the population under study. In fact, the history of the automobile (Courty, 1990; Foreman-Peck, 1987) shows that licensed drivers, depending on their proportion in the population, do play a role in the setting of authorized speed limits both for themselves and for those who do not have a licence and represent a hindrance to traffic on the road network. For example, the highway code is established by public authorities in close collaboration with the Automobile Clubs, which justifies the term of 'club effect' in this particular case.

Thus, the more members there are in the licensed drivers' club (for a given population), the more the speed differential (and thus the accessibility differential) favours those drivers. One can suppose that individuals preparing to take the driver's licence examination consider that the benefit to be gained in terms of speed surpasses the cost of preparing the licence. This benefit is represented by a function of proportion l of licensed drivers, such as:

$$\theta(s-s_0) = \theta l^\alpha$$

where s is the authorized speed for licensed drivers, and s_0 is the authorized speed for non licensed drivers. θ is a parameter distributed evenly over the population and representing a more or less marked interest in speed, in the sense that it increases the accessibility. This functional representation is inspired from models used in the telecommunications sector (see Curien & Gensollen, 1989; Curien & Dupuy, 1996).

However, the gain in accessibility enjoyed by a licensed driver is defined here in relationship to the accessibility for non-members. Consequently, the elasticity of accessibility relative to l, E_c, is lower than

$$\Delta a/a/\Delta l/l = 2\Delta s/s/\Delta l/l = 2\alpha$$

Suppose that what is gained by members of the club in terms of authorized speed equals what is lost by non-members, one can point out that

$$E_c = (1 - s_0/s)\alpha$$

Given the current speed limitations set by the highway code on French roadways, the elasticity of accessibility in relation to the number of members in the club of licensed drivers would therefore be close to

$$E_c = 0.6\alpha$$

Given the following French data; that 75 percent of people of driving age (at least 18) have a driver's licence (according to French National Survey of 1994) and that the average cost of learning to drive was approximately 6000 FF (ca. 900 euro), we established a maximum acceptable cost of learning to drive at 8000 FF (ca. 1200 euro). The function which links the acceptable cost of obtaining a driver's licence to the proportion l of licensed drivers among the total population reaches a stable point of equilibrium for the aforementioned values when the a parameter has a value of 0.8 (see illustration 10.2). Another model, where a depends on l, gives about the same value for E_c.

The elasticity of accessibility in relation to the number of members in the club of licensed drivers would therefore be:

$$E_c = 0.5$$

In other words, an increase of 1 percent in the number of driver's licence owners (in the whole of a given population) leads to a 0.8 percent relative speed advantage over non-owners and an actual accessibility advantage of approximately 0.5 percent. This data corresponds to the data in a highly

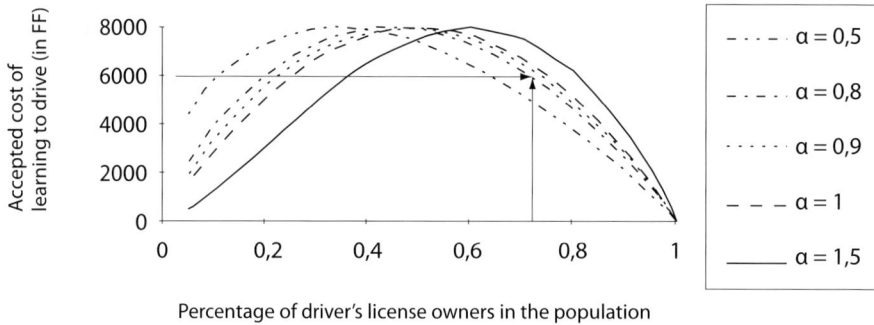

Illustration 10.2   Determining the club effect parameter (a)

motorized country (France), where the proportion of non-licensed drivers is explained by various cultural or demographic reasons (Madre & Pirotte, 1997) with little or no relation to the club effect. This elasticity was probably even greater in the past. In any case, this result corresponds to what can be observed concerning the driving restrictions progressively imposed on non-licensed drivers and users of two-wheeled vehicle driving.

Fleet effect: automobile acquisition

Once in possession of a driver's licence, the second step towards entry into the automobile system consists in acquiring a vehicle that can be driven at the authorized speed and according to the rules fixed by the driving code. The benefit of owning a car increases as the number of cars already on the road (the fleet) increases. In order to measure the advantage because of the fleet effect, we chose to study the services provided to automobile owners by dealers and agents in charge of sales, after-sales services, maintenance and emergency repairs.

In France, as a result of both tradition and present legislation, each large automobile manufacturer has its own network of dealers and agents. Thus, the simultaneous observation of the fleets of the various makes of car present in France and of the networks of corresponding dealers and agents allows us to measure the positive fleet effect. The acquisition (or at least the use) of a make of car with a large fleet offers the driver more services than would a less well-known make – even if agents of one make can perform certain types of repairs on cars of another make. This difference can be illustrated by maps giving the locations of dealers and agents of more and less well-known makes. In France, Renault used to have nearly 7000 dealers and agents, Peugeot 4000, Toyota only 250. Illustration 10.3 shows the differences in the Auvergne region, already chosen as an example in the preceding section. In terms of density of service availability, there is obviously an advantage to owning a well-known make with a large fleet.

The corresponding model is very simple. Statistically, at a given date, there is a proportionality between the number of dealers and agents of a certain make in the country and the number f of registered cars of that make. The elasticity E_p of the services offer (and therefore of accessibility as

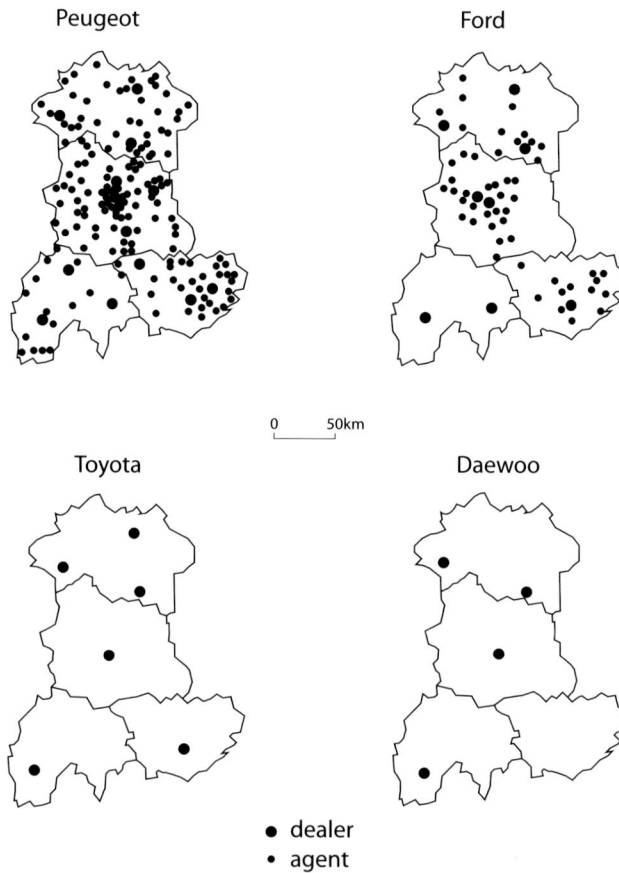

Peugeot   Ford

0 50km

Toyota   Daewoo

• dealer
• agent

Illustration 10.3   **The fleet effect. Density of automobile distribution services in the Auvergne region**

well) in relation to the fleet is 1. An increase of 1 percent in the fleet of a given make will therefore correspond to an increase of 1 percent in the number of dealers and agents in France and thus the accessibility of services provided to the car owner. With a few adjustments, this result can be applied to other regions. Thus, as far as fleet effect is concerned, the Auvergne region would have an elasticity of fleet

$$E_f = \Delta d/d/\Delta f/f$$

$$E_f = 1$$

We have chosen to limit the analysis to intra-sectorial effects, those internal to the automobile sector. However, in this category we could also take into account road signs, maps (Ribeill, 1991) or gas stations, even if the services provided there belong rather to the network effects studied in the following section, as in many cases more services are provided to the driver than to the car. Shopping centres, parks, sportsground and cinema theatres also seem to spring up according to the same principle, except that in the latter case, the effect is because of the whole fleet, all brand names included, and not to the fleet of a single make. Car parks, for instance, which provide an essential service, are built in relation to fleet. In this regard, it should be noted that in France, a car is parked on an average 95 percent of the time. The parking supply must thus correspond directly to the size of the fleet (and not to the amount of traffic), without disregarding geographic distribution.

Thus, the value of the actual fleet effect seems much greater than that calculated by the method mentioned earlier.

Network effect: road traffic

The owner of a driver's licence (member of the club) having acquired a car (belonging to a fleet) will probably want to use the road network. The benefit that the driver will gain on entering this network depends on the number of drivers already using it. This first calls to mind a negative externality, the result of traffic congestion: the more dense the traffic, the more tie-ups the new driver will encounter, hence, the slower he will go. In fact, though this effect exists, it only does so to a limited extent in time and space. It is minor compared to the positive network effect, whose workings can be explained in the following way.

The denser the traffic on a road network, the more money is devoted to improving that network. This is the main principle of the *Roadworks Investment Fund*, which has been in existence for several years now in many countries (Roth, 1996). A special budget for road investment is supplied by the taxes levied on fuel consumption, car oil, and so on, the total amount of which is just about proportional to road traffic. Where such a fund does not exist, there is nonetheless a close relationship between the amount of taxes and the amount of road investment. Improvements come in the form of an increase in possible – but not real – speed on certain parts of the network, precisely those with the heaviest traffic.

Contrary to the previous effects, in this case there is no isotropy, because of which we used the term network effect. Heavy or light traffic depends on where the drivers are coming from and where they are going, and on the structure of the existing network. Money for improvements is set aside for one road or the other according to traffic. Improvements may be justified for reasons of capacity, security or environment, but in all cases, improvements make for increased efficiency on the infrastructure in question, particularly as concerns speed. On the contrary, when less used, a road is often not maintained, in which case it deteriorates and is less efficient.

Let us return to the Auvergne region, and journeys made starting from the town of Gannat. Illustration 10.4 illustrates the effect of this network effect. We compared distances from Gannat in all directions of the road network that could be travelled in one hour in 1977 and in 1997. The map shows the considerable increase in the efficiency of the road network.

Precise modelling is much more complex in the case of the road network. For a telephone network, the non-isotropic problem was accurately formulated, but modelling only leads to operative solutions with extremely restrictive hypotheses, which tend back to the case of isotropy. Precise modelling of the

1977
Shows the part of the network accessible
in less than 1 hour by car from Gannat

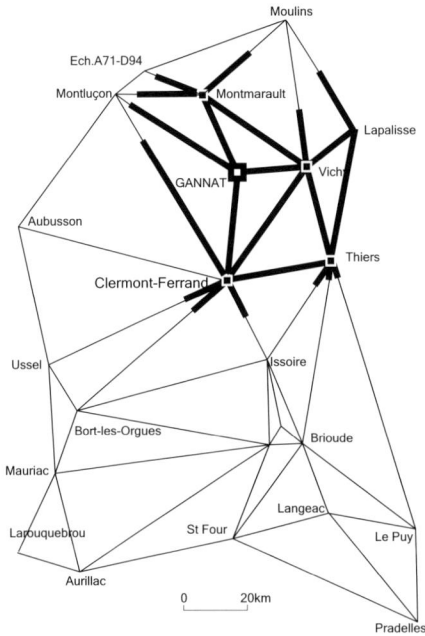

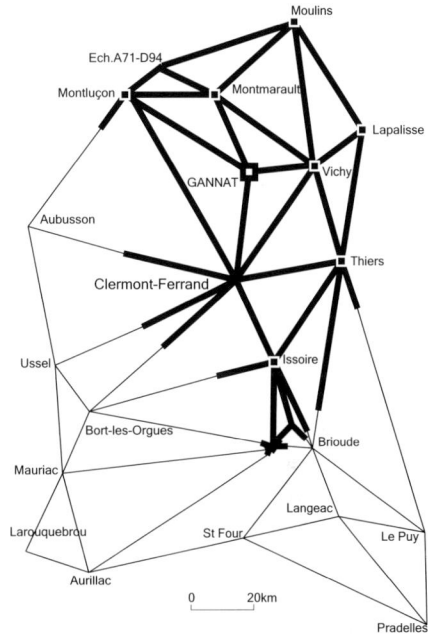

1997
Shows the part of the network accessible
in less than 1 hour by car from Gannat

The bold lines show the distances that can be travelled in one hour departing from Gannat on each of the possible itineraries

Illustration 10.4   **The network effect. Accessibility gain 1997/1977 owing to improvement of the network**

road network takes into account both the design of the road network and the structure of movements – in transportation engineering terms, the origin-destination matrix, which represents users' *desire lines*. In the telecommunications sector, the term *affinities matrix* is used. As Steyer and Zimmermann note concerning telecommunications – in connexion with the spread of fax machines – for the user, benefits depend not only on the actual or probable number of other users of the network, "but also on the choices… made by the other users he is in relation with…. In this case, a network is the topology of the users' intercommunication needs and of the expected benefits" (Steyer & Zimmermann, 1996).

However, we can show where such an effect comes from by considering the simple example of a road network allowing communication between three points in a region, i, j, and k. Let us look at the effect of a global increase $\Delta C/C$ in traffic on the network. The rule, which the operator will adopt in our hypothesis, is the following: invest in one segment in such a way as to increase speed (by $\Delta s/s$) if the traffic increase ΔT on that segment exceeds the threshold T_h. Then

$$\Delta s/s = \delta A \Delta T/T$$

with $\delta = 0$ or 1 according to whether $\Delta T > T_h$ or not on the segment considered. A is a constant called the adaptation factor of the network. According to the topology adopted for the network – and in certain

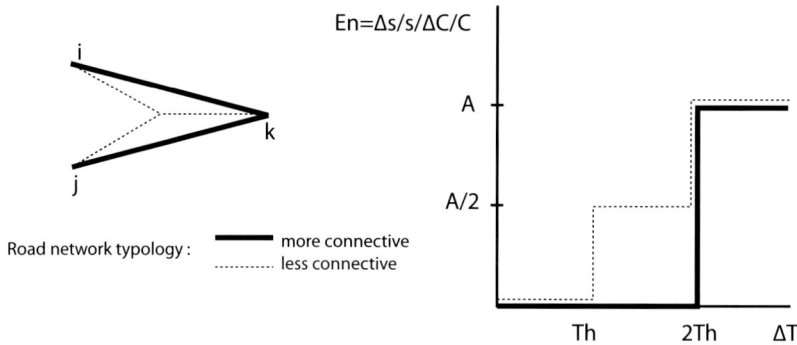

Illustration 10.5 **Speed/traffic elasticity in function of traffic variation and network topology**

simplifying hypotheses of traffic symmetry and kilometric equality of trip distances – if the average increase in speed $\Delta s/s$ is divided by the global increase in traffic $\Delta C/C$, in other words, by a factor of 2, then the elasticity E_n varies according to the graph shown in illustration 10.5.

From the point of view of accessibility, the increase in speed made possible on the various segments can be interpreted as an increase in the distance that can be travelled in a given amount of time. The connectivity of such networks can be measured according to the theory of graphs by the index y (Curien & Dupuy, 1996). Here, the most connective topology corresponds to a $y = 2/3$, the least connective to a $y = 1/2$.

In the case of the most connective road network topology, the area accessible from point k is unchanged as long as $\Delta T < 2T_h$; and in the case of the least connective road network, the area accessible from point k is farther when $\Delta T > T_h$. Coming into play here are the global increase $\Delta C/C$ in traffic on the network, the adaptation factor A and a topological, matrix factor, which expresses the adequation between the topology of the road network and that of itineraries. As a result of the hierarchy of roads and traffic regroupings, the greater the difference between the road network design and the O/D matrix – in terms of the theory of graphs, the weaker the connectivity – the greater is the positive impact of traffic on speed (see the least connective topology in illustration 10.5) and therefore, the greater is the positive effect of the network.

This model shows the importance of the phenomena of anisotropy and polarization, which, by orienting the flow of traffic, favour the building of major trunk roads and motorways which in turn drain the flows. In illustration 10.4, there is a noticeable anisotropy in the north-south direction and around the centre constituted by Clermont-Ferrand, the capital of Auvergne.

As we were not in possession of sufficient data to separate the incidence of the topological factor and the adaptation factor, we globalized the two factors by measuring network effect by means of the E_n speed elasticity in relation to traffic on the French network, using data from French national surveys (1981 and 1993). These surveys provide traffic values and average driver speed on the road network. A particular difficulty can be avoided by taking the whole of the French road network: indeed, the discontinuities in accessibility variations resulting from threshold effects are smoothed out when we consider the whole of the network rather than efficiency on a particular itinerary. In this sense, the elasticity calculation retains its meaning despite local discontinuities owing to threshold effects.

A comparison of network speed – actual driving speed including time lost slowing down and stopping to respect priorities (André, 1997) and not the speed theoretically allowed on the network – on the one hand and traffic on the other over an interval of 12 years, gives us an elasticity for the advantage of using a network, and therefore of accessibility,

$$E_n = \Delta a/a/\Delta C/C = 2\Delta s/s/\Delta C/C$$

$$E_n = 0.8$$

This same value also holds true for the Auvergne region on the basis of observations made over an interval of 20 years. Here, it is doubtless a matter of a lower estimation of the E_n elasticity. In fact, the overall speed increase of approximately 25 percent registered on French roads in general covers quite different contexts. In city centres, speed remained stable during the period. However, the creation of bypasses and their increasingly frequent use by drivers has increased speed considerably. A study of bypasses put in service about ten years ago shows that they allowed a speed increase of approximately 50 percent. The rapidity of the journey from Gannat to Saint-Flour (see illustration 10.4) increased by almost 60 percent owing to the building of motorways A71 and A75. These two figures are a good illustration of the model mentioned earlier and lead us to believe that the effect of the topological factor mentioned earlier would bring about network effects measured by E_n elasticities significantly higher than 0.8 on the most frequented parts of the network.

Combinations of positive effects: chain reactions

We showed that the automobile system affords the user the benefits of club, fleet and network effects and we quantified the latter by calculating the elasticities. Positive effects go hand in hand and thus accumulate. On obtaining one's driver's licence, one benefits from the size of the club made up by those who already possess theirs. On acquiring a car, one benefits from the size of the pre-existing fleet. Finally, when driving at the maximum speed allowed, one takes full advantage of a road network whose efficiency depends on its being used by other car owners and, in particular, one enjoys the services provided to one's make of car.

Going back to the example of the Gannat area, the benefits gained by the three positive effects together is shown in illustration 10.6 by the superimposition of several maps. On the first, we see a non-licensed *voiturette* driver on the road network as it was in 1977, within the one-hour isochrone. On the road he finds the service points (few in number) provided by his make of car. The example is that of Aixam, the French leader on the *voiturette* market with a fleet of approximately 25000 cars (out of a total *voiturette* stock of 67000 cars in France).

On the second map, we see a driver at the wheel of a standard car 20 years later in 1997. He is driving at the speed allowed by his license and by the present state of the network and finds the services provided by Peugeot (second largest French make), of which the fleet in France consisted of about five million vehicles. Visually, the difference is considerable.

The fleet effect produces Δd. Δs is the result of club and network effects, or

$$\Delta s = (\Delta s)_c + (\Delta s)_n$$

Accessibility of Aixam *voiturettes* services in less than 1 hour from Gannat for a non-holder of a driver's licence

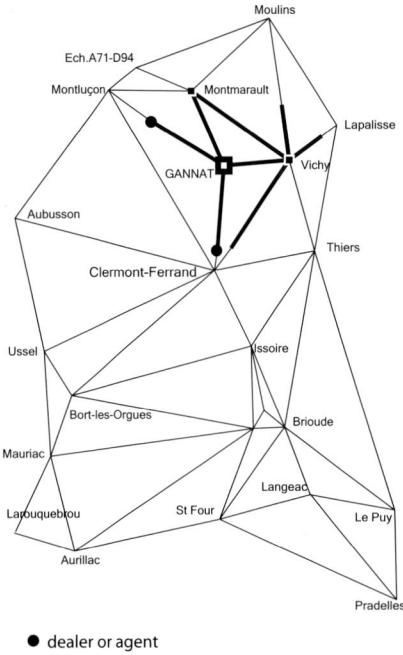

Accessibility of Peugeot services in less than 1 hour from Gannat for driver's licence holder

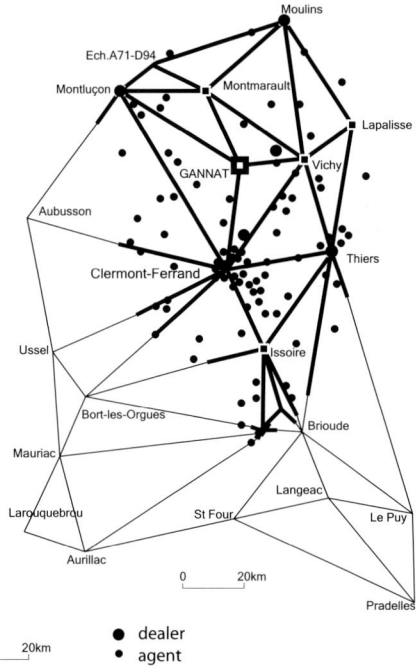

● dealer or agent

● dealer
• agent

Departing from Gannat, in one hour the driver can cover the distance shown in bold lines on each itinary and have access to the service points indicated on the maps.

Illustration 10.6   **Combination of club, fleet and network effects**

By definition of accessibility as given earlier

$$\Delta a/a = E_c \Delta l/l + E_n \Delta C/C + E_f \Delta f/f$$

If all driver's licence owners acquired a car and if all car owners drove the same way on the network, we would have

$$\Delta l/l = \Delta f/f = \Delta C/C = q$$

from which

$$\Delta a/a = q(E_c + E_n + E_f)$$

Taking into account the previously obtained values ($E_c = 0.5$, $E_n = 0.8$, $E_f = 1$) and taking $q = 1\%$

$$\Delta a/a = 2.3\%$$

In fact, the hypothesis of equality of the relative variations of *l*, *f*, and *C* cannot be accepted. Data collected in the United States clearly invalidates it. Between 1969 and 1977, the number of driver's licences increased by 24 percent, the fleet by 13 percent and total traffic by 40 percent. Thanks to the analysis of the data from the United Kingdom, we can understand some of the interactions occurring between the three variables (RACS, 1995). In particular, the learning period tends to slow the increase in the total number of kilometres or miles covered, in relationship to the number of licenses delivered. Thus, drivers who have been licensed for less than two years drive an average of 73 miles per week. Those who have been licensed for more than ten years and less than 20 years drive an average of 130 miles per week. The demographic characteristic of the population under consideration makes the issue of learning processes even more complex. However, we can roughly estimate intermediate elasticities necessary to the calculation of the expression (I) using data from French surveys made in 1982 and 1994.

$$\Delta l/l \Delta f/f = 0.8$$

$$\Delta C/C/\Delta f/f = 0.6$$

which leads to a global positive effect measurement in the automobile system (club + fleet + network):

$$\Delta a/a = 0.8 E_c \Delta f/f + 0.6 E_n \Delta f/f + E_f \Delta f/f$$

$$\Delta a/a = (0.8 \times 0.5 + 0.6 \times 0.8 + 1)\Delta f/f$$

the E_a elasticity (in relation to automobile fleet) of accessibility provided to the user entering the system is thus

$$E_a = \Delta a/a/\Delta f/f = 1.9$$

In other words, all things being equal, in France, *a 1 percent increase in motorization gives the driver an accessibility gain of close to 1.9 percent.*

To gain an even more precise idea of the value of these positive effects of the automobile system, a dynamic model taking into account the effects of anticipations could be made. Actually, it is quite probable that fleet and network effects come into play as positive anticipations in the decision to obtain a driver's licence. Also to be taken into account are recent analyses linking the decision to buy a car to the number of kilometres travelled, and therefore to traffic on the road network (de Jong, 1997). De Jong's model shows, in fact, using data from the Netherlands, Norway and Israel, that a household's purchase of a second car can be interpreted as an economic choice. The calculation assumes that the fixed cost of an additional car is amortized owing to the number of kilometres travelled. Other effects also come into play that we were unable to consider. The increase in speed resulting from network effect has an impact not only on driving itself and choice of roads, but it probably strengthens the club effect as well (for a given number of driver's licence owners), i.e. the difference between the authorized speed limit for licence owners and that imposed on the others. Finally, the cumulative result of positive effects as described can be represented as shown in illustration 10.7.

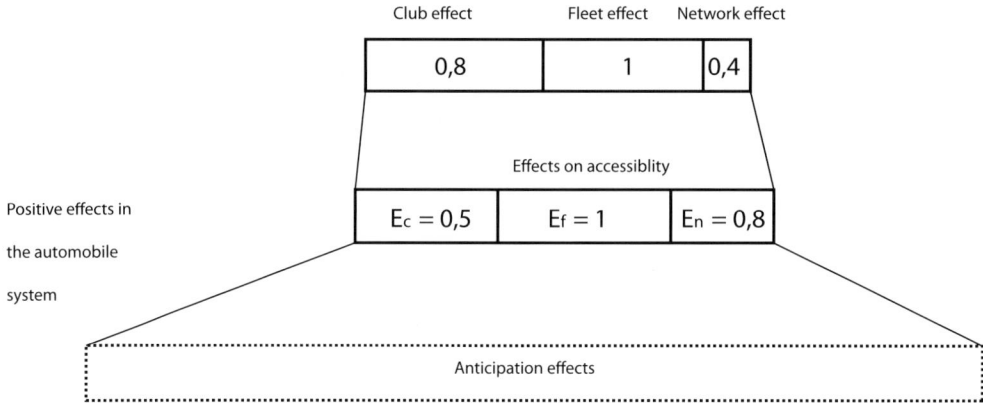

	Club effect	Fleet effect	Network effect

0,8	1	0,4

Effects on accessiblity

$E_c = 0,5$	$E_f = 1$	$E_n = 0,8$

Positive effects in the automobile system

Anticipation effects

Illustration 10.7   **Combination of positive effects in the automobile system**

Despite the methodological limitations explained earlier, the result is significant. The globally positive effect (in terms of accessibility) is considerable such as to bring about strong motivation to join the automobile system (or not to leave it). If the accessibility gain thus proposed were to have an impact on demand with an elasticity of 1, according to French data, the effect would be much greater than that of factors usually assumed to have direct impact on the increase of automobile use as shown in the table in illustration 10.8.

The effect would therefore be four times greater than that of income, six times greater than the cost of using a car, and nine times greater than the effect of the price of fuel – using the (short term) elasticity values (RACS, 1995) would hardly have any influence on the extent of the measured effects. Even if we suppose that demand would react to the increase in accessibility no more than it does to the expansion of the road network (in other words, the corresponding elasticity would only be 0.15), according to our calculations, system effect (expressed in terms of the elasticity of automobile demand) would still be almost as great as the direct effect of cost, usually considered an important factor.

Of course, certain constraints do limit demand, but on the whole, not enough to prevent positive effects from playing their role in the explosive growth of the automobile system. In particular, so far, scale economies in automobile production have lowered costs (Womack, 1990). Each new driver added to the system contributes to heightening its interest (here, in the form of accessibility) for those about to enter – and so, on and on rolls the same magic circle which was identified in America back in the 1960s and led to today's automobile dependence – the same snowballing effect observed in the expansion of the telecommunications networks.

Elasticity of automobile demand In [vehicles] × [km] in relation to	
Price of fuel	-0.22
Cost of using a car	-0.30
Household income	+0.45
Positive accessibility effects	+1.90

Illustration 10.8   Elasticity of automobile demand

The magic circle and automobile dependence

The results of this study lead to a few conclusions and suggestions concerning the point of view upheld by Newman. The use of the term 'automobile dependence' shows that Newman and his colleagues see things clearly. Doubtless there is a virtuous (magic!) circle of positive effects spurring the growth of the automobile system, which, in turn, generates negative externalities: traffic congestion, pollution, the irreversible consumption of fossil oils, space, and so on. But it must be added that the importance of club, fleet and network effects and the combination of all three has made it increasingly difficult to do without the automobile (dependence). To belong to the system has become essential, and to a large extent it is the fact that many others are in the system – independent of fashion, which is not studied here – that motivates us to enter it (or to remain in it), to use a car, and thus to become dependent on it.

Given the value of the positive effect as described earlier, it would be impossible to adopt a Manichean point of view. It would be no simple matter to stop the magic circle from rolling in order to be rid of its indirect negative consequences. All the more so because accessibility increases benefit not only to individuals – some authors have shown the importance of accessibility for economic activity in general (Prud'homme, 1997). It is important to understand the links between the virtuous circle and automobile dependence.

The increased use of automobile, brought about by the magic circle of positive effects, creates negative externalities of different sorts. Road congestion is an intra-sectorial negative externality that concerns traffic and parking. As we have said, the network effect means that a global accessibility increase will cause temporary and localized traffic congestion on main roads until they are rebuilt to adapt to the increase in traffic. In city centres, the fleet effect also creates problems because of cars parked on the streets, thus reducing speed and accessibility.

These negative externalities have been implicitly taken into account in our model. Their effect is to reduce elasticity values compared to what they would have been without traffic congestion. Noise and other disturbances are extra-sectorial negative externalities. As we have said, the model does not take them into account. From our point of view, they cannot be directly linked to the notion of dependence.

Dependence must be seen as a negative externality which is extra-sectorial from the point of view of the automobile sector, but nevertheless closely tied to the automobile system. The dependence externality affects those who cannot enter the automobile system or who are obliged to leave it. Dependence concerns those whose age, health, handicap, or economic situation prevent them from acquiring an automobile. It also concerns drivers unable to use their cars because of a serious and prolonged energy or environmental crisis, such as would be the case when there is another oil crisis or a major climatic alarm caused by the greenhouse effect. From the point of view of available space, the Netherlands is now in just such a critical situation. For this reason, at a given time, it depends directly on the positive effect that we characterized by the E_a elasticity. As indicated in the RAC Foundation for Motoring and the Environment report: "Car dependence grows rather than simply existing" (RACS, 1991). Dependence is all the greater when a large number of people are concerned and it can become a political issue. The elderly, adolescents, inhabitants of rural areas, ethnic minorities and disadvantaged social classes are all relevant in this case (Taylor & Ong, 1995; RACS, 1995; Nutley, 1996). Even if the members of these social groups partially benefit from the development of the automobile system when they borrow someone else's car (RACS, 1995).

Can we overcome automobile dependence? – the role of physical planning

The radical suppression of the automobile would put an end to both the magic circle and dependence. Yet it is hard to imagine how such a policy could be justified, given the fact that for the most part, the automobile system is part and parcel of the market economy. In contrast, because of the positive effect, entry into the automobile system – beyond the benefit to the individual of acquiring a commodity and using it – means a *bonus* of a collective type, one which has a backlash effect on the collectivity if dependence on it becomes too great.

Laissez-faire is not a solution. On the short or medium term, the so-called Mogridge conjecture is often considered as a justification for *laissez-faire* (Derycke, 1997). In the long term, it would surely lead to a lessening of positive effects and perhaps to substitutes that would get round the effects of dependence. But the weight of positive effects is such that *laissez-faire* can only reduce negative externalities after an extremely intense and prolonged period of growth (Madre & Pirotte, 1997). It is doubtful whether this sort of *laissez-faire* would guarantee sustainable automobile development.

A more realistic and satisfactory policy would be to reduce the bonus owing to positive effects in such a way as to keep dependence within acceptable limits. In short, to slow down the rotation of the magic circle in order to reduce automobile dependence. But how? Purely economic policies, via prices, do not seem to be enough. First of all, from a theoretical point of view, it is difficult to define an optimum point which would balance out accessibility advantages and dependence drawbacks. Further, as things stand today and considering the importance of certain advantages, it seems impossible to counterbalance the positive effects in this way. If we make car owners pay for the advantages they obtain from the positive effects of the automobile system, we might hope to reduce, if not suppress automobile dependence. In this respect, it is interesting to look at the theory and experience of tariff systems in the telecommunications network.

Increased prices did, in fact, make it possible to momentarily curb the avalanche caused by club effects until supply was able to cope with demand, but the analogy ends there. In the case of telecommunications, it was possible for a single operator to impose a price and, taking positive effects into account, vary it in such a way as to adapt the acceleration of demand to supply until saturation. In the automobile system, faced with a complex combination of several types of positive effects, there is neither a single operator nor a simple tariff system. The price of learning to drive is set on a market composed of numerous driving schools and does not seem to depend directly on the proportion of driver's licence owners. The price of a car only very indirectly reflects the size of the fleet in a given territory. Taxes on vehicles and fuel are based on horsepower and the number of kilometres travelled but not on the topology of traffic on the road network. Only motorway tolls could be seen as corresponding to a form of positive network effects. The aim of inter-city highway tolls is mainly financing and not dissuasion from dependence. However, in France, a balancing-out policy allocates part of the revenue from tolls to the construction of motorways in less travelled areas. Theoretically, the effect would be to lessen the positive effects of toll roads, yet, tolls are hardly imposed with that in mind. Despite new inner city congestion charge systems policies, there are very few toll roads in and around cities (Derycke, 1997), which significantly limits the results that might be expected from such a policy – in particular to counterbalance the effect of bypasses, mentioned earlier.

Newman and his colleagues are thus justified in putting physical planning back into the centre of the debate. If we refuse the total banishment of the automobile and discard the idea of laissez-faire and if we admit that a solely economic policy is insufficient and impracticable, then we can only hope to overcome automobile dependence by actions on the constituent elements and mechanisms of these effects, of which physical planning is one.

From this angle, to what sort of action do our results lead? We can look at the problem from three points of view. The first is limited to the automobile sector, the framework of our analysis. A second point of view would enlarge the approach to include the automobile-based system, and a third would examine in a yet broader manner communications systems other than the automobile system. We will first deal with these communications systems, then with the automobile-based system, and finally, with the automobile sector, which, it would seem, should be the focus of policy measures aiming to restrain automobile dependence.

Political implications outside the automobile system

Our analysis leads us to consider other communication systems apart from the automobile system: public transportation and telecommunications networks. These systems have one thing in common with the automobile system in that they too may possess positive club, stock and network effects and therefore, magic circles. To the extent that they may constitute alternatives to automobile transportation, their development can be of interest in the reduction of automobile dependence. Without getting into analyses beyond the framework of this Chapter, we would like to make two remarks concerning the efficiency of policies in this domain and the role of physical planning.

The efficiency of policies aimed at reducing automobile dependence through public transportation or telecommunications depends both on the extent of the positive effects generated by each of the latter, and on their substitutability. In France, the relative decline in public transportation over a number of years means that extremely deliberate policy-making is necessary to ensure positive effects. As far as telecommunications are concerned, the fact that they generate greater positive effects would increase the efficiency of such policies, at least in countries highly developed in the field of telecommunications (Mitchell, 1995; Drewe, 1997).

There remains the question of substitutability. As far as public transportation is concerned, substitution rates in relation to the automobile are very low (often less than 5 percent, according to observations made when new tramway or regional railroad lines are put in service). As concerns telecommunications, experts agree on a substitution rate no higher than 15 percent.

As a result of the low level of substitutability of the automobile by public transportation or telecommunications, these systems' positive effects are not obviously sufficient to overcome automobile dependence. Given the limited efficiency of policies based on these effects, physical planning can thus definitely play an important role. However, in order to be efficient, the positive effects of physical planning must lead to a reduction of automobile dependence. Even a very rapid public transportation system, if it does not ensure service to the desired destination, will not create positive accessibility effects. A telecommunications system can only reduce automobile dependence if communication and transportation facilities are taken into account when planning the relocation of activities (Capello, 1994; Drewe, 1997). Otherwise, the positive effects of the telecommunications networks will not reduce the advantages of physical accessibility, and therefore, of automobile dependence. In any case, policies in this domain have limited efficiency and are extremely dependent on the context of public transportation and telecommunications systems in each country.

Political implications within the automobile system

Our analysis opens out onto two different policy avenues that concern the automobile system: we either discourage those not yet in the automobile system from entering it, or we encourage some of those already in it to leave.

The first would seem to pose no problem. Those not yet in the system are doubtless attracted by it, but in most cases, for reasons of income, age, physical or intellectual capacity, or for cultural reasons they are not yet part of it. This is particularly the case for women and elderly persons, for whom, even in highly motorized countries, access to the automobile is not a general rule (see for example Lee-Gosselin & Pas, 1997; Madre & Pirotte, 1997). They can thus be left outside the automobile system, while remaining assured, locally, of what Newman proposes: density, accessibility to pedestrians, public transportation and convenient service. A good example of this exists in France: Saint-Denis, a suburb north of Paris with a population of 91000, where 48 percent of households do not own a car.

This policy, however, has one serious drawback, which is that of segregation. Those who remain outside the automobile system can certainly survive and are less dependent; however, they do not benefit from the same advantages as others do. For example, as far as accessible facilities are concerned, the segregation effect as measured by Nutley is evident (illustration 10.9; Nutley, 1985).

As far as job access is concerned, Taylor and Ong's study on outlying metropolitan areas in the United States gives a clear description of the segregating effects of the suburbanization of jobs. Black minorities have less access to jobs not because they live for the most part in the central areas, but to the extent that their access to car ownership is limited, compared to that of white people. Moreover, the study shows that commuting time for those who depend on public transport is on an average 75 percent longer than for those who drive to work (Taylor & Ong, 1995).

However, in order for Newman's densification policy – applied in the framework of the Australian programme *Better Cities* – to be efficient, it would have to be enforced in all the zones where it is needed. The accessibility problem in rural zones, which has been raised by several authors in connection with countries such as the United States, Great Britain and France remains unsolved (RACS, 1995; Nutley, 1996; Dupuy, 1996).

The second policy, that of encouraging a certain number of those already in the automobile system to leave it, is *a priori* more difficult to put in place even if we count on important effects as a consequence of what we have shown earlier. Owing to the effects measured earlier, such a policy's success would reverse the movement of the magic circle. For those not yet in the system, the advantage of entering it would decrease with an elasticity of about 2 in relation to the flow of those leaving it.

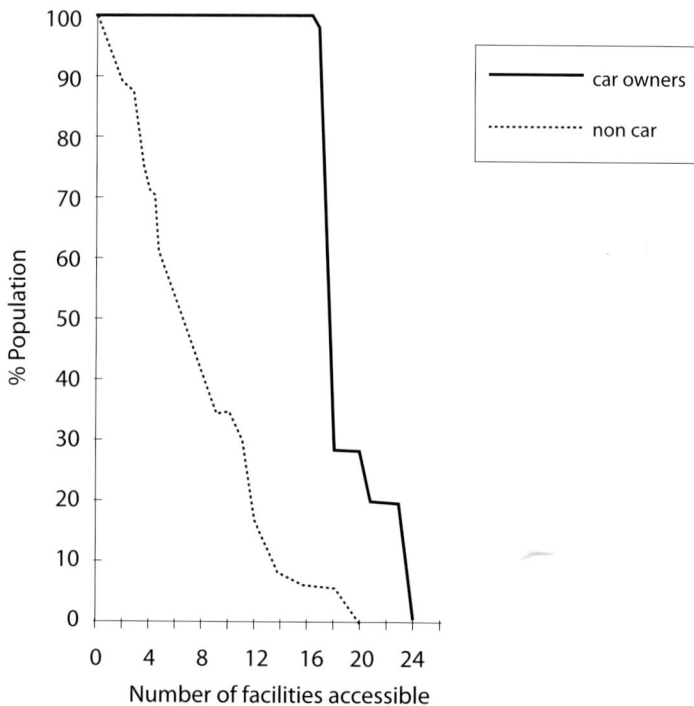

Illustration 10.9   **Local accessibility by social groups.** Source: based on Nutley (1985)

This sort of policy would involve a high-quality transformation in the organization and layout of the city, making automobile accessibility almost useless. For routine journeys, highly efficient public transportation would satisfy demand (Deakin, 1991). For certain types of trips, car rental would replace ownership. By combining residential, commercial and other functions and activities in one area, one would also reduce the need for travelling from one place to another. An example of this can be found in large European cities (Paris, for instance, or, more recently, Stockholm) (Cervero, 1995). The compact cities of the Netherlands illustrate such physical planning policies in a context where, because of lack of space, it is absolutely necessary to reduce automobile dependence (Drewe, 1997).

Thanks to a strong historical tradition and to a virtuous circle turning over a longer period of time, choices unfavourable to the automobile along with a lessening of dependence can actually be observed in city zones of this type. Such transformations must be of extremely high quality (therefore very costly) to match the quality of access provided by the automobile. Thus, because of their cost and owing to certain irreversible factors, mentioned by Goodwin (RACS, 1995), in their early stages, transformations of this sort only concern a small part of the population, and carry a risk of segregating effects (Troy, 1992). But unlike the preceding case, it is the wealthier part that would be segregated here, rather than the reverse.

All told, the economic and social difficulty of implementing these policies stems from the need to increase their scope to an exceedingly great extent, because the automobile system has become too vast. As a result, they are of limited efficiency in countries which are already highly motorized. For this reason, we do not believe that 'the overall message... cautiously optimistic' of the RAC Foundation for Motoring and the Environment, concerning the possibility of reducing car dependence, is correct as regards the automobile system as a whole. However, we fully agree with its conclusions regarding policy-making in the automobile sector *per se*.

Political implications within the automobile sector

Within the automobile sector, there are four possible ways to reduce automobile dependence. First, diminish the club effect by reducing the gap between members and non-members of the club. Achieving this would involve authorizing different categories of drivers to drive different categories of vehicles at different speeds. This would lessen both the attractiveness of a driver's licence and the club effect. Measures favouring two-and three-wheeled vehicles, motorized or non-motorized electric or non-electric mini-cars support this aim and the Japanese example proves the efficiency of such a policy. It is simply a question of adapting legislation and facilitating the use of such vehicles parallel to the use of ordinary cars. Physical planning obviously has a role to play here, by creating bicycle paths, parking facilities for small vehicles, recharging stations for electric cars, and so on. These conclusions converge with the prospective analyses of automobile market specialists (Nieuwenhuis & Wells, 1997).

Second, reduce the fleet impact by favouring forms of automobile access generating fewer external effects. Short-term rental and car-sharing cooperatives (as in Switzerland) promote better use of a given fleet and reduce fleet effect. A more limitative public parking policy (as in German city-centres) would also have considerable impact.

Third, increase the connectivity of the road network in such a way as to reduce the effects of heavy traffic and the network effects they generate. This would mean building more, and less rapid, roads in the aim of making the overall design of the road network correspond more closely to the desired lines. With a stable fleet, this sort of design would reduce the number of vehicles × kilometre, thus reducing speed increases caused by the modernization of the network. Such a policy could be enforced by setting up a well-planned tolling system which would discourage heavy traffic on main roads and favour the construction, maintenance and use of slower but more direct roads.

Fourth, control the capillary spreading of the road network. Roads are often built in anticipation of the future construction of housing or other facilities (in rural areas, for example). By limiting this expansion, one diminishes the importance of speed (club and network effects) in determining accessibility levels, and the positive effect is thus reduced.

It should be noted that as a general rule, the physical planning actions we suggested for implementation within the automobile sector and which are aimed at lessening dependence by reducing positive effects, tend to facilitate travel as far as the individual driver is concerned, rather than the reverse. We are therefore talking about policies which are both efficient and realistic.

A few concluding remarks

So far, we have discussed the situation in the developed countries. In the case of developing countries, where automobile use is growing rapidly but remains limited, policy-making aimed at reducing dependence is an easier task (Gakenheimer, 1997): differentiations between types of vehicles and licences (with an effect on accessibility), restrictions linked to the fleet effect (parking in particular), restrictions connected with network efficiency, favouring connexity and connectivity of networks rather than capillary spreading. In areas where the automobile system is still at a moderate stage of development, the wisest course is to lead a policy of density combined with a strong public transportation supply. The telecommunications system can also be mobilized. The cost of such policies can remain within reasonable limits and there is no fear of an increase in segregation. The efficiency of such policies can be illustrated by a number of interesting examples, both present and past. For decades, they were implemented in the Soviet Union. In its own way, China favoured spatial density, combined with an extraordinary increase in the use of bicycles, tricycles and other similar modes of transportation. However, an evaluation of the political regimes that supported these policies is left to the reader. Some developing countries are already counting on telecommunications systems as a solution to transportation problems.

Thus, in terms of policy, a study of the positive effects of the automobile system leads us to conclude that physical planning is doubtless one of the more efficient ways of fighting against automobile dependence, especially in countries in the process of becoming motorized. Elsewhere, in the developed countries, its efficiency has likewise been proved, but its advantages must be weighed over and against the risks of its segregating effects.

Three remarks should be made in conclusion to this Chapter. First, that Newman focuses his analysis and recommendations on cities (Newman, Kenworthy & Vintila 1995; Newman 1996; Newman & Kenworthy, 1998). Goodwin's report on car dependence adopted a much wider perspective (RACS, 1995). Our study shows that the positive effects of the automobile system are felt way beyond the limits of the city: the club, fleet and network effects studied earlier are defined and hold true on a regional, national, even on an international scale, and not only on an urban scale. Such a fact must be taken into account when deciding at which level of government the task of making and implementing policies aiming to restrain automobile dependence should be carried out.

Secondly, the automobile system is in the process of becoming a world system, first of all from the production point of view, but also from that of consumption (Lung, 1997). For this reason, countries still at the early stages of motorization are susceptible to the impact of fashion and prestige, a phenomenon generating significant effects, although these have not been discussed in our analysis, they should be reintroduced at this point. Indeed, the demand for cars today in Eastern Europe and in China is most likely to be influenced by these phenomena, a fact which should be taken into account in the definition of policies.

Thirdly, if it is for the purpose of protecting scarce resources such as air, space and oil that Newman proposes densification as a means of reducing automobile dependence, the positive effects at the root of automobile dependence reveal yet another resource to which modern society attaches increasing importance, and that is time. The results of our measurements seem to correspond not to some sort of anarchic behaviour or systematic waste, but to a new rationale of 'space-time densification' which reflects the scarcity of time, as had been previously suggested in the research of Zahavi (1976; 1982) and also in research on time value, adopted in traffic engineering studies. It may be that the premises of Newman and his colleagues' reasoning are more debatable than their conclusions. Can there be any doubt but that the revolution in modern societies is that of having made time incredibly scarce? Automobile dependence is only a reflection of this, and no policy should remain unaware of it.

11   Mobility of the Poor in Two European Metropolises: Car Dependence versus Locality Dependence*

Introduction

In highly motorized societies, the urban mobility of poor households – fewer of whom tend to own a car than better-off households – is an issue that raises questions in regard to the need for and/or the nature of specific public policy-making. Thinking on the matter suffers from an enormous lack of insight into how poor households use and move around their urban space. Do they all seek to acquire a car for the same reasons, irrespective of local contexts? What role does commuting play in structuring their travel patterns? Does this constitute an area that calls for particular kinds of public policies?

We have sought to shed light on these questions through a comparative survey based on in-depth interviews with around a hundred low-income households in the urban areas of Paris and London (Coutard, Dupuy & Fol, 2002). To facilitate comparison between two countries – France and Great Britain – we selected households inhabiting similar districts: a city-centre neighbourhood dominated by social housing estates; and a community on the outer suburban fringe, largely populated by poor households (see illustration 11.1). The interviews enabled us to fine-tune our analysis of the sample households' travel habits and the constraints hindering their mobility.

The analysis is rounded off with a wider-ranging statistical study aimed first at pinpointing the general social and demographic characteristics of poor households in France and Britain, together with their economic status and residential location; and second at identifying the factors underlying the various patterns of mobility: the urban history of the two regions under consideration; the housing, transport and social security policies implemented. These two areas are clearly interdependent: a country's social security guidelines, for instance, have a major effect on the socio-demographic characteristics of poverty. [1]

France and Great Britain: differing contexts

While the past 20 years have seen the British government withdrawing from the fields of housing, transport and urban planning on a national level (with the emergence of quasi-autonomous NGOs – quangos, the sale of social housing, the deregulation and/or privatization of public transport, and so on), in France the state is still the key actor. In social policy terms, the British have placed a far greater emphasis on the introduction of powerful incentives designed to encourage the unemployed to return to work. Meanwhile, in Britain more poor households tend to own their own homes than in France, largely in inner-city areas. Also, more of them consist of families than in France, featuring higher levels of child poverty and lower levels of unemployment. With regard to mobility, the British poor appear

*   Previously published in *Built Environment*, 30 (2), 2004, pp. 138-145. http://www.informaworld.com. Included with permission; co-authors: **Olivier Coutard, Sylvie Fol.**

	Central area neighbourhood	Outer area locality
Paris	Salvador Allende estate in Saint Denis	Chaumont-en-Vexin
London	De Beauvoir estate in Hackney	Shelley estate in Chipping Ongar

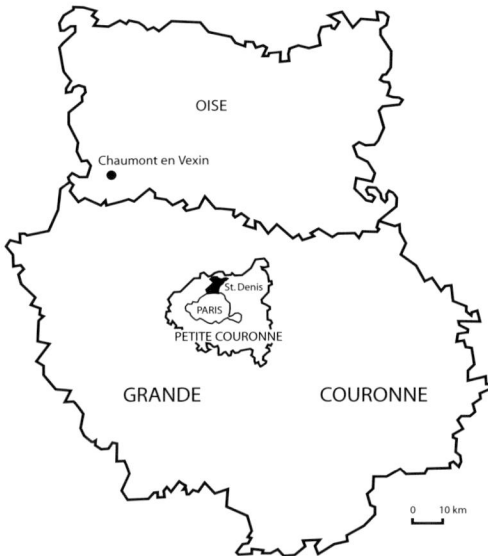

a. St. Denis and Chaumont-en-Vexin in the Paris agglomeration

b. Hackney and Chipping Ongar in the London agglomeration

Illustration 11.1 **The four central and outer area districts where surveys were carried out and their spatial context: Paris' central area neighbourhood *Salvador Allende* estate in Saint-Denis and the outer area locality *Chaumont-en-Vexin* and London's central area neighbourhood *De Beauvoir* estate in *Hackney* and outer area locality *Shelley* estate in *Chipping Ongar*.** Original visualisation by A.M. Barthelemy, Dpt. de Geo. , Université Paris X

to be under greater pressure to acquire a motor car, while the working poor account for a comparable and growing share of the population in both France and Great Britain.

At the level of regional urban areas, the spatial functioning and layout of London is more metropolitan (polycentric) in nature than Paris, and of a larger spatial scale in terms of planning policy as well as the travel patterns that the policies in question are partly responsible for producing. While the transport systems may differ in structure, broadly similar patterns can be noted (e.g. in line with the modal split pertaining to each urban area as a whole). There are significant differences in the spatial distribution of poor households in London and Paris – with those in the former concentrated in areas closer to the urban core and those in the latter more scattered – which does not mean that poor households in the Paris area are spatially isolated, as we shall see later on.

Noting how the poor in Britain appeared under greater pressure to acquire a car than those in France led to us wondering whether poor British households are not more car-dependent than their French counterparts. If so, what are the reasons for the differences in their respective situations and how likely is it to last?

France: daily practices based on locality dependence

In terms of mobility, most interviewed household members of the Île-de-France (Paris region) do not tend to travel very far from home. Virtually none of those residing in Chaumont spend any time in Paris, and some have never even been there. A significant proportion of the residents of the Salvador Allende estate rarely go to Paris either. In both cases, this has less to do with their not having a car – since Paris is within easy reach by public transport – than the fact that they are simply becoming less and less inclined to leave the familiarity of their immediate surroundings. This situation is often ascribed to a lack of money or transport. But locality-centred practices also tie in with the presence in the home neighbourhood of resources that help alleviate poverty-related constraints.

Indeed, both sites feature shops and key public services and facilities. Chaumont – probably on account of its county town status – offers a wide range of shops and services: food shops, banks, a post office, a taxation centre, a family welfare centre, the offices of the national electricity company and an especially large number of public facilities for a town of its size: several schools, two colleges, a social centre, a centre run by the regional organization providing for the welfare of mothers-to-be and infants, and even a hospital. Similarly, residents of Salvador Allende have a mere fifteen-minute walk to access the very wide range of shops and services on offer between the pedestrian precinct and shopping centre of Saint-Denis town centre. The concentration of services, in both Chaumont and Saint-Denis, represents a further advantage for non-car-owning residents: a relative abundance of local job opportunities. Indeed, a sizeable proportion of the working population among interviewees in Chaumont (a third) and Salvador Allende (close to 40 percent) were employed locally. A good deal of local jobs is linked to public facilities: posts at the town hall, caretakers on the social housing estates, hospital workers, ancillary staff of local schools, nursery assistants, and so on. This pool of public sector employment opportunities represents another reason why poor households can survive without a car.

When travelling is unavoidable, public transport can offset the disadvantages of not having a car. Residents of Chaumont, for instance, can reach the neighbouring town of Gisors thanks to the state-run railway line from Paris, which is also used by high school pupils and people looking for more specialized shops and services. Salvador Allende residents enjoy access to a clearly far more extensive transport system: with the extension of a metro line to central Paris, the upgrading of the bus services a new bus station now being located quite close to the estate – they have a number of different lines to choose from in order to travel to neighbourhoods throughout Saint-Denis and other towns in the region. Local people approve of the new metro station, which some see as a *bona fide* opening to the outside world. And even though few of our interviewees are actually using it to travel to Paris on a regular basis, they appreciate having it there should they wish to do so.

That said, public transport is not the answer to all of the local population's travel needs. Weekly shopping trips, for instance, are not always practical by bus or by metro. When non-motorized households find themselves in need of a car, they have to call on outside resources. Relatives and, to a lesser extent friends constitute a crucial source of such resources for many of the low-income households interviewed. Their importance hinges first and foremost on spatial proximity. More than half of our Salvador Allende estate sample households have relatives living in Saint-Denis (half on the estate itself) and a further 25 percent have family in other neighbouring towns.

The family plays a major part in the residents' activities, and they devote much of their spare time to it. What is more, it is a major source of mutual aid. Relatives can help to avoid trips through such services as child minding. They can also help to increase the mobility potential of non-car-owning households by offering a lift to those that have trouble carrying heavy loads of food shopping home on foot or on public transport. The family provides clearly the most easily , or at least most frequently mobilized support.

Poor households without cars have a limited range of resources available to them and these must be used in a measured way. Recourse to each type of service is carefully managed in accordance with constraints specific to each individual set of circumstances and travel needs. The balance struck in the use of the various resources is manifestly complex and delicate. Residential location is a key component of that balance. Indeed, inhabiting places equipped with a wealth of 'conveniences' lessens the need to resort to other resources, especially public transport and relatives or friends. Our survey has revealed a clustering of poor households around these convenience-rich areas, stemming in Saint-Denis and Chaumont alike from local policies geared to building social housing for low-income earners.

The clustering was also found to tie in with two complementary forms of residential strategy implemented by the poor households themselves: a *static* form, where those living in the heart of their 'resource base' seek to stay put; and a *mobile* form, where households make a conscious effort to gravitate towards places capable of satisfying their resource needs. The *static* form is common in Saint-Denis – with a good many households having been there for years on end – as well as in Chaumont, albeit to a somewhat lesser degree. These are the households with the local family connections and the least trouble in mobilizing solidarity-related resources. The proximity of their relatives (or friends) has combined with the familiarity with the places and their inhabitants that has gradually built up over the years to create a reassuring environment and to produce relational ties. Working-class relationships hinge on spatial proximity. This is conducive to the growth of far stronger local roots than may be found among households belonging to other social classes. Alongside the *well-rooted* residents are other households adhering to the second, *mobile* form of residential strategy, i.e. those who have arrived more recently in a conscious endeavour to be closer to the resources on offer locally. For some families, Chaumont represents one of a limited range of possible residential locations featuring a sufficient supply of services. A significant number of recent arrivals happen to be former residents who already have relational ties in the town. These include several divorced women returning to be close to their families after having moved away from former husbands.

So the concentration of a minimum resource base is crucial to poor households with limited, if any, access to a car. The towns studied feature adequate public services – including public transport – while the proximity of family and friends and familiarity with the places create conditions conducive to residents establishing local roots and, at the same time, developing certain forms of locality dependence. It is hardly unusual to find such features in Saint-Denis, a typical suburban (innercity) neighbourhood. It comes as more of a surprise in Chaumont, whose peri-urban environment might lead one to expect more spatially scattered practices and, hence, a greater degree of car dependence. Analysis of the British study areas will, as we shall see, reveal quite a different picture.

Great Britain: daily practices based on car-dependence

The surveys carried out in the London area pinpointed a number of especially influential constraints shaping the urban mobility patterns of low-income households. Poor public services, not least insofar as transport is concerned, significantly undermine the self-sufficiency of such households when they do not own a car, thus putting them in a position where they have little choice but to acquire one.

Few of the interviewed De Beauvoir households use the limited number of shops available on the estate because they find them too costly. The Shelley estate is relatively better served, with shops located on the estate itself or at the nearby Chipping Ongar centre. But these are small and medium-sized businesses whose prices are known to be higher than the outlying hypermarkets, and which tend to be used only by residents without cars. The latter usually take the bus and unanimously complain about the slowness, unreliability and extremely poor quality of services. De Beauvoir estate residents are especially unhappy about the lack of an underground station and the endless waits at bus stops. But their situation is nowhere near as bad as it is for residents of Shelley, where buses are even fewer and farther between and where the Chipping Ongar underground station is sorely missed, depriving locals of a really useful link to central London. Its closure some years ago has sparked a chain reaction with a highly damaging effect on urban life: closure of local shops and businesses, closure of schools, and people leaving in droves. Non-car owning households, however, scarcely ever seek to alleviate their local travel problems by appealing to their relatives or friends. Indeed, even though some interviewees have some family living nearby, their relationships appear far less close-knit than is the case among French households. They hardly mentioned their family networks. Relatives rarely visit one another, and not a single non-car-owning household admits to asking the family for help with its transport problems. Moreover, many are not inclined to ask their friends. Given the accumulation of problems and the apparent risk of social isolation, even the poorest non-motorized households find themselves unavoidably pushed into acquiring a car.

Motorized households regard car ownership as a matter not of choice but of compulsion. This is primarily because of where the jobs are located. The De Beauvoir estate is the neighbourhood with the largest number of long-distance commuters. Since most of the Shelley residents working locally (over a third) are unskilled women doing insecure, part-time jobs, a greater share of the burden is being shifted onto the male wage-earner, as far as the household's sources of income are concerned. And, as almost every working member of an interviewed, motorized household points out, the best paying jobs are those located farthest from home. This makes it essential to own a car. Without a car, many would have had to settle for lower-paying jobs in the neighbourhood (e.g. at the local supermarket). Owning a car is also very often said to be a must for working women with children and others having to cope with complex, demanding trip-chains.

Car ownership, however, accounts for an enormous share of the household budget among our interviewees, especially the residents of Shelley, who clearly have no other alternative. Virtually every motorized household in Shelley finds it hard to drive a car without making sacrifices in other areas of the family housekeeping. They often say that they worry about their cars breaking down, since they cannot afford to buy a new one or to have them repaired as regularly as they might like. That said, not every car owner uses his or her vehicle with the same degree of intensity. Indeed, poor people tend to limit the use of their cars to essential purposes (mostly trips to work). Several interviewees – especially Shelley residents – point out that they hardly ever go out in them because they are too old and because petrol is far too expensive.

The seemingly inevitable motorization of the peri-urban poor of Britain appears to have produced a form of car dependence that is quite unlike the situation found to exist among their counterparts in France, for whom alternative solutions still appear possible.

The role of public policies

Our surveys have highlighted two distinct and at times conflicting models in regard to the spatial practices of the poor in Great Britain and France. We now need to take a more detailed look at the specific role that employment policy plays, via its effects in terms of home-to-work mobility, in structuring poor people's spatial practices and in sustaining those two national models.

The poor of both Britain and France face employment difficulties of a nature that can be manifest (unemployment) or latent (remote workplaces, job insecurity, and so on). Endeavours to tackle poverty can aim at promoting jobs for people facing either of these employment difficulties. In addition, they can seek to provide the people in question with sustainable welfare support for as long as it takes them to return to the employment market. Policy-makers waver between these two approaches (when they are not seeking to combine them). Over the past two decades, British policy-makers have favoured an incentives-based welfare-to-work policy aimed at encouraging poor people of working age to return quickly to or make a first appearance in a flexible and fast-changing jobs market. Meanwhile, their French counterparts have established a socially sensitive approach providing out-of-work poor people with specially designed, long-term assistance.

Opting for either one of these policy approaches is bound to affect poor people's mobility. To find jobs that match their skills and abilities quickly, they are driven to widen their job-hunting horizons and to be ready either to move home or to agree to long-distance commuting. Alternatively, they can stay put. The metropolitan areas of Paris and London feature far more extensive employment markets than smaller cities. What is more, their transport systems render the workplace far more accessible. Three-quarters of jobs in the Paris area, and almost as many in and around London, can be reached in under an hour on public transport.

Overall figures such as these, however, mask the fact that the jobs for which the poor are most eligible are not necessarily located within easy reach of home. This is the European version of America's 'spatial mismatch'. In the United States, the problem is relatively simple. Largely suburbanized jobs are relatively inaccessible to the deprived population groups that remain confined to inner-city areas. Although the situation in large European metropolises such as Paris and London may differ, the spatial mismatch is just as real. In London, the better-off classes first of all moved out of areas in and around the city centre and the less well-off moved in (see the example of Hackney). More recently, a number of centrally located neighbourhoods have undergone an intense degree of gentrification, forcing the poor into other neighbouring areas or even, more rarely, to outlying areas such as Shelley (Atkinson, 2000). In

Paris, most of the poor have remained in or around the capital. The large-scale construction of public social housing estates in the suburbs with a view to accommodating struggling population groups has led to a situation where social housing accounts for some 30 percent of the stock in the inner suburbs. So much so that the poverty rate recorded in 1999 by the French family allowance office[2] came close to 17 percent in Seine-Saint-Denis (an inner suburban borough) as opposed to less than 10 percent in Val d'Oise, which is still the outer suburban district where the rate is at its highest. Only more recently has there been a marginal increase in the number of poor people moving into more remote outlying areas (see Chaumont-en-Vexin).

In London, all but the highly skilled service sector jobs have relocated away from the city centre. These now cover a vast area encroaching on the green belt in the regions of the Outer Metropolitan Area. In Paris, the workplace for manual labourers and low-level office workers is located further from the city centre than it is for more highly skilled workers (see Wenglenski & Orfeuil, 2004). So "the *banlieue rouge*[3] model, with its social housing located close to the workshops, has collapsed" (Massot, Armoogum, Ledily, Madre & Orfeuil, 1995). Furthermore, while the metropolitization of the London and Paris urban areas has gone hand-in-hand with a growth in employment opportunities, few of those opportunities actually concern the sorts of low-skilled jobs that are chiefly of interest to the poor.

Nowadays, the poor of Paris and London alike are increasingly having to live in areas located some distance away from the centre, while the jobs for which they can consider themselves eligible have become both few and far between. Under such circumstances, the French policy, advocating density and mixing, boils down to the reproduction in outlying towns of the locality-dependence model initiated in and prevailing over the social housing estates of Paris' inner suburbs. In Great Britain, the promotion of welfare-to-work incentives has resulted in a growth in mobility that, in such a highly motorized country, was always bound to amount to a growth in automobility.

Therefore, recent employment policy (or measures to tackle unemployment) in the two countries has tended to confirm our observations vis-à-vis the two national models. One is struck, for example, by the consistency of each country's public policy affecting the mobility of the poor. In France, the reliance on local resources goes hand-in-hand with efforts to provide the people concerned with community-level facilities, services and transport. In Britain, on the other hand, policy-makers bank on people's mobility; and they have not chosen to provide them with efficient public transport networks. A growing confidence in the market's ability to supply transport services has put neighbourhoods with few car owners at a disadvantage. And when those neighbourhoods are located on the outskirts, it further bolsters the obstacles to their participation in an extended urban society and economy (MacGregor, 1997). Public transport in France, especially in and around Paris, has been maintained at a good level of efficiency in spite of the difficulties such as under-funding and security problems. The same cannot generally be said to be true in and around London.

Assessing the policies in terms of sustainability

Comparison between France and Great Britain has therefore brought out two national models of spatial practices among poor households (see illustration 11.2). These models undoubtedly stem from – and have in any event been bolstered by – the gradual implementation of a body of public policies concerning not just travel, but also welfare benefits, housing, infrastructure and services. How can one conduct a comparative assessment of the two models and their underlying policies? Does France

Model	Sustainability criteria		
	Environmental	Economic	Social
Car dependence (G.B.)	–	–	+
Locality dependence (Fr.)	+	+	–

Illustration 11.2   **Assessment of sustainability criteria by national model**

have good grounds for maintaining an approach that leaves the poor somewhat immobile? Has Britain made a greater success of it by compelling its poor to adhere to a state of automobility? In other words, should a country facing the task of tackling poverty within a context of general motorization seek inspiration from the British or the French approach? Is car dependence ultimately preferable to the locality dependence model or *vice versa*?

Our survey has led us to assess the two models (and their underlying policies) in terms of sustainability, in the light of three sets of criteria: economic, environmental and social. From the economic point of view, car dependence burdens the poor with heavy costs that undoubtedly undermine their ability to cope with other basic expenses (e.g. food), which hardly looks very sustainable. From the environmental point of view, locality dependence is clearly more sustainable insofar as it tempers overall car dependence. From the social point of view, however, our studies have shown that young people do not appear overly keen, to say the least, on the locality dependence model, thus threatening to undermine the sustainability of that approach.

It is not the researcher's job to weigh up these three criteria to rule in favour of one particular approach or another. That said, we do need to underscore one key factor to emerge from our research. In countries featuring widespread motorization (to a degree that exceeds the European average), the poor can only cope with a reliance on local resources (locality dependence) if they have constant access to help from third parties – relatives, friends and neighbours who generally tend to be car owners. Keeping up such forms of solidarity is a *sine qua non* for any policy geared to curbing car dependence. At the same time, it generally involves a high level of car ownership within society. This leads to the conclusion that it is doubtful whether a radical choice of either policy can lead to sustainable development. If poverty cannot be eradicated, one sustainable solution would clearly involve a balance being struck between car dependence and locality dependence.

Notes

Note 1   The definition of poverty used in this survey hinges on the following criterion: that the household's 'equivalized' income (a measure incorporating the size of the household into income comparisons) places it among the poorest 20%.

Note 2   The family allowance office (*Caisse d'Allocations Familiales*) defines the poverty rate as the share of a town's residents living in a welfare beneficiary household whose income is below the poverty line.

Note 3   Literally 'red suburb', which refers to the dominance of the communist party in local government in many municipalities around Paris in the post-1945 period.

"According to General Systems Theory, the different components of a simple set need the complement of some relationships to constitute a system. Every city, every urban, metropolitan, regional or continental agglomeration is by essence a system and hence their relationships cannot be ignored, as has been and continuous to be the case in most urban plans, which are obsessed by forms and static elements. Relationships imply the exchange of goods, energy and information flows and the networks of transports and services are the space-channels that make possible the circulation of those flows. To understand the primary purpose of the networks and their development processes is a fundamental question for the organization of the territory. The networks that occupy space, much space, have been neglected in urban plans, although aside from being the channels of flows they are the main structuring elements of the territory and the city. The efficiency of the system and its capacity to adapt to the changing technological and social realitieswill depend on them."

From: Prologue *by Alberto Serratosa, to the book by Dupuy, G.,* El Urbanismo de las redes, teorías y métodos, *Oikos-Tau, Barcelona, 1998*

12 Car Dependence: Prospective Studies and Avenues of Research*

Are longer-term policies flexible enough to adapt to the changing nature of the issue? What is the outlook as far as future trends are concerned (see illustration 12.1)?

Half of all motorists in the G-7 countries think they will be paying more for their cars in the coming five years. Just under half reckon they will have to use lower emission vehicles.

Prospective studies on car dependence are fairly scarce. One of the first in France – where just over a quarter of car owners do not think that anything is going to change (FIA Foundation, 2005) – used econometric modelling to study the impact of selective pricing in persuading commuters in the Lyons region to leave their cars at home and travel to work by train (Schéou, 1997). The basic scenario predicted that a doubling in price at the petrol pump and motorway toll-both, a 70 percent increase on parking meters and a €1.50 charge for entering the Lyons urban area – La Courly – would lead to less than a one percent decrease in car use by the year 2010.

Car dependence

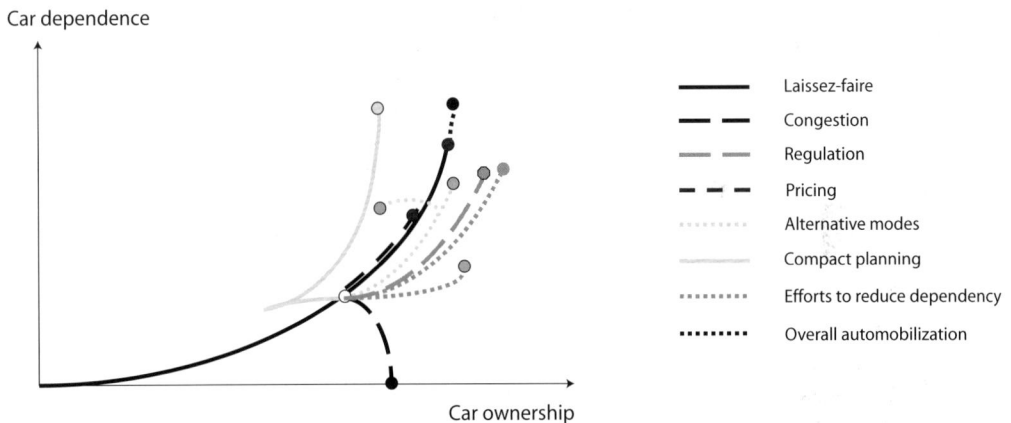

———	Laissez-faire
– –	Congestion
– –	Regulation
– – –	Pricing
··········	Alternative modes
———	Compact planning
··········	Efforts to reduce dependency
■■■■■■■■■	Overall automobilization

Car ownership

Illustration 12.1   Effectiveness of various policies that aim to reduce car dependence

More recently, the interdepartmental Program of Research, Experimentation and Innovation in Land Transport (PREDIT) commissioned the *Application de Techniques Nouvelles* (ATN) consultancy to test a 20-year simulation of changes in urban mobility in the Greater Lyons area – selected because it offered comprehensive, fresh and reliable data on the key fields under consideration: transport, population, economic activities/employment, housing and the environment – using the latest MobiSim mobility simulation model (Casanova, 2003).

---

*   Previously published as Dupuy, G., 2006, « *Prospective et pistes de recherche* ». In: *La Dependance a l'Egard de l'Automobile*. Paris, PREDIT / La Documentation Francaise. Included with permission.

ATN were supplied with a set of five scenarios drawn up by the *Groupe de Batz* working group, set up by DRAST, the French department of scientific and technical research and development (Crozet, Orfeuil & Massot, 2001; Wachter, Theys, Crozet & Orfeuil, 2005). The results were somewhat mixed, but one of the five scenarios nonetheless proved promising from the sustainable development point of view.

Meanwhile, Marie-Hélène Massot of the *Institut National de Recherche sur les Transports et leur Sécurité* (INRETS) sums up a prospective study for the DRAST science and technology watchdog, CPVS, with the following conclusion: " The socio-economic stakes in terms of car dependence and public costs are so high that speed limits and increases in the cost of car use – especially through urban toll-booths, which serve as a source of funds for public transport investment – should be considered not just from the viewpoint of their short-term impact on current traffic control and the enhancement of infrastructure capacity and safety, but also from that of their potential long-term impact on urban redevelopment. The scenario to test is that of the costs of car use being ploughed back into strategies concerning the location of people and economic activities, and the redensification of urban forms within the framework of urban projects enabling such redevelopment – public transport and housing policy, control over the land and property markets, and so on" (GPU, 2003).

Clearly, there is a question of irreversibility – a key feature of dependency – and no satisfactory answer appears likely to emerge in 20 years given how little latitude the government has, according to the experts, to take the necessary action to tackle car dependency.

Yet forward studies also suggest a need for thinking on possible turning points, or at least significant shifts in emphasis. In the *Groupe de Batz* scenarios it was considered that major shifts would be required over the coming 20 years (Crozet, Orfeuil & Massot, 2001): challenging the value attached to mobility and controlling the mobility through private transactions, i.e. by the market. What should one make of those scenarios? On the whole, they clearly point to a reduction in car dependence. Next, challenging the 'value attached to mobility' would involve changes in activity scheduling: cancelling out – or merely reducing – the time savings made then reinvested, in liaison with increasing car dependence, would mean having to reduce the time needed for other activities: which? Finally, moving to regulation by the market would, in the light of the above-mentioned studies, lead to increasingly unequal access and, hence, greater social exclusion: how far can society allow this to progress?

True, the shift could be facilitated by means of such strong messages as the disastrous environmental impacts of greenhouse gases. But increasing the price of petrol would send out an even clearer message. How would significant and continuously rising petrol prices affect car dependence? Can those now feasible increases alter the thrust of forecasting?

Over and above the occasional agitation linked to geopolitical events in the Middle East, readily available stocks of black gold will eventually run dry due to growing demand on the part of the emerging countries. So a significant rise in oil fuel prices is conceivable in the long term. Hybrid engines, fuel cells and other alternative technologies may have become competitive by then; and the relative Malthusianism of the producer countries may have been overcome through a show of strength on the part of some consumer countries. But let us assume that increases in crude oil prices will be the prevailing trend.

Previous experience of oil crises has shown that in the short run, motorists do not cut down on their mileage a great deal: a 10 percent rise in the price of petrol at the pump bringing about somewhere in the region of a one percent decrease in road traffic. What is more, sensitivity to the price of crude is three to four times lower due to levels of taxation on oil fuel (INRETS, 2005). The effects are, of course, more marked in the long term: a similar 10 percent increase in oil fuel prices leading to a seven percent fall in consumption, with one percent due to a decrease in the numbers of cars on the roads, two percent to reduced mileage and the rest to people switching to more sensible vehicles. So there are grounds to expect a slight decline in car sales, which would help restrain, or even reduce, car dependency. Let us remember, however, that these are long-term forecasts subject to a host of technological and geopolitical conditions.

The most likely outcome would be a restriction in demand for car ownership, with the poor realizing that it is simply unaffordable and dropping the idea of joining the motorists club. This would serve *ipso facto* to put a cap on car dependence. However, it would also result in significant inequalities between those able to pay the extra cost of petrol and to continue enjoying the same accessibility as before, and those compelled to make do with other modes of transport.

Mobility is linked to city forms. So it would be interesting from the prospective studies point of view to follow the example of PREDIT (2005) and look into a variety of models or ideas: e.g. the 'power city', the middle-class bohemian 'bobo city', yuppielands, landlands or restlands like the retirement Valhalla of Kotkin (2000), architect of the utopian Nerdistan (see box 12.1).

Box 12.1 Nerdistan

Inconceivable half a century ago, Silicon Valley has become a vast urban area. The unplanned concentration of activities and homes has led to the emergence of heavy automobile traffic accompanied by various forms of pollution. Technological research is still being done in the Valley, but software development is now the core economic activity. While the most mundane share of this kind of work is being relocated to India and so on, there are still enough jobs to sustain the frenetic activity that has turned Silicon Valley into an area where the peaceful landscape of the early days has tended to give way to agitation and stress.

Yet competition between this kind of 'suburb' and the 'historic' big cities, especially here in San Francisco, is fierce. Where will the technological activities of the twenty-first century be based? Richard Florida (2002) stresses the lure of the 'community'. Silicon Valley can meet this challenge by describing itself as a Nerdistan, at term coined by Joel Kotkin (2000). Nerd, on the one hand, is an acronym for No One Ever Dies, but it also denotes the creative brains behind the new technologies, people whose passion for their research leaves them somewhat cut off from the real world. Nerds are looking for a pleasant environment where they can work and live together without having to conform to the rules of ordinary urban life. They do not want Silicon Valley to become like any other suburb. So they would be ready to accept building regulations, landscape protection measures and traffic restrictions favouring soft transport modes with which that are completely out of kilter with car-dependent American suburbanization. Given the increasing intellectual and economic power of this creative class, we could join Kotkin in regarding Nerdistan – or rather nerdistans, since other similar kinds of places are being devised near Madison, Wisconsin, for instance – as a new urban image. Can such an image be incorporated into prospective studies and challenge the current, overly realistic and, hence, pessimistic thinking on urban sprawl and car dependence?

As a matter of fact, the transformation of some spaces – under the influence of economic, sociological or cultural factors that have nothing to do with the transport system – can serve to change the conditions of car dependence. Developments in the sociological make-up of the Parisian population or in economic activities in London, for instance, definitely have helped further policies geared to reducing dependency, in central areas at least.

After first appearing in a 1979 American journal article (Carpenter, 1979), the term 'automobile dependence' was used extensively, without really being defined, by Peter Newman, Jeffrey Kenworthy and Felix Laube of Murdoch University in Western Australia (Newman & Kenworthy, 1991; 1998; Newman, Kenworthy & Vintila, 1995; Newman, 1996; Kenworthy & Laube, 1999; Kenworthy, Laube, Raad, Poboon & Benedicto, 1999). Its success clearly stems from the suggestive power of the contrast between dependency – a form of subservience – and the car, a symbol of freedom. Success, that is, in the non-French-speaking world. France, as has so often been the case with other such Anglo-Saxon concepts as governance, the digital divide and so on, was around ten years late in adopting that of car dependence. French researchers preferred to talk about car captives, a term harking back to the 1960s concept of 'public transport captives' (Madre, 1995). So the French were also slow to use the actual concept and, hence, to begin formulating the policies needed to address the problem. Strangely enough, French researchers were producing some highly interesting work drawing on the fields of game theory or sociology some 30 years earlier (Duclos, 1976; Dupuy & Robert, 1976). One of the reasons why those approaches failed to make their mark is that they were swathed in ideological straightjackets that made them hard to disseminate among transport experts and planning practitioners in France and, what is more, abroad. It begs the question of how contemporary French research can highlight its distinctive nature and gain recognition at the international level. Which brings us back to the matter of interpreting the concept of car dependence.

Dependency here is neither a personal trait nor the by-product of the warped or spiteful nature of motorists. Even in the most 'individualistic' research approaches, car dependence appears linked to the history, the experience, the social setting and geographic milieu characterizing the propagation of the motor car as a mode of transport. Which, incidentally, is why many researchers – when not opting for a broader, more holistic, approach – have sought to link it to types of territory or socio-economic variables (Rousseau, 2001). It is similarly pointless trying to blame a particular culprit or miscreant. The car industry, for instance, may well go to great lengths to sell its products but it only manages to do so because they are in such massive demand. One could pin the blame on the economies of scale that have always typified this industry and made it possible to cut costs and, hence, prices. But is there anything wrong with that?

What about the authorities? Have their policies been misguided? They have only done as much as society has been willing to accept. Flonneau (2005) plays down the overly harsh criticism levelled at Georges Pompidou, president of France from 1969 to 1974, for his allegedly pro-car approach to urban development in Paris.

Rather than some great 'culprit' or 'conspiracy', car dependence stems from a host of relatively rational decisions leading to significant system effects that have, in turn, generated a cumulative, self-sustaining process.

It is tempting to draw parallels with drug addiction. Researchers at Paris I University working within the framework of an ADEME-PREDIT contract have used econometric 'addiction' models designed to forecast future trends in alcohol and tobacco consumption in order to study car ownership in Europe (Gardes & Starzec, 2002). But it amounts to a methodological ploy using statistical models. One must bear in mind that car dependence is a social, not a personal, phenomenon. People are dependent not on themselves or a particular product, but on others and on the community. It is thanks to other motorists that a driver enjoys a bonus unavailable to non-motorists. It is because of – and in relation to – motorists that the non-motorist is marginalized. The fact that inhabited areas have grown too large to cross by foot has made the motor car, in many cases, a must. Given that car dependence is inherently social in nature, all personal, local or overly focused attempts to reduce that dependency, despite having the potential to produce other interesting results, are bound to fail. In other words, the battle to combat car dependence will be won only if society at large can be persuaded that it is a just cause. Only then can the action be comprehensive enough to be truly effective.

But is it a just cause? Why is car dependence so bad?

System effects are not specific to the motor car. The fashion effect and 'club effect' which are rooted in the same basic principle, are found in many other areas. People are as reliant on the telephone, on electricity and on high-speed trains as they are on cars. Any form of transport can give rise to a vicious or virtuous circle. Take the virtuous circle of the bicycle, for instance: increasing numbers of cyclists leading to more bicycle-oriented planning, thus stimulating a further increase in the number of new cyclists, and so on and so forth. No fear of any danger to the environment there, some may say. Maybe not, but what about in the case of electricity or the telephone? Electricity production can generate nuclear waste and/or air pollution; and mobile phones emit waves that may be harmful to the health. Yet car dependence, despite being incurable to some, causes a far greater degree of concern than any such dependency on electricity or the telephone. This is probably due to the fears stoked up by images of the countryside no longer resembling the rural landscapes of yesteryear, for instance or of the city losing touch with its historical roots – something that nobody, in Europe at least, wants to see happening and which justifies the current crusade against car dependence. So it is an issue that goes well beyond the confines of the transport sector. In the future, researchers might be well advised to take an interest in the creation, reproduction and dissemination of such images.

	1975	1985	1995
Sleep, meals, personal hygiene	75.8	74.7	74.6
Work, study, domestic duties	40.2	40.4	42.4
Leisure	49	50	48.1

Illustration 12.2   **Time use in the Netherlands: hours per week among the over 18s (month of October).** Source: Social and Cultural Planning Office of the Netherlands, Time Use Survey (1975-1985-1995)

Basically, though, car dependence stems from the strict time frames involved in the overall social organization determining the roles, duties and obligations of each and every member of society in the fields of study, work, home life and leisure. As a matter of fact, illustration 12.2 shows how variations in the main time-budget categories tend to be negligible over a long-term period (20 years).

The point is that human nature does not change a great deal, and neither do the physiological needs of human beings or the time required to meet those needs and to perform the roles of workers, students and domestic actors within the overarching, slowly evolving, framework of social organization. Leisure time too remains surprisingly constant. So the time restrictions placed on behaviour patterns are highly rigid. The travelling required to fulfil the various roles and duties also takes time. Cutting the distances and, hence, the time spent in transit, is one way to save time. But it is not an option open to most people. It depends far too much on the forms of physical planning adopted, on the labour market and on structures over which individuals have no influence. The other alternative is to increase travel speeds. When a mode of transport like the motor car makes this possible, it is bound to be approved on account of the fact that it is within the purview of the individual and it helps make the rigid time frame imposed by social organization a little more flexible. People regard its speed and accessibility – factors seen to have played a key role in fostering dependency – as their only means of realizing a deeper-rooted desire to loosen the temporal yoke without having to drop out of society altogether. The car gives them a little more time and leeway, helping them to cope and to fulfil themselves. One survey interviewee questioned on the issue of car dependence replied "what are you talking to me about that for? Why are you asking if I'm dependent? On the contrary, the car makes me more independent, less reliant on others or on the circumstances". According to Crozet and Joly (2004), working from Zahavi's hypothesis, car speeds may no longer be such a critical factor in the scenarios centring on an 'extensive model' of economic development and spatial organization, as witnessed in the United States.

Clearly, there are no short-term, quick-impact, solutions. In recent comparative analysis of transport infrastructure evaluation methods produced by PREDIT at the behest of the CGPC French civil engineering authority, user time savings was found to be the overriding factor in favour of infrastructure production in France – and indeed in most other developed countries – irrespective of the negative impacts on the environment. The final report concurs with the experience of economic evaluation experts that "most [transport] infrastructure investment in the developed world is geared to improving the transport system on the fringes and is essentially designed to increase journey speeds" (Conseil Général des Ponts et Chaussées, 2005).

Conventional wisdom long held with the paradigm of a rational choice between different modes of transport for a particular journey. The concept of 'transport choice' originally stemmed from the number and frequency of daily journeys made throughout the year within the framework of urban commuting, which happens to remain the rationale underlying its relevance today. But growing awareness of the existence of journey chains involving trips made for a mixture of different reasons made it clear that the transport choice for a particular journey depended on others and especially on such 'weak links' as public transport, which could only lend weight to the argument in favour of the motor car. The focus of attention then turned to the role of parking, which is mandatory for the availability of cars and, hence, their superiority over other modes of transport.

Meanwhile, observers noted how most journeys no longer seemed to have anything to do with commuting. Widespread car ownership, increasingly individualized lifestyles and the growing proportion of the non-working population with the means to travel had given rise to a proliferation of circuitous journeys that no longer seem to tally with the usual 'transport choice' criteria. Lately, questions began being raised about the time factor too. In view of the increasing number of jobs with flexible and irregular workings hours, and what with nocturnal leisure activities, was there still a choice between public and private transport? So it was that the first signs of car dependence appeared on the radar of urban transport experts.

Urban planners and developers, for their part, have gradually succumbed to the feeling that control has been lost over forms of urban development. People and economic activities are no longer located where one might have wished them to be, but in places made accessible to them by rapid means of transport, mostly cars. Actions aimed at remodelling the city and backing it up with a vigorous pro-public transport programme have proved limited, failing to contain suburban sprawl and to bring about a major shift away from car use. Car dependence has clearly been too strong for such policies to vanquish.

Recent studies on car dependence have largely remained confined to urban areas, which are home to around 80 percent of the population in developed countries and a significant share of economic activities. Some respected experts in the field continue to defend such a focus on the grounds that it is in "cities [that] the majority of world population will live. This is where the concept of urban development becomes important as cities are seen as being the source of economic wealth and prosperity, and the centres of sustainable development. It is only in cities that many of the activities essential to the creation of wealth and well-being can take place" (Banister, 2005). As soon as one broaches the underlying reasons of car dependence, however, it becomes necessary to raise the issue of spatial scale well beyond the city limits. What does this involve?

Now that local leisure-time activities are taken into account in urban transport surveys, attention needs to turn to 'tourism', in the statistical sense of the term, i.e. including at least one night spent away from home and involving variable distances (mostly regional), with often free accommodation (staying with family or friends); for a variety of reasons: to consult a specialist, to make one-off purchases, to drop the children off at their grandparents' house, to go hunting, simply for fun, and so on. The preferred form of transport in such cases tends to be the car. Surveys have shown the surprising skills of car drivers here, even when it is a matter of going out to 'explore' unfamiliar parts of the country (Sajous, 2003).

Journeys for pleasure or 'tourism' are far less frequent than those made between the home and the workplace or to take the children to school. The extra mileage involved carries greater weight in people's minds, making the car more meaningful to them by enabling them to expand their territory (Dupuy, 1995a). Car manufacturers have long been aware of this, which explains their deep-rooted reluctance to market cars designed exclusively or even primarily for the urban environment.

Assuming that pleasure and 'tourism'-related mileage represents, at a guess, around half of the distance covered in cars, that particular half goes further towards explaining the reasons for car dependence than the mileage devoted to routine journeys. It is what attracts people to joining the ranks of the motorists; and most probably why they see no antithesis between freedom and dependency (Auphan, 1999). Dependency is just the price to be paid for the freedom gained in terms not just of residential location but also – and perhaps moreover – of medium and long-distance journeys.

Unlike the Swiss, however, the French are rather ill-informed – and lacking in statistics – on the subject of journeys for pleasure and 'tourism', at scales way beyond that of the city. Urban transport surveys may now embrace leisure-time activities, and there may well be research done on tourism-related mobility, not least by PREDIT, but it is all still far too fragmented. Approaches would need to be harmonized and the scales of analysis, which remain overly focused on urban areas, to be routinely expanded – if not to the national level then at least to the regional, as in the pioneering article by Madre and Pirotte (1997) – in order to grasp the underlying causes of car dependence and, *ipso facto*, the obstacles preventing its reduction.

The most plausible scenario, given the major trends in terms of both car ownership and future policy-making, is that of society's continuing automobilization and increasingly deeper addiction to the motor car. In which case, researchers should be looking into how to alleviate the dependency. Take the example of another mode of transport: walking. Human beings have, since the emergence of *homo erectus*, learned to walk as a means of occupying their territory and gaining access to the world. Spatial organization has been designed to provide access to walkers. Yet one tends to forget that it is, by nature, a tiring and precarious way to travel. While we all may rely on walking, nobody discusses that particular dependency because it is natural, taken for granted by all but those with a mobility impairment who are unable to walk. As they cannot always take the bus or enjoy access to wherever they want to go, efforts have had to be made to come up with the means to assist them: wheelchairs, specially adapted buses, and so on. In the case of the car, with current trends conceivably set to continue towards universal automobilization, palliative measures would need to be found for those with an (auto)mobility impairment; meaning that policies to reduce car dependence would have ended in failure.

Furthermore, a tacit yet widespread acceptance of the dependence could be regarded as a kind of collective pact to produce a new territory with the help of cars. The inability to shake off that essentially social addiction demolishes our modern approach to freedom. On the other hand, the term 'dependence' testifies to the strength of the trend: the dependence is accepted only because it is a prerequisite for real territorial change. In which case, it would amount to a silent revolution that transport policies would be powerless to prevent. This is plainly an avenue of research not to be ignored.

Part IV

ICTs:
Interconnections and
Divides

13   The Icelandic Miracle: The Internet in an Emergent Metropolis*

Iceland is a patch of volcanic land just below the Polar Circle in the remote reaches of the North Atlantic, a tiny island nation no larger than the state of Kentucky but inhabited by 93 percent fewer people. Its main source of sustenance and prosperity has long been the cod-rich surrounding seas.

To those who see this as a wild and rugged land of volcanoes and glaciers with unpaved roads and a smell of fish dominating the ports, it may come as a surprise to find that Iceland has actually developed into one of the most sophisticated nations in the world in terms of Internet diffusion. It had the third largest number of host computers (i.e. capable of accommodating applications for browsing, e-mail, e-commerce, and so on) per capita by 1998, behind Finland and the United States, yet ahead of Sweden and Canada; in addition some 60 percent of the population were frequently accessing Internet services from offices, homes, the university, cybercafes and other establishments by 2000 (Paltridge, 1999). Given the country's geographical isolation, its shift from the fringes of global activity to centre-stage on the network of networks may even seem little short of a miracle.

This Chapter proposes to lift the veil from the Icelandic miracle. We begin with a reminder of the factors commonly considered conducive to Internet diffusion and of the limited scope of analyses based mainly on statistical correlations. Next, we look at Iceland's historical and geographical characteristics and how they have served both to enhance and to impede the spread of the Internet, before going on to underline the importance of the so-called 'metropolitization' of the capital city Reykjavik. Attention then turns to the key factor that has propelled the country to the heights of the Internet charts: the concerted decision making of public and private telecommunications sector operators, a gamble that appears to be paying off. We conclude with a roundup of what is being done to sustain the miracle and useful input the Icelandic case offers for policy making elsewhere.

Conventional factors and their drawbacks

Internet diffusion in any given country is usually measured, amongst other factors, by numbers of host computers, frequent Internet users, connected households, or registered domain names. Each of these provides useful yet partial indicators. Certainly one of the least contested and most commonly used measures has been the percentage of the population benefiting from Internet connectivity in the home. Icelanders have been leading this field, ahead of the Swedes, Danes, and Americans, since 1999 (see illustration 13.1).

But how can one explain why Internet diffusion in the late 1990s was so much greater in some countries than in others?

---

*   Previously published in *Journal of Urban Technology*, 10 (2), 2003, pp. 1-18, http://www.informaworld.com. Included with permission.

Year	Percentage of population connected
1995	3.8
1996	12.3
1997	19.0
1998	51.2
1999	58.0
2000	60.0

Illustration 13.1   Icelanders accessing Internet from home. Source: Statistics Iceland (2000)

Hargittai (1999) – in a study limited by a lack of comparable data to a sample of 18 OECD countries (not including Iceland) – pinpoints a number of explanatory variables, testing her assumptions through statistical analysis. She explores the characteristics of each sample country, measuring Internet connectivity by the number of host computers per 10,000 inhabitants, and then subjects this and the other variables to regression analysis. Internet diffusion in any given country, she concludes, hinges on economic wealth, income equality, standards of education, fluency in English, telecommunications infrastructure, and free competition in the marketplace.

How far do those factors go to explaining the miraculous growth of the Internet in Iceland? *Per capita* GDP is close to that of Switzerland; *per capita* earnings are among the highest in the world; there is a remarkably even distribution of income, and the population is generally very well educated. But even though the same can be said of Luxembourg, another small and still wealthier country, for example, the latter had three times fewer connected households than Iceland in 1999. And proportionately half as many Swiss as Icelanders were classed as frequent Internet users in 2000.

As far as English fluency is concerned, while Icelandic youth may, as a rule, be quite familiar with the language, older members of the population with an average level of education are far less so. Furthermore, Iceland recently had to import immigrant labour from Eastern Europe and Asia, and the new arrivals are hardly very fluent in English either. The first language taught in schools is Icelandic, followed by Danish with English coming only third. And Icelanders see their mother tongue as a symbol of national identity, making constant efforts to ward off what they regard as the harmful influences of other languages, especially English.

In terms of telecommunications infrastructure and equipment, Iceland is in a very strong position. In 1995, for instance, it became the first country in the world to have a completely digital public telephone network. But before the advent of the Internet, the equipment found in Icelandic homes was average and conventional compared to that of the Danes, Finns, or Swedes. So infrastructure and equipment were apparently not influential factors in the early stages of Internet diffusion there (see illustration 13.2).

Nor was there free competition among telecom operators. Deregulation of the Icelandic telecommunications sector has been slow and cautious. INTIS (Internet Iceland Inc.), the public body responsible for Net-based scientific and technical communications, remained the country's one and only Internet service provider (ISP) until 1996; the national phone company (established in 1906)

	Denmark	Finland	Sweden	Iceland
Teletext	80	83	85	67
Fax	22	25*	18	11
Cell phones	49	73	64	40**

*1997

** GSM only

Illustration 13.2   Private access to telecom services in 1998 (percentage of population). Source: Statistics Iceland (2000)

remained wholly state-owned until 2000. Since then, only 5 percent of its shares have been sold to the public, and its monopoly of the telephony market remained intact until 1997. So Internet diffusion in Iceland did not benefit from a competitive telecom market as early as it did, for example, in the United States, Canada, or Great Britain. But neither was it handicapped by the delay, as we shall see below. In any case, there is generally some debate as to whether a deregulated telecommunications sector really is a *sine qua non* of Internet diffusion. Argentina was quick to open the sector up to free competition, but the spread of the Internet there has been slow; however, Singapore has become one of the leading countries in the world in this field with its state monopoly intact (Guillén & Suárez, 2001). Also, even though the Internet in Saudi Arabia is subject to state control and censorship, as opposed to the open trading regime prevailing elsewhere, the country has a remarkable record in terms of increasing public access to the network – the service having accumulated some 60,000 subscribers within two years of its launch in January 1999 (Al-Tawil, 2001); whereas in France, the state's monopolistic policies staved off Internet penetration while it continued the highly effective development of a longer-running competitor: the text-based Minitel (Hargittai, 1999).

So despite the existence in Iceland of what statisticians regard as favourable factors, statistical correlations fail to fully account for the success of the Internet in Iceland. Both Hargittai (1999), and Guillén and Suárez (2001), happen to reach conclusions that concur with this view: the former stressing the limited scope of the statistical approach, arguing that "…the quantitative aspects (…) need to be supplemented by qualitative information about country-specific attributes that may also affect connectivity" (Hargittai, 1999: 712), and the latter actually citing Iceland as counterevidence to the argument that Internet diffusion relies on deregulation.

Besides, the operating conditions of telecommunications networks alone certainly could not have been responsible for triggering Internet diffusion. An increase in private Internet use on such a scale as in Iceland is only possible if accompanied – or even preceded – by the supply of equipment and services. Would telecom operators and ISPs have taken an interest in Iceland simply because it had a population of young, prosperous, and educated people who spoke a little English? Not likely. Such companies only agree to invest when they sense significant market potential (Downes & Greenstein, 1999). And given that this remote, 90-percent barren island nation located 1,800 km from Copenhagen and 4,000 km from Montreal is inhabited by fewer than 300,000 people, it does not have the necessary critical mass to justify large-scale investments. Rapid entry into the modern age has been no straightforward matter for a country still reliant on its fisheries, proud of its cultural and linguistic identity, and jealously guarding its independence, not least from the world's leading promoter of the Internet, the United States.

Authors adopting a more monographic approach and delving into the favourable factors that macroscopic statistical analysis tends to obscure, stress the key role of the metropolis in the growth of Internet diffusion. Several draw attention to the extraordinary clustering of Net-based activities in the large metropolises of California and the northeast coast of America, which have long figured as sources of economic wealth, financial activities, and technological innovation, boasting great potential in terms of creativity and communication (Kellerman, 2000; Moss & Townsend, 1997; 2000). But finer analysis comparing Internet activity growth to the size of the metropolis and, moreover, focusing on the actual rate of growth, brings to light a number of outsiders: Seattle, Phoenix, Atlanta, and Denver. On closer inspection, the success of some of these metropolises in the 'Internet galaxy' can be seen to have been the result of a blend of capitalizing on opportunities and sensible policy-making geared to interlinking the growth of the Internet with metropolitization (Castells, 2002; Walcott & Wheeler, 2001; LeBlanc, 2001). This is clearly what occurred in Atlanta and Denver.

In Iceland's case, we need to offset the shortcomings of macroscopic correlation-based reasoning by leaving the realm of statistical aggregates and turning our attention to the country's geography and, more importantly, to the metropolitization of the capital city, Reykjavik, home to some 60 percent of the population.

The emergence of a modern metropolitan state

Few foreign tourists, visiting Iceland out of a love of nature and an appreciation of its vast landscapes, will notice the country's discreetly concealed factories, power plants, and industrialized fisheries. Many, on the other hand, will be struck by the low population density, the seventh lowest in the world in 2001 according to the U.S. Census Bureau's International Database. In the countryside outside Greater Reykjavik and the other large towns and cities, they may not see another human being for miles. Even the urban landscape of the capital itself – which, notwithstanding the early influences of Scandinavian-style planning, has been developed according to the highly relaxed standards of American cities since the end of the Second World War – reinforces the impression of wide, open spaces. Most, therefore, return home with an image of the country that is worlds away from the reality of Internet connectivity success. A highly scattered distribution of people and activities is not usually considered a factor conducive to Internet diffusion. But that, as we hope to show below, is a misleading premise in Iceland's case.

Iceland was first populated in the Middle Ages by the Vikings, who were followed by the Scots and Irish. It long remained self-sufficient, living on fish from the sea, meat from sheep raised on sparse pasture lands, and root vegetables grown, with some difficulty, in and around a handful of villages. Under the colonial rule of Denmark, from the late fourteenth century through to independence in 1944, Iceland's autarky crumbled into a dependency that arguably held back the Icelandic people's development.

During the early twentieth century, however, as Danish control slackened, a quiet revolution took place. A French diplomat taking up a post at his nation's consular offices in Reykjavik in 1930 had previously pictured Iceland as an isolated and backward land of "fishermen and farmers concerned solely with feeding themselves on the produce of the sea and a few meager patches of land, a place where trading activity was less than minimal and monopolized by the Danes, and where all contact with Europe passed via Copenhagen. There were no Icelandic shipping lines, and the first cable link with Denmark only came into service as recently as 1906" (Condroyer, 1931: 104). Much to his surprise, however, he discovered a close-knit people deeply attached to traditional values yet showing an equally deep interest in – and openness to – the outside world. He found Icelanders to be lively traders with a remarkable appetite for the trappings of modern life: electricity, the automobile, sewing machines, phonographs, and the telephone. And their desire for independence had translated into a flurry of capacity-building projects in the sectors of, among others, hydroelectric power, communications, and manufacturing. Reykjavik had become a thriving town of 25,000 inhabitants, compared to the mere 6,700 living there in 1900, and there were plans to open a commercial airport. As far as telecommunications were concerned, the capital was served by 2,400 phone lines, and the first automatic exchange had opened within the space of four years. The telegraph and telephone age soon spread beyond the capital and the main coastal ports. Indeed, on a visit to a remote and seemingly isolated *baer* (farm), Condroyer spotted a yellow telephone set in the corner of the room and realized that "modern times have even reached a place as remote as this" (Condroyer, 1931: 163).

Icelandic society's openness to modernity and to the outside world happens to have been one of the main factors that, within 65 years, would help fuel the metropolitization of Reykjavik and turn Iceland into highly fertile ground for Internet diffusion. Meanwhile, Iceland's limited independence in the 1930s left it heavily reliant on its own basic resources, mainly fish stocks and hydroelectric power. The latter was useful and already doing much to facilitate life on the island, but it was not exportable and capable of providing the economy with a desperately needed staple. Thankfully, fish stocks were plentiful and, with the increasing hauls being brought in by the newly generalized trawlers, soon buoyed the balance of payments and established Iceland as a diminutive yet active presence in global trade.

Iceland's international relations saw a slight change in course with the Second World War. For strategic reasons, England, the United States, and then NATO successively sought to secure a foothold there. This eventually led to the setting up of Keflavik military base, which in 2000 employed some 5,000 people (a fifth of them Icelanders) and provides a livelihood for four times as many more. This in turn led to the opening of a modern international airport that has done much to bring the country into contact with the rest of the world. The Gorbachev-Reagan summit meeting of 1986 symbolized Iceland's newfound position as an intermediary between the East and West. Gradually, Iceland normalized its rather strained relations with the United States, enabling it to build alliances during the cod wars and, hence, keep Russian trawlers away from its coastlines. Its refusal to join the European Union meant that it could avoid the fishing quotas imposed on EU member states. These unique circumstances boosted Iceland's position on the world stage. Fish products still make up a good share of its exports and, at the same time, secure a comfortable living for the population. Denmark, which accounts for no more than 8 percent of Iceland's imports and 5 percent of its exports, has become just one of a number of trading partners headed by Germany, Sweden, the United States, Japan, and France.

By the time the commercial Internet burst onto the scene, Iceland was already a longstanding global trader. There was more to its adoption of Information and Communication Technologies (ICTs) than an insularity complex of the kind cited in the cases of Mauritius, Réunion, some of the Caribbean islands or the Balearics (Bakis & Segui Pons, 1998; see Chapter 14).

In 2000, Internet connectivity rates in Mauritius and Réunion, although equivalent to those of Switzerland, were half as high as in Iceland. Similarly, a smaller proportion of households in the Saint Pierre et Miquelon islands off the Newfoundland coast (see next Chapter) – i.e., 50 percent, just over the French average – were connected to the Internet via television cable; users there were complaining that the telecom operator and public authorities lacked the technical and commercial expertise to foster the qualitative progress needed for the opening up and economic development of the islands (Institut de l'Audiovisuel et des Télécommunications en Europe, 2001).

It may be true to say that Icelanders are encouraged to indulge in global communication by the desire to remain in close contact with a sizeable diaspora: an estimated 200,000 people of Icelandic origin are currently living overseas, with one city in Manitoba (Canada), for instance, being known as *Little Reykjavik*, due to its large Icelandic community. But beyond that, the Internet serves to underpin the country's ambitions in terms of international economic development.

Iceland is a nation. But it should now be regarded as a metropolis, i.e. a hub of international economic networks, a place of innovation and intense exchange within a context of globalization. The urban area of Reykjavik is home to 180,000 of the island's 290,000 inhabitants. The rest of the population lives mainly in the satellite towns of Akranes, Borgarnes, and Akureyri in the north, Hveragerdi and Selfoss in the southeast, and Vik in the south. The remaining towns, situated on the coast, account for a total of just a few thousand people, and even these are well linked (especially by air) to the capital.

On the economic front, Reykjavik has undergone a genuine transformation since the beginning of the 1990s (see text box 13.1). Fishing activities still prevail in the ports, but they account for less than half of Iceland's exports – down from 90 percent in the early 1960s – and employ a little over 10 percent of the working population (Country Reports.Org, 2003).

Meanwhile, a host of electronics, IT, telecommunications, and biotechnology companies have sprung up in the Reykjavik urban area. Gardabaer, south of Reykjavik, is already regarded as the Icelandic Silicon Valley, specializing in the production of software and equipment (accounting programs, barcode readers, graphical user interfaces, antivirus software, video scanning, and so on). The companies there have an international client base, including Citibank, Kodak, Volvo, Ford, Southwestern Bell Telephone, Microsoft, Unisys, Navision, IBM, Hughes, Marconi, and others.

Box 13.1   Examples of Icelandic Expertise

DeCode Genetics has gained worldwide renown since its creation in 1996, employs a workforce of over 200 people, and works, among others, for Hoffman-LaRoche in the biotechnologies field.

OZ Interactive Inc., a Reykjavik-based firm set up in 1990, specializes in 3-D interactive graphics software. Its flagship product, the OZ Virtual browser, provides users with three-dimensional surfing capacity and counts Microsoft, Soft Image (USA), and Mental Image (Germany) among its major clients. It employs several dozen people and has expanded operations to Tokyo and California.

Iceland's national electronic fish auctions system was developed by a Reykjavik-based firm and is now exported throughout the world.

Urban Networks – Network Urbanism

More generally, a seedbed of new businesses has paved the way for activities in the fields of computer-assisted education, research and development consultancy, and so on. Some, capitalizing on Iceland's location midway between Europe and America, also take advantage of time zone differences to supply remote computer maintenance services: when it is 8 A.M. in Reykjavik, the offices in Chicago are not yet open; and at 5 P.M. in Iceland, they are already closed in Berlin or Stockholm. The development of these new activities definitely has had an impact. The population of Greater Reykjavik has grown 15 percent from 1990 to 2000, and economic growth stands at around 5 percent per year.

It should also be said that Reykjavik's outstanding international airport – together with the runways of Keflavik military base, which are also used for civilian traffic – has done much to boost the growth of tourism (now Iceland's second biggest industry after fishing). Reykjavik, therefore, has enormous potential in this field and plays host to a good many international conferences, and so on. It is also beginning to develop a name as a media and cultural centre thanks to the international success of the singer Björk, the American film *101 Reykjavik*, the Vestmann Islands rock festival, and so on. Harsh weather conditions may hamper road and even air links, but such communication difficulties have been offset in Iceland by the fact that the country's activities revolve around the capital, despite its location in the far southwest of the island.

Meanwhile, Iceland has modernized its retail trade to a remarkable extent. Icelanders make more than 90 percent of their purchases via electronic means (smart cards, e-banking, and so on); Iceland holds the world record for *per capita* points of sale terminals, and some 25 percent of Icelanders are regular e-commerce users, another record (CFCE, 1998).

Iceland has, therefore, grown into an integrated, mini-metropolis centering on the capital, Reykjavik. And the success of its Internet also stems from its success as a metropolis. Indeed, 70 years after the arrival of Condroyer, the Icelandic writer, Einar Màr Gudmundsson, wrote: "You think you are arriving in a small town [Reykjavik] only to find yourself in a city that is, in its own way, an active participant of the global economy" (Gudmundsson, 2002: 45).

Icelandic governance

Another key factor explaining the miraculous growth of the Internet in Iceland has been the decision making of the authorities and telecom operators, which – given that the Icelandic society is small in size and bound to the same core values – has perhaps been rather more straightforward here than in many larger and more culturally diverse nations (Lorentzon, 1998). As mentioned earlier, the Icelandic government did not decide to deregulate the telecommunications sector until relatively late – 1996 for the Internet and 1997 for telephone services. The telecom markets, however, are still dominated by a small number of Icelandic companies, most of them stemming from existing public services. It has since transpired that this delay helped pave the way for Iceland's surge to the top of the world's national Internet connectivity charts.

Development of the home user market was primarily achieved by the state-run *Postur og Simi* (Post and Telegraph) company and the banks. Recognizing the benefits of their customers' having easy access to the Internet, they managed to rationalize their networks, which, in a country with such a low-density population, had been very costly to run. It was not long before they began developing home services. In 1996, *Islandbanki* launched the first secure home banking scheme and was soon offering its customers free Internet access. This sparked a trend that saw free access also being made available to the customers of other banks, the Post Office, and then to practically everybody else. It was made possible thanks to Iceland's low telephone charges, the fifth lowest of thirty OECD countries in 1998 according to an international comparative study of Internet access rates. These were kept down by the government and telecom operators' policy of considering all national calls as local. With 65 percent of households computer-equipped, free and easy access enabled Internet diffusion to grow at a far more spectacular rate than one might have imagined possible in 1996, going solely by the commercial Internet services being offered at the time (Wilhelm, 1999).

Meanwhile, the key player in the corporate user and ISP market has been Internet Iceland Inc. (INTIS), which was originally formed by the largely public Association of Research Networks in Iceland (SURIS) to operate what has become the country's longest-running Internet network, ISnet. INTIS subsequently became wholesale transmission capacity supplier to a significant share of the Icelandic business community and to around twenty ISPs, including the exclusive server at the Keflavik NATO base (300 user lines). In 2000, INTIS was taken over by the country's leading value-added telecommunications service provider, *Islandssimi* (established in 1998). While fixed-line telephony continues to be dominated by Iceland Telecom (*Siminn*), *Islandssimi* currently handles some 60 percent of Icelandic Internet traffic.

Infrastructure-wise, the joint decision making of the authorities and the handful of private operators emerging from liberalization of the telecom sector – culturally committed to the idea of Internet services for all Icelanders – developed a form of governance that steered clear of fruitless competition and confinement in market niches and turned the Internet into a modernizing tool for the newly emerging metropolis. Every Icelandic telephone was connected to an automatic exchange by 1986 and fibre-optic cable had begun being laid nationwide in 1985. The Reykjavik Energy subsidiary, Lina.Net, and *Islandssimi* subsequently worked together to build and operate the advanced Greater Reykjavik fibre-optic Metropolitan Area Network (1 Gbps) used by government departments, the University, businesses, ISPs, and so on. In 2001 it had been extended as far north as Akureyri and southeast to Hveragerdi and Selfoss (see illustration 13.3).

In terms of international communications, however, the geographically isolated Icelanders remained relatively poorly connected with the rest of the world until the 1990s. The first submarine cable to open up a route for telegraph and telephone communications between Reykjavik and Western Europe had reached the country from Scotland via the Faeroe Islands in 1906. The next major breakthroughs came in 1962 and 1963 with the opening of the SCOTICE and ICECAN telephone cables to Scotland and Canada, the first to benefit from subsequent specialized data transfers being the military at the Keflavik base and the Icelandic scientific community, which had the capacity to interact with counterparts in Scandinavia and North America at speeds of around 10 Kbps. Skyggnir Earth Station began relaying international satellite telephone communications in 1980, but the advanced transatlantic undersea cables (TATs) were still passing Iceland by, mainly because their builders/owners considered the island too remote and underpopulated to represent a market warranting the necessary investment.

Then, in the early 1990s, Iceland Post and Telegraph joined the leading European telecom companies in the capital structure of CANTAT 3, a pioneering U.S.$600 million fibre-optic cable route built by Teleglobe Canada and extending 7,104 km from Pennant Point in Nova Scotia (Canada) to Denmark, Germany, and the United Kingdom (see illustration 13.4).

Urban Networks – Network Urbanism

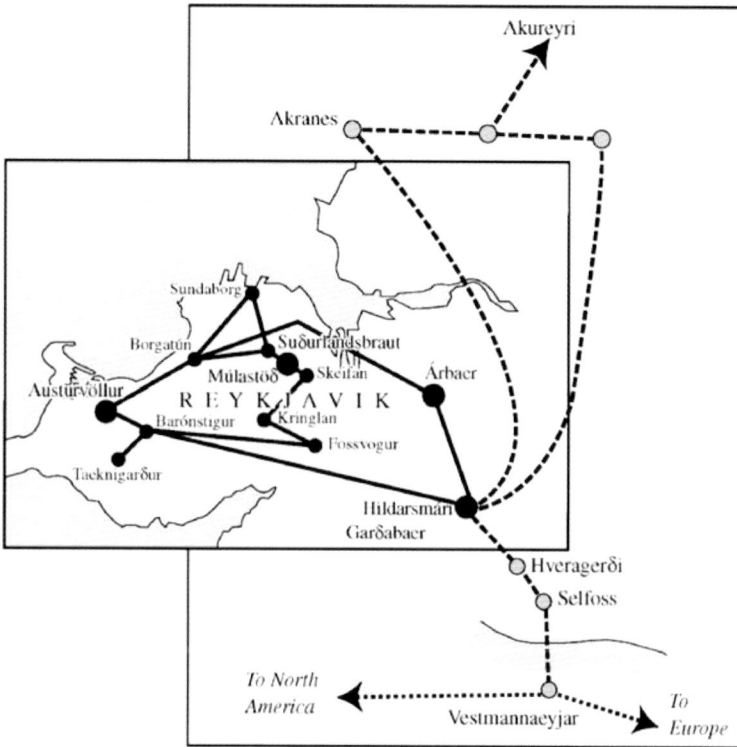

Illustration 13.3   **Backbone of Islandssimi's Greater Reykjavik Metropolitan Area Network (MAN) in October 2000.** Source: Lina.Net (2003)

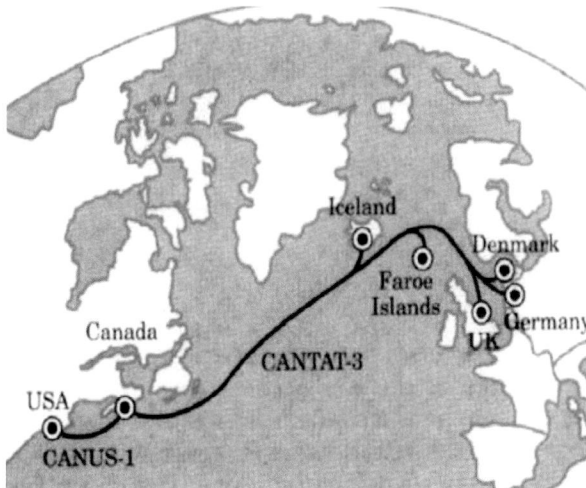

Illustration 13.4   **Gateway geography of CANTAT 3.** Source: http://library.cs.tuiasi.ro (accessed August 2003)

With North America via	1986	1989	1990	1997	1998	1999	2000	With Europe via
	0.3 Kbps	1.2 Kbps						Amsterdam
		2.4 Kbps						Copenhagen
			9.6 Kbps	2 Mbps	2 Mbps	4 Mbps		Stockholm
							34 Mbps	London
Montreal				2 Mbps	8 Mbps	10 Mbps		London
New York							48 Mbps	London

Illustration 13.5   **Growth in Iceland's International Communications Capacity.**
Source: Newman (2000)

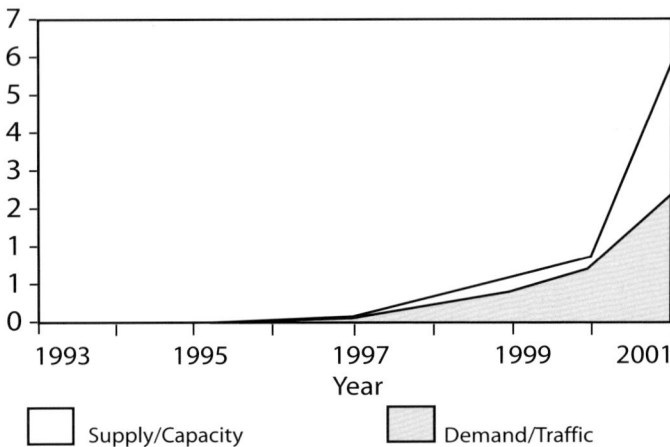

Illustration 13.6   **When Supply Anticipates Demand: Growth of Capacity and International Internet Traffic in Iceland.** Source: www.intis.is (accessed August 2003)

Urban Networks – Network Urbanism

The decision to locate the Icelandic landing station on the Vestmann Islands, 10 km off the south coast, was clearly not intended solely to cater to the communications needs of their 5,300 inhabitants. Indeed, it was part of a key strategic move, banking on the future and ultimately leading to the Greater Reykjavik Metropolitan Area Network (MAN) being linked up to CANTAT 3 in 1999, connecting the fledgling metropolis directly to Europe (especially London) and North America (New York). When it came online in 1994, CANTAT 3 was the first system to use synchronous digital hierarchy technology, with the capacity to carry both broadband integrated services digital network (ISDN) and asynchronous transfer mode (ATM) traffic at 155 Mbps: a greater capacity than all of the other TATs of the day put together (see illustration 13.4).

The enormous amount of communication capacity created (see illustration 13.5 and 13.6) was in excess of demand, and it gave the Icelandic economy an opportunity to speed up its transformation. Bloomberg financial services have since been made available throughout the land via a private virtual network, for instance, and businesses have been quicker to adapt to the Internet in Iceland than elsewhere – a fact reflected by a remarkable increase in host-computer and domain-name density, which is far greater than the OECD country average (Zook, 2000).

Through tight, monopolistic, and *metropolitanizing* governance, the public-private partnership has managed to supply the infrastructure needed to sustain economic development centering on a metropolis that, though still in the process of formation, has already gained recognition and a place in the sphere of global interactivity. Without it, the metropolis might easily have been handicapped by the country's size, low population density, and geographical isolation. Avoiding the risk of being left out of the investment required at the global level in the face of giants like the United States, and ending up confined to the fringes of the Internet, however, that governance turned potential weaknesses into strengths in spectacular fashion. It capitalized on such favourable factors as the population's wealth and high levels of education – regarded by sociologists as the most conducive to Internet diffusion in any given country – as well as a pursuit of modernity, an openness to the outside world, and a faith in technology to match the Scandinavian countries that set the pace in the fields of telecommunications in general and the Internet in particular. These circumstances have produced a nation of well-equipped, frequent Internet users and have enabled Iceland to establish itself as an outstanding presence on the Web, as measured, amongst other factors, by connectivity rates and international exchanges and by numbers of links to Icelandic Web sites.

The key, then, to the mystery of the Icelandic miracle is that Icelanders are beginning to reap the rewards of judicious policy making within a favourable context of metropolitization.

Sustaining the miracle

History did not end in 2000. The public authorities and operators, taking the economic and institutional changes stemming from liberalization in their stride, have kept up their strategy of joint decision making geared to prudently opening up to competition and fostering a dynamic domestic market, while enhancing international relations with a view to establishing Iceland, and especially Reykjavik, as a new global metropolis. Iceland may have been hit by the worldwide recession and the collapse of the Internet economy, but its determination remains strong and investment continues.

With several cuts in CANTAT 3 traffic having caused major disruptions in international tele-communications and, above all, Internet connectivity, *Islandssimi* set out to safeguard against future incidents by setting up a new satellite earth station and building the new FARICE fibre-optic cable to Scotland via the Faeroe Islands. Large-scale network capacity-building and performance-improvement projects have since been underway across the metropolis. Several hundred households have already been benefiting from high-speed Internet access (100 Mbps) as part of the Greater Reykjavik 'Fibre to the Home' pilot project jointly run since 2001 by Lina.Net and the Swedish company Ericsson. That same year, Marconi installed an advanced optical network covering Greater Reykjavik based on its SmartPhotonix technology (80 channels of 10-Gbps each), and it has already served to bolster the capital's position as an international Internet hub.

These are challenging times to be making such investments. But the signs point to there being no shortage of demand: in the education sector, for instance, 3,000 students signed up for a major e-learning program in 2001, by which time some 35 percent of Icelanders had taken courses on the Web.

Pointers for policy making elsewhere

The success of the Internet in Iceland may have had much to do with uniquely Icelandic historical and geographical characteristics, as outlined above. Aside from that, however, urban policy makers in other parts of the world could find that there are a number of useful pointers to be gleaned from that success. Here, for a start, are three (Gorman & Malecki, 2000).

First, new communications networks like the Internet are growing thanks to economies of scale. To foster the development of such networks, policy makers must be willing to expand the scope of urban policies well beyond the usual institutional boundaries. The very term 'urban policy' needs to be broadened. The Icelandic metropolitization process described earlier tallies with a change in scale. Internet diffusion has been a success not just for the city or municipality of Reykjavik, but for the entire Greater Reykjavik area, linked to satellite towns located dozens or even hundreds of miles away, and taking in rural areas. Indeed the whole country has become a metropolis with a position on the global networks of exchange with North America, the rest of Europe, the Far East, and so on. Electronic communications will not erase the many territorial boundaries that exist from grassroots to international levels. And those boundaries may continue at times to protect economic or social advantages (Al-Tawil, 2001; Graham & Marvin, 2001). But if the Internet and other such networks are to continue to grow, urban policies will need to be geared to openness and partnership rather than isolation and withdrawal.

Second, the Internet may often be associated with economic liberalization and competition, but its development has also been secured through highly regulatory and interventionist policy making (Petrazzini & Guerrero, 2000): the proactive approach of the local authorities in the field of telecom infrastructure in Amiens (France), for example, which has led to the rapid creation of thousands of jobs (Flichy & Zarifian, 2002); the prevailing state monopoly in Singapore, which has produced record Internet penetration rates (Guillén & Suárez, 2001); or the incentives offered in some South Korean cities that have helped turn them into 'high-speed Eldorados' with connectivity rates of around 60 percent (Cho Sung Hye, 2002). Is there a case for implementing such policies within a liberalized global context? In Iceland, public-sector action has been vindicated by the role that the Internet plays in key noncommercial sectors such as education, research, economic development, urban and regional planning, and international relations. The knock-on effects in favour of network-building at every level, including the commercial, have been considerable. These are grounds not for a stubborn defence of longstanding monopolies but for policies geared to prudent deregulation and governance of an oligopolistic environment in which the operators are most likely to invest (Antonelli, 1997).

Third, the Internet is associated with an extraordinary pace of change in the field of telecommunications and information technology. Sound policy making, therefore, calls for the capacity to capitalize on and keep up with the changes (Rutkowski, 2000). Iceland managed to seize on the technological opportunities arising first from its completely digital telephone network, then from the CANTAT 3 cable and, more recently, it has begun preparing the way for high-speed local access (100 Mbps end to end). Meanwhile, for many years it has been a member of what is known as NORDUnet, the Internet highway to Nordic science and technology, research, and education networks in Denmark, Finland, Norway, and Sweden, countries at the cutting edge of the telecommunications sector. Icelandic policy makers, therefore, had the up-to-date knowledge needed to be able to foster popular acceptance of, and faith in, ICTs across-the-board, including in other sectors such as new energies, e.g., the use of non-polluting fuel cells for running parts of the public transport system (Icelandic New Energy Ltd, 2003). The authorities, especially in the large metropolises, need to promote urban policies geared to spreading that faith by demonstrating how ICTs bring progress for all, not just the few, and by steering clear of those that give rise to urban splintering – in other words, by establishing policies that prove that ground-breaking ICTs are not synonymous with the digital divide (Graham & Marvin, 2001).

"Do consumers enjoy a *club effect*?

The network concept tallies with that of interdependence in production – due to economies of scale and scope – and in consumption, in the 'club' of users.

The club effect can be direct as in the case of point-to-point communication services like the telephone or fax, where each subscriber represents a potential correspondent and, hence, a direct benefit for the others.

It can also be indirect as in the case of the information services accessible via the French Minitel system, for instance, or the collection/distribution services provided by infrastructure networks, where usefulness to the individual does not depend directly on the number of other users but on the range of services available – a range that is all wider when rendered economically viable by an extensive user base."

From: Réseaux de Communication, Marchés et Territoires *by Nicolas Curien; in Curien, N. & Dupuy,* G., Presse des Ponts et Chaussées, Paris, 1996

14   Networks and Borders: The Resistible Rise of ICTs in Saint Pierre et Miquelon*

Over the past few decades, the potential provided by the new information and communication technologies (ICTs) has opened up new prospects for territorial planning and development. Ever-greater data storage and transmission capabilities and ever-lower costs have made it possible to conceive of effective ways to overcome the isolation of remote, relatively inaccessible places, especially islands such as those of Saint Pierre et Miquelon, a French territory in the North Atlantic some 4,500 km west of Paris. Other, on the face of it comparable, cases like Iceland and the Faroe Islands have been quick to embrace ICTs, with an estimated 60% of the Icelandic population, for example, using the Internet by 2002. ICT take-up has energized those countries: Reykjavik, the capital of Iceland, has undergone a process of what can be described as metropolitanization (see Chapter 13); and a number of highly ambitious projects are already under way in the Faroe Islands. So what is the situation as far as Saint Pierre et Miquelon is concerned?

After a brief introduction to the territory, its history and current circumstances, this Chapter goes on to examine the state of ICT development there, and seeks to explain why there has been no ICT 'miracle' of the kind seen in Iceland or the Faroe Islands. The first reason lies in the fact that the territory is very small. The networks serving this tiny French territory would need to cooperate with those of its close neighbour, Canada, to give genuine momentum to the development of ICTs. But the chances of that happening are limited by the existence of a border separating not just Saint Pierre et Miquelon from Newfoundland, but also France and even Europe from North America. This has led to some highly distinctive policy-making that hinders ICT development and diminishes the benefits it might be expected to have for territory. We conclude with a look at some of the prospects for the future.

Saint Pierre et Miquelon past and present

Saint Pierre et Miquelon consists of two main islands and a number of smaller ones amounting to a total surface area of 242 km2 inhabited by a population of around 6,500 people, 90 percent of them based in Saint Pierre, a port town on the smaller of the two main islands. The archipelago is located east of the vast Saint Lawrence estuary, just twenty or so kilometres off the south coast of Newfoundland, part of the Canadian province of Newfoundland and Labrador (see illustration 14.1).

Visited for centuries by French seafarers, the islands were formally recognized in 1536 by the navigator Jacques Cartier, and declared a French possession in 1670. Ceded to the British by the Treaty of Utrecht in 1713, they were then restored to French control some fifty years later under the Treaty of Paris, and became a French territory once and for all under the Treaty of Vienna in 1815.

---

*   Previously published as « Réseaux et frontière: le résistible développement des NTIC à Saint-Pierre et Miquelon ». *Annales de Géographie – Réseaux et Frontières : Internet aux Marges*, 114 (645), Septembre-Octobre 2005, pp. 531-549. Included with permission.

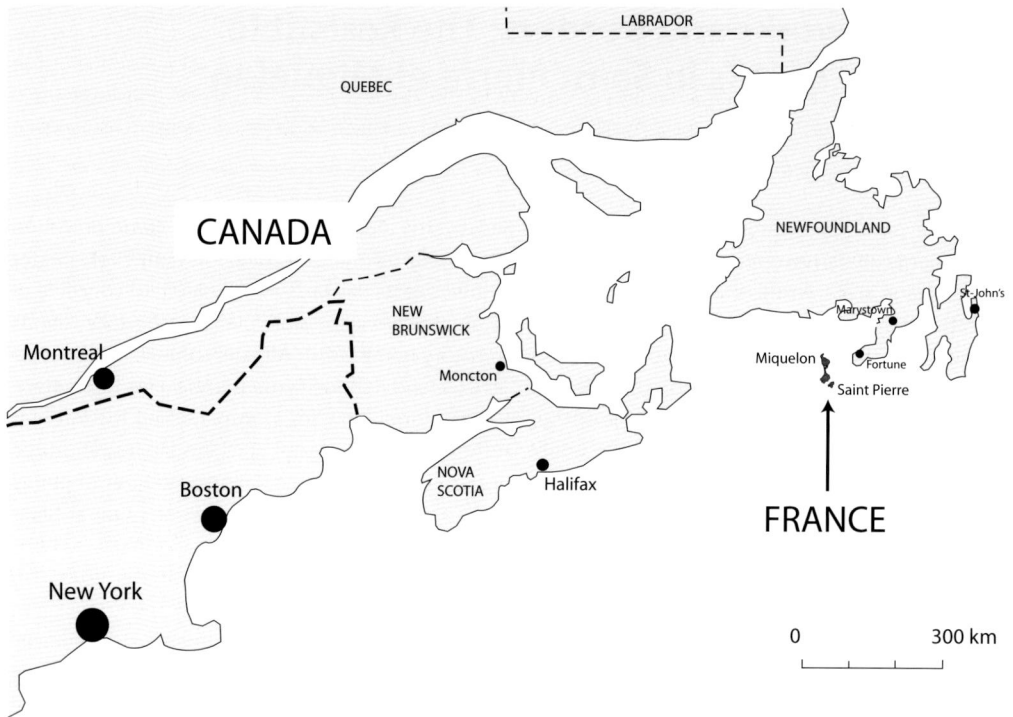

Illustration 14.1   Saint Pierre et Miquelon: outpost of France off the coast of Canada

Ancient relics attest to the presence of the Beothuk and Mi'kmaq indigenous peoples from across the water. Much later, the islands provided refuge to the Acadians driven out of Nova Scotia by the British during the Great Expulsion of 1755-1763. While 20 percent of today's population consists of metropolitan French people, most of them sent to the territory to take up temporary civil service posts, the other 80 percent were actually born there as the latest in a long line of islanders stretching back to the early settlers from Brittany, Normandy and the Basque regions of France and – in a minority of cases – Spain. In addition to which, they also feature traces of Irish ancestry stemming from the large number of marriages that have taken place with Newfoundland women.

Basically, what drew the European settlers to the islands first and foremost were the rich fishing grounds of the Grand Banks of Newfoundland (Fleury, 2004). Because the fishing vessels from Europe needed special logistics in order to be able to harvest the plentiful resources, Saint Pierre et Miquelon long prospered on the back of the businesses that sprang up to provision the ships, to dry and salt the cod, and so on. However, the modernization of the trawling fleet, with the advent of the steam then the diesel engine, on-board freezing, and so on, signalled the start of a gradual decline in the general 'service station' activities of the port of Saint Pierre, a trend boosted at the turn of the twentieth century by changes in the customs rules which served to slow the flow of supplies from America to local fishing companies and ship owners. Despite a brief boom in the golden age of prohibition in the United States (1920-1933), when the French authorities allowed the islands to become the hub of a thriving trade in bootleg alcohol from Canada and Europe, the economic fate of Saint Pierre et Miquelon looked grim. But the beginning of the end really came in the 1970s, by which time the threat to the fish stocks due to

Urban Networks – Network Urbanism

over-exploitation had grown so great that a number of countries, led by Canada, took steps to impose restrictions. A serious dispute over the quotas later culminated in Saint Pierre et Miquelon having to accept a drastic cut in its industrial fishing activity in the 1990s. On-site fish processing too shrank virtually to nothing. As a result, fishery-related activities in the islands now stand at just 10 percent of what they were in the 1980s.

The economic plight of the local population prompted the French government to come up with stopgap measures in the shape of subsidies and public works programmes to build a new airport, renovate the hospital, overhaul the drainage system, and so on. Today, Saint Pierre et Miquelon is inhabited by a relatively youthful population with a high standard of living but an extremely weak economic base that is wholly dependent on aid from metropolitan France – the territory imports 13 times as much as it exports, and the biggest employers are the civil service followed by the public buildings and works sector. Institutionally, Saint Pierre et Miquelon is in the unique position of being an OCT – according to the European Union definition of overseas countries and territories – with all of the administrative attributes of a French department inhabited by a hundred times as many people: a prefecture, various branches of local government, a gendarmerie, border police, a Chamber of Commerce, a general council with extensive – especially tax-raising – powers, town councils, and so on. As much political posturing goes on here as in France, although it is certainly less ideological, more 'domestic' and even, at times, more violent (Gay, 2003).

But what of ICT development in this socially, economically and politically unusual setting?

ICTs in Saint Pierre et Miquelon

Telegraphy first arrived in Saint Pierre et Miquelon when the transatlantic submarine cable reached the islands in 1867. They soon assumed the role of a node between Europe and North America but had to wait another 65 years before the telephone made an appearance. Urgent messages were sent by telegram, and the post was delivered just once a month by sea. The first modern means of communication, radio, arrived after the First World War, followed by television, via satellite, in 1960, and the first colour broadcasts in 1981.

Saint Pierre et Miquelon has come a long way since then. The French overseas broadcasting network, *Réseau France Outre-Mer* (RFO), runs a major station there staffed by around 70 people and broadcasting a selection of French channels together with local radio and television programmes. A coaxial cable TV network set up in 1991 across most of the Saint-Pierre et Miquelon urban areas now offers access not just to RFO programming but also to channels in Canada and the United States.

Telephone density is higher than in some parts of France: 4,600 lines for 2,400 households and 6,300 inhabitants in 2004, i.e. 65 percent of the population versus 53 percent for the French department of Haute-Garonne, for instance. And the main mobile phone operator, SPM Telecom, had built up a customer base of over 2,200 subscribers by 2002 (rising to 2,340 in 2003), at which time another few hundred people were signed up with its Canadian competitor, NewTel.

Computer density too is higher than in France. Although exact figures are unavailable, an IDATE report published in 2002 reckoned nearly every household and business in the islands to have been equipped with at least a single computer by 2001 (IDATE, 2002). With respect to the Internet, SPM

Telecom had 1,600 subscribers in 2004 (28 percent of the population), around 43 percent of whom enjoyed broadband access via the TV cable. Once again, these figures are above average in comparison to metropolitan France where subscription rates in March 2004, according to the French telecoms regulator, ART, stood at just 16 percent of the population (40 percent of them on broadband).

However, one cannot take this relatively positive picture at face value. For a start, the Saint Pierre et Miquelon population is unique in that it is predominately young, wealthy, urban, and even connected to the cable network – features that happen to match what global statistics commonly deem to be the ideal conditions for ICT penetration (Hargittai, 1999). So there are no grounds for saying that the territory had the 'lead' over France.

Furthermore, the ICT indicators do not mean to say that the local community has adapted to the technologies or incorporated them into their plans. Indeed, a number of shortcomings appear to suggest that ICTs have yet really to become part of life in the islands. Internet access in particular has been hampered since the start by low speeds and higher prices than in France. One electronic discussion forum reflects the numerous complaints of active users. A petition launched in 2000 garnered 1,300 signatures, stirring up many strong feelings and prompting reactions on the part of elected officials. The fact is that Internet development in Saint Pierre et Miquelon has struggled to keep up with the demanding expectations in regard to standards and prices.

When a satellite Internet connection launched in 1997 proved ill-suited to the interactive nature of Web-based practices, France Telecom brought out a scaled-down version of its Wanadoo service operating via the metropolitan French telephone network. Using the TV cable for Internet access has made broadband available to a good share of the local population. But SPM Telecom's proposed link-up to the Canadian backbone, which could, in theory, secure the capacity needed to provide users with their promised speeds, has run into economic difficulties. The backbone connection charges incurred by SPM Telecom are very expensive and based on the amount of capacity sought. From the subscribers' point of view, this has translated into very high rates that, when added to their mandatory cable TV subscription fee, come to nearly three times what people pay in France. IDATE (2002) confirms the prohibitive nature of subscription and communication rates in 2001 and describes the technology provided by French suppliers as 'overloaded and obsolete'.

Any progress recorded since then must be weighed against the overall development of what is on offer in terms of broadband technology, which has boomed in France thanks to the performance of ADSL and the significantly lower prices stemming from competition among operators around the globe. Internet access in Saint Pierre et Miquelon remains reliant on the coaxial cable TV network because the territory's only operator, SPM Telecom, cannot compete with itself by offering ADSL at prices that undercut its cable subscription fee. Connection to the Canadian backbone is still hampered by the challenging economic and technical conditions. And the extension of services to Miquelon has proved problematic due to it being such a small and relatively remote community.

Beyond – yet probably linked to – these basic barriers to what has come to be considered as routine use of the Internet, there are weaknesses and deficiencies as far as the websites are concerned. It is hard to know exactly how many active sites there are located in Saint Pierre et Miquelon. Plans to develop a '.pm' domain to identify them was remaining at a standstill in 2004; and although a directory produced by local website design and hosting company, Azimut, is supposed to list every site in the islands, it provides details only on those belonging to its own customer base. However, if we cross this with other data – a few dozen personal, i.e. non-commercial or administrative, sites plus the many branches of local government and the relatively large number (some 440) of businesses – we arrive at an estimated total of around hundred active sites at most. Proportionally, in 2005 there were around 7 times fewer personal sites here than in France. Businesses, for their part, have been unable to see why they should spend some €3,000 on an Internet site when RFO will broadcast their radio commercials across the islands for free. Any that do have a site tend, by and large, to use them strictly to provide information rather than for online orders and sales. This tallies with the failure of mail-order selling in Saint Pierre et Miquelon. Even the airlines and shipping companies – long standing models of Web-based information and booking services in other parts of the world – have ignored these highly effective means of access. Another noteworthy feature here is the low number of virtual private networks (VPNs) for secure payment of commercial transactions in online shops and stores. As a matter of fact, Visa and Mastercard are the only credit card companies with a VPN based in Saint Pierre et Miquelon.

At the institutional level, the Chamber of Commerce, the Social and Economic Committee and other such bodies did not have a website of their own by 2005. Neither did FrancoForum, the organization promoting French language and culture in the region and around the world, or the tourism development association, *Loisirs-Accueil Saint-Pierre et Miquelon*. What is more, barely a single branch of the French government present in the islands enjoyed access to its departmental intranet site in France. In most cases, the telephone, fax and Minitel remained the most commonly used administrative communication tools, and the vast majority of state services were relatively 'backward' in ICT use (IDATE, 2002).

So while the population of Saint Pierre et Miquelon may be more than adequately equipped with ICTs, the territory as a whole has yet to capitalize on the technological opportunities. Its economic, administrative and cultural actors are still holding back. ICTs have not managed to crystallize or underpin development projects, either in industry or in the service sector. Indeed, the "organizations involved in economic development have yet to place a premium on the leverage of Internet technologies [and] no initiatives likely to foster projects and partnerships between the various actors have materialized to date" (IDATE, 2002).

Lacking the critical mass

Why is it that despite the factors in their favour – not least the extent to which individuals are equipped with the hardware – and their potential for giving the territory a genuine chance to end its isolation, the ICTs have not yet managed to serve as a lever for local development?

The first hypothesis is, of course, linked to the fact that the Saint Pierre et Miquelon community is so small. Geographers have long known how the diffusion of innovations tends to occur in keeping with the urban hierarchy, as confirmed by most existing Internet diffusion studies based on domain name density or other criteria (Moss & Townsend, 2000; Malecki, 2002; Duféal & Grasland, 2003; Alvergne & Latouche, 2003). ICTs in general, and the Internet in particular, are adopted first in very large cities and then, somewhat later, by increasingly smaller cities and towns and so on before finally making inroads into rural areas.

In mainland Europe, the ICT lag between rural and urban areas has even been measured: twelve months in the case of the Internet and six for mobile telephony (ESPON, 2004). As far as Saint Pierre et Miquelon is concerned, the spread of innovation has been hampered not only by its size, but also, significantly, by its distance from the French urban hierarchy. What is more, the viability of any prospective technical network, especially when geared to transmitting and communicating information, is governed by pre-existing networks of social and economic relationships. Such relationships are always extremely sensitive to physical proximity, and in this case they are undoubtedly intense yet obviously confined to a small population and business community. In addition, the fact that these are islands means that the networks of relationships are enclosed, as it were, in a tiny virtual bubble that is hardly expanded at all by its diaspora, with just 180 or so youngsters a year leaving to study in France or in Canada, for example.

So Saint Pierre et Miquelon would appear to lack the critical mass without which it is impossible to induce the effects normally associated with the early stages of network development: the economies of scale needed to reduce costs, and the club and network effects that pump up the relevance of the services on offer (Curien & Dupuy, 1996; Curien, 2000).

Here are two clear-cut examples to illustrate the point:

- In the field of education: while Saint Pierre et Miquelon may boast, among other things, a high school and an information and guidance centre (CIO) equipped since the day they opened with an ample enough supply of computers – no fewer than 100 in 2003 – and Internet connections, the student body is too small for the territory to warrant having a university centre of the kind found in the Faroe Islands, whose population is seven times bigger. The high school and CIO may be key places for local youngsters to be able to consume information from France, Canada, the United States and so on via the Internet, but unlike a university centre, they do not have a great deal of information to share with the outside world, which does not help generate much in the way of network effects and interactivity;

- And in the field of healthcare: the Saint Pierre et Miquelon hospital may have been renovated, but its level of expertise tallies with the size of the population. It simply cannot handle a good number of illnesses and operations. So patients are transferred to other, better equipped, hospitals in Canada or France. Over a thousand such medical evacuations take place each year, at an average cost of €1,700 a time. Because serious conditions are treated elsewhere, the Saint Pierre et Miquelon hospital has little to exchange with other establishments in terms of telemedicine. In 2002, it had just two Internet lines – one for medical and the other for administrative purposes – and was considered, from the medical ICT point of view, to be in a 'prehistoric' state (IDATE, 2002).

At the same time, a number of other examples show that not even the implementation of exogenous means can help overcome the difficulties in promoting ICT development from too small a base. An optical fibre and videophone pilot project run by the French ministry of telecommunications in the town of Biarritz in the 1970s, for example, produced very little in the way of positive results; and the knell appears to have sounded for a more recent, and ultimately unsuccessful, project to create a 'digital city' showcasing the very latest in ICTs in Parthenay, a town of 18,000 inhabitants, when the mayor lost his bid for another term in office at the last elections.

So one might be tempted, in the light of the above, to give full credit to the theory that Saint Pierre et Miquelon is simply not large enough to have the critical mass needed for ICT development. But other small communities have managed to achieve outstanding results in this field – the towns of Klaksvik on Bordoy Island in the Faroes (5,000 inhabitants), for instance, and Selfoss and Akureyri in Iceland

(6,000 and 16,000 inhabitants respectively) – which suggests that another, complementary, theory is required. Selfoss may lack the necessary critical mass, but Iceland's unique form of governance has seen the town incorporated into a nationwide ICT development programme run from the capital, Reykjavik (see Chapter 13).

So the problem of critical mass can be overcome by expanding the area over which ICTs are deployed and used. Their corresponding networks naturally facilitate such an expansion by freeing them, partially at least, from the obstacles posed by distance. As far as Saint Pierre et Miquelon is concerned, the expansion has gravitated historically towards metropolitan France, irrespective of the thousands of kilometres that lie between them, with RFO and France Telecom providing the connections that produced the situation described earlier regarding low speeds and economic monopolization.

Another alternative would be to consider redirecting that expansion towards its closer neighbours, Canada and the United States, not least because North America is a global hub of ICTs in general, and the Internet in particular (Castells, 2002). Newfoundland and Labrador is not a very prosperous Canadian province, perhaps, but its level of ICT development is high in comparison with French standards, and its capital city, St. John's (population 170,000), is a leading resource centre. Further afield are a host of other possible relay points in terms of infrastructure, expertise and training – Moncton in New Brunswick (population 115,000), Halifax in Nova Scotia (pop. 400,000), Boston in Massachusetts, New England (600,000), and Montreal in Quebec (3 million) – and it would be well worth linking up with them in order to have access to the economies of scale and the club or network effects required to enable the islands to cross the critical mass threshold, which they could never hope to achieve on their own.

This is much more than a purely theoretical view. A good number of stakeholders in Saint Pierre et Miquelon have given it substance over the past few years by endeavouring to play the international expansion card in the field of ICTs.

Networks and the quest for synergy

As mentioned earlier, Saint Pierre et Miquelon's communication with the outside world began to improve slightly with the arrival of television broadcasting a selection of French programmes in the late 1960s. In the 1980s, however, came the enticing prospect of being able to enjoy Canadian programmes, which were easy to pick up due to the islands' proximity to Newfoundland. Guillot (1986) draws attention to the fact that the differing standards led to many Saint Pierre et Miquelon households having two television sets – one for watching RFO and the other for the Canadian channels. Even at that time "some houses had satellite dishes which, despite being very expensive, look likely to become very popular because they make it possible to pick up the American channels"; and, notwithstanding the language barrier, the latter's sports and entertainment programmes were already competing with the output of the French broadcasting company (Guillot, 1986).

In 1991, doubtlessly based on his observations of this behaviour, a local entrepreneur named Charles Landry set up a cable television network based on the model of those operating in North American cities and offering access to an extensive range of channels from France, Canada and the United States. Every Saint Pierre et Miquelon household now has cable television. But the network is facing renewed competition from satellite television, with Canadian operators offering a most enticing choice of programmes at an attractive price. While the islanders cannot, in theory, subscribe to those services, a scheme allowing them to give an address in Canada makes it quite easy for them to circumvent the rules. This example in the case of television highlights a newly emerging tendency to capitalize on the existence of networks beyond the strict confines of the territory and the control of the French government, or to extend domestic networks towards the increasingly appealing services on offer in North America.

A similar trend can also be seen in the field of telephony. SPM Telecom has found itself competing in the mobile phone market with the NewTel network belonging to the Canadian operator Cellutel. Once again, the infrastructure used is based in Newfoundland. As there is nothing to prevent electromagnetic waves from reaching the shores of Saint Pierre et Miquelon, NewTel has been able to offer a competitively priced service that allows users to contact subscribers around the globe via North America, as long as they have a physical address in Canada, albeit with a restriction on those living in Saint Pierre et Miquelon where the Canadian network has no legal right to operate. Meanwhile, under a new Canadian Internet protocol telephony system called Vonage, subscribers in Saint Pierre et Miquelon have only to dial a low-rate phone number in America in order to speak, via the Web, to any other Internet user anywhere in the world, and are charged for the call independently of its distance and duration. Vonage is a two-way service, with subscribers in the islands able to receive calls mainly from the United States or Canada.

Even though there is nothing wrong with SPM Telecom's services relayed via satellite to France by France Telecom, then, trends in the telephony sector too reflect a move towards expanding the core area in order to empower the networks to operate in a more efficient or economical manner.

As for the Internet per se, when it first arrived on the islands in 1997 the absence of a French ISP allowed the Canadian operator CanCom to step into the breach and to deliver a rather rudimentary service using telecommunications satellites, with signals being picked up by a communal satellite dish and transmitted to individual users at very low speeds via the telephone network. In 2000, SPM Telecom – a private company owned largely by France Telecom but managed by Landry AVI – was awarded a French ISP licence and set out to use its cable network to provide regular Internet access, especially broadband. This ended up putting satellite connectivity to the islands in the shade, and attention turned back to Canada and the rest of North America. A microwave link was established to Newfoundland via dedicated lines to Marystown (in the direction of St. John's) where the nearest node of the CanCom backbone network was located, thus ensuring a link-up to the major US operators (MCI-UUNet).

Faced with increasing demand for connectivity and the high cost of leasing the microwave lines to Marystown, SPM Telecom has begun once again to consider solutions involving foreign companies, the aim this time being to have an 80 km fibre-optic link built from the Newfoundland coast to Marystown by another Canadian operator, a competitor of CanCom. SPM Telecom hopes to be able to persuade CanCom, given how much business it would be in danger of losing as a result, to bridge the gap between its backbone node and Saint Pierre et Miquelon. Otherwise, it will have no other alternative than to press ahead with the costly fibre-optic solution.

Meanwhile, SPM Telecom, in conjunction with the newer Canadian operators, is considering plans for a more direct undersea link from St. John's in Newfoundland to the east coast of North America via Saint Pierre and Halifax, which is a major entry node for transatlantic traffic from Europe.

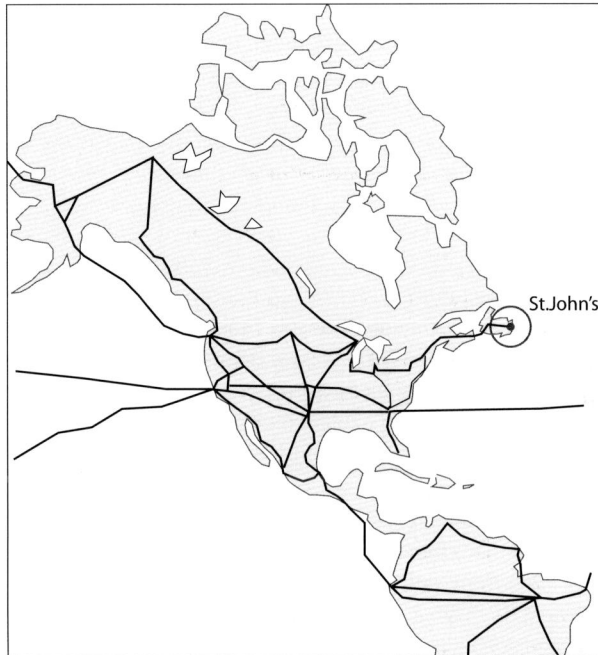

You have reached the end of the internet.

*You will have to turn around. Use your brower's backbutton to do so. This is
the final directory entry of the easternmost web server located in the city of St
John's, Newfounland (circle). The Internet's fiber optic junction nodes (drawn
in black) of North America all have ingoing / outgoing limbs numbering more
than one. Except for Newfoundland. You can find out all kinds of neat stuff about
Newfoundland on the Internet. But not here, because you've reached the end.*

Sorry

Illustration 14.2   **The above map and its accompanying message, which have appeared on a number of
different websites, express a simple idea: seen from America, St. John's of Newfoundland is the end of the world as far as the Internet is concerned. When seen from Saint
Pierre et Miquelon, however, the image is reversed: St. John's, once one has crossed
the French Canadian border, can act as a gateway to the vast North American Internet
'hub' dominating the global 'network of networks'.** Source: opalda.com

Efforts to seek synergies with North American capacity can also be seen in the field of ICT-based services. The main two private websites providing information on Saint Pierre et Miquelon – www. grandcolombier.com and www.mathurin.com – are hosted in Canada and the United States. As a rule, Saint Pierre et Miquelon website designers source their images directly from North American picture libraries. What is more, the islanders tend more readily to seek information on house-building or motor cars, for instance, on American websites such as www.floorplan.com or www.ford.com than on their less well-designed French counterparts. That growth in foreign contacts through the Internet shows clearly how actors in this sector are compelled to transcend the confines of Saint Pierre et Miquelon and metropolitan France in order to enter into a multi-layered, global environment turned toward North America (see illustration 14.2).

Blocked at the border

Why is it that the quest for synergies with North American networks beyond the territorial confines of Saint Pierre et Miquelon has not helped boost ICT take-up in the islands? More often than not, the plans of the various actors in the field of ICTs have been held back by one obstacle in particular: the border. Fleury (2004) shows how in the case of fisheries and underwater resources, the – singularly geographical – concept of borders can explain much of what goes on in this part of the world. His findings can be applied to the case of ICTs (Kahin & Nesson, 1996; Dupuy, 2002).

Saint Pierre et Miquelon's border with Canada amounts first and foremost to that narrow stretch of sea so easily crossed on so many occasions down the ages that even though the islanders are keen to stress what sets them apart from *Nioufis* – the Quebeckers' nickname for inhabitants of Newfoundland – the family ties between them are countless. Not everybody takes cooperation between neighbours for granted. The first signs of a dividing line that lowers expectations as to what one can expect from those on the other side of the fence can be seen in the sense of superiority, or even pity, shown toward the day trippers from southern Newfoundland arriving on Saint Pierre when the weather is fine, but without a great deal of money to spend during their stay.

Further afield – an hour by plane – is St. John's, a largish city visited for trips not just to the hospital, as mentioned earlier, but also to the shops. Due to its distance (350 km away), size, differing customs, and language – with most people speaking only English and the French-speaking community numbering no more than 600 or so individuals – it seems, in the eyes of the islanders, like another world with whom cooperation, once again, cannot be taken for granted. The impression is made all the stronger in the light of the fact that 60 percent of small and medium-sized businesses in Newfoundland have been on the Internet since 1998; that public access to the Net has been available to residents of St. John's for an equally long time; and that Cable Atlantic, acting on behalf of Time Warner, has just provided 52,000 of that city's households with highly reliable broadband connections. Indeed, they continue to regard St. John's as a foreign town, with a degree of mistrust and little hope of trouble-free, cooperative relationships.

Next is Moncton, with its radical, French-speaking Amerindian community. New Brunswick has a French-speaking population of 300,000 out of a total 800,000 inhabitants. Although cooperation offers clear advantages here as far as the Canadians are concerned, the cultural and political motives behind it may appear a little suspect to some islanders. Then there is Halifax, the capital of Nova Scotia, a truly international port and an economic hub that has long served Saint Pierre et Miquelon as a key place for acquiring resources; then Montreal, Boston, Toronto, and New York.

Feelings may be divided as to whether it is worthwhile or even possible to go beyond the strict confines of territorial boundaries in order to join an ICT development process that has become a potent force in North America. But the French government continues to stand guard at the border, clearly unwilling to commit itself to any course of action likely to undermine it. In the meantime, Saint Pierre et Miquelon ranks no higher than fifth on the list of French overseas departments and territories in regard to ICT policies and levels of Internet development (IDATE, 2002).

So recent history has seen a catalogue of missed opportunities and near-conflicts that show, when all is said and done, how hard it is to transcend the border and expand the ICT area in order to achieve the necessary critical mass. Take, for a start, France Telecom's disinterest in Canada's plans to build the CANTAT 3 transatlantic submarine cable which, following its completion in 1994, provided a tremendous boost to ICT development in Iceland and the Faroe Islands. As the route ran between Halifax and Iceland, it could easily have passed via Saint Pierre et Miquelon and, hence, given the territory the chance to enjoy similar levels of success. Decision-makers at the time, however, preferred to concentrate on meeting the needs vis-à-vis telephone communications with metropolitan France, and the existing satellite link sufficed for that. More recently, Bell Canada was planning to set up a French-language call centre in Saint Pierre et Miquelon involving the creation of around 500 new job opportunities, but it came to nothing. Without knowing the exact details of the negotiations, it is safe to say that this was because of an apparent lack of any real commitment to the project on the part of the French authorities, national and local alike.

Similarly, negotiations in this field have been no less problematic at government level too. In 1994, the French and Canadian governments signed an agreement to foster cooperation between Saint Pierre et Miquelon and the Atlantic provinces of Canada. A Franco-Canadian joint regional cooperation commission has met each year since 1996 to discuss a range of issues of common interest relating to the environment, tourism, cultural exchanges, and so on. Only once, at its third meeting in 1999, has there been any firm agreement on the subject of ICTs: "New information technologies were seen by the delegations as an essential tool for developing exchanges. They decided to develop a Web site and promote the exchange of information and expertise in this field" (http://www.acoa.ca/e/business/spm/communique3.shtml; accessed June 2008). Since then, regardless of the need to tackle such matters, the French authorities have appeared distinctly unenthusiastic about seeing the issue back on the agenda – for fear, no doubt, of a focus on cooperation in the field of ICTs showing the country to be over-reliant on Canada.

Progress, in the meantime, has remained more or less at a standstill. The fact that the ICT development area has yet to be expanded beyond the territory's borders, for instance, has hampered efforts to create a special '.pm' Internet domain which, as things stand at the moment, would be hard to fill. Moreover, the government appears confined to the role of a border guard with a duty to protect the islands against global or cross-border ICT trends. The so-called 'Faraday cage' episode is most illuminating. RFO programmes can be picked up in neighbouring Canada and rebroadcast across the land, all the way to Vancouver, by Canadian operators who are allowed to do so under that country's laws. When the French productions being broadcast free of charge were resold in North America, however, the licensees were up in arms over their loss of earnings. To ensure that justice was done in the eyes of French law, the government decided to encase the RFO transmitter in a Faraday cage so as to prevent the signals from reaching Newfoundland. The affair caused quite a stir, and the local population and their member of parliament managed to block the plans in the interests of the need to increase the global reach of the French-speaking world. As a result, the much-vaunted Faraday cage remains nowhere to be seen. But the current *status quo* smacks less of a *bona fide* global strategy than a lack of decision-making, ostensibly out of respect for the French conception of its borders.

Among the other problems one could mention are those encountered by website development projects that, despite being likely to increase the range of French influence around Saint Pierre et Miquelon, have had trouble securing support from the government. SPM Telecom's legal action against NewTel is typical of an attitude aimed more at rigorous border enforcement than at becoming involved in international cooperation and at expanding the area in an effort to foster ICT development.

Hence, the border – not just of Saint Pierre et Miquelon but also of France and even Europe – clearly acts as a real barrier to projects genuinely capable of paving the way for future progress and having a positive impact on the development of ICTs. A good share of the islands' actors appear satisfied with the current state of affairs, where a local operator – 'historic' in many ways more than just the legal sense of the term attributed to it by the French telecommunications regulator – is given the task of attending to the prudent management of ICT development in the territory. But IDATE (2002) notes the "absence of any initiatives on the ground to help promote the emergence of activities conducive to economic development and to building the partnerships required for the emergence of new projects". So the border holds firm against the ICT networks, maintaining the territory's identity in its relationship with France while asserting France's identity in an increasingly open global environment.

Prospects for the future

The current situation may seem to convey a certain sense of balance, but there is no ruling out the onset of major, rapid, changes. Saint Pierre et Miquelon enjoys below-average access to ICTs, and a sustained upsurge in demand could upset that fragile balance and, hence, prompt calls for stronger links with Canada and the United States. This, to some extent, would undermine the border, not least because the above-mentioned concept of critical mass is open-ended. Global operators are beginning to turn their attention to pockets of demand that they would never have considered worthy of consideration a few years ago (Dupuy, 2004).

But let us take a look as another possible scenario that appears to tally with what is already a significant trend in Saint Pierre et Miquelon. The need to find a means of replacing economic aid from France has sparked efforts to find alternative solutions in the fields of tourism and global business services. As far as tourism is concerned, the potential market lies in Canada and the United States and efforts to capitalize on that market will hinge on major growth in Internet development. Already, a 2004 tourist guide produced by the province of Newfoundland and Labrador in conjunction with the Consulate General of France – and covering both the Atlantic provinces and Saint Pierre et Miquelon – makes use of a wide range of links to websites (Le Gaboteur, 2004). As for business services, the idea is to turn Saint Pierre et Miquelon into a gateway to Europe, a testing ground to provide North American businesses anxious to develop a European exports market with a means of familiarizing themselves with European procedures.

North American actors definitely are taken by the idea. And it has the backing of the French authorities. But it is hard to see how it can bear fruit without a genuine commitment to opening up Saint Pierre et Miquelon to the North American ICT networks. In other words, it must be a two-way partnership: on one side, the North American companies acclimatizing themselves to Europe via Saint Pierre et Miquelon; and on the other, Saint Pierre et Miquelon, France and Europe having no qualms about learning to work with the powerful information and communication machinery of North America.

Once that happens, barriers to ICT development in Saint Pierre et Miquelon would become a thing of the past. And geographers and land planners alike would have no choice but to rethink the concept of the border from A to Z.

"... spaces whose very form is networkesque and whose structural properties find expression in those of the network. A network whose links consist of terrestrial, subterranean, maritime and aerial channels of communication (including telephone cables and even radio waves) carrying people, goods (including energy) and data, where cities are no longer discreet, more or less self-contained, units but areas of consolidation centring on its nodal points: the points where the said channels of communication intersect ...

When set against this networkesque οκουμένη [œcumene or inhabited world] the 'countryside' is what is caught between the links. (...) The more relational, continuous, open and unconfined the urban space, the more non-relational, discontinuous, closed and confined is that of the countryside as such (cut up, moulded and delimited as it is by the connecting links of urban space).

A farm, insofar as it is connected to the network-space, is located in the urban οκουμένη and as much an integral part of it as any other human settlement."

From: Anthropologie de l'Habiter: Vers le Nomadisme *by Georges-Hubert de Radkowski, PUF, Paris, 2002*

15   The Urban-Suburban Divide[*]

Data for comparing urban and peri-urban areas are too scarce to give much more than a glimpse of the significant differences between them as far as both the availability and the uses of new information and communication technologies (ICTs) are concerned. ICT development first begins in large cities whose suburbs often remain excluded from the economic and cultural wealth of the centre. When the cities are – as in the United States – polycentric in structure, the nature of the gap is more complex. In France, communities in the north of the Hauts-de-Seine department are less well equipped in ICTs than the neighbouring La Défense business district, which is on a par with inner Paris. But a survey of the socio-economically more disadvantaged residential areas around La Défense has shown them to have access to its excellent equipment. This does not seem to be the case everywhere. In the more deregulated setting of Santiago (Chile), for instance, the trickle-down effect works to the advantage of none but the better-off neighbourhoods. Generally speaking, deregulation of the telecommunications sector can be regarded as having a tendency to accentuate disparities between some urban areas that enjoy access to premium networks and others with nothing but basic and, as it happens, deteriorating services – the ICT version of the *splintering urbanism* theory (Graham & Marvin, 2001). Increasing peri-urbanization leads to increasingly complex disparities, with some relatively sparsely populated peri-urban areas inhabited by young, relatively high-income, households.

However, satisfactory access to – and extensive use of – ICTs is possible in peri-urban areas after all, as seen in the following extract from an article by Dominique Malécot, published in the 9 June 2006 edition of the French equivalent of the Financial Times, *Les Echos*:

> *Peri-urban areas enter the ICT age*
>
> *Seine-et-Marne General Council, with the support of the Ile-de-France regional authorities, has just finished equipping the entire department for ADSL coverage. The €60 million committed to the project, which has paved the way for the construction of very high-speed broadband infrastructure in 2007, has helped produce a mix of technologies – fibre optic, Wi-Fi, powerline, and WiMAX – to offer the best possible Internet access to residents of the department's 514 towns and villages, 80 percent of which are inhabited by fewer than 2,000 people, and few of which are covered by the operators' commercial networks.*
>
> *"Originally," explains Gérard Eude the Socialist Vice-Chairman of Seine-et-Marne General Council and Chairman of the Seine-et-Marne Development agency, "the aim was to meet the quite strong demand and provide every resident of the department with ADSL access. But there was an economic side to it, too. We enjoy a very high quality of life in our area, and many freelancers and senior executives may be tempted to move here if they have the chance of an ADSL line. This, in turn, would help create new activities."*
>
> *Without disowning its rural image, Seine-et-Marne has opted for the new technologies…*

---

[*]   Previously published as « La Fracture Ville-Banlieue ». In: Dupuy, G., 2007, *La Fracture Numerique*. Series *Transversale Débats*. Paris, Editions Ellipses, pp. 66-70. Included with permission.

Gómez-Barroso and Pérez-Martínez (2007), in a study of ADSL development in the outskirts of Madrid, help identify the operator's strategy and the risks of a possible divide. Population density definitely does appear to be the key factor, although its influence is tempered when household wealth is taken into account. The wider-ranging work of Grubesic and Murray (2002) tends to reach similar conclusions. Suburbs may be less advanced in ICT terms than the city centre – or centres – but they can also be more so than rural areas with low housing density. So where does one have to place the divide?

At the same time, the suburbs are underequipped for technical reasons. In the case of ultra high-speed broadband, for instance, access to services is available only within a two-kilometre radius of a telephone exchange. So the suburbs lose out to the centre due to the spatial distribution of telephone exchanges as a result of the density not just of the population and economic activities, but also of telephone lines.

Differences between the centre and the suburbs stem also from socio-economic factors. Social housing districts, despite being densely populated, do not meet the minimum social and economic conditions for ICTs to be able to flourish there. Notwithstanding which, there arises the issue of their cultural significance: what kind of progress or chances of social advancement do they enable in those neighbourhoods? Where is the point in adopting ICTs if they are used merely to meet basic communication needs – already satisfied quite inexpensively by cellphones and SMS – or for strictly recreational purposes (games consoles)? Questions like these are increasingly prevalent given that public service supply, which is often all that is available via community 'cybercentres', goes hand-in-hand with strict orders. Official texts talk about the 'need for scrupulous supervision and monitoring'.

This puts quite a dampener on efforts to encourage the adoption of ICTs. Nevertheless, other issues need to be taken into account here. A number of studies have shown contemporary musical creation to be an extremely selective process, with just one in a hundred new releases managing to turn a profit. Yet there are places that act as a breeding ground for creativity in this field: not only large cities around the world such as Memphis or Stockholm, but also often isolated or outlying urban areas featuring a concentration of alternative cultures whose representatives are spawning new musical genres and maintaining standards of excellence by means of the cluster effect. So the suburbs appear to be conducive to the production of contemporary music, meaning that their inhabitants are acquiring digital technologies, especially for recording. Hence a quarter of the Ile-de-France region's record companies and labels are located in peri-urban areas – mainly in Hauts-de-Seine and Seine-Saint Denis – and as many records are recorded and pressed in those areas as in Paris (Calenge, 2002).

Urban regeneration policies – now a leitmotif for local political authorities – frequently hinge on the assumption that ICTs can take over from outmoded or relocated manufacturing activities. The new technologies are promoted as being an engine for growth and for improving the quality of urban life. It is by no means certain that magic formulas like these are enough to overcome the reluctance of inhabitants who, unable to identify with them, fear that they will yet again be the have-nots of urban change. Firmino (2005) points to the need to communicate these futuristic visions, and to show that they are not based on a risky form of technological determinism. A "more receptive and mature environment [must be created] for the acceptance of new paradigms of the virtual city and the network society", which is some challenge given how the causes of the resistance are most probably the same as those that gave rise to the digital divide in the first place.

Recent studies on the layout of the Wi-Fi network seem to corroborate the inhabitants' suspicions. Tony Grubesic and Alan Murray provide quite an accurate account of Wi-Fi coverage in the American city of Cincinnati, linking it to the spatial distribution of inhabitants and economic activities. The fact is that the location of certain activities and/or population groups is a key factor in regard to Wi-Fi coverage; and technological advances in Cincinnati do not help narrow the digital divide (Grubesic and Murray, 2004).

When there is a *clear* digital divide between urban and peri-urban areas – i.e. distinguishable from the complex forms of spatial differentiation found in the contemporary urban environment – it is, more often than not, double-edged: a rift in terms both of the levels of ICT development and how the technologies are used.

16   The Digital Divide: Primarily a Matter of Geography? *

ICT development boils down to an extension of the networks relaying information to various parts of the country and making it possible to communicate. From that point of view, nothing really new has happened since Alexander Graham Bell first invented the telephone in 1876. Even Bell felt that these technologies would reduce space to nothing. Communication via the telephone or Internet is now instantaneous, in stark contrast to the prolonged wait and sometimes tedious journeys required for letters to arrive through the post. The late *Ancien Régime* mail coach, regardless of the quality of the royal highway system, needed up to a week to reach some parts of the kingdom from Paris; and the early nineteenth-century *Aéropostale* airmail service took days to assure the link between Paris and Buenos Aires or Santiago de Chile. Delivery times today are measured in a matter of milliseconds.

Is it not slightly absurd, then, from the geographical standpoint, to be talking about a digital divide with respect to technologies that are doing more to bring remote places together than ever before? Those railing against the digital divide tend to forget – or, perhaps, draw a veil over – this particular aspect of telecommunications networks. Each new cellphone subscriber or Internet surfer and every cybercafé is helping create an ever-better connected space. One does not have to buy into the utopian ideal of a global village to wonder about the meaning of a digital divide that tends to divide people and places once held asunder by geography but now brought together by ICTs. In other words, talk of a 'geographical' digital divide is little short of an abuse of language.

There is some truth to this line of argument. Laying a fibre-optic cable costs €50,000 a kilometre compared to €1 million/km for a sewer and drainage network and €35 million/km for a motorway or high-speed railway tracks; a computer costs ten times less than a car; a mobile phone is so cheap that 95 percent of youngsters in Europe now own one; and while GPS satellites may be very expensive, their global use makes it possible to spread the burden in a genuinely cost-effective manner. So ICTs represent a highly economical means of interconnecting people and helping them overcome spatial barriers. This has been understood full well by the local authorities or cable operators deploying networks at every scale – from the SIPPEREC system[1] covering the suburbs of Paris to the SAT3/WASC/SAFE submarine communications cable linking Europe to the Far East via Africa[2]. Technological progress and the relatively low cost of network deployment would appear to rule out the possibility of the digital divide, unlike in the case of transport, being primarily geographical in nature.

Yet things are not quite as simple as they seem. Ideally, ICTs should be able to reach any point in any territory and to eliminate geographical distances. But the fact is that geographic disparities continue to persist. Why? There are two reasons. On the one hand, the speed of technological progress is such that genuine breakthroughs are soon rendered obsolete. Access to fixed-line telephony, for instance, is no longer the most relevant yardstick now that mobile telephony is the norm almost everywhere; and being an Internet subscriber in France is meaningless without broadband access.

---

*   Previously published as « La Fracture Numérique est-elle d'Abord Géographique? ». In: Dupuy, G., 2007, *La Fracture Numerique*. Series *Transversale Débats*. Paris, Editions Ellipses, pp. 104-111. Included with permission.

So the disparities are fading in basic service provision yet resurfacing for more sophisticated services. The dividing line may shift but the digital divide still prevails.

On the other hand, the operators have yet to find a satisfactory business model for providing total territorial coverage. The older networks formerly playing more or less the same role – telegraph, fixed-line telephone, drinking water, electricity, roads – took quite some time to come up with stable models, mostly within the framework of private or public monopolies: the road system covers a substantial share of its costs by making motorists pay parking taxes, road tolls and, first and foremost, fuel tax; telephone, water and electricity networks charge customers a set subscription fee plus a variable amount corresponding to their consumption; radio companies took quite a while to find a suitable model before advertising revenues came to the fore; terrestrial television, in France at least, still draws on a mix of licence fees and advertising revenues, albeit with increasingly less of the former and more of the latter; and the promoters of the Minitel system settled on the highly original, practical and lucrative *kiosque* information service.

So far, neither mobile telephony nor the Internet has yet found the right business model. The Internet, for its part, has tried everything from direct and indirect advertising to the sale of hardware, software and value-added services and more. But users are loath to pay for something presented as free when their mere participation has market value. As long as this issue remains unresolved, the operators are going to continue holding back on the investment front – refraining from, among other things, the general introduction of costly yet, in some areas and on some routes, increasingly cost-effective 'last-mile' delivery. At some point, this state of affairs is bound to result in clear geographical differences, and the fact that less densely populated areas are the worst served definitely does seem to suggest that the digital divide is fundamentally a matter of geography.

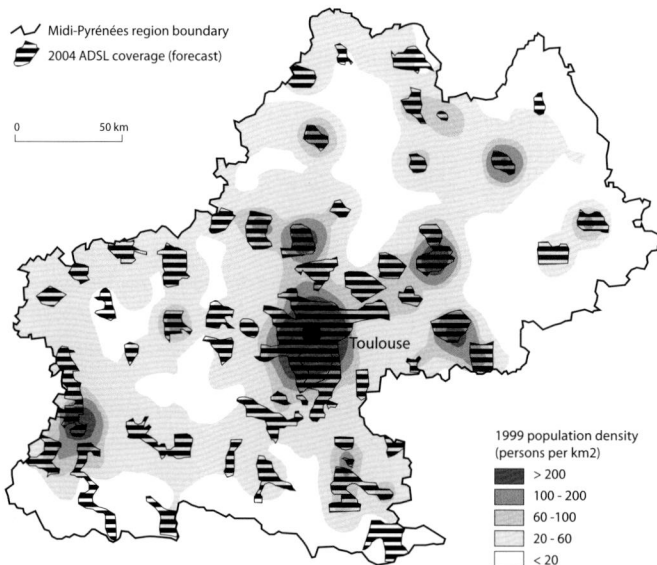

Illustration 16.1   Comparison of population distribution and Internet services in Midi-Pyrénées.
Source: Dupuy (2004); data sources: Cabinet JCA ON-X et Conseil Régional Midi-Pyrénées, 2003 (ADSL); ® INSEE 2003 (population density)

A quick solution to the problem seems unlikely. Developing value-added services is a long and costly process for the operators. Periods of intense competition are followed by a tendency to consolidate, meaning that the business model is certain to be oligopolistic or even monopolistic. The most likely outcome as far as ICTs are concerned is that they will follow the example of the huge airline companies that came to monopolize the market in the wake of competitive liberalization, leaving just a few niches for smaller, low-cost, companies. In which case, services may gradually be extended to sparsely populated and/or isolated areas, thus reducing the geographical dimensions of the digital divide at some geographic scales, at least. But this is obviously just one possible scenario for the future. For the time being, the operators' economic rationales, in spite of the various regulatory mechanisms in place, are therefore giving rise to geographical disparities liable to lead to a digital divide.

While it may well be true to say that less densely populated regions – density being the usual yardstick of differentiation, over and above the harder to identify rural/urban distinctions – are less well served than others, are they in actual fact receiving any less than might be expected in the light of their population density?

Fortunately, there are some answers to that key question. Internet service provision, for instance, is not consistent throughout the land. It is more limited in places inhabited by fewer people. But variations in Internet connectivity have been shown to follow strictly the same laws as variations in population density. At the global scale, spatial settlement patterns – in the countries of the North, at least – have been seen to adhere to a so-called 'fractal' law. In other words, the more one enlarges the space being studied, starting from a highly populated area in northern Europe, Japan or on the north-eastern seaboard of the United States, for instance, the sparser becomes the population in proportion to the surface area under consideration. This is no random decrease in density. It tallies with a well-established statistical law characterized by a stable parameter – the fractal dimension – that is independent of the area in question (see box 16.1). The fractal dimension for the population is 1.5, which is extremely close to that of the distribution of the nodes and key links of the Internet networks serving the various spaces and populations (Yook, Jeong & Barabási, 2002).

Box 16.1

What is a network's fractal dimension?

In geometry, a line is said to have a dimension of 1 and a surface a dimension of 2. The mathematician Benoît Mandelbrot has taken this further in suggesting that some flat figures could have a fractal dimension of between 1 and 2. Such is the case of extensively branching networks whose branches are reproduced in the exact same shape yet at different scales.

A network's fractal dimension can illustrate how well it 'covers' or 'serves' a particular geographical space. If the dimension is close to 2 it covers almost the entire surface area. If the dimension is closer to 1 it only serves a selection of lines across that area.

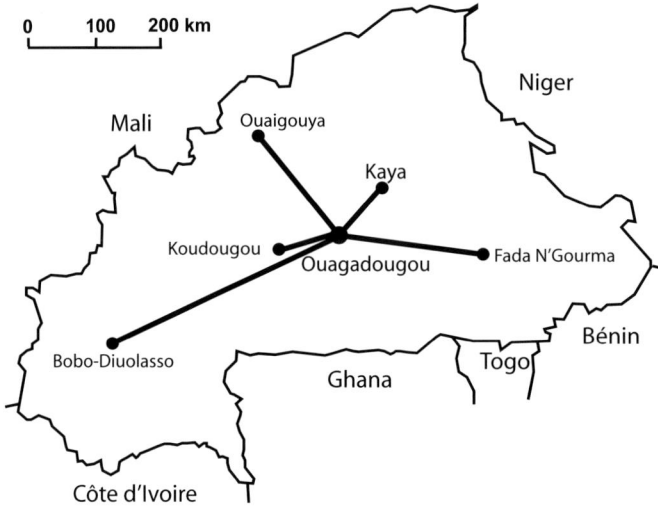

Illustration 16.2   Topological structure of backbone networks in Burkina Faso. Source: Bernard (2003)

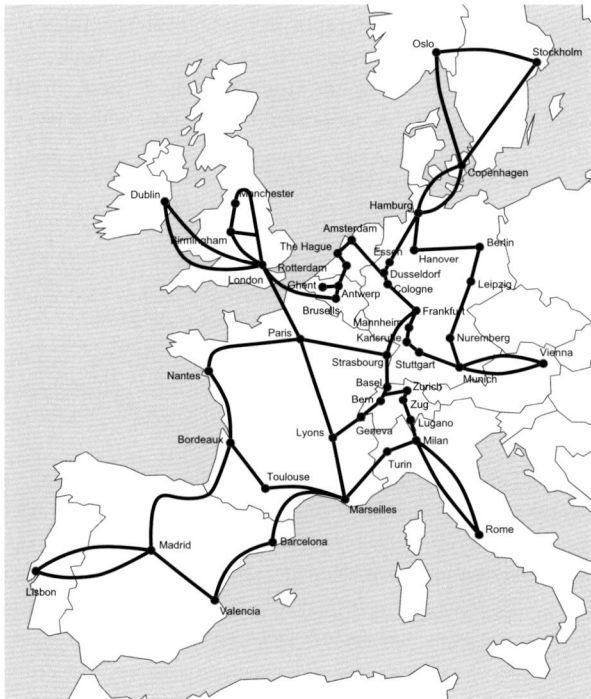

Illustration 16.3   Topological structure of backbone networks in Europe. COLT EuroLAN network (2005). Source: after http://www.colt.net/fr/fr

Urban Networks – Network Urbanism

Applying this rule to the Midi-Pyrénées region of France, which many officials regard as receiving limited coverage and blighted by a digital divide of a distinctly geographical nature, the Toulouse urban area is clearly far better served by the main Internet routes than the 'digital deserts' of Aveyron and Gers (Dupuy, 2004). But the fact is that the difference in service provision merely reflects the size of the population drawn to Toulouse and a few other districts in the region. As at the global scale, the fractal dimension for the distribution of the Midi-Pyrénées population was 1.36 in 2003, with an almost identical 1.44 for Internet coverage by the major providers (see illustration 16.1), meaning that Midi-Pyrénées was not suffering from a digital divide of a primarily geographical nature. On the contrary, the region even enjoyed slightly better services than its population distribution might have led one to expect.

So the digital divide cannot as a rule be regarded as a matter first and foremost of geography. ICTs have helped overcome some geographic obstacles, especially that of distance, but they have not been the answer to the dreams of those that wanted to see them totally eliminate space. Indeed, space still figures as a factor in the rationales of present-day operators setting their sights on short-term economic gains.

Illustration 16.2 shows a radial network in Burkina Faso where the primary concern was to save as much as possible on infrastructure costs, resulting in a highly vulnerable network part of whose territory will be completely deprived of Internet services in the event of a cut link. The COLT corporate telecommunications EuroLAN network in Europe, on the other hand (illustration 16.3), consists of a series of connected rings with an alternative traffic path for each link ensuring against such eventualities. This kind of network is highly reliable and, of course, very expensive to build.

Both in the North and the South, then, Internet and mobile telephony networks, as seen in the illustrations, adhere quite closely to human settlement patterns regardless of any geographical barriers to territorial service provision. Even in the South, where there is a *bona fide*, full-fledged digital divide, that divide is not just of a geographical but also of a socio-economic nature. In spite of the geographical barriers on territorial service provision, however, the Internet and mobile telephony networks adhere quite closely to human settlement patterns, except in the countries of the South where there really is a digital divide of both a geographic and socio-economic nature (see illustration 16.2).

Notes

Note 1   SIPPEREC: *Syndicat Intercommunal de la Périphérie de Paris pour l'Electricité et les Réseaux de Communication*. This is an intermunicipal authority coordinating electricity and telecommunication services in the Ile-de-France region.

Note 2   SAT3/WASC/SAFE: South Atlantic 3/West Africa Submarine Cable/South Africa-Far East.

17   Around Ile-de-France: In the Grips of a Digital Divide or Merely Lagging? *

The growth of any network – be it in the fields of transport, power supply or ICTs – is spatially inconsistent: somewhere along the line, some areas and places are always going to be better equipped than others. But there are two ways in which the ICTs in particular are in a league of their own.

On the one hand, the pace of innovation and its corollary, obsolescence, is much faster: the commercial Internet in France has been up and running for barely a decade; and even though mobile telephony is still more recent, third generation (3G) cellphones are already set to make second generation (2G) phones a thing of the past. On the other hand, ICT network deployment occurs across a vast geographic scale, with international infrastructures providing for (very) long-distance communications. It is therefore quite hard to determine how well equipped a geographic unit is exactly in ICTs because some of them belong to a far larger scale (Dupuy, 2002; Dupuy, 2004). Google, for instance, provides its much appreciated services to Internet users in the Loir-et-Cher department, but it would be a waste of time trying to spot traces of the global scale to which it owes its qualities as a search engine in the cantons of Mondoubleau or Romorantin.

Hence, ICT service supply must be studied over a long enough period to smooth out the effects of technological innovation, and over vast enough areas to avoid any strictly localized effects. Surveys carried out on these issues in various countries around the globe have come up with broadly similar findings. The indicators may differ depending on whether the focus is on hardware (computers, telephones, and so on), Internet connectivity or the number of websites, but researchers all recognize that the same processes are at work. ICT development begins in the rich-country megalopolises before gradually spreading out, according to the usual laws of geography, in line with the human settlement systems and the urban hierarchy. At any given moment, large, economically powerful, urban areas enjoy high standards of service supply while remote rural or mountainous areas with low population densities and sparse economic activities will remain 'digital deserts'.

A number of French metaphors spring to mind when considering the likelihood of a digital, among others, divide in France: *Paris et le désert français* or 'Paris and the French desert' (Gravier, 1947), a phrase illustrating the huge inequalities separating the capital from the rest of the country; *la diagonale du vide* or 'the barren oblique', a sparsely populated, economically weak stretch of land extending more or less diagonally from the north-east to the south-west of the country; *la France profonde* or 'deepest France" reflecting the profoundly French cultural identity of towns and villages.

This Chapter sets out to show that those images do not tally with the nature of the digital divide in France from the geographical point of view, and seeks to find out why.

---

*   Previously published as « Autour de l'Île-de-France: Fossé ou Fracture Numérique? ». In: Dupuy G. & I. Géneau de Lamarlière (eds), 2007, *Nouvelles Échelles des Firmes et des Réseaux. Un Défi pour l'Aménagement*. Paris : L'Harmattan, pp. 131-150. Included with permission.

Drawing on measures taken at the European level within the framework of the European Spatial Planning Observatory Network (ESPON), it will show how France is characterized by levels of ICT development that are acceptable in the Ile-de-France region. Yet it is clearly below par in its surrounding regions – the so-called *circumfrancilian* belt (CFB) – whereas even very rural areas further from Paris have demonstrated a great deal of drive and vitality in this field. Why is it that the CFB regions are lagging behind? After highlighting the conventional variables affecting ICT diffusion, and how they have put those regions at a disadvantage, the Chapter goes on to show why the action taken so far has failed to close the gap, concluding with a look at how the situation is affecting national and regional development, and a round-up of best practices.

The ESPON report

In 2003, a consortium of research consultants delivered its report on a survey commissioned by the European ESPON project on telecommunications services and networks (CURDS, 2004). Despite not extending to medical, educational and e-government applications, its comments and conclusions remain the most wide-ranging to date. Any pan-European assessment of ICT supply and demand relies on coherent data for each and every country forming the focus of attention – in this case the 27 Member States of the European Union. This one used statistics published by the International Telecommunications Union (ITU, 2002), and a 2004 report by the INRA market research agency (INRA, 2004). Both sets of data are somewhat outdated now, the latter having probably been based on older data, meaning that they no longer reflect the true situation in regard to mobile telephony or even fixed-line telephony – given the recent trends vis-à-vis subscription cancellations. Nor do they attest to recent broadband penetration in France. Nevertheless, the survey can still be credited with having produced comparative analysis of the NUTS 2 regions of all 27 EU Member States by means of an 'overall typology of combined household and business telecommunications development' comprising the following six indicators, with the figures in brackets indicating their weightings: fixed telephony (1), mobile telephony (2), Internet access (3), broadband Internet access (4), fibre backbone access (1), proportion of firms with their own websites (1). The regions were sorted into categories ranging from 'highly advanced' to 'highly lagging', and the picture conveyed in the corresponding maps is much as expected: a vast tract of highly-to-moderately advanced regions stretching north-south from the Nordic states and the British Isles down through Germany and the Benelux countries to much of Italy; the western 'peninsula' of France, Spain and Portugal lagging, on average, quite some way behind; and the block of eastern European states, not least the newcomers to the EU, mostly bringing up the rear (see illustration 17.1).

Although the overall picture at the European level is relatively unsurprising, the same cannot be said for France. Only Ile-de-France has managed to haul itself up to 'moderately advanced' level, which still leaves it lagging well behind the 'highly advanced' regions of south-east England, northern Germany and Denmark; the CFB – together with Auvergne and Basse-Normandie – are classed as 'lagging', on a par with parts of Poland or the Czech Republic; and the rest of France falls into the 'moderate' category.

The situation presented in illustration 17.2 is confirmed by the table in illustration 17.3, which was compiled by using the ESPON indicator to divide all the French regions save Ile-de-France and Corsica into two levels of ICT uptake, and then applying another indicator to show their proximity to Ile-de-France: regions bordering on Ile-de-France (1); regions reached directly from Ile-de-France via a single

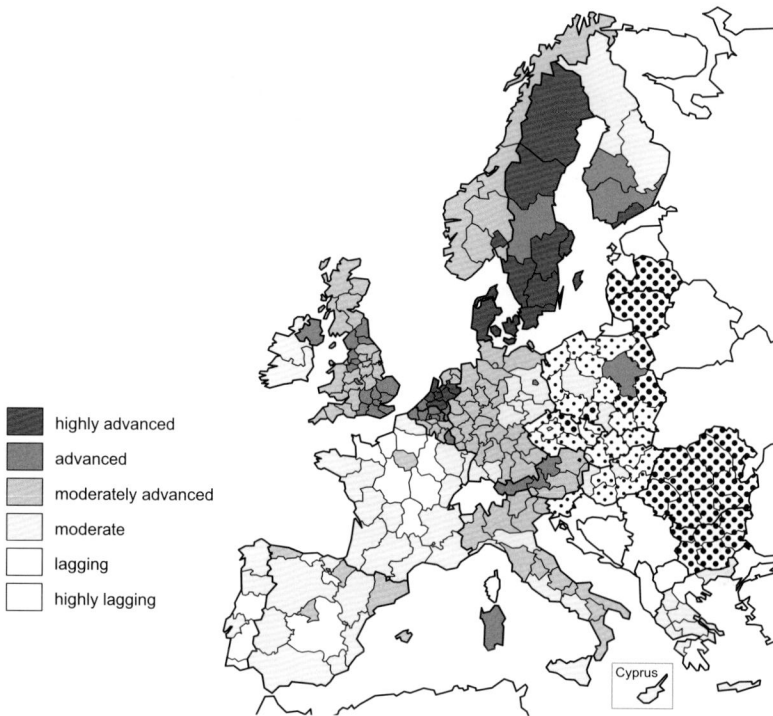

Illustration 17.1 **Telecommunications development: infrastructure and services in Europe.**
Source: CURDS (2004)

Legend:
- highly advanced
- advanced
- moderately advanced
- moderate
- lagging
- highly lagging

Cyprus

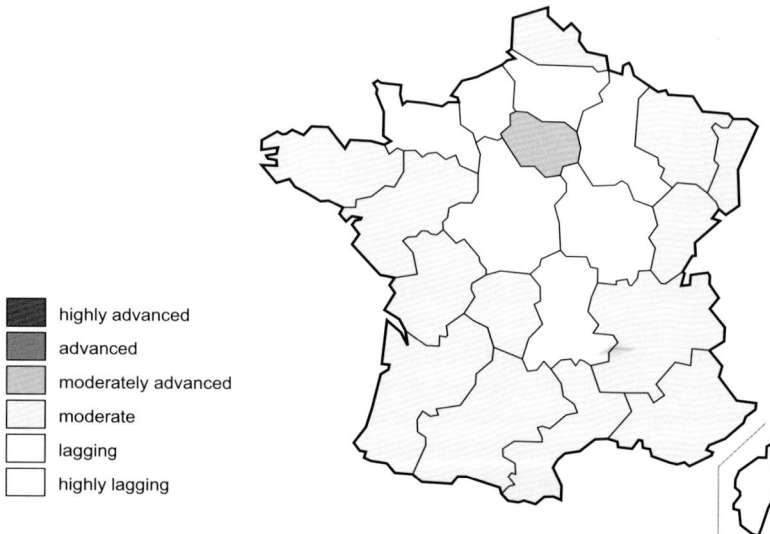

Illustration 17.2 **Telecommunications development: infrastructure and services in France.**
Source: CURDS (2004)

Legend:
- highly advanced
- advanced
- moderately advanced
- moderate
- lagging
- highly lagging

Distance from Ile-de-France	Positive ICT uptake	Negative ICT uptake
1		Bourgogne Centre Champagne-Ardennes Haute-Normandie Picardie
2	Franche-Comté Limousin Lorraine Nord-Pas-de-Calais Pays de la Loire Poitou Rhône-Alpes	Auvergne Basse-Normandie
3	Alsace Aquitaine Bretagne Languedoc-Roussillon Midi-Pyrénées Provence-Alpes-Côte d'Azur	

Illustration 17.3   ICT uptake versus distance from Ile-de-France. Source: based on CURDS (2004)

other region (2); and regions reached directly from Ile-de-France via two other regions (3). Clearly, the greater the distance from Ile-de-France the more digitally advantaged the region. Not one of those in the outer band figures in the negative ICT uptake column, while none of its immediate neighbours figure in the positive column.

It is as if the relatively ICT-rich Ile-de-France is preventing innovation from diffusing beyond its borders, thus encircling itself with a vast digital moat. Only the regions far on the other side of that moat enjoy satisfactory levels of ICT development.

Why are the CSB regions lagging behind?

According to the now abundant amount of literature on the subject, ICT development clearly begins in areas that are densely populated and economically vibrant, with the main activities revolving around the upper echelons of the service sector – finance, science, publishing, audiovisual production, and so on – and the key factors underpinning that development include levels of education and even age (Downes & Greenstein, 1999; Hargittai, 1999; Moss & Townsend, 2000; Zook, 2000; Malecki, 2002; Grubesic & O'Kelly, 2002; Duféal & Grasland, 2003; Jacquin, 2003; Duféal, 2004a; Grubesic, 2004). Yet analysis of the dynamics of ICT networks show that they have a natural tendency to expand: the operators are always seeking to increase their market share and subscriber base; innovation diffuses; and the diffusion is fuelled by economies of scale and the 'club effect'. Even less wealthy areas with smaller and less youthful or well-educated populations will therefore gradually end up being provided with services and becoming involved in the use of the new technologies. So what is happening in the regions around the outskirts of Ile-de-France?

A set of simple yet sound indicators helps reveal the impediments affecting those regions from the point of view of the factors conducive to ICT development (Cordellier & Lau, 2004).

Population age, sometimes regarded as a major barrier to innovation diffusion, seems to have had little impact here: the over 60s accounting for between 18.3 and 24 percent of the CFB population, depending on the region, compared to a national average of 20.6 percent. Population density, on the other hand, is between six and seventeen times lower than in Ile-de-France, with just 57.3 to 69 percent of people inhabiting urban areas according to the 1999 census versus a national average of 75.5 percent. The employment market in all five CFB regions is characterized by a persistently high proportion of farm and labouring jobs (DATAR, 2002). Otherwise, their relatively scarce economic activities – representing just four percent of the overall national value added – are found in the service sector, whose contribution to the GDP of France stands at between 60.8 and 68 percent, compared to a national average of 73 percent (Cordellier & Lau, 2004). Finally, educational standards are lower, with between 12.6 and 14 percent of boys and between 12.5 and 13.7 percent of girls managing to pass their baccalaureate and to advance beyond the first two years of higher education, versus a national average of 18.4 and 17.3 percent respectively.

Some might say that the national averages are 'bumped up' by the figures from the highly urban, highly educated and service sector-oriented Ile-de-France, and that it would be better to compare the CFB regions with the rest of the country, not including Ile-de-France. There are two ways to respond to that particular argument.

For a start, they are also lagging behind most other French regions based on the same criteria: their urban populations, for instance, are smaller than those of Midi-Pyrénées and Aquitaine, and larger than none but a handful of mainly rural regions such as Poitou-Charentes or Basse-Normandie; their service-sector contribution to GDP is outstripped by Midi-Pyrénées, Aquitaine and even Poitou-Charentes; and education in all five CFB regions figures right at the bottom of the national charts, even lower than Nord-Pas-de-Calais – for the number of boys in upper secondary education, at least – and Auvergne, for the number of girls.

Secondly, even if the demographic and economic superiority of Ile-de-France does 'bump up' the national averages, one might reasonably expect its neighbouring regions to be benefiting from their proximity to such a thriving hub and, hence, to be posting much closer figures in terms of indicator readings. Far from it. According to a CFB labour market survey, they "remain underqualified and underequipped in terms of IT activities" (Alvergne, Lazzeri & Planque, 1999). In actual fact, their proximity to Paris has even been described as one of the main reasons for their current state of ICT underdevelopment (Thiard, 2001). As it is not within the scope of this Chapter to delve into the historical reasons behind that underdevelopment, let us now move on to the present-day rationale of the ICT network operators, the lack of private-sector initiatives, and what the local authorities have done to step into the breach.

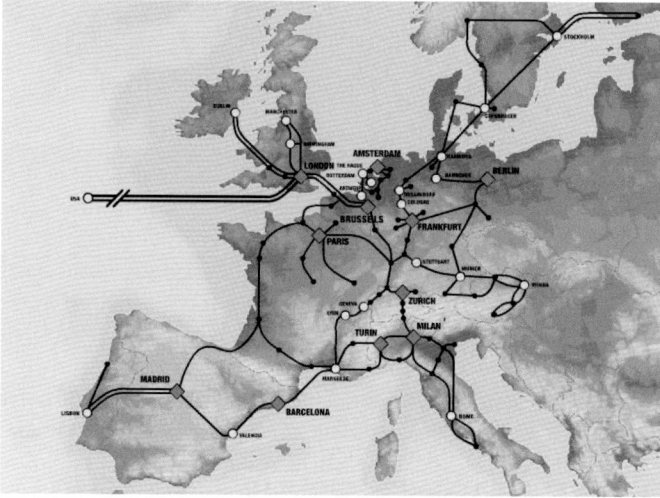

Illustration 17.4   **CFB regions 'overlooked' by the operators: the COLT EuroLAN network (2008).**
Source: http://www.colt.net

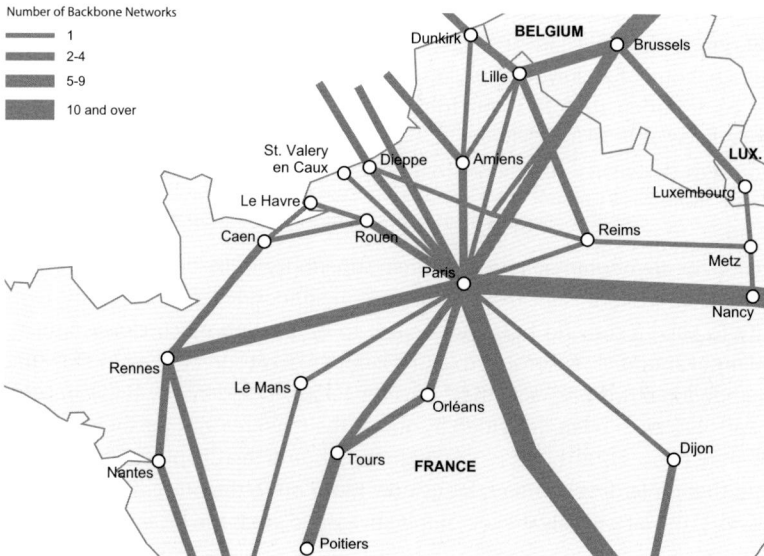

Illustration 17.5   **CFB regions neglected by the backbone networks.**
Source: Rutherford, Gillespie & Richardson (2004)

Urban Networks – Network Urbanism

Is the gap being bridged or continuing to widen?

The situation described above hardly makes the CFB regions an attractive proposition from the point of view of the telecoms operators. Strategy-wise, their interests are known to lie first and foremost in a combination of large urban populations and thriving service-sector activities. The fact that website hosting companies, for example, adhere to a simple set of ground rules stipulating that they set up shop exclusively in large cities and a few major 'corridors' means that the CFB naturally lose out to Ile-de-France, Nord-Pas-de-Calais, Lorraine, Alsace or Brittany (Jacquin, 2003). Amiens city council had to put up a really hard fight at the negotiating table to persuade the operators to incorporate local service provision into the lines designed to carry traffic between Paris and northern Europe. But while the Internet backbone networks have to pass through the CFB to reach Paris – a major European hub – rarely do they ever equip those regions with connecting nodes (CURDS, 2004). An especially telling example of how the CFB and other apparently unprofitable regions are left out in the cold can be seen in the route of the corporate telecommunications operator COLT's EuroLAN network, which links up the major European nodes but provides nothing in between (illustration 17.4).

Every backbone network of the operators using the Parisian hub clearly tends to cut across the outer fringes of the Paris Basin to reach the areas where the traffic is heaviest (illustration 17.5).

As far as household service provision is concerned, let us take the example of broadband Internet access, one of the key ESPON indicators. According to Grubesic (2004) and Gómez Barroso and Pérez Martínez (2004), such access depends on a variety of criteria: geographic (density), demographic (urban centres) and socio-economic (GDP). This puts the CFB regions at a real disadvantage since none of the various ICT service providers are likely to be keen to invest in places scoring as poorly as they do vis-à-vis each of those criteria.

As for private-sector initiatives, illustration 17.6 shows how the proportion of CFB firms with their own websites in 2000 – an indicator that is highly indicative of ICT development – was, according to a conclusive survey based on the Yahoo! Directory, significantly smaller than that of firms not only in Ile-de-France but also in all 16 of the other regions of metropolitan France (Duféal, 2004b). The CFB economic fabric, perhaps on account of its constituent activities, seems to be struggling more than any other to gain a foothold on the World Wide Web. Given the lack of private-sector initiatives on the part of either the operators or local economic actors, one might reasonably expect local government to step into the breach.

	Websites (Yahoo! Directory, 2000)	Population (INSEE, 1999)	Number of sites per capita (10-5)
Ile-de-France	14,341	10,952,011	131
CFB	4,191	9,030,785	46
Other regions	27,088	38,535,952	70

Illustration 17.6   **Regional corporate website density in metropolitan France (December 2002).**
Source: Duféal (2004b)

The authorities do indeed appear to regard ICTs as a matter of prime importance, warranting efforts to mobilize the private sector or civil society when possible, or even to substitute market forces with public action (Cohendet & Stojak, 2005). It is not as if they have been idle in the regions concerned: alternative infrastructure projects have been carried out in Haute-Normandie, for instance (Frémont-Vanacore, 2004); telephone call centres have been set up in Orléans, Tours, Blois, Rouen, Amiens, Reims and Troyes, creating thousands of jobs in the process (Moriset & Bonnet, 2005); and the *Technopole de l'Aube* science and technology park has been opened at Troyes University of Technology. In the light of the ICT development indicators, however, those efforts do not appear to have produced the expected outcomes. On the one hand, they are often far too recent to have had time to bear fruit. Frémont-Vanacore (2004) observes that although the Technopole de l'Aube project was first launched as long ago as 1994, nothing much happened in Haute-Normandie before 2002-2003. On the other hand, a more realistic view must be taken of the impact of some of the initiatives. Moriset and Bonnet (2005) draw attention to the fact that the call centre jobs created in the CFB regions are far less numerous not only than in Ile-de-France – 2,000 operator's posts created in Tours, for instance, versus 46,000 in the Paris urban area – but also in the provincial urban centres of Lille, Bordeaux or Lyons. In addition to which, this is an opportunistic, hence 'fickle', line of business: a call centre can easily pack up and relocate to places offering greater opportunities in workforce recruitment.

Furthermore, local government policies in the CFB regions seem incapable of meeting the challenges in this or indeed any other field. Frémont-Vanacore (2004) provides a highly enlightening comparison between Haute-Normandie and Basse-Normandie: when the latter – which is located far from Paris and close to Brittany, a region showing a great deal of vitality in ICTs – found itself facing the threat of serious economic decline, it wasted no time in implementing strong and effective policies to address the issue; whereas the authorities in Haute-Normandie, because of the region's proximity to Paris and its rich industrial and commercial traditions, saw no need for any particular policy-making and have therefore been very slow to take action (Frémont-Vanacore, 2004).

The fact is that over the period 1975-1990 the metropolitan area of Paris seemed to become 'increasingly disconnected from the rest of the Parisian Basin' (Alvergne, Lazzeri & Planque, 1999), and studies of regional policy-making since the 1960s show the CFB regions to have been "more concerned about managing their own internal equilibria than about positioning themselves to combat the competitive forces of other French or European regions" (Thiard, 2001). This tallies with the conventional view that most of the regional boundary changes mapped out in post-war France created rather unconvincing territories.

More than half a century later, there is a strongly felt sense of territorial inconsistency around the outskirts of Ile-de-France. Champagne-Ardennes and, moreover, Centre are still lacking in unity; Haute-Normandie and Basse-Normandie remain divided, in spite of measures to combine them; and Picardy is torn between a share of Oise – now a satellite of Paris – the regional capital, Amiens, and the deeply troubled department of Aisne. Even in 1994, CFB regional capitals were still "struggling to govern largely artificial spaces that do not square with their historical spheres of influence" (Lieutaud, 1994). This is in stark contrast to other such regions as Midi-Pyrénées, Franche-Comté or Rhône-Alpes, which really do appear to have acquired a shared sense of destiny.

A challenge for national and regional development

Anyone seeking to root out the reasons why the CFB is lagging will soon see that they are plainly structural in nature: the decline in farm labour, a dwindling population, a manufacturing base hammered by de-industrialization, weak urban networks and so on. According to a joint report by the Ile-de-France regional government and the state national development commission (DATAR), "the Paris Basin, not including Ile-de-France, remains a social and economic problem area. Internal disparities are on the increase. None but a handful of the larger towns and cities are dynamic enough to evolve into metropolitan areas capable of underpinning and ensuring balanced development. The lack of adequate opportunities in higher education and research looks set to continue and to grow still worse" (DATAR/Préfecture de l'Ile-de-France, 1999).

Under these conditions, it is doubtful whether national and regional development policies will manage to rectify structural drawbacks that could not be put right in more favourable times; and whether ICT development can, in one fell swoop, miraculously offset the lack of jobs, the shortcomings in education, and so on. A more reasonable policy goal would be to concentrate on preventing the lag from developing into a full-blown digital divide, so as to secure the CFB regions' chances of development on both a national and a European scale.

As for the actors best placed to achieve that goal, the local and regional authorities in the CFB and Ile-de-France – together of course with the state – can play a leading role in the relevant ICT-related policy-making. The CFB authorities, as seen earlier, have been slow to recognize the problems and their initial actions were rather disorganized. Some broad policy lines now seem to be emerging in this field. But given that the policies themselves remain somewhat uncoordinated they are unlikely to prevent the entrenchment of a digital divide or to stave off any possibility of the CFB regions being 'left out' of the European ICT landscape.

Meanwhile, the authorities in Ile-de-France too have problems of their own to deal with as regards consistency and uniformity, with Paris and the department of Hauts-de-Seine putting the rest of the region in the shade (DATAR, 1999). Paris alone has 18 percent of French websites for just 3.5 percent of the country's population, while the Paris urban area has 30 percent of French sites for 15 percent of the population (Duféal, 2004b).

What about the role of the state? In 1992, an official report on the telecommunications networks in the Paris Basin asserted that "France is fortune enough to have a relatively modern and homogeneous network. Its few weaknesses concern the Paris urban area and are due to congestion, and it is Parisian businesses that are suffering as a result – from connection delays, disruptions and problems in accessing wireless telephony networks. In the long run, these disparities will be ironed out. But for the new services – e.g. high-speed fibre-optic ISDN or GSM – specific conditions and timescales will be introduced for large companies, SMEs and domestic subscribers respectively, and will vary according to the economies of scope that the urban areas may or may not be able to offer depending on their density and market potential. (…) So deploying and ensuring access to fibre-optic broadband networks throughout the Paris Basin represents a tool for regional development" (DATAR, 1992).

In the early 1990s, the government was therefore quite proactive and optimistic. Standardized service provision had been extended throughout the entire country, and the sole operator – France Telecom – was entrusted with the task of keeping it that way, no matter what.

Just a few years later, however, the government had to come to terms with deregulation. The withdrawal of state support led to the collapse of public teleport projects in Ile-de-France (Rutherford, 2004), but the impact has been far greater on other regions, not least in the CFB. The recent introduction of ADSL and broadband, including in the CFB regions, must not be mistaken for a renewed commitment to national and regional development on the part of the government, or a concerted effort to bring about a dramatic reversal in the situation. It has been due largely to the quality of the existing networks of France Telecom and the urban cable operators (see illustration 17.7), and the fact that they have been relatively easy to upgrade. Even so, the demand for their new broadband services can hardly be described as overwhelming.

Hence, public actors at both national and local government levels now appear fully capable of handling national and regional development policy in the traditional sense of the term. But in the present-day climate of decentralization, and in the light of the upheavals caused by the extraordinary scale at which the deregulated networks are operating (Dupuy, 2004), it may well be time to consider new forms of national and regional development.

Best practices for staving off the digital divide

While a digital lag refers simply to a temporary disparity in ICT equipment and access, a digital divide is the end product of a cumulative vicious circle in which the ICTs play a key part. In a nutshell, when a particular area is having trouble accessing ICTs on account of a particular set of characteristic features, it will serve to strengthen those features and make the access even harder to gain, and so on. Low

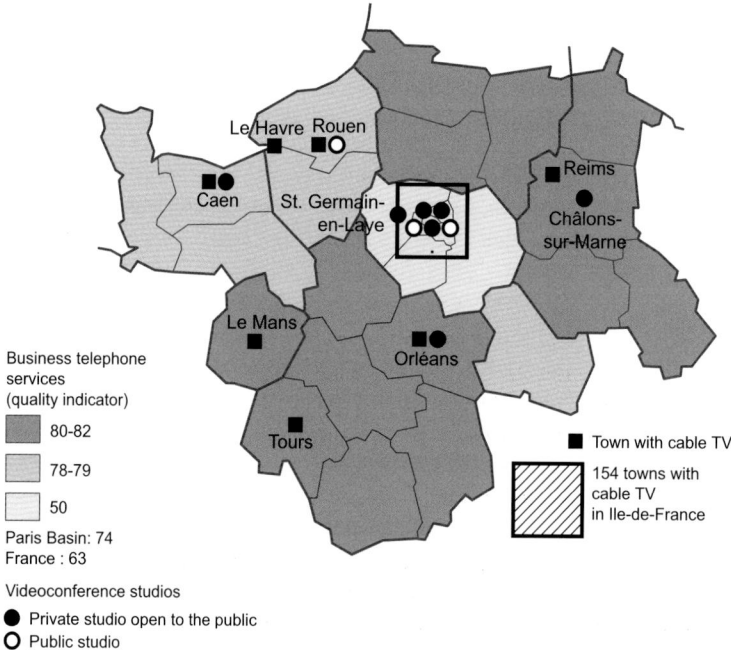

Illustration 17.7   **Telecommunications supply in the Paris Basin before deregulation (1992).**
Source: DATAR (1992)

Urban Networks – Network Urbanism

population density and activity rates, for example, constitute a definite impediment to service provision by telecommunications networks. The resulting paucity of services may be described as regrettable evidence of a digital divide, but there is still a chance that the situation will eventually improve as a result of falling prices or technological progress. If, however, the lack of ICTs were to drive people and businesses out of the area, it would bolster the barrier to service provision, which would in turn increase the exodus and so on and so forth until there really was a full-blown digital divide.

Let us apply this to the realm of university research. Standards in CFB regions as far as postgraduate studies are concerned are low. Given that this probably helps account for their low level of ICT development, the university research system is a very important issue. With the ICTs playing an ever-more prevalent role in that system, if CFB universities, technical schools and colleges succumb to ICT underdevelopment, more and more students are going to desert the regions for Ile-de-France and Paris, thus further undermining the CFB higher education system, leading to an increasing shortage of training opportunities, a decreasing likelihood of ICT uptake, and so on and so forth. It is worrying to note that the business, service, tourism and other sectors in the CFB are probably in the grips of similar such cumulative processes indicative of a digital divide. Fortunately, however, they have been held in check in the academic research system by the national telecommunications network for technology, education and research (RENATER) (see illustration 17.8). The French government set up RENATER in 1993 as a public interest group of bodies working in the fields not just of technology, education and research but also of culture – research institutes, universities and *grandes écoles*, together with the respective ministries in charge – the aim being to enable those bodies to communicate with each other and with counterpart organizations around the globe via the World Wide Web.

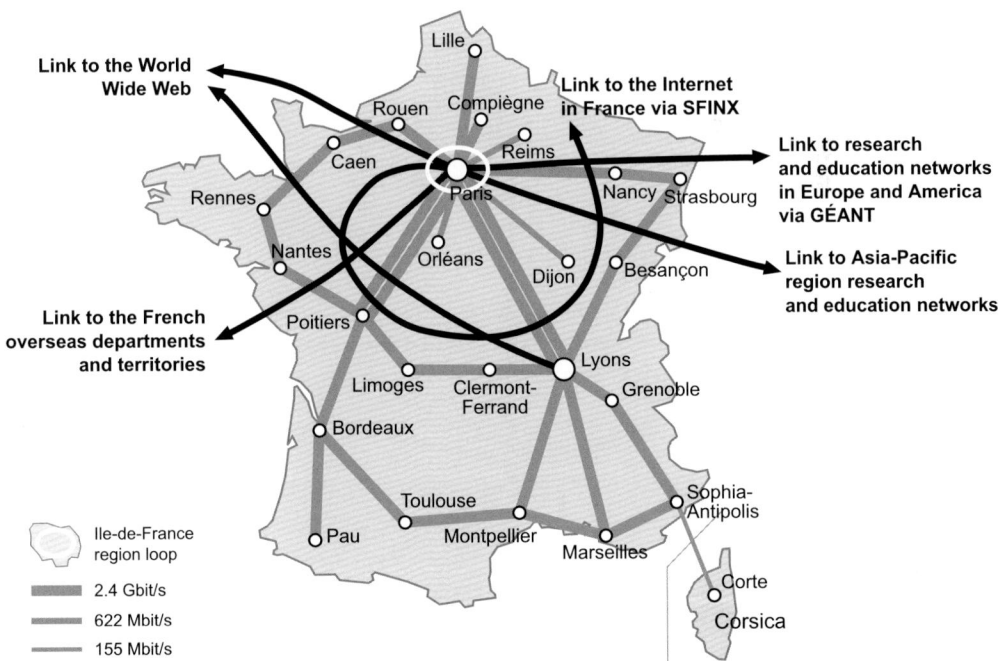

Illustration 17.8   **The RENATER network (2005).** Source: www.renater.fr

For over a decade, RENATER has actively helped improve national and regional development, not least in the CFB regions, producing in the process a set of best practices that can be of enormous assistance to present-day policy-makers in the fields of physical planning and ICT development. RENATER has enabled the government to provide almost unlimited connection capacity and to build on its commitment to ensure service provision for every region in France. From the outset, the network's architecture – which broadly resembles that of any other French backbone, with Parisian hub and strong links between Paris and other large cities – took in four of the five CFB regions, and was extended to Burgundy in 2005 (see illustration 17.9 and 17.10).

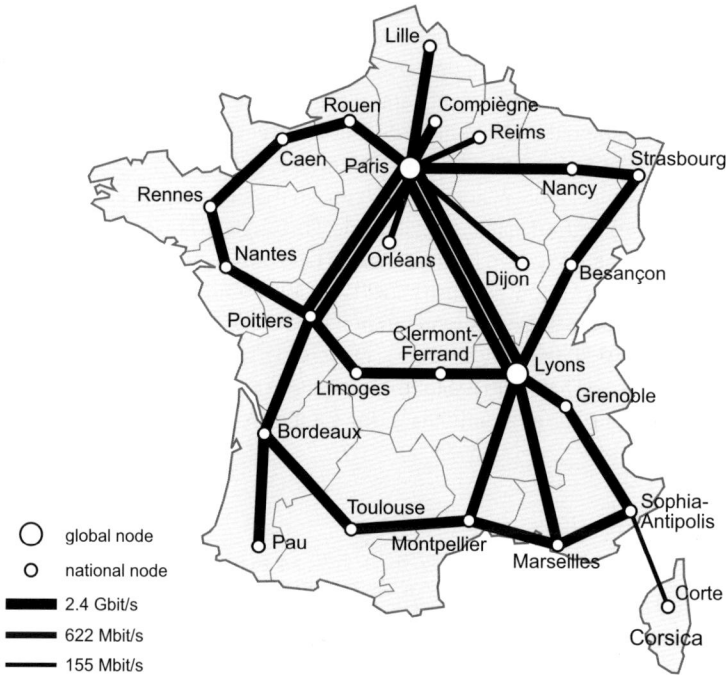

Illustration 17.9 **RENATER 3 network (2005).** Source: www.renater.fr

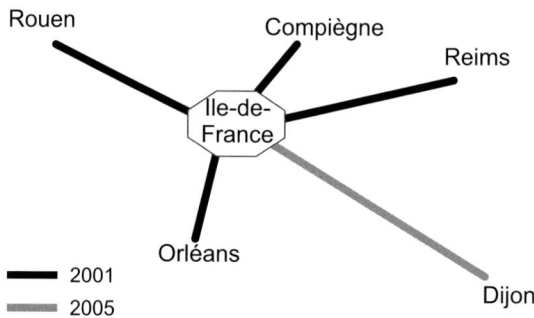

Illustration 17.10 **CFB regions incorporated into the RENATER network (2005).** Source: www.renater.fr

Urban Networks – Network Urbanism

As a matter of fact, the original interregional contract between the state and the Paris Basin regions had already provided for Picardy and Champagne-Ardennes to be linked up to RENATER as long ago as in the period 1994-1998. It was then left to the local authorities to relay the services, using their own means, to the research and education establishments in their region. So the regions were expected to extend the services not only to the large urban areas that were ready to take up the baton, but also across the entire regional fabric – which is what happened very early on with the RRP Picardie regional network, and then later with the Haute-Normandie network system (SYRHANO). So the combined action of the state and the CFB regional authorities in the fields of technology, education and research has prevented the lag from evolving into a digital divide.

Conclusion

The further back one steps, and the larger the geographic scale, the clearer become the rationales for – and the territorial impacts of – network deployment. On a European scale, one can see why those rationales have created what could broadly – and deservedly, perhaps – be described as a digital divide between Ile-de-France and the underserved regions of its surrounding 'ICT exclusion zone'. In short, the CSB regions have suffered because of the 'tunnel vision' of operators deploying their networks with their sights set on hub connections and on serving wealthy, densely populated, areas. Crippled by their socio-economic past and their dependence on the capital, they have been sidelined. Meanwhile, regional development has continued, at varying scales, in line with the rationales of the newly decentralized local authorities, which lack the capacity to redress the digital lag on their own. Interconnectivity between cities, regions, the nation and Europe means there is still a chance of the issue being addressed through coordinated development action. Going by the evidence so far, however, it is pretty slim. Development scales are being enlarged – to pan-European level – but the policies remain compartmentalized and territory-specific.

So RENATER and its unique way of managing ICT networks come across as a 'best practice', with the state concentrating fully and exclusively on its role in preventing the lag from evolving into a digital divide, in the RENATER fields of competence, at least. Some regions definitely would have appeared in a less negative light in the ESPON report had ICT use been mainstreamed into technological innovation, education and research. The fact is, however, that this is one particular field where the state still manages to preserve its prerogatives. What are the chances of RENATER best practices, and their positive impact on regional development, being extended to other fields? It is hard to tell in the prevailing climate of decentralization and economic competition. But there is one field likely to lend itself well to such best practices or policies, and that is e-government. France is commonly singled out as a 'lagger' with respect to e-government, meaning that it theoretically has much room for manoeuvre. The longer it continues to lag, however, the greater the danger of CSB and other borderline regions being subjected to a worsening digital divide. Ideally, work should begin without further ado to capitalize on RENATER-inspired best practices as enablers of progress in CFB regional e-government.

Part V

New Tools for Planners

"What principles guided the expansion of the railroad network? Some decision rules were concocted, and it was found that network expansion could be modelled quite well. The key decision rule was a simple one, the next intercity rail link to be added goes to the nearest large place not yet served. Some additional but not very important rules bore on the measure of 'nearest large place' and the filling in of links between nodes already served but not directly linked.

That was an interesting study, as was a study done some years later of the waste water collection network of Allegheny County, Pennsylvania, where decision rules appeared to mirror the political need for a network focused on a single large water treatment plant."

From: Networks: Reminiscence and Lessons *by William Garrison; in* Flux, N° 1, Spring 1990

18   Networks and Urban Planning: Evolution of a Two-Way Relationship*

The early networks: discreet beginnings

The first of a series of technical systems designed to supply urban populations with the services, that are now regarded as the basic necessities of city life emerged in the mid-19th century. These systems included running water, sanitation, power, transport, and communications. In view of their spatial organization – meshed or branching cables, conduits and so on – they came to be known as 'networks'.

The new networks emerging in the mid-1800s often stemmed from technological breakthroughs of the Industrial Revolution, for example, using compressed air technology to create a supply of motive power, or gas for public lighting (*gaz de ville*, or 'city gas'). Subsequent breakthroughs have continued to spawn a succession of networks, of which, perhaps the most outstanding example in recent times is the Internet, which developed from the telephone. This spawning process that has been gradual, and at times extremely slow, is extending across the entire urban area. For instance, it was more than a century before every building in Paris was connected to the main sewers.

Many of the early networks appeared in the days when urban planning was beginning to establish itself as a doctrine and a professional practice; and for quite some time, urban planners failed to recognise the importance of their role. Indeed, all but a handful of visionary pioneers (e.g. Ildefonso Cerdà) consigned those networks to a lower order of logistics. The technicians who worked on them were considered to be there strictly to ensure that the networks were properly maintained, and not to meddle in the more noble business of planning or policy-making. To be fair to the mainstream urban planners of the day, it must be said that those early networks were really rather discreet. Their construction caused barely a ripple in the urban fabric. Conduits and cables were slipped discreetly into its unoccupied chinks and crevices – on, or often beneath, the public highway – and, equally discreetly, fed into buildings and homes, without significantly altering the architecture or urban shape.

Take the garage, for instance: with the advent of motorized vehicles in the early 20th century, this became a terminal of the road system. Previously, people usually went out and returned home on foot, or sometimes by horse or horse-drawn carriage. Having to park a car before entering a building marked a dramatic departure from earlier practices. Le Corbusier was one of the first architects in Europe to grapple with the ramifications of the automobile revolution. His Villa Savoye, built in Poissy near Paris in the 1930s, was designed with the motor car in mind: it had a driveway so that passengers could be dropped off at their front door, before driving the vehicle into a built-in garage. By and large, however, the main entrances of the vast majority of buildings continued for a long time to be designed strictly with pedestrians in mind. Architects seemed to want to banish the car to covert garages concealed

*   Previously published in Hulsbergen, E.D., I.T. Klaasen & I.Kriens (eds), 2005, *Shifting Sense in Spatial Planning.: Looking Back to the Future*. Series Design/Science/Planning,   Amsterdam: Techne Press, pp. 125-130. Included with permission.

at the bottom of a back garden or in a basement. The façades of Eugène Hénard's modern Parisian apartment buildings, designed at the turn of the 20th century, scarcely give a hint of a garage, even though the architect-planners, bent on reform, were very aware of the parking-space factor. Mathieu Flonneau, in his thesis on the history of the motor car in Paris, observes the many ways in which public spaces had to be adapted to cater for the ever-growing volume of automotive traffic (Flonneau, 2002). He also draws attention to the deference paid to the urban shape, which continued through to the 1960s and the presidency of Georges Pompidou.

While there may have been a great demand for efficient urban networks, in the modern sense, architect-planners were 'put in their place' and made to feel that they could not encroach upon the built environment and/or significantly alter the aesthetics, structure or shape of the city. At the time, these considerations were regarded as being far more important than being able to move around town at speed, or even having a home equipped with modern conveniences. For quite some time, then, urban planners could sit back and watch the new networks spread through the city without feeling any need to revise their approaches or ways of thinking.

New network urbanism

From the 1970s and 1980s onwards, the work of historians began to create an awareness of the true role of these new networks in the organization and functioning of cities (Tarr & Dupuy, 1988). Engineers started to describe how their techniques had developed over time, and how they were related to urban space. In fact, a host of historians addressed the network issue (see Tarr & Dupuy 1988): Thomas Hughes and Alain Beltran with respect to electricity (see also Beltran 1990); Letty Anderson and Jean-Pierre Goubert to water (see also Goubert 1986); Joel Tarr and André Guillerme to sanitation; Clay McShane and Dominique Larroque to transport; and Seymour Mandelbaum and Pascal Griset to communications, to name but a few American and French examples. All of them reveal the importance of these networks in the making of the modern city. Most of these writers contrast the unobtrusive way in which networks were physically incorporated into the built environment, with their considerable impact on urban life. This relatively recent observation has certainly prompted contemporary urban-planning practices to acknowledge the significance of networks and take their role into account. Examples of the ways in which the old networks have benefited from progress can be seen in the new tramlines or parking restriction policies in some cities, and the enhancement of public lighting or running water systems in others.

Despite this, the old networks are now being replaced or completely transformed by the new. Partial or total automation is improving efficiency, reducing operating costs and radically changing the relationship between operators and users, as, for example, in underground transport systems. The newly enriched range of Information and Communication Technologies (ICTs) is also providing urbanites with untold means of harnessing the potential of the city's physical space and of becoming integrated into its social space.

In the 1960s, the idea that progress in the realm of ICTs would do away with the need to travel to work every day, leaving people free to choose where to live or locate a business, gave rise to the concept of the 'electronic cottage'. Then, after the advent of the Internet, all the talk was about the 'cybercity'. Nowadays, attention has turned to the 'digital city' and the links between metropolization and the major nodes of global communication networks.

It is unrealistic, however, to say that the immediate and tangible effect of ICTs on a city will bring about its rapid transformation. True, the shopping malls of American cities may be losing some 2,000 travel agencies a year due to direct bookings over the Internet; but urban commerce as a whole continues to stand firm in the face of e-commerce. The numbers of teleworkers remain relatively small, and the structure of the 'digital city' is still one of bricks and concrete.

Let there be no mistake, though, ICTs are making a dramatic difference to the ways in which urban space is used. So we really do need to reappraise the relationship between cities and networks; root and branch. The changes are enormous.

A change of scale

The networks serving urban populations used to be called 'urban networks' or 'urban technical networks'. Those names meant something in the past, in the early days of DC (direct current) electricity networks, pressurized water supply, sewerage systems, gas, trams, metros and so on. Not only were their users urbanites but also, as they were technically self-contained, they were managed by the municipal authority. Their scale was resolutely urban. Since then, major changes have taken place in most sectors, but nowhere more markedly than in that of ICTs. Take the Internet, for example. The growth of the Internet hinged on the capillarity of the telephone network, which was first deployed in cities. But the Internet is a global, not an urban, network. Its main infrastructure, like many of its operators, is not urban but international. Internet operators do not decide to move into a particular region without considering the picture at the global level: they operate in other countries too; they have to comply with international technical standards; they are competing with other international operators; and they need access to global financial markets. Their capacity to supply broadband Internet services at a reasonable price, at local level, depends on global Internet-related trends. Events at the local level cannot deviate too far from those global trends without giving rise to a digital divide. This means that urban centres now have to keep up with global trends. At first, this requirement was confined to large global metropolitan areas, but, subsequently, this requirement has spread to smaller well-placed cities that now act as waypoints or gateways.

Geographical scale is not a recent problem. It was already an issue in the 19th century, with the railways, especially with regard to the siting of stations. The railways were a large-scale network and urban planners and policy-makers learnt to work with it. In France, they produced solutions such as the Paris metro, which was implemented in 1900, and then, some 60 years later, the RER high-speed city-suburban link. Nowadays, some interesting new solutions are being found for the problem of how to combine the urban with the national (or international) scale. The Karlsruhe Tram Train, for example, Milan's Passante or their equivalents in Brussels and Barcelona have effectively turned the metropolis from a terminal into a waypoint.

Technological progress

The pace of technological change is fast with ICTs, even more than with transportation or drinking water supply technologies. In the not so distant past, people were amazed at the speed of Internet penetration. Less than 10 years later, with the arrival of ADSL and broadband connections via an ordinary telephone line, the situation has changed again. Before long, it looks as though UMTS will make fixed-line Internet access obsolete.

The effect of these rapid technological changes has been great. In the past, ongoing network expansion, with the same technologies and standards for all, maintained the principle that, in the course of time, every citizen would gain access to the service. Right of access to the networks went hand in hand with the right of access to the city. Such considerations now seem almost meaningless. In France, the deregulation of the telecommunications sector led to the introduction of a universal, strictly fixed-line phone service (with the continuing provision of call boxes and directories) that just happened to coincide with the cell phone and Internet boom. The service instantly lost appeal. Everyone today expects broadband. Tomorrow, it will be UMTS.

This issue of the timing of technological developments has led to marked differences in service provision to different urban areas or population groups. Graham and Marvin (2001), albeit with some arguable generalizations, expose the undesirable effects on urban cohesion of premium networks – water, electricity, telecommunications, transport – that offer better services to those who can afford to pay. Some may persist in imagining or expecting cities eventually to enjoy a full and homogenous range of services, but the fact is, as far as networks are concerned, new technological developments and the socio-economic demand are giving rise to the 'two-track' city. Such differentiation is not a passing phase. Each successive new development opens up a new rift, often before the last can be bridged.

Deregulation versus planning

More importantly, ICTs are deployed in an amazingly competitive, free-market environment. The world of networks has changed greatly since the early 1980s; since the days when Judge Harold Greene ordered the dismantling of the monopoly of the American Telephone and Telegraph Company (AT&T). Rutherford (2004) shows how, in the case of Paris and London at least, the operators, old and new, and the political authorities are playing a difficult game in an ever-changing context where mistrust is the rule, for want of perfect competition. Notwithstanding the operators' penchant for discretion, there is no hiding how they act: hunting for niches, claiming territories, putting up passive resistance when the regulators step in. As for the political actors, they change regulations frequently to advance such legitimate issues as social cohesion and national and regional development, to run pilot projects and so on. In a period of transition, however, one cannot always be sure that the self-declared actors are actually up to the part that they claim they are meant to be playing.

In many cases, the institutional environment has changed, not only due to the deregulation of the telecommunications sector, but also for other reasons (such as decentralization in France, reunification in Germany, new administrative regime regulations in London, and so on). This affects the distribution of roles. To take another French example, the Institute for Urban Planning and Development for the Ile-de-France Region (IAURIF) was an active promoter of the Francilian[1] teleport project of the early 1990s. One would have been inclined to take the agency seriously, at the time, when its public statements hailed the teleport as a balanced means of coordinating regional telecommunications infrastructures. In fact, the project hinged on an agreement between the (then monopolistic) operator and the public authorities, and it was very soon eliminated by deregulation. Today, nobody talks about the Francilian teleport any more, and it is clear that IAURIF is not up to the job of regional telecommunications development planning.

There is nothing historically new about deregulation. The first railway and electricity companies were privately owned and in competition with each other. Nevertheless, the public authorities managed to work with that situation. In Paris, in the early days of electricity, planners mapped out geographical areas for which concessions – or partial monopolies – were awarded. Each operator was allotted a share of urban territory known as a 'sector'. Each sector's boundaries were determined by the public authority in such a way that they encompassed zones that contained a mixture of dense, animated and wealthy areas, and less dense or poorer ones. The hope was that it would be in the operator's interests to deploy its network across the entire sector and thereby ensure a degree of spatial equalization. But it later became common in Europe, and especially in France, to see the authorities assuming responsibility for both urban planning and the administration of networks run by public-sector monopolies. For a while, they managed to dovetail the two with relative ease. It was the golden age of network urbanism (Dupuy, 1991a & 2000).

Now, when the networks occupy a more recognized place in urban planning, everything is changing again: geographical scales are dilating to the edge of infinity; technology is developing at ever faster speeds; and, with the liberalization of the network utilities, monopolies are giving way to almost uncontrollable competition. Urban planning may be able to overhaul its practices and thinking enough to adapt to the first two changes (in scale and technology), but the third (network liberalization) has sent its paradigms reeling and destabilized its action. Can a new network-oriented form of urban planning take shape in this new context? History offers a wealth of encouraging examples. But first of all, European planners will need to abandon their nostalgia for the post-Second World War golden age, for urban planning that embraces public networks as a basic requirement. Tomorrow's network urbanism is bound to be very different from that of yesteryear.

Notes

Note 1   'Francilian' trefers to the Ile-de-France region as 'French' refers to France.

"Growth and preferential attachment should be sufficient to explain the scale-free topology discovered by the Faloutsos brothers. On the Internet things are a bit more complicated, however. While not the primary consideration, distance does matter. Undeniably, it is more expensive to lay down two miles of optical cable than half a mile. We must also take into consideration that nodes do not appear randomly across the map. Routers are added where there is a demand for them, and demand depends on the number of people wanting to use the Internet. Thus there is a strong correlation between population density and the density of the Internet nodes. The distribution of routers on the map of North America forms a fractal set, a self-similar mathematical object discovered in the 1970s by Benoit Mandelbrot. Therefore, when trying to model the Internet, we must simultaneously acknowledge the interplay of growth, preferential attachment, distance dependence, and an underlying fractal structure.

Each of these forces alone, if taken to the extreme, could destroy the scale-free topology. For example, if the length of the wire were the main consideration when deciding where to link, the resulting network would have an exponential degree distribution, developing a topology very similar to the highway system. But the amazing thing is that these coexisting mechanisms delicately balance each other, maintaining a scale-free Internet. This very balance of power is the Internet's own Achilles' heel."

From: Linked: The New Science of Networks *by Albert-Laszlo Barabási; Perseus, Cambridge, MA, 2002*

19 Progressive Network Urbanism: The Way Ahead for Urban and Physical Planners

Various developments over the past twenty years have given plenty of food for thought on the concept of network urbanism. This Chapter cannot embrace all of those connected with the many social, economic, ideological and other changes affecting the relationship between human beings and the spaces in which they live. So let us focus instead on three particular aspects that make it a must to reappraise the concept in order to extend its scope into a forward-looking approach:

-   The sudden emergence of ICTs among the networks involved in urban planning, not least the Internet and mobile telephony;

-   Urban forms and the debate on suburban and peri-urban development, with a particular emphasis on the utopian ideas associated with network urbanism;

-   The need to shift network urbanism from the realm of general debate to that of identifying the task-specific tools and techniques required for its implementation.

The methodological and scientific advances of the past few years are starting to bear fruit, and now it is time to build on them.

ICTs: routine networks

The phenomenal growth of the ICTs over the past few years has stirred the imagination of teachers, researchers and practitioners in the fields of urban and physical planning, and has even rekindled a propensity for utopian thinking of the kind prevalent among planners since the early days of Ildefonso Cerdà (1815-1876). The idea that ICTs would release people from the daily bind of commuting to work, leaving them free to choose where to live or to locate economic activities, gave rise in the 1960s to the concept of the 'electronic cottage'. Then, with the arrival of the Internet, attention turned to the 'cybercity'. And today, with links being forged between metropolization and the major nodes of the global communications networks, people talk about the 'digital city'.

It is unrealistic to expect that the city can be transformed overnight as a direct and tangible result of the influence of ICTs: American shopping malls may be losing some 2,000 travel agencies a year to direct bookings via the Internet, but urban businesses have thus far managed to withstand the challenge of e-commerce; teleworkers remain relatively few and far between; and the so-called 'digital city' still looks very much like a bricks-and-mortar structure. However, ICTs definitely are having a profound effect on the use of urban space, and anyone unable to see the changes must need their eyes testing.

So let us recapitulate the conventional, historical perceptions of the ways in which networks affect the city and, after showing how they fail to account for what is happening with ICTs today, suggest some pointers for addressing the professional concerns of planners.

Networks in the city

In the past, historical research and the experience of urban planners led to the view that the city was gradually modernized by a variety of networks according to a simple paradigm that, once formalized in 1990, went on to experience an unexpected degree of success as a widely-held tenet of latter-day urban planning. Basically, the diffusion of innovations or network expansion according to time is represented as an S-curve: growth begins slowly, as if held back by the newness of the phenomenon, then picks up speed until the exponential curve reaches an inflexion point beyond which it slows down before culminating, asymptotically, in complete diffusion. This, in a nutshell, illustrates the past emergence and spread of a host of rich-country networks in the fields, among others, of water supply, sanitation, electricity, fixed telephony and transport (see illustration 19.1). But now, in the ICT age, it is time to revisit that paradigm and to question a number of aspects of the S-curve model:

- Do the curves still correspond over time to the same networks given the speed of technological change with the ICTs?

- Are they not a lot steeper for ICTs than for the other, older, networks?

- By what criteria does one calculate the percentage of connected users on the vertical axis? By housing stock? A particular population (constant or variable)? A particular territory (fixed or variable)? The fact is that Internet users are defined not by where they live but by their use of the Internet, wherever they may be.

One should also bear in mind that the time values on the horizontal axis are relatively long, several decades in some cases.

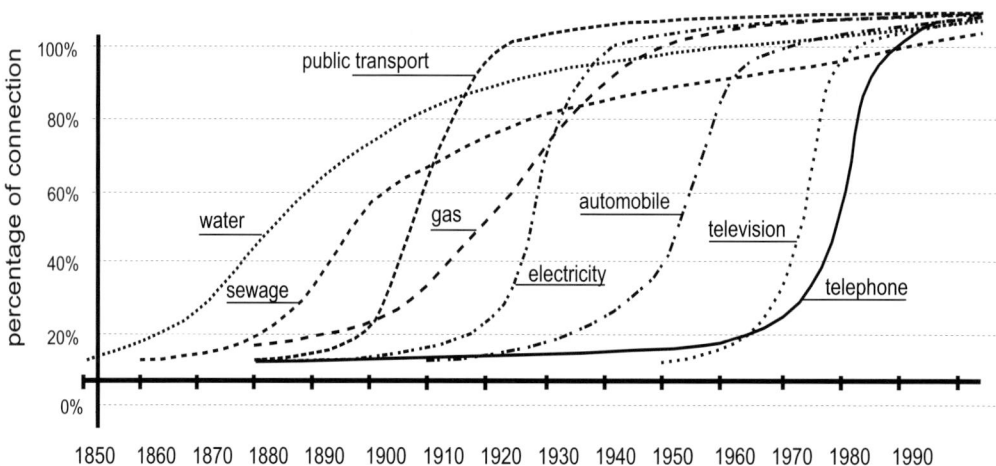

Illustration 19.1   Development of infrastructure networks in Western cities. Source: Dupuy (1991a: 42)

Changing scales

It has become customary to call the networks serving city residents urban networks or urban infrastructure networks. Those names make sense from an historical point of view, as the users of the early pressurized water supply, sewerage, city gas, DC (direct current) electricity, tramway or metro systems lived in the city. Furthermore, the networks themselves were technically independent and operated by the city authorities. The prevailing scale was, in every respect, well and truly urban.

Major changes have occurred since then in most network sectors, not least in that of the ICTs. Take the case of the Internet, for example. Although at first developed using the capillary telephone network already deployed in cities, the Internet is not an urban but a global network many of whose operators are multinational corporations, and the scale of whose core infrastructure is anything but urban. Internet operators do not decide to move into a particular region irrespective of the global context. They also operate in other countries; they have to comply with universal technical standards; they are competing with other global operators; and they rely on a global financial system. Their capacity to provide broadband services at a reasonable price is determined by the rationales of the global Internet.

The core Internet infrastructure is represented in the graph shown in illustration 19.2 by the three characteristic features indicated on its three axes:

- Spatial coverage – the relative density of a network's territorial service provision;

- Reach – the average length of a link between two nodes

- Polarization – the frequency of nodes acting as starting points or endpoints for large numbers of links.

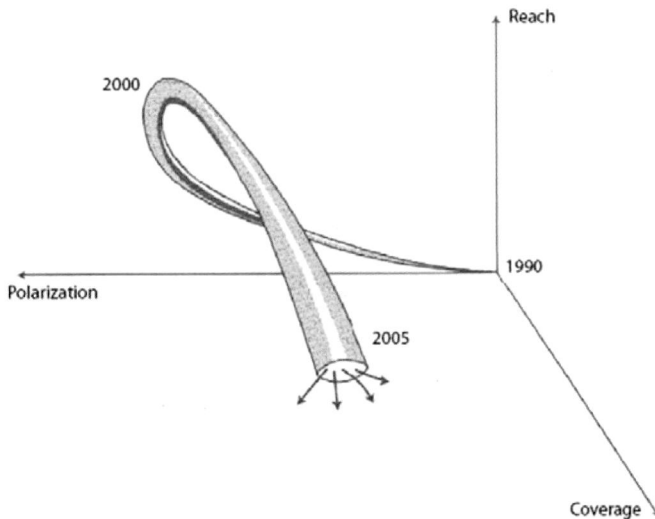

Illustration 19.2   The core Internet infrastructure represented by the three characteristic features on its three axes: spatial coverage, reach and polarization. Source: Dupuy (2004)

It is in relation to those three axes that the particular position of the Internet at a particular point in time can be determined at a global scale. That position marks the starting point of its ensuing trajectory, which can be interpreted as follows: growing as a network via a twofold annual increase in traffic; creaming off the wealthier customers in more densely populated areas; striving to expand its spatial coverage by concentrating on ever-larger hubs; compelled, after the collapse of the Internet economy in 2000, to adopt a fresh approach in order to ensure the continuation of quality service provision in an economic climate that was tough yet rich in technological innovations; and subsequently managing to boost its spatial coverage while at the same time maintaining service levels by means of more dispersed, less polarized, hubs and shorter internodal distances.

This is a statistical summary, a kind of average. Clearly, though, what happens locally cannot be too far removed from the global trend without running the risk of creating a digital divide. Large cities have therefore had to adhere to a global rationale that once placed a premium on large global metropolises, but which has now become more conducive to ever-smaller yet well-placed cities, waypoints or gateways.

First-class networks in a two-track city

The pace of technological change has been faster with ICTs than with transport or drinking water supply technologies. Not so long ago, people were marvelling at the speed of Internet diffusion, then, within the space of a decade, ADSL changed the shape of things by providing high-speed access via a regular telephone line; and fixed installation Internet access may soon be rendered obsolete by advanced mobile telecommunications technologies.

These rapid changes have had a significant impact. Ongoing network expansion used to hinge on universal techniques and a universal standard, sustaining the principle that every citizen could gradually have access to a universal service. The right to the networks went hand-in-hand with the right to the city. Clearly, this has become almost meaningless. The liberalization of telecommunications in France has resulted in a universal service for none but the users of fixed-line telephony – together with phone boxes and directories – at a time of explosive growth in Internet and mobile phone use. Meanwhile, the appeal of universal fixed-line telephony has declined in the face of increasing demand for access to broadband. Tomorrow people will be clamouring for UMTS.

The differing pace of technological innovation has led to striking differences in service provision depending on the type of urban area or population. Graham and Marvin (2001) condemn the undesirable effects on urban cohesion of the premium networks offering better water, power, telecommunications and transport services to those that can afford to pay for them. Although cities are still believed or expected to provide a full – and fully standardized – range of public services, the realities of technological innovation and socio-economic demand have produced a two-track city as far as networks are concerned. This is no temporary situation. With one technology replacing another, the speed differential tends to be reproduced before the gap can be closed; and ICTs have exacerbated that trend.

From the city to urban space and beyond

Networks may have begun by easing their way discretely into the existing urban fabric, but the new practices emerging in the course of their expansion have in the long run profoundly changed the face and, more broadly, the shape of urban planning, architecture and the built environment.

American suburbanization, for example, has gone through a number of different phases. Each has been underpinned by network service provision. Rail and tramway systems made it easier to move away from urban centres; and the electricity networks helped promote the widespread distribution of amenities formerly confined to densely populated areas. Meanwhile, a good deal of the suburban development between 1850 and 1950 went hand-in-hand with the establishment of factories, which did much to help local residents gain access to so-called 'urban' networks (Lewis, 2004). Later, especially in the 1950s, the proliferation of cars on suitable road networks helped foster extensive suburbanization. Electricity came to be taken for granted – as reflected in the key place of the refrigerator in suburban life and homes – including in formerly rural areas. Television and, moreover, the telephone ensured that suburban households were not cut off from the communication, information and even culture that used to be the preserve of city-dwellers. Nowadays, the spread of ICT networks from urban centres to peri-urban and even near-rural areas is continuing to make life easier for the businesses and households that settle there.

Despite stopping short of the utopian electronic cottage of the 1960s, ICTs have nonetheless been instrumental in the spatial redistribution of the population and the emergence of a variety of peri-urban forms: 'emerging cities', 'edge cities' and 'metapolises'. The networked city no longer bears any resemblance, morphologically or geographically, to the cities of the past (see box 19.1).

As a matter of fact, the urban space where networks are deployed is no longer confined to the city. They spread, it seems, within ever-expanding urban areas while at the same time changing the morphological nature of the city, making it much larger and more diffuse. So talking about a "digital city" these days seems somewhat paradoxical, not because we are still awaiting the advent of digital technology but because the city as we knew it is already a thing of the past.

Box 19.1

"Virginia and Eric Chatain left Limoges a year and a half ago with their 13 year-old daughter, Ludivine, and eight year-old son, Jeremy. They moved into a renovated farm house in Miremont, 30 km south of Toulouse, which costs them €750 a month in rent, and travel to work every day by car. The 'cultural richness' and 'human touch' of the locals, and the educational opportunities in Toulouse, have persuaded the Chatain family to stay there for good. Given the prices on the property market, they are now looking to buy a house within a 40-80 km radius around Toulouse. What's the betting they'll have a high-speed ADSL Internet connection when they move in?"

Source: L'Express magazine, 19 April 2004

New network urbanism for the ICT age?

What history has taught us about how transport, power and other 'historical' networks have affected the city is not easily applied to the new ICT networks. Given the sheer speed of ICT development, its reliance on global trends and the fact that it forms part of an overall context of liberalization, it is safe to say that those networks affect the city in completely different and more drastic ways, even though we have yet to see the full extent of their impact. Some similarities can probably be detected in the past development of the electricity network, for instance (Hughes, 1983). But ICTs have caused such wider ranging upheavals that we are compelled to rethink the whole relationship between networks and the city, and indeed the meaning of network urbanism.

Network urbanism originally stemmed from a hundred and fifty years of urban planning in cities through which many different networks were spreading in what was assumed to be a relatively continuous, locally manageable way. Now, in the age of ICTs, however, we must revisit those assumptions if we want the planners and developers to have a hand in the changing nature of cities in the twenty-first century.

Broadacre City: a utopian dream come true?

Utopianism is the lifeblood of urban planning. Theorists and practitioners alike have always relied on a critical detachment from the real-life city and on projecting their thoughts into other, imagined, contexts to facilitate the 'spatialization of common goods' (Choay, 1965).

The great planners – from Cerdà and Godin to Howard, Garnier, Wright and Le Corbusier – are very much part of the utopian tradition. Fishman (1977) shows how the work of Frank Lloyd Wright, Ebenezer Howard and Le Corbusier, in spite of their differing personalities and national backgrounds, was inspired by the power of that thinking. This, incidentally, prevented them from having much of an influence over contemporary urbanization in their day. Indeed, Wright and Le Corbusier made their name in the field of architecture, and Howard was known first and foremost as a property developer.

Let us take the case of Frank Lloyd Wright (illustration 19.3). Fishman (1990), in a study of late twentieth century suburbanization in America, concluded that Wright's utopia was already on the way to becoming a reality by the end of the 1980s. Has he been proved right? Has the utopian dream of *Broadacre City* come true?

Illustration 19.3   Frank Lloyd Wright

To answer these questions, let us recapitulate Wright's key ideas. The *Broadacre City* concept, first presented in his 1932 book *The Disappearing City*, hinges first and foremost on a rejection, or at least an abandonment, of the traditional urban form which Wright likened to generalized cancers, berating the *laissez-faire* attitude for having created a metropolis in its own image: disorganized, hideous and inhuman. *Broadacre City* offsets the centrality and density of urban areas with rapid transport systems, helicopters and communications networks: radio, telephone and others. As an architect with a great feel for landscape, Wright also wanted it to provide access to his country's most beautiful sites, places formerly so far off the beaten track as to have been almost uninhabitable. Now, thanks to the motorways, they could become part of everyday life. Fallingwater, a house in rural south-western Pennsylvania, is a prime example of this approach. Furthermore, Wright regarded *Broadacre City* as a utopian 'freedom city', empowering individuals to live where they liked and to travel as they wanted. Every American should have an acre of land, which roughly works out at a minimum of a hundred possible locations for the average family home.

Based on the above, Fishman reckoned American suburbia to be more densely populated in the late 1980s than all of the country's urban centres put together, claiming that *Broadacre* did indeed exist and that most Americans were already living there. His analysis of human settlement patterns in that vast suburban space noted the critical role of power, transport and telecommunications infrastructure in enabling individual households to develop their own travel, relational and service networks revolving around what had now become the centre of urban life, redefined at another scale: the home. Suburbia, then, had evolved into a self-constructed, self-centred networked city; a *mallopolis* of decentralized power devolved to each and every family and citizen in each and every micro-centre, allowing them to decide for themselves how to organize the network of places they frequented and, ultimately, their own living environment. So the *mallopolis* was, in Fishman's words, a 'genuine form of a plastic democracy'. Subsequent research has borne out Fishman's assessment and highlighted the nature of this velvet revolution in urban development (Garreau, 1990; Dupuy, 1995a).

Large-scale peri-urbanization has long since become prevalent in many other countries, especially in Europe (Dupuy & Sajous, 2000; EEA, 2006) (illustration 19.4). Some reckon the size of the peri-urban population in France – not counting the rural areas transformed in many respects by extensive urban sprawl – to stand at around 15 million people (Dible, 2006). Such trends had been widely predicted as long as 30 years ago (Bauer & Roux, 1976). French peri-urbanites now enjoy greater access than ever to the multiple networks described by Fishman, and a good many surveys have confirmed the pivotal role of the home in travel and relational networks (Pinson & Thomann, 2002).

American suburbanization and European peri-urbanization may represent a major change in the urban form, but do they amount to an actualization of *Broadacre City*? There are three main reasons to doubt it.

First, there has been no clear-cut *decentralization* of the kind envisaged by Wright and observed by Fishman. Peri-urban lifestyles may tally increasingly with that particular model, but city centres have survived in terms of their physical form and, in Europe, their vitality. They continue to have significant pulling power for jobs, commerce and, what is more, political interests, especially in France. Density, centrality and agglomeration remain strong. And the redistribution of power – Wright's vision of a plastic democracy (Fishman, 1990) – has yet to materialize. Present-day metropolitan governance may have given rise to unprecedented forms of public choice but *Broadacre*, from that viewpoint, is still a utopian dream; all the more so given that now sparsely populated rural areas appear more dependent than ever on central areas.

Illustration 19.4   *Broadacre City* in a European context: Upper Bavaria

Second, the decreasing densities seen to emerge from urban sprawl, including in those countries claiming to have curbed it, definitely do seem to tally with the *Broadacre City* model, meaning that the trend observed by Fishman remains to be disproved. According to statistical findings, however, that model is still a long way from being realized. In France, for instance, spatial density in peri-urban areas is five times greater than foreseen by Wright in respect of *Broadacre*. Disentangling the factors responsible is not easy. The complex workings of the land market bear some of this responsibility: circumstances differ from one country to the next, but the safeguarding of natural landscapes and upkeep of productive farmland, together with efforts to curb house-building on greenfield sites – now something of a national cause – have made peri-urban and not rurban property development commonplace in France. In any event, Wright's utopian vision of a host of scattered, diversely landscaped sites remains, once again, a dream.

Third, the emergence of networked territories in Fishman's *mallopolis* hinges, insofar as transport is concerned, on extensive ownership and use of cars, i.e. *automobility*. The road infrastructure supports a host of travel networks, and the corresponding growth in mobility is possible only because of car speeds keeping travel times down to an acceptable level. But the increasing automobility associated with decreasing densities and the relocation of economic activities has led to ever more space being adapted for people in cars (expressways, parking lots and so on). So motorists enjoy significant advantages over non-motorists in terms of accessibility, meaning that more of the latter seek to acquire a car and fewer of the former can do without theirs. This, in turn, leads to ever-larger numbers of cars on the roads; and the heavier the traffic the greater the spatial replanning catering to motorists and, in turn, the more extensive the *automobility*, and so on and so forth. This vicious circle is commonly known as car dependence (see Part III), which is a hard habit to break, thus undermining *Broadacre*'s prevailing ideas of freedom and choice. American suburbanization or European peri-urbanization cannot be held responsible for all of the planet's ills. After all, they do offer households resident in the areas in question some advantages. But can an urban space with such a dependence on one particular form of transport be described as a 'freedom city'? Given the doubts surrounding this point, *Broadacre City* can still be considered a utopia.

Network urbanism revisited: new concepts, new methods

The sudden emergence of networks

The growth of transport, power and communications networks since they first emerged in the mid-nineteenth century has been spectacular. Techniques stemming from the industrial revolution often provided an unbeatable means of meeting existing needs at an acceptable cost. The steam pump gave urban areas access to alternative sources of drinking water that had become crucial due, for example, to groundwater pollution; electricity enabled instant communication via telegraphy and then the telephone, which played a key role in economic development. Meanwhile, longstanding urban traffic problems were addressed through the development of the tramway. From the highly unsatisfactory system of horse-drawn wagons on unsurfaced roads to the laying of steel tracks, then the installation of coal and steam-powered motors the length of what amounted to a genuine 'railroad' to provide the power for independent movement. The ensuing economies of scale and falling costs contributed to the success of that major public transport system in the large cities of North America and Europe.

Network techniques gave rise to in-depth changes. In spatial terms, the networks paved the way for widespread urban development, modernization and decreasing population density in rural areas, thus transforming the geography of human settlements. In temporal terms, they generally brought speed, sometimes instantaneousness, and often directness: enabling consumers to gain direct access to water at the turn of a tap, for instance, instead of having to use a middleman, i.e. the water carrier.

Adapting to the networks

In spite of the depth of the changes, urban planners and developers gradually managed to come to terms with those techniques as seen in the example of Arturo Soria y Mata's *Linear City*, a prototype networked city in Madrid which, although hardly revolutionary, allowed inhabitants to capitalize on advances in the fields of transport, public lighting, and so on (illustration 19.5) (see also Chapter 1).

Illustration 19.5   **Cross-section of the main street in the first *Linear City* neighbourhood in Madrid.**
Source: Soria Y Mata ((1913) 1979: 13)

Central and local governments have often been known to harness network development for the benefit of physical planning at various levels. Calabi (1979) shows how between 1880 and 1910 the average Italian city used the networks as an effective urban planning policy tool in the absence of an overarching master plan of the kind already in place in the large cities. Striving to uphold the compact radio-concentric model in the face of a strong tendency towards anarchic suburban sprawl, while seeking to secure financial resources without having to resort to raising taxes, they decided to municipalize the networks, thereby taking over their running and earning power, which were in the hands of profit-making companies at the time. As such, they ended up practising a form of network urbanism consistent with the policy options of contemporary municipal socialism. In 1894 in Paris, the city's governing Seine County Council granted control of the electricity sectors to the companies operating in central areas with a view to using their profits to serve the suburbs (illustration 19.6).

At a wider level, the French government joined forces with the railway companies in order to provide a suitable national rail service. In the late 1930s, it went on to plan the construction of the country's road system to help achieve its national and regional development goals. Those limited yet *bona fide* efforts to utilize the potential of the networks resulted in the spatial organization now familiar in France today.

A new state of affairs for network urbanism

Nowadays, at a time marked by the emergence of new ICT networks, the older networks – their position transformed by privatization and the shift to competition in sectors formerly dominated by territorial and economic monopolies – are experiencing major changes in their *modus operandi*. Even the remaining 'old-style' networks have had to embrace automation, remote management and some of the other rapid technological developments introduced by ICTs in order to keep up with changing demand in a newly competitive environment: "the next generation of infrastructure systems needs to be in full convergence with information technologies" (Zimmerman & Horan, 2004). Networks are now interconnected at a continental and even a global scale, and such sweeping economic and political

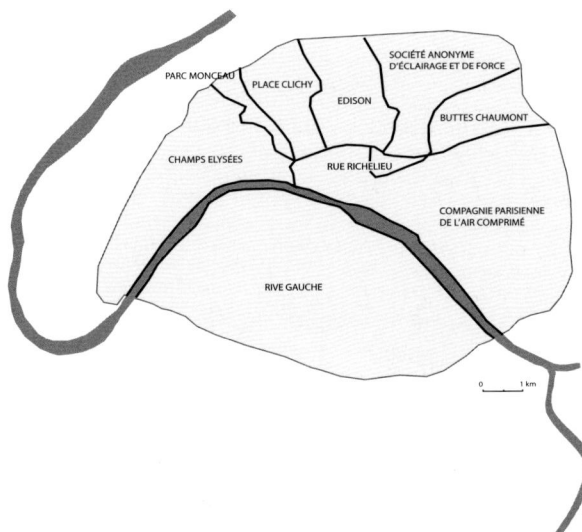

Illustration 19.6   **The perimeters of the concessions for electricity operators at the end of the 19th century. The City Government intended to equalize power distribution.**
Source: after Daumas, M. & J. Payen, 1976: Atlas, planche 47

Urban Networks – Network Urbanism

processes as decentralization and globalization have blurred the authorities' role as much in their development as in their management. According to Graham and Marvin (2001) the various changes have resulted in a new kind of segregation between the more or less neglected public networks and the premium networks serving selected cities, neighbourhoods or population groups, thus producing what is called urban fragmentation.

What can be done to help planners to adapt to the situation in the light of this new state of affairs? The answer is to revisit the networks and to show how they can act in the interests of the community. Network urbanism is not fixated on the networks of the past. It is ever-more open to the evolution of modern networks and, more importantly, to the changing geographic scales that affect them.

Planners may argue that they have no control over the rationales currently advancing network development owing to the fact that the actors are operating in a free-market economic environment, the pace of technological innovation is extremely fast and, what is more, the scales involved are of a continental/global order. Yet they can also seek to exploit those networks and their strategic goals – to increase or decrease their coverage – and even to sway their development in order to better organize the territory under their responsibility. But for that to happen they need simple yet relevant models to represent the laws governing network growth and deployment. They can no longer work with the model that used to guarantee universal access to a network: the S-curve (illustration 19.1). This curve has served to characterize the increase in a particular network's service provision to a particular space or population as a function of time:

$$x = a/(1 + e^{-akt}),$$

where x represents the proportion of the space or population served, t stands for time, and a and k are constants peculiar to the network in question.

New concepts

More than 20 years ago, Dancoisne (1984), in her Thesis on the French railway system, not only identified real long-term changes in its topology but also suggested that it was evolving morphologically according to its own timescales.

Illustration 19.7 shows distinct phases in the system's development over the period in question:

- First, expansion hand-in-hand with efforts to add further links to the network (connectivity);

- Next, a continuing increase in length alongside a slowdown then decline in the addition of new links; and finally;

- The decision to close lines while enhancing the newly modernized network's connectivity.

Fortunately, new conceptual tools make it possible to break away from the problem of scale divergence and to capitalize better on the opportunity for an operator to connect a particular zone or territory or to provide services to a particular population. Stemming from a variety of sources, these tools epitomize the contribution of scientific interdisciplinarity to the field of physical planning. Let us take a look at a few examples.

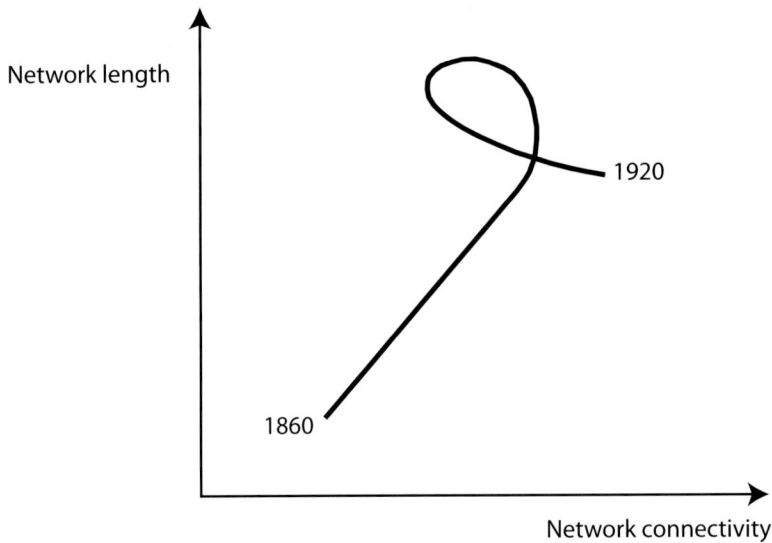

Illustration 19.7   Development of the French railway network (1874-1920). Source : Dancoisne (1984)

Adhesion

The preferred model up to now has centred on the distinction between the seamless network, e.g. the road system, which serves a particular space from one end of its paths to the other, and the point-to-point network such as the telephone system, whose services are restricted to subscribers in specific locations. The tendency today is to refer more to another concept: *adhesion*. A network's adhesion to the space through which it passes is determined in relation to the interface between it and that space, i.e. the number of potential access or service points made possible by the extent of its presence in the field (see illustration 19.8 a and b). This tallies with the 'space syntax' obtained by representing networks such as the urban road system as abstract graphs describing the opportunities they afford in urban spaces (Hillier & Hanson, 1984; Salingaros, 2005).

The seamless/point-to-point dichotomy can be replaced by a 'scale of adhesion' (Brès, 2005). In the case of transport networks, for instance, it would extend from *terminal adhesion* in air transport – the quintessential origin/destination model, with no interface between the plane travelling from one place to another and the space through which it is flying – through to *longitudinal adhesion*, where a person travelling by foot can, at each step, stop and gain access to the space through which they are walking. It should be noted that the adhesion concept challenges not only the infrastructure of the network in question, but also the nature of the services it provides.

Other forms of adhesion can be seen in the fields of mobile telephony or Wi-Fi. Wi-Fi technology provides a wireless means of connecting a computer remotely to the Internet. Although designed it is

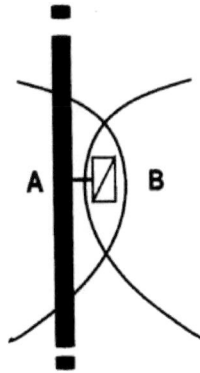

Illustration 19.8a   **Dual adhesion: the rectangle represents a space located alongside a road that is accessible by car and forming part of both the road system (A) and a residential area (B)**

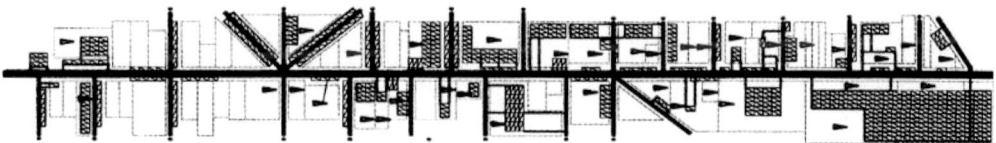

Illustration 19.8b   **Physical adhesion of the road network to the built environment as illustrated in this plan of a trunk road running through residential and commercial areas south of Paris. In black: the road infrastructure. In grey: parking areas.** Source: Brès (2005)

designed to be used as a rule under the supervision of the owner of a main Wi-Fi enabled computer – in the home or in restaurants, airports and other public places, with password-restricted access – outsiders can pick up the signal and have a connection in the street, in the vicinity of an office or apartment building. In the United States there are groups of so-called *warchalkers* that go around marking out the areas where connections can be had free of charge by chalking lines drawn on pavements and walls (illustration 19.9a&b). These are the visible signs of Wi-Fi network adhesion in public spaces.

In the case of mobile telephony, adhesion is limited only by the capacity of cell sites to provide channels of communication (see illustration 19.10). If the network is well-proportioned there is never any shortage of capacity, the user perceives no limits, and the adhesion is infinite. With Wi-Fi technology, on the other hand, adhesion mapping shows a remarkable array of areas of continuity and discontinuity. It should also be noted that adhesion is linked to a two-tier notion characterizing the manner in which a surrounding space establishes relations with a particular network, as reflected in the 'residents only' streets in the case of the urban road system.

What should planners make of this concept? Adhesion, in our view, is consonant with the changing shape of network governance in which the user, previously regarded as a passive subscriber, is

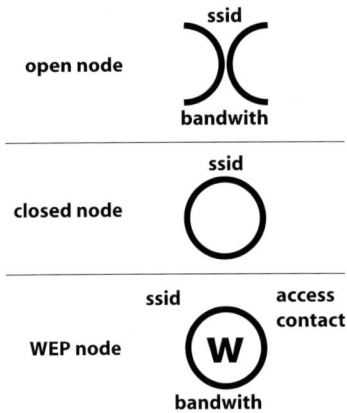

Illustration 19.9a/b   **Warchalking signs.**
Sources: http://en.wikipedia.org/wiki/Warchalking ;
http://www.visuallee.com/weblog/2002_06_01_archive.html (accessed 4 March 2008)

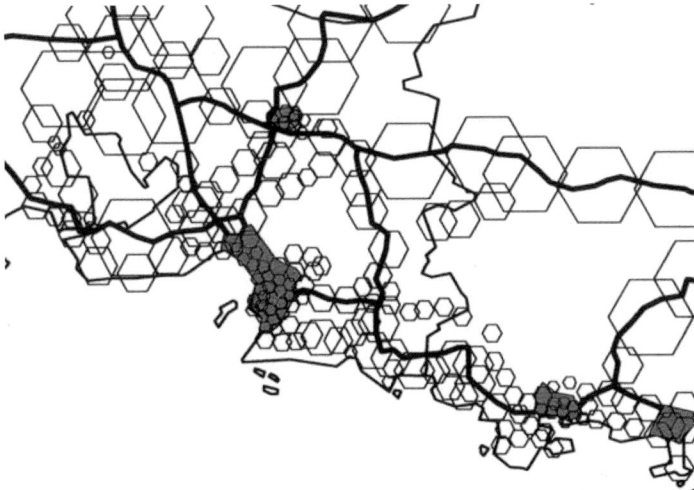

Illustration 19.10   **Network of mobile phone cell sites covering the Marseilles urban area.**
Source: Bouygues Télécom (1997)

acknowledged as playing a proactive role. It is paving the way for new forms of network co-production that the planner must not ignore.

Preferential attachment

'Preferential attachment' means that new nodes added to an existing network preferably link to nodes that already have a lot of links to other nodes. *Vice versa* nodes with a lot of links in a network are more likely to attract new links than nodes with less links. This concept stems from the simple rules that one can recognize in the construction of some of the older networks. Every new section added to the Irish or Dutch railway systems, for example, had to be designed to reach the nearest large town not yet benefiting from rail services (Garrison, 1990; Rietveld & van Nierop, 1995). Likewise, the construction of the Alleghany County public sanitation system in Pennsylvania was geared, at all times, to ensuring that all the pipelines led to a single large purification plant (Garrison, 1990).

Barabási (2002) has crystallized the concept in a theoretical premise distinguishing the scale-free networks with just a few nodes and a large number of links – e.g. airline networks, with their hubs and

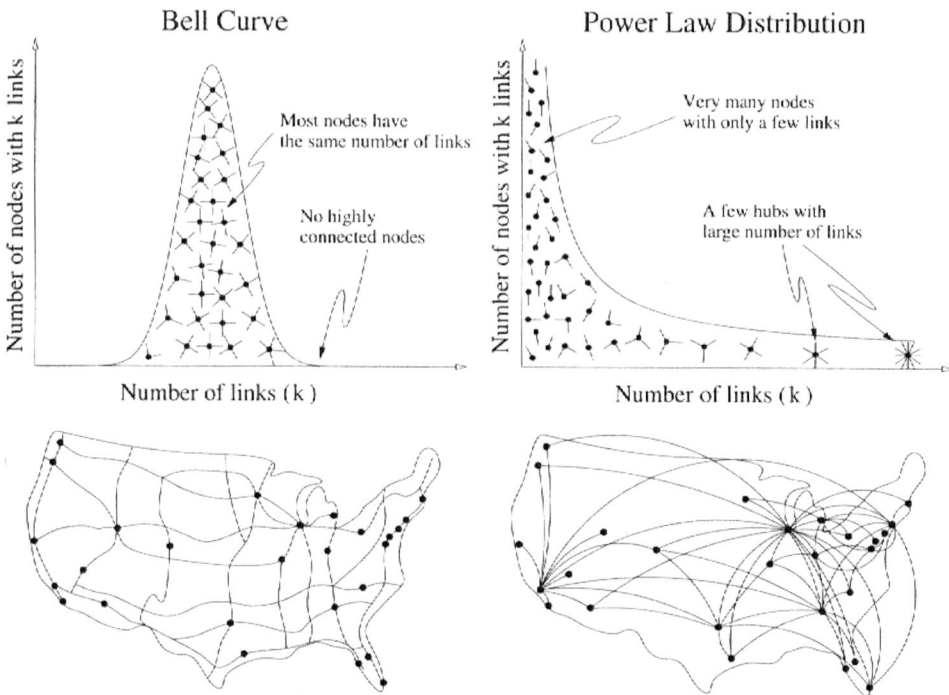

Illustration 19.11   Random networks follow a bell curve, while scale-free networks follow a power law degree distribution. Source: Barabási (2002: 71)

Box 19.2

"The degree distribution of a random network follows a bell curve, telling us that most nodes have the same number of links, and nodes with a very large number of links don't exist (top left). Thus a random network is similar to a national highway network, in which the nodes are the cities, and the links are the major highways connecting them. Indeed, most cities are served by roughly the same number of highways (bottom left). In contrast, the power law degree distribution of a scale-free network predicts that most nodes have only a few links, held together by a few highly connected hubs (top right). Visually this is very similar to the air traffic system, in which a large number of small airports are connected to each other via a few major hubs (bottom right)." Barabási (2002: 71).

"Note that there is an important qualitative difference between the power law and a bell curve when it comes to the tail of the distribution. Bell curves have an exponentially decaying tail, which decreases much faster than the decrease seen under the power law. This exponential tail is responsible for the absence of hubs. In comparison, the power law causes a much slower rate of decay, which allows for 'rare events' such as hubs." (Rooij 2005: 241)

spokes, and Internet backbones – from those with many varied nodes and a variable number of links (see illustration 19.11; box 19.2).

The fractal approach

Barabási also calls attention to another concept that has been around for some time but whose usefulness with respect to network topology has yet to be appraised beyond the confines of the Lyons stormwater drainage system, i.e. the fractal approach (Thibault, 1995). Fractal images are now so familiar that the Parisian urban heating system, for instance, smacks of a fractal topology or geometry (see illustration 19.12). But what exactly is a fractal topology and what does the fractal approach tell us about how a particular network came into being?

Once again, this concept has emerged from the repeated use of a set of simple rules. The expansion of the urban heating system has hinged on the principle that a building requesting a connection is only served if it meets two basic conditions: that it signs up for a specified minimum amount of heating; and that it is located within a given distance of the network. Interestingly, the same sorts of rules have applied in the construction of high-speed ADSL networks, as seen in a recent study on service provision by the Spanish operator Telefonica in the outskirts of Madrid (Gómez Barroso & Pérez Martínez, 2004). At one particular stage of development the operator set a minimum threshold whereby only towns with a population of at least 20,000, for instance, were considered eligible to join the network. Given that there were too many towns above that threshold, however, not all of them could be served at once. So a set of secondary criteria was introduced: number of households, phone lines or secondary residences or average income, for example. Generally speaking, one or two of those criteria were enough to be able to adjust the network to the company's service provision capability.

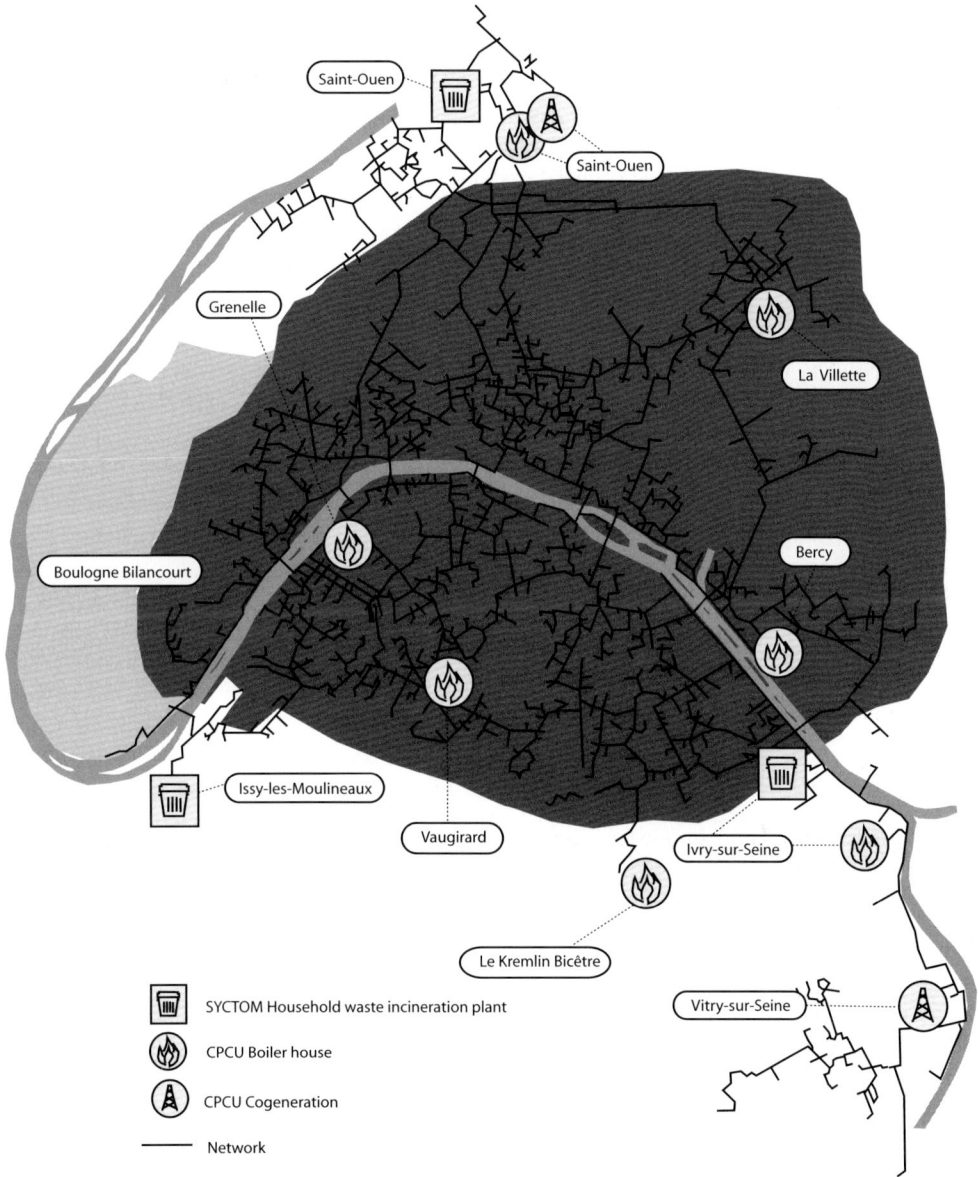

Illustration 19.12   Paris heating network. Source: after http://www.cpcu.fr (accessed May 2008)

The following labels appear on the map:

Saint-Ouen

🗑 Saint-Ouen

Grenelle

🔥 La Villette

Boulogne Bilancourt

🔥 Bercy

🔥

🔥

🗑 Issy-les-Moulineaux

Vaugirard

🗑 Ivry-sur-Seine

🔥

🔥 Le Kremlin Bicêtre

Vitry-sur-Seine

Legend:

🗑 SYCTOM Household waste incineration plant

🔥 CPCU Boiler house

🅐 CPCU Cogeneration

—— Network

Applying such rules produces a fractal topology that ultimately provides a particular space with services that are regularly distributed yet dependent on their population density.

Network time

Networks are not set in stone. They evolve over time as their topology adapts to new economic or political conditions and their infrastructure is adjusted to guarantee their 'stakeholders' uninterrupted provision of ever-changing services. But there are differences between network time and ordinary – or, in other words, social – time. The fact is that each network has its own development clock, so to speak.

Urban and physical planners must grasp this crucial new concept before taking any action in the field of network urbanism. It requires an in-depth understanding of the nature of the various networks and their place in the city, i.e. knowledge of their past history. The key means of acquiring such knowledge is through diachronic analysis, which is useful for:

- Mapping out the transition from a virtual 'maximal' network to the real network, and to pinpoint the territorial constraints – earlier boundaries and other existing networks – that compel the operator in charge of that transition to eliminate some of the original projected transactions (see Chapter 2);

- Identifying the role of the economic factors, technological options, legal restrictions and political intentions now assimilated into the networks and, hence, virtually undetectable through analysis of their current state; and

- Clarifying such recursive processes as a network's expansion to new points or the emergence of new links, especially in the light of the fact that the rules by which the operators handle the tensions and enforce the necessary regulations in developing or adjusting their networks become clear only over relatively long periods.

What kind of diachronic analysis is best suited to the work of network urbanism? Basically, it calls for the same types of geographical or plot surveys usually carried out, in theory, within the framework of conventional planning. It does not require a comprehensive study of the networks' past history. Planners are not historians. They draw instead as much as possible on research done by others. More often than not, this produces qualitative analyses highlighting the factors responsible for shaping one or more networks. In the case of the French road system, for example, planners have been able to use the distinction identified by historical researchers between two main categories of roads leading into and out of cities: valley roads and plateau roads. The former – which tend to be narrow and winding and to create links between towns and villages – are lined with relatively small plots of land and attract small-scale businesses and workshops. The latter, on the other hand, are straight, lined with larger plots and attract large-scale economic network operators. So the valley roads, in a sense, hark back to the system's past, developing at a far slower pace than the rapidly evolving plateau roads.

At another scale, a whole city's infrastructure networks can evolve according to a unique intrinsic 'clock', as in the example of Buenos Aires (see Chapter 7). That city's networks, originally built with heavy investment in the late nineteenth/early twentieth century, have helped keep it going in the face of dramatic economic decline, thus staving off the onset of an infrastructure network crisis of the kind experienced in other cities, especially in Latin America.

Recent advances in research have made it possible to move on from such qualitative analyses towards more quantitative approaches combined with representations of network temporalities through model-building – at first with more rudimentary means and then with computers – as seen in the cases of the French, Irish and Dutch railways (Dancoisne, 1984; Garrison, 1990; Rietveld & van Nierop, 1995), the Alleghany County sanitation network (Garrison, 1990), the Lyons stormwater drainage system (Thibault, 1995) and the water supply systems of New England (Anderson, 1988).

Hence, while the development of the Internet – or, to be more precise, its backbone networks – is widely hailed as having been completely random and subject to no master, a combination of the fractal and preferential attachment models has shown it to have been governed by the hidden laws of its own intrinsic timescales, as reflected in the three distinct phases: all-out growth, followed by growth within the framework of a restructured topology, through to the current growth of a more moderate and considered nature (see illustration 19.2).

Concluding remarks

Adhesion, preferential attachment, the fractal approach and network time are new concepts set to revitalize network urbanism, to foster the emergence of new tools and, ultimately, to enable urban and physical planners to come to terms with the true nature of the networks, thereby putting them in a better position to capitalize on the latitude provided by their development, and paving the way for positive change in future urban and physical planning practices.

References

A

Akierman, L., 1988, *Représentations Graphiques des Réseaux*, PhD Thesis, Ecole nationale des ponts et chaussées, Paris.

Al-Tawil, K. M., 2001, The Internet in Saudi Arabia, *Telecommunications Policy,* 25, pp. 625-632.

Albini, D. & L.A. Costa, 1987, Le Réseau Deborde: les Inondations de Buenos Aires. In: Dupuy, G. (ed.), *La Crise des Réseaux d'Infrastructure: le Cas de Buenos Aires,* Presses de l'école nationale des ponts et chaussées, Paris, pp. 99-140.

Altshuler, A., M. Anderson, D. Jones, D. Roos & J. Womack, 1984, *The Future of the Automobile: The Report of MIT's International Automobile Program*. MIT Press, Cambridge, Mass.

Alvergne, C. & D. Latouche, 2003, Le Système Urbain Nord-Américain à l'Heure de la "Nouvelle Économie", *Mappemonde,* 70 (2), pp. 21-23.

Alvergne, C., Y. Lazreri & B. Planque, 1999, Évolutions des Structures Régionales de Qualification du Travail (1975-1988). In: Gilli, J-P. & C. Dupuy (eds), *Industrie et Territoire en France: Dix Ans de Décentralisation*, Les Études de la Documentation Française, pp. 37-55.

Amar, G., 1988, Essai de Modélisation Conceptuelle d'un Réseau de Circulation. In: Dupuy, G. (ed.), *Réseaux Territoriaux*, Paradigme, Caen.

Amar, G. & N. Stathopoulos, 1987, Les Réseaux à Organisation Polaire, *Cahiers Scientifiques du Transport,* 15-16.

Anderson, D.D., 1981, *Regulatory Politics and Electric Utilities: A Case Study in Political Economy*, Auburn House, Boston, Mass.

Anderson, L., 1988, Fire and Disease: The Development of Water Supply Systems in New England, 1870-1900. In: Tarr, J. A. & G. Dupuy, *Technology and the Rise of the Networked City in Europe and America*, Temple University Press, Philadelphia, pp. 137-156.

André, M., 1997, Vehicle Uses and Operating Conditions: On-board Measurements. In: Stopher, P. & M. Lee-Gosselin (eds), *Understanding Travel Behaviour in an Era of Change*, Pergamon/Elsevier Science Ltd., Oxford.

Antonelli, C., 1997, A Regulatory Regime for Innovation in the Communications Industries, *Telecommunications Policy*, 21 (1), pp. 35-45.

Armstrong, G. & A.V. Nelles, 1986, *Monopoly's Moment: The Organisation and Regulation of Canadian Utilities 1830-1930*, Temple University Press, Philadelphia.

Asphalt Institute, 1966, *Asphalt Institute quarterly*, Issue April 1966, Asphalt Institute, New York.

Atkinson, R., 2000, Measuring Gentrification and Displacement in Greater London, *Urban Studies*, 37 (1), pp. 149-165.

Auphan, E., 1999, Liberté ou Dépendance? La Mobilité Partagée entre l'Automobile et les Transports en Commun. In: *Géographie et Libertés. Mélanges en Hommage à Paul Claval*, L'Harmattan, Paris.

B

Bailly, A., 1994, Existe-t-il Encore une Géographie Rurale?, *Les Nouveaux Espaces Ruraux, Sciences Humaines*, 4, hors série, 1994, p. 42.

Bakis, H., 1989, Les Réseaux Privés de Télécommunications: L'Exemple de la Réservation Aérienne, *Netcom*, 3 (1).

Bakis, H. & J. M. Segui Pons (eds), 1998, Geospace and Cyberspace, *Netcom*, Special Issue, 12 (1-3).

Banister, D., 2005, *Unsustainable Transport: City Transport in the New Century*, Routledge, Londen/New York.

Barabási, A.L., 2002, *Linked: The New Science of Networks*, Perseus, Cambridge, Mass.

Bardet, G., 1947, *L'Urbanisme*, PUF, Paris.

Bardou, J.-P., J.-J. Chanaron, P. Fridenson & J.-M. Laux, 1977, *La Révolution Automobile*, Albin Michel, Paris.

Barjonet, P.-E. (ed.), 1989, Transports et Sciences Sociales: Question de Méthode, *Journée d'Étude de l'Institut National de Recherche sur les Transports et leur Sécurité*, Paradigme, Caen (Fr.).

Barth, F., 1978, *Scale and Social Organization*, Universitets Forlaget, Oslo.

Bassand, M., P. Rossel, 1989, Métropoles et Réseaux, *Espaces et Sociétés*, 57/58, pp. 196-208.

Bauer, G. & J.M. Roux, 1976, *La Rurbanisation ou la Ville Éparpillée*, Le Seuil, Paris.

Bedarida, M., 1984, Quand les Chevaux Vapeur s'en Mêlent: Ville d'Automobile, *Monuments Historiques*, 134, August-September 1984.

Beauchard, J., 1988a, *Trafics*, Eres, Toulouse .

Beauchard, J., 1988b, Trafic de Masse et Figures de la Marginalité, *Quaderni*, 6, Winter 1988-1989.

Beltran, A., 1990, Création et Développement du Réseau Electrique Parisien (1878-1939). In: F. Caron, J. Derens, L. Passion, Ph. Cebron de Lisle (eds), *Paris et ses Réseaux, Naissance d'un Mode de Vie Urbain, XIX-XX-ème siècles*, Bibliothèque historique de la Ville de Paris (BHVP), Paris.

Benevolo, L., 1979, *Histoire de l'Architecture Moderne*, Dunod, Paris.

Benoît, P. & P. Irrmann, 1989, *Enquêtes 1989 sur 23 Millions de Rurbains*, Nathan-Agora-Ipsos, Paris.

Bernard, E., 2003, *Le Déploiement des Infrastructures Internet en Afrique del'Ouest*. PhD Thesis under direction of H. Bakis & A. Chéneau-Loquay, Université Montpellier III.

Berque, A., 1982, *Vivre l'Espace au Japon*, PUF, Paris.

Besson, P., M. Savy, A. Valeyre & P. Veltz, 1989, *Gestion de Production et Transport*, Paradigme, Caen (Fr.).

Beyeler, C., 1991, *Alimentation en Eau Potable et Élimination des Déchets: des Systèmes en Crise? Analyse Comparative France / États-Unis sur la Période 1960-1990*, PhD Thesis, Université Paris XII.

Bodard, T., 1987, Du réseau au bombeador. L'alternative critique pour l`eau potable. In: Dupuy, G. (ed.) *La Crise des Réseaux d'Infrastructure: le Cas de Buenos Aires,* Presses de l'école nationale des ponts et chaussées, Paris.

Boissevain, J., 1979, Network Analysis: A Reappraisal, *Current Anthropology*, 20 (2), pp. 392-394.

Boltanski, L., 1975, Les Usages Sociaux de l'Automobile, A*ctes de la Recherche en Sciences Sociales* 1 (2), pp. 25–49.

Bonatti, M., 1992, Nouvelles Tendances de la Mobilité, *Déplacements*, 7.

Bonnafous, A. & Plassard, F., 1974, Les Méthodologies Usuelles de l'Etude des Effets Structurants de l'Offre de Transport, *Revue économique*, 25 (2), March 1974.

Bonnet, M., 1980, L'Automobile Quotidienne: Mythes et Réalités. In: Ministère Transport, *L'Automobile et la Mobilité des Français*, La Documentation Française, Paris, pp. 199-214.

Bonnin, J., 1984, *L'Eau dans l'Antiquité*, Eyrolles, Paris.

Bornot, F. & A. Cordesse, 1981, *Le Téléphone Dans Tous Ses Etats*, Actes Sud, Le Paradou (Fr.).

Bouley, J., 1990, Le Réseau à Très Grande Vitesse Européen se Construit, *Revue d'Histoire des Chemins de Fer*, 2 (spring), pp. 165-169.

Bouygues Télécom, 1997, *Le Déploiement du Réseau* (in-house document).

Bouvier, P., 1986, *Paris-New York: Étude Comparative des Transports Urbains de Masse 1900-1955*, Centre d'Etudes Sociologiques, Paris.

Brès, A., 2005, *Inscription Territoriale des Mobilités et Riveraineté des Voies: Faire Halte Aujourd'hui*. PhD Thesis under the direction of G. Dupuy, Université Paris I.

Bricnet, F. & P.A.Mangolte, 1990, *L'Europe Automobile, Virages d'une Industrie en Mutation*, Nathan, Paris.

Bressand, A., C. Distler & K. Nicolaidis, 1989, Vers une Économie de Réseaux, *Revue de Politique Industrielle*, 3 (winter), pp. 155-168.

Bunn, L.A. & P.A. David, 1991, L'Économie des Passerelles Technologiques et l'Évolution des Réseaux, *Flux*, 4 / 6, April-June / October-December, 1991.

C

Calabi, D., 1979, I Servizi Tecnici a Rete e la Questione della Municipalizzazione nelle Città Italiane (1880-1910). In: Morachiello, P. & G. Teyssot, *Le Machine Imperfette: Architettura, Programma, Instituzioni nel XIX Secolo*, Officina Edizioni, Rome.

Calatayud, J.B., 1989, Con la Ingeniería Urbana Como Pretexto, *CEUMT*, 109 (May-June).

Calenge, P., 2002, Les Territoires de l'Innovation: Les Réseaux de la Musique en Recomposition, *Géographie, Economie, Société*, 4, pp. 37-56.

Capello, R., 1994, *Spatial Economic Analysis of Telecommunications Network Externalities*, Avebury, Aldershot (UK).

Carpenter, J., 1979, Lessening Automobile Dependance Through Land Use Planning, *Practising Planner*, 9 (1).

Casanova, Y., 2003, *Travaux de Recherche Destinés à l'Etude Prospective des Systèmes de Déplacements Quotidiens Urbains et Interurbains de Voyageurs - MOBISIM III*, ATN-PREDIT, Paris.

Castells, M., 1989, *The Informational City: Information Technology, Economic Restructuring and Urban-Regional Process*, Blackwell, Oxford.

Castells, M., 2002, *La Galaxie Internet*, Fayard, Paris.

Cauquelin A., 1979, *Cinévilles*, Union Générale d'Editions, Paris.

Cauquelin A., 1987, Les Portes de la Ville. Presentation at the seminar *Voie de Communication: Espaces Transitifs*, Montpellier, March 1987.

Cerdà, I., 1867, *Teoría General de la Urbanización*, Instituto de Estudios Fiscales, Ariel, 3 vols.

Cerdà, I., 1979, *La Théorie Générale de l'Urbanisation* (presentation and adaptation of the book published in 1867, by A. Lopez de Aberasturi), Le Seuil, Paris.

Cervero, R., 1995, Stockholm's New Towns, *Cities*, 12 (6), pp. 41–51.

CFCE, 1998, *Internet et Commerce Électronique en Europe du Nord*, Centre Français du Commerce Extérieur, Paris.

Chaline, C., 1989, *Evaluation Comparative du Réaménagement des Fronts Fluviaux et Portuaires en Aire Métropolitaine*, LEDALOR/IUP, Paris.

Cho Sung Hye, 2002, Telecommunications and Informatization in South Korea, *Netcom*, 16 (1-2), pp. 275-291.

Choay, F., 1965, *L'Urbanisme, Utopies et Réalités, une Anthologie*, Le Seuil, Paris.

Choay, F., 1969, *The Modern City. Planning in the 19th Century*. Planning and City Series, George Braziller, New York.

Choay, F., 1979, Preface. In: Cerdà, I., 1979, *La Théorie Générale de l'Urbanisation* (presentation and adaptation of the book published in 1867, by A. Lopez de Aberasturi), Le Seuil, Paris.

Ciuró, J., 1970, *Historia del Automóvil en España*, CEAC, Barcelona.

Clark, C. & G.H. Peters, 1965, The Intervening Opportunities Method of Traffic Analysis, *Traffic Quarterly*, 19, pp. 101–119.

Claude V., 1987, *L'Association Générale des Hygiénistes et Techniciens Municipaux: École et/ou Lobby, 1905-1930*, Rapport de Recherche pour le Plan Urbain, ARDU/Université Paris VIII.

Claval, P., 1973, *Principes de Géographie Sociale*, Éditions M.Th Génin, Paris.

Claval, P., 1981, *La Logique des Villes,* Litec, Paris.

Claval, P., 1987, Réseaux Territoriaux et Enracinement, *Cahiers du Groupe Réseaux*, 7.

Coing, H., 1980, Le Transfert et Les Techniques Urbaines Vers Les Pays du Tiers Monde, *Les Annales de la Recherche Urbaine*, 7.

Cohendet, P. & L. Stojak, 2005, La Fracture Numérique en Europe, *Futuribles*, 305.

Collin-Delavaud, A., 1984, Espace et Pouvoir dans la Restructuration de l'Aire Métropolitaine de Buenos Aires, *L'Information Géographique*, 2.

Condroyer, E., 1931, *L'Ermite de l'Atlantique*, Editions de la NRC, Paris.

Conseil General des Ponts et Chaussées, 2005, *Analyse Comparative des Méthodes d'Evaluation des Grandes Infrastructures de Transport*, July 2005, Paris.

Cordellier, S. & E. Lau, 2004, *L'État des Régions Françaises: Espace et Territoires*, La Découverte, Paris.

Corn, J. J., 1992, Works and Vehicles: a Comment and Note. In: Wachs, M. & M. Crawford (eds), *The Car and the City: The Automobile, The Built Environment and Daily Urban Life*, University of Michigan Press, Ann Arbor, Michigan.

Cottereau, A., 1969, L'Apparition de l'Urbanisme comme Action Collective: l'Agglomération Parsienne au Début du Siècle, *Sociologie du Travail*, 4, October-December 1969.

Country Reports.Org, 2003, Iceland. *www.countryreports.org/content/iceland/htm*; accessed August 2003.

Courty, G., 1990, Le Sens Unique: la Codification des Règles de Conduite sur Route, 1894-1922, *Politix*, 10-11, pp. 7-20.

Coutard, O., G. Dupuy & S. Fol, 2002, La pauvreté périurbaine: dépendance locale ou dépendance automobile, *Espaces et Sociétés*, 108-109.

Coutras, J., 1993, La Mobilité des Femmes au Quotidien: un Enjeu des Rapports Sociaux de Sexe, *Les Annales de la Recherche Urbaine*, 59-60, November 1993.

Cribier, F., 1994, Parcours Urbains de Deux Génerations de Parisiens, *Le Courrier du CNRS*, 81 (summer) 1994, pp. 61-63.

Crozet, Y. & I. Joly, 2004, Budgets Temps de Transport: les Sociétés Tertiaires Confrontées à la Gestion Paradoxale du 'Bien le Plus Rare', *Cahiers Scientifiques du Transport*, 45, pp. 27-48.

Crozet, Y., J.-P. Orfeuil & M.-H. Massot, 2001, Mobilité Urbaine: Cinq Scénarios pour un Débat, *Notes du Centre de Prospective et de Veille Scientifique,* 16, Centre de prospective et de veille scientifique, Paris, pp. A-66.

CURDS, 2004, *Telecommunication Services and Networks: Territorial Trends and Basic Supply of Infrastructure for Territorial Cohesion*. Final Report on ESPON project 1.2.2. University of Newcastle, Centre for Urban & Regional Studies (CURDS)/ESPON, Newcastle Upon Tyne.

Curien, N., 2000, *Économie des Réseaux*, La Découverte, Paris.

Curien, N. & G. Dupuy, 1996, *Réseaux de Communication, Marchés et Territoires*, Presses de l'école nationale des ponts et chaussées, Paris.

Curien, N. & M. Gensollen, 1989, *Prévision de la Demande de Télécommunications: Méthodes et Modèles*, Eyrolles, Paris.

D

Dancoisne, P., 1984, *Théorie des Graphes et Constitution du Réseau Ferré Français*, PhD Thesis under the direction of Philippe Pinchemel, Université Paris I.

Danger, R., 1935, La Circulation de Grand Trafic dans la Traversée des Agglomérations, *Urbanisme*, 35, April 1935.

Dascal, G., 1986, *Urbanisme*, post-graduate diploma, Institut d'Urbanisme de Paris, Université Paris XII.

DATAR, 1992, *Livre Blanc du Bassin Parisien*, La Documentation Française, Paris.

DATAR / Préfecture de l'Ile-de-France, 1999, *Pour une Métropolisation Raisonnée*, La Documentation Française, Paris.

DATAR, 2002, *Aménager la France de 2020, Le Bassin Parisien*, La Documentation Française, Paris.

Daunton, M.J., 1981, Public Place and Private Space: The Victorian City and the Working Class Household. In: Fraser, D. & A. Sutcliffe, *The Pursuit of Urban History*, Edward Arnold, London.

Daunton, M.J., 1983, *House and Home in the Victorian city: Working Class Housing 1850-1914*, Edward Arnold, London.

de Jong, C. , 1997, A Microeconomic Model of the Joint Decision on Car Ownership and Car Use. In: Stopher, P. & M. Lee-Gosselin (eds), *Understanding Travel Behaviour in an Era of Change*, Pergamon/ Elsevier Science Ltd., Oxford.

de Radkowski, G.H., 2002, *Anthropologie de l'Habiter: Vers le Nomadisme*, PUF, Paris.

de Solla Pool, I. (ed.), 1977, *The Social Impact of the Telephone*, MIT Press, Cambridge, Mass.

Deakin, E., 1991, Congestion, Air Pollution, Greenhouse Gases, Energy Use: the Effectiveness of Transportation and Land Use Strategies for Impact Management. In: *Proceedings of Transport and Greenhouse: Towards Solutions*, Office of the Environment, State of Victoria, Australia.

Dekindt, J., 1986, Notes Sur la Sociabilité des Réseaux, *Actions et Recherches Sociales*, 4.

Derycke, P.H., 1997, *Le Péage Urbain*, Economica, Paris.

Devillers, C., 1988, De la Logique de Secteur au Projet Urbain, *Villes en Parallèle : Formes Urbaines,* 12-13, November 1988, pp. 245-259.

Dézert B., 1989, De la ZALA à l'Aéroville: Une Nouvelle Révolution Technologique, *Cahiers du CREPIF*, 27.

Di Meo, G. & X. Piolle, 1989, Structures Sociales et Espaces: Essais d'Approche Complexe des Espaces Actuels de la Territorialité. Paper delivered at the *6e Colloque Européen de Géographie Théorique et Quantitative*, Royaumont (Fr.), October 1989.

Dible, P., 2006, *Le Village Métamorphosé: Révolution dans la France Profonde*, Plon, Paris.

Downes, T. & S. Greenstein, 1999, Do Commercial ISPs Provide Universal Access? In: Gillett, S. & I. Vogelsang (eds), *Competition, Regulation, and Convergence: Current Trends in Telecommunications Policy Research*, Lawrence Erlbaum Associates, Mahwah, NJ, pp. 195-212.

Drewe, P., 1997, The Network City, Contribution of Information Technology to New Concepts of Spatial Planning. *Western Regional Science Association, 36th Annual Meeting*, Hawaii.

Drewe, P., 2008, *The Experience of French Futurology – Some Lessons*. Publication forthcoming.

Duclos, D., 1976, *L'Automobile Impensable: Objet-technique, Effet d'un Code Idéologique ou Rapport Contradictoire aux Forces Productives. Pré-étude sur les Conditions d'Évolution des Pratiques et des Idéologies de l'Automobile par les Ménages*, ATP Socio-économie des Transports, SAEI, Mission de la recherche, Centre de Sociologie Urbaine (CSU), Paris.

Duféal, M., 2003, *Les Sites Web: Marqueurs et Vecteurs de Dynamiques Spatiales et Économiques dans l'Espace Économique Français*, PhD Thesis under the supervision of L. Grasland, Université Avignon (Fr.).

Duféal, M., 2004a, Mesure de la Diffusion Spatiale des Sites Web dans les Régions Méditerranéennes Françaises. In: Guichard, E. (ed.), *Mesures de l'Internet*, Editions Les Canadiens en Europe, Paris.

Duféal, M., 2004b, *Les sites web, marqueurs et vecteurs de dynamiques spatiales et économiques dans l'espace méditérranéen français*, PhD Thesis under the direction of Gabriel Dupuy, Université Paris I.

Duféal, M. & L. Grasland, 2003, La Planification des Réseaux à l'Epreuve de la Matérialité des TIC et de l'Hétérogénéité des Territoires, *Flux*, 54, pp. 49-69.

Dupuy, G., 1975, *Une Technique de Planification au Service de l'Automobile: les Modèles de Trafic Urbain*, Document de travail, Action concertée de recherche urbaine, ATP, Paris.

Dupuy, G., 1977, *Histoire du 'Tacot': Le Petit Train de Pontoise à Poissy par Andrésy (1912-1935)*, Club Historique d'Andrésy, Andrésy (Fr.).

Dupuy, G., 1978, *Urbanisme et Technique: Chronique d'un Mariage de Raison*, CRU, Paris.

Dupuy, G., 1984, Pour Une Génétique des Réseaux Urbains, *Bulletin de l'IDATE*, 5.

Dupuy, G., 1986, *Systèmes Réseaux et Territoires*, Presses de l'école nationale des ponts et chaussées, Paris.

Dupuy, G. (ed.), 1987a, *La Crise des Réseaux d'Infrastructure: le Cas de Buenos Aires,* Presses de l'école nationale des ponts et chaussées, Paris.

Dupuy, G., 1987b, Vers Une Théorie Territoriale des Réseaux: Une Application au Transport Urbain, *Annales de Géographie*, n° 538.

Dupuy, G., 1988a, Utility Networks and Territory in the Paris Region: the Case of Andresy. In: Tarr, J. & G.Dupuy (eds), *Technology and the Rise of the Networked City in Europe and America*, Temple University Press, Philadelphia, pp. 295-306.

Dupuy, G., 1988b, La Crise des Infrastructures Urbaines aux Etats-Unis. In: Lefèvre, C., S. Body-Gendrot, G. Dacier, L. Davezies, G. Dupuy & J.C. Mathio, *Les Villes des Etats-Unis*, Masson, Paris.

Dupuy, G., 1991a, L'*Urbanisme des Réseaux: Théories et Méthodes*, Armand Colin, Paris.

Dupuy, G., 1991b, S'Habituer à des Étudiants Motorisés: Universités-parkings, *Urbanisme*, 250, September 1991.

Dupuy, G., 1995a, *Les Territoires de l'Automobile*, Anthropos Economica, Paris.

Dupuy, G., 1995b, *La Ville et l'Automobile*, Anthropos-Economica, Paris.

Dupuy, G., 1996, L'Automobile entre Villes et Campagnes. In: *Nouveaux Espaces et Systèmes Urbains: Livre Jubilaire en Hommage au Professeur Bernard Dezert*, SEDES, Paris.

Dupuy, G., 2000, A Revised History of Network Urbanism, *OASE,* 53, Network Urbanism / Netwerkstedenbouw, Uitgeverij SUN, Nijmegen.

Dupuy, G., 2002, *Internet, Géographie d'un Réseau*, Ellipses, Paris.

Dupuy, G., 2004, Internet: une Approche Géographique à l'Échelle Mondiale, *Flux*, 58, pp. 5-19.

Dupuy, G., 2005, Challenging the "Old" Urban Planning Paradigm: The Network Approach. In: L. Albrechts and S. Mandelbaum (eds), *The Network Society, a New Context for Planning*, Routledge, London/New York.

Dupuy G. & F. Germinet, 1992, Les Effets de la Motorisation Étudiante: Diagnostic et Perspectives. *6ème Congrès Mondial de la Recherche dans les Transports*, Lyons, July 1992.

Dupuy, G. & P. Sajous, 2000, L'Etalement Péri-urbain: Perspectives Internationales. In: Mattei, M.F. & D. Pumain, *Données Urbaines*, 3, Anthropos-Economica, Paris.

Dupuy, G. & J. Tarr (eds), 1984, Les Réseaux Techniques Urbains, *Les Annales de la Recherche Urbaine*, 23-24, July-December.

Dupuy, J.-P. & J. Robert, 1976, *La Trahison de l'Opulence*, Presses Universitaires de France, Paris.

Dutton, J.M. & W.H. Starbuck, 1974, Diffusion of an Intellectual Technology. Presented at the *Conference on Communication and Control in Social Processes*, University of Pennsylvania, November 1974.

E

Economides, N., 1996, The Economics of Networks, *International Journal of Industrial Organization*, 14, pp. 673–699.

EEA (European Environment Agency), 2006, *Urban Sprawl in Europe: The Ignored Challenge*, EEA Report 10, EEA, Copenhagen.

Emanuel, C., 1989, Le Transformazione Recenti delle Reti Urbane nella Padania Centro-occidentale, *Consiglio Nazionale delle Recerche, Progetto finalizzato Economia, Sotto Progetto 4, La diffusione territoriale dello Sviluppo*, Tema 8, Cuaderno 8.

ESPON, 2004, *Telecommunication Services and Networks: Territorial Trends and Basic Supply of Infrastructure for Territorial Cohesion*, CURDS, Newcastle Upon Tyne.

F

Faivre d'Arcier, B., J.M. Offner & A. Bieber, 1979, *Les Plans de Circulation. Évolution d'une Procédure Technique*, IRT, Paris.

Faure, H., 1959, Un Modèle Prospectif du Marché de l'Auto, *Consommation,* 4, October-December 1959.

FIA Foundation, 2005, *The Automobile and Society*, FIA, London.

Fichelet, R., M. Fichelet & N. May, 1970, *Pour une Approche Ecologique de l'Utilisation des Moyens de Transport: Contribution à une Psychosociologie des Comportements Urbains*, SERES-DAFU, DGRST.

Filderman, R., 1992, Commentaires sur le Phenomene du Rejet de la Boîte Automatique en Europe, *Revue Culture Technique,* 25, Automobile et Progrès.

Firmino, R.J., 2005, Planning the Unplannable: How Local Authorities Integrate Urban and ICT Policy Making, *Journal of Urban Technology*, 12 (2), pp. 49-69.

Fischer, C., 1992, Appels Privés, Significations Individuelle: Histoire Sociale du Téléphone Avant-guerre aux États-Unis, *Réseaux*, 55.

Fishman, R., 1977, *Urban Utopias in the Twentieth Century: Ebenezer Howard, Frank Lloyd Wright and Le Corbusier*, Basic Books, New York.

Fishman, R., 1990, Metropolis Unbound: The New City of the Twentieth Century, *Flux*, 1 (spring), Paris, pp. 44-55.

Fleury, C., 2004, Saint-Pierre et Miquelon, Îles et Frontières, *Norois*, 190, pp. 25-40.

Flichy, P. & P. Zarifian, 2002, Les Centres d'Appel, *Réseaux*, 20 (114), pp. 9-19.

Flonneau, M., 2002, *L'Automobile à la Conquête de Paris, 1910-1977. Formes Urbaines, Champs Politiques et Représentation*, PhD Thesis, Université Paris I.

Flonneau, M., 2005, *Paris et l'Automobile, un Siècle de Passion*, Hachette, Paris.

Florida, R., 2002, *The Rise of the Creative Class*, Harper Business, New York.

FNAU (Fédération Nationale des Agences d'Urbanisme), 1987, *La Ville et l'Eau*. Document handed out at the 9th annual FNAU meeting, October 1987, FNAU, Nantes.

Foreman-Peck, J., 1987, Deaths on the Roads: Changing National Response to Motor Accidents. In: Barker, T. (ed.), *The Economic and Social Effects of the Spread of Motor Vehicles*, MacMillan, London.

Frémont, A., 1988, *Géographie d'une Société*, Flammarion, Paris.

Frémont-Vanacore, A., 2004, Réseaux de Télécommunications et Aménagement du Territoire en France: Les Collectivités Locales au Cœur du Débat, *Flux*, 58, pp. 20-31.

Fridenson, P., 1991, La Société Française et les Accidents de la Route (1890-1914), *Ethnologie Française*, XXI, 3.

Frybourg, M., 1990, Transports: Les Mille et Une Manières d'Innover, *Politique Industrielle*, 19.

G

Gakenheimer, R., 1986, The Plight of American Infrastructure: What Reasons for the Neglect. In: Terny, G. & R. Prud'Homme (eds), *Le Financement des Équipements Publics de Demain*, Economica, Paris.

Gakenheimer, R., 1997, Rapid Motorization in the Developing Countries: Correlates and Consequences. In: Dupuy, G. (ed.), *Géographies de l'Automobile et Aménagement des Territoires*, Université Paris X / INRETS, Paris.

Gardes, F. & C. Starzec, 2002, Evidence on Addiction Effects from Households Expenditure Surveys: the Case of the Polish Panel. Presented at the *Econometric Society European Meeting*, Venice, August 2002.

Garreau, J., 1990, *Edge Cities*, Anchor Books, New York.

Garrison, W., 1990, Networks: Reminiscence and Lessons, *Flux*, 1 (spring), pp. 5-12.

Gay, J.C., 2003, *L'Outre-Mer Français, un Espace Singulier*, Belin, Paris.

Georgano, G.N., 1990, *Les Voitures de 1970 à 1990* (adaptation to French by D. Blanc), Editions Gründ, Paris.

Gibelli, M.C., 1988, Urban Planning Strategies and Tools to Cope with Technological and Socio-Economic Change in Metropolitan Areas. In: OECD, *Urban Development and Impacts of Technological Economic and Socio-Demographic Change: Report of an Expert Meeting*, OECD, Paris, June 1988.

Gille, L., 1989, La Société de Consommation: Naissance d'Une Nouvelle Economie, *Telecoms Magazine*, 28.

Giovannoni, G., 1931, *Vecchie Città ed Edilizia Nuova*, Unione Tipografica Editrice Torinese, Turin.

Gökalp, I., 1988, Les Systèmes Technologiques à Grande Échelle: les Réseaux et leur Impact, *Annales du Levant*, 3.

Goldfield, D., 1988, The Future of the Metropolitan Region. In: Schaffer, D. (ed.), *Two Centuries of American Planning*, Johns Hopkins University Press, Baltimore.

Gómez Barroso, J.L. & J. Pérez Martínez, 2004, The Geography of the Digital Divide: Broadband Deployment in the Community of Madrid, *Universal Access in the Information Society*, 3 (3-4), pp. 264-271.

Gómez Barroso, J.L. & J. Pérez Martínez, 2007, ADSL Deployment in the Community of Madrid: Investigating the Geographical Factors of the Digital Divide, *Telematics and Informatics*, 24 (2), pp. 101-114.

Gomez Ibanez, J.A., 1991, A Global View of Automobile Dependence, *Journal of the American Planning Association*, 57 (3), pp. 376–379.

Gorman, S.P. & E. J. Malecki, 2000, The Networks of the Internet: An Analysis of Provider Networks in the USA, *Telecommunications Policy*, 24, pp. 113-134.

Gossiaux, L.F., 1989, La Notion de Terrain et l'Approche Anthropologique: Mobilité des Jeunes dans les Ardennes et Automobilisme. In: Barjonet, P.E. (ed.), *Transports et Sciences Sociales: Questions de methode*, Paradigme, Caen (Fr.).

Gossiaux, L.F. & P.E. Barjonet, 1990, *Automobilisme et Société Locale: les Jeunes et l'Auto dans la Vallée de la Meuse. Une Approche Anthropologique*. Rapport INRETS 113, INRETS, Paris.

Gottman, J., 1972, Megalopolis and Antipolis: The Telephone and the Structure of the City. In: de Solla Pool, I. (ed.), *The Social Impact of the Telephone*, MIT Press, Cambridge MA.

Goubert, J.P., 1986, *La Conquête de l'Eau*, Robert Laffont, Paris.

Goubert, J.P., 1988, The Development of Water and Sewerage Systems in France, 1800-1850. In: Tarr, J.A. & G. Dupuy (eds), *Technology and the Rise of the Networked City in Europe and America*, Temple University Press, Philadelphia, pp. 116-136.

Goytisolo, J.A., 1993, El 'Seiscientos' en el Recuerdo, *Tribuna Libre*, October 1993.

GPU (Groupe Prospective et Usages sociaux de l'automobile), 2003, Séminaire 'Automobile, environnement et société à l'horizon 2010-2020 ', *Cahiers du CPVS*, 6, April 2003.

Graham, S. & S. Marvin, 2001, *Splintering Urbanism: Networked Infrastructures, Technological Mobilities and the Urban Condition*, Routledge, London/New York.

Gravier J.-F., 1947, *Paris et le Désert Français*, le Portulan, Paris.

Green, J., 1963, *Partir Avant le Jour*, Grasset, Paris.

Grubesic, T.H., 2004, The Geodemographic Correlates of Broadband Access and Availability in the United States, *Telematics and Informatics*, 21 (4), pp. 335-358.

Grubesic, T.H. & M.E. O'Kelly, 2002, Using Points of Presence to Measure Accessibility to the Commercial Internet, *The Professional Geographer*, 54 (2), pp. 259-284.

Grubesic, H. & A.T. Murray, 2002, Constructing the Divide, Spatial Disparities in Broadband Access, *Papers in Regional Science*, 81 (2), April 2002, pp. 197-221.

Grubesic, H. & A.T. Murray, 2004, 'Where' Matters: Location and Wi-Fi Access, *Journal of Urban Technology*, 11 (1), April 2004, pp. 1-28.

Gudmundsson, E.M., 2002, Au Pays des Poètes, des Elfes et des Troll, *Courrier International*, 616, pp. 44-45.

Guermond Y., 1994, La Poste et Ses Territoires, *Bulletin de l'IREPP*, April 1994.

Guillén, M.F. & S.L. Suarez, 2001, Developing the Internet: Entrepreneurship and Public Policy in Ireland, Singapore, Argentina, and Spain, *Telecommunications Policy*, 25, pp. 349-371.

Guillerme, A., 1988, The Genesis of Water Supply, Distribution and Sewerage Systems in France, 1800-1850. In: Tarr, J.A. & G. Dupuy (eds), *Technology and the Rise of the Networked City in Europe and America*, Temple University Press, Philadelphia, pp. 91-115.

Guillot, D., 1986, *Les Îles Saint-Pierre et Miquelon au XXéme Siècle*, PhD Thesis, Université Paris I.

H

Hall, P., 1988, Impact of New Technologies and Socio-Economic Trends on Urban Forms and Functioning. In: *Urban Developement and Impact of Technological Economic and Socio-Demographic Changes. Report of an Expert Meeting*, June 1988, OECD, Paris.

Hargittai, E., 1999, Weaving the Western Web: Explaining Differences in Internet Connectivity Among OECD Countries, *Telecommunications Policy*, 23 (10-11), pp. 701-718.

Haumont, N. & F. Wintersdorff, 1990, *Les Pratiques de l'Habitat Français 1960-1990*, CRH, Paris.

Haussmann, G., 1879, *Memoires, 1853-1870. Grands Travaux de Paris*, Paris.

Haussmann, G., 1893, *Memoires III. Grands travaux de Paris*, Paris.

Hayashi, K., 1992, From Network Externalities to Interconnection: the Changing Nature of Networks and Economy. In: Antonelli, C. (ed.), *The Economics of Information Networks*, North Holland, Amsterdam.

Hibbs, J., 1983, Urban Bus Transport in Buenos Aires: The Colectivos, *Transportation Research Record*, 914, Transportation Research Board, Washington D.C.

Hillier, B. & J. Hanson, 1984, *The Social Logic of Space*, Cambridge University Press, Cambridge.

Hirsch B., 1990, *L'Invention d'une Ville Nouvelle*, Presses de l'école nationale des ponts et chaussées, Paris.

Hughes, T.P., 1983, *Networks of Power. Electrification in Western Society*, Johns Hopkins University Press, Baltimore.

Hughes, T.P., 1987, Visions of Electrification and Social Change. In: *1880-1980, un Siècle d'Electricité dans le Monde, Actes du Premier Colloque International d'Histoire de l'Electricité*, PUF, Paris.

I

Icelandic New Energy Ltd., 2003, *Ecological City Transport System (ECTOS)*, Icelandic New Energy Ltd., Reykjavik.

IDATE, 2002, *Etude sur les TIC: Préparation au Programme d'Action du SEOM pour le Passage de l'Outre-mer à la Société de l'Information. Synthèse: la Situation à Saint-Pierre et Miquelon*, IDATE, Montpellier (Fr.).

Illitch, I., 1974, *Energy and Equity*, Harper and Row, New-York.

INRETS, 1983, *Travailler à Paris, Vivre à 100 km: Les Migrants SNCF en Grande Région Parisienne*, Note d'Information, 27, Paris.

INRETS, 1989, *L'Amélioration de l'Offre de Transport: De l'Induction Directe à l'Apprentissage de la Mobilité à Longue Distance*, Rapport INRETS, 97, Paris.

INRETS, 2005, Hausse du prix du pétrole, quels impacts sur les comportements?, *Axes*, 2, November 2005.

Institut de l'Audiovisuel et des Télécommunications en Europe, 2001, *Synthèse de l'État des Lieux des NTIC dans les DOM, Saint-Pierre et Miquelon et Mayotte*, Institut de l'Audiovisuel et des Télécommunications en Europe, Montpellier (Fr.).

ITU (International Telecommunication Union), 2002, *Yearbook of Statistics: Telecommunications Services Chronological Time Series 1992-2001*, ITU, Geneva.

INRA, 2004, *Telecoms Services Indicators 2002*. Produced for the European Commission, DG Information Society.

J

Jacobson, C., S. Klepper & J. Tarr, 1985, Water, Electricity and Cable Television: A Study of Contrasting Historical Patterns of Ownership and Regulation, *Urban Resources*, 3, pp. 9-18.

Jacquin, C., 2003, Les Services d'Hébergement d'Internet en France, *Netcom*, 17 (1-2), pp. 23-34.

Jaillet, M.C., 1981, L*es Pavillonneurs: La Production de la Maison Individuelle dans la Région Toulousaine*, PhD Thesis under the direction of G. Jalabert, Université Toulouse-Le Mirail (Fr.).

K

Kahin, B. & C. Nesson (eds), 1996, *Borders in Cyberspace, Information Policy and the Global Information Infrastructure*, MIT Press, Cambridge, Mass.

Kellerman, A., 2000, Where Does It Happen? The Location of the Production and Consumption of Web Information, *Journal of Urban Technology*, 17 (1), pp. 45-61.

Kenworthy, J.R. & F.B. Laube, 1999, Patterns of Automobile Dependence in Cities: an International Overview of Key Physical and Economic Dimensions with some Implications for Urban Policy, *Transportation Research Part A*, 33 (7-8), pp. 691-723.

Kenworthy, J., F. Laube, T. Raad, C. Poboon & G. Benedicto, 1999, *An International Sourcebook of Automobile Dependence in Cities, 1960-1990*, University Press of Colorado, Denver, CO.

Kotkin, J., 2000, *The New Geography: How the Digital Revolution is Reshaping the American Landscape*, Random House, New York.

Kristan, M., 2002, *Otto Wagner: Villen, Wohn- und Geschäftshäuser, Interieurs; ausgeführte Bauten*, Album Verlag, Vienna.

Krost-Lapierre, E., 1993, *Les Déplacements Motorisés des Étudiants. Problematique du Stationnement a l'Université de Paris-X Nanterre*, Masters Thesis under direction of Gabriel Dupuy, Universite de Paris-X Nanterre.

Kunstler, J.H., 1993, *The Geography of Nowhere, The Rise and Decline of American Man-Made Landscape*, Touchstone, New York.

L

La Rochefoucauld (de), B., 1982, *L' Anbondance Foncière*, Paris, Dunod.

Lacoste, X., 1991, *La Ville du Service: Le Service de Distribution d'Eau et son Territoire dans l'Agglomération de Rabat-Salé au Maroc*, PhD Thesis under direction of H. Coing, Université Paris XII.

Lamure, C.B., 1995, *Quelle Auto dans la Ville?* Presses de l'école nationale des ponts et chaussées, Paris.

Larroque, D., 1988, Economic Aspects of Public Transit in the Parisian Area 1855-1939. In: Tarr, J.A. & G. Dupuy (eds), *Technology and the Rise of the Networked City in Europe and America*, Temple University Press, Philadelphia, pp. 44-66.

Lassave P., 1987, *L'Expérience des Plans de Déplacements Urbains (1983-1986)*, CETUR, Ministère de l'Equipement, Bagneux (Fr.).

Lauraire R., 1987, *Le Téléphone des Ménages Français: Genèse et Fonctions d'un Espace Social Immatériel*, La Documentation Française, Paris.

Lauvray, M.-C. & D.Pascal, 1995, *La Renault 4 de Mon Père*, E.T.A.I., Boulogne-Billancourt (Fr.).

LeBlanc, G., 2001, Les Nouveaux Districts Industriels des Technologies de l'Information: l'Exemple de Denver aux Etats-Unis. In: DATAR, *Réseaux d'Entreprises et Territoires, Regards sur Les Systèmes Productifs Locaux*, La Documentation Française, Paris, pp. 97-116.

Le Gaboteur Inc., 2004, *Terre-Neuve-et-Labrador & Saint-Pierre-et-Miquelon: Guide Touristique 2004-2005*, Le Gaboteur Inc., St John's (OCT St. Pierre et Miquelon).

Lee-Gosselin, M. & E. Pas, 1997, The Implications of Emerging Contexts for Travel Behaviour. In: Stopher, P. & M. Lee-Gosselin (eds), *Understanding Travel Behaviour in an Era of Change*, Pergamon/Elsevier Science Ltd., Oxford.

Leralta, J., 1991, *Madrid, Villa y Coche*, Ediciones La Libreria, Madrid.

Lévy, J., 1994, Oser le Désert? Des Pays sans Paysan, *Les Nouveaux Espaces Ruraux, Sciences Humaines*, 4, hors série, 1994, pp. 6-9.

Lewis, R. (ed.), 2004, *Manufacturing Suburbs: Building Work and Home on the Metropolitan Fringe*, Temple University Press, Philadelphia.

Libby, W.L., 1969, La Fin du Trajet Quotidien, *Analyse et Prévision*, 7.

Lieutaud, J., 1994, L'Ile-de-France et l'Aménagement du Grand Bassin Parisien, *Cahiers du CREPIF*, 57.

Lina.Net, 2003, *Internet*; www.lina.net/Forsida/Fyrirteaki/Internet, accessed 2003.

Lorentzon, S., 1998, The Role of ICT as a Locational Factor in Peripheral Regions: Examples from 'IT-Active' Local Authority Areas in Sweden, *Netcom*, Special Issue 12 (1-3), pp. 303-331.

Lung, Y., 1997, New Automobile Spaces, *La Lettre du GERPISA*, 115.

M

MacGregor, A., 1997, La Lutte contre l'Exclusion dans les Quartiers en Difficulté: l'Expérience Britannique (The struggle against exclusion in areas in difficulty: the British experience), *2001 Plus*, 43, pp. 7-41.

Madre, J.-L., 1995, Les Nouveaux Captifs de l'Automobile, *Cahiers de l'IAURIF*, 122.

Madre, J.L. & J. Armoogun, 1994, *Motorisation et Mobilité des Franciliens dans les Années 2000*, INRETS, Paris.

Madre, J.L. & A. Pirotte, 1997, Regionalisation of Car-fleet and Traffic Forecasts. In: Stopher, P. & M. Lee-Gosselin (eds), *Understanding Travel Behaviour in an Era of Change*, Pergamon, Elsevier Science Ltd., Oxford.

Malecki, E.J., 2002, The Economic Geography of the Internet's Infrastructure, *Economic Geography*, 78 (4), pp. 399-424.

Martinand, C., 1986, *Le Génie Urbain*, La Documentation Française, Paris.

Massot M.-H, J. Armoogum, P. Ledily, J.-L. Madre & J.-P. Orfeuil, 1995, *Espaces de Vie, Espaces de Travail: 15 Ans d'Evolution* (Living Spaces, Working Spaces, 15 Years of Evolution), INRETS, Paris.

Mayoux, J., 1979, *Demain l'Espace. L'Habitat Individuel Péri-urbain*. Rapport de la Mission d'Étude Présidée par Jacques Mayoux, La Documentation Française, Paris.

McShane, C., 1994, *Down the Asphalt Path*, Columbia University Press, New York.

McShane, C., 1993, The Roots of Traffic Control, 1897-1929. Paper presented at the *XIXth International Conference of the History of Science*, Zaragoza, Spain, August, 1993.

Mellet, F., 1971, Méthodes Modernes de Préparation des Décisions Appliquées à l'Aménagement, *Bilan Raisonné de l'Expérience Française*, Cahiers de l'IAURP, 25, octobre 1971.

Mende, H.-U. von & M. Diete, 1994, *Kleinwagen - Small Cars - Petites Voitures,* Taschen, Köln.

Menerault, P., 1994, Contribution à une Analyse Morphologique des Réseaux Viaires, *Flux*, 16, April-June 1994, pp. 49-67.

Merdrignac, C., 1989, *Les Centres de Proximité: Un Nouvel Enjeu pour les Gestionnaires Urbains: Le Cas d'Orgemont à Epinay-sur-Seine*. Post-graduate Thesis under the direction of Anne Fournié, Institut d'Urbanisme de Paris.

Merlin P., 1984, *La Planification du Transport Urbain*, Masson, Paris.

Michon, R. et al., 1989, PRAO, Planification des Réseaux Assistée par Ordinateur. Paper delivered at the *Représentation Graphique des Réseaux seminar*, Cahiers du GDR Réseaux.

Miliutin, N.A., 1974, *Sotsgorod. The Problem of Building Socialist Cities*, MIT Press, Cambridge, Mass.

Ministère des Affaires Étrangères, 2006, *Spatial Planning and Sustainable Development in France*. Ministère des Affaires Étrangères, Paris.

Mitchell, W.J., 1995, *City of Bits*, MIT Press, Cambridge, Mass.

Moles, A.A., 1987, La Cité Cablée: une Nouvelle Qualité de Vie, *Les Annales de la Recherche Urbaine*, 34, Spring-Summer 1987, pp. 80-86.

Moriset, B. & N. Bonnet, 2005, La Géographie des Centres d'Appel en France, *Annales de Géographie*, 641, pp. 49-72.

Moss, M.L. & A. Townsend, 1997, Tracking the Net: Using Domain Names to Measure the Growth of the Internet in U.S. Cities, *Journal of Urban Technology*, 4 (3), pp. 47-60.

Moss, M.M. & A.M. Townsend, 2000, The Internet Backbone and the American Metropolis, *The Information Society*, 16 (1), pp. 35-47.

Mumford, L., 1964, *The Highway and the City*, Seeker and Warburg, London.

N

Neret, G. & H. Poulain, 1989, *L'Art, la Femme et l'Automobile*, E.P.A., Paris.

Neuschwander, C., 1988, Villes et Réseaux, *Alternatives Économiques*, 62, December 1988, pp. 22-23.

Newman, P.W.G., 1996, Reducing Automobile Dependence, *Environment and Urbanization*, 8 (1), pp. 67-92.

Newman, C., 2000, Iceland Technology Landscape. In: *MOGIT, Information Technology Landscape in Nations, Management in Global Information Technology Program [MOGIT]* at American University, Washington, D.C.

Newman, P. & J.R. Kenworthy, 1991, *Cities and Automobile Dependence,* Gower Technical, Brookfield, Vermont.

Newman, P., J.R. Kenworthy, 1998, *Sustainability and Cities: Overcoming Automobile Dependence*, Island Press, Washington, D.C.

Newman, P.W.G., J.R. Kenworthy & P. Vintila, 1995, Can we Overcome Sutomobile Dependence? Physical Planning in an Age of Urban Cynicism, *Cities*, 12 (1), pp. 53-65.

Nieuwenhuis, P. & P. Wells, 1997, *The Death of Motoring? Car Making and Automobility in the 21st Century*, Wiley, Chichester.

Nutley, S.D., 1985, Planning Options for the Improvement of Rural Accessibility: Use of the Time-space Approach, *Regional Studies,* 19, pp. 37–50.

Nutley, S.D., 1996, Rural Transport Problems and Non-car Populations in the USA, *Journal of Transport Geography,* 4 (2), pp. 93–106.

O

Offner, J.M., 1990, La Représentation Graphique de Réseaux: Outil Heuristique ou Innovation de Gestion?, *Flux*, 2, pp. 61-65.

Offner, J.M. & A. Sander, 1990, *Les Points-Clés d'Autrement Bus. Des Théories à la Pratique: Analyse de la Mise en Oeuvre d'une Innovation à la RATP*, RATP, Paris.

Orfeuil, J.P., 1993, France: a Centralized Country in between Regional and European Development. In: Salomon, I., P. Bovy & J.P. Orfeuil (eds), *A Billion Trips a Day - Tradition and Transition in European Travel Patterns*, Kluwer Academic, Amsterdam/Dordrecht, pp. 241-256.

P

Paché, G., 1989, L'Organisation Spatiale de la Firme: Modes de Transaction et Technologies de l'Information. Paper delivered at the *International Geographical Union, Commission on Communications and Telecommunications Geography*, Geneva, 7-8 November 1989.

Paltridge, S., 1999, OECD Regulatory and Statistical Update, *Telecommunications Policy*, 23, pp. 683-686.

Patterson, R.W., 1966, *Forecasting Techniques for Determining the Potential Demand for Highways*, University of Missouri.

Perry, C., 1929, *Neighborhood and Community Planning*, Regional Plan of New York and Its Environs, New York.

Petrazzini, B.A. & A. Guerrero, 2000, Promoting Internet Development: The Case of Argentina, *Telecommunications Policy,* 24, pp. 89-112.

Pinaud C., 1988, Trans, Inter, Com, Pac: Petit Abécédaire de la Communication. In: Dupuy, G. (ed.), *Réseaux Territoriaux*, Paradigme, Caen (Fr.).

Pinson, D., 1987, Nantes, Chantenay: l'Installation du Service d'Eau contre l'Indépendance Communale. In: Burlen, K. (ed.), *La Banlieue Oasis, Henri Sellier et les Cités-jardins, 1900-1940,* Saint-Denis, Presses Universitaires de Vincenne (Fr.).

Pinson, D. & S. Thomann, 2002, *La Maison en ses Territoires: De la Villa à la Ville Diffuse*, l'Harmattan, Paris.

Piveteau, J.L., 1990, La Voiture, Signe et Agent d'une Nouvelle Relation de l'Homme à l'Espace, *Cahiers de l'Institut de Géographie de Fribourg*, 7.

PREDIT, 2005, Idées de Villes en Italie, *Recherches et Synthèses*, 18.

Prud'homme, R., 1997, Urban Transport and Economic Development, *Régions et Développement*, 5.

R

RACS, 1995, *Car Dependence*, RAC Foundation for Motoring and the Environment, London.

Raffestin, C., 1980, *Pour un Géographie du Pouvoir*, Litec, Paris.

Raffestin, C., 1987, Repères Pour Une Théorie de la Territorialité Humaine, *Groupe Réseaux*, 7.

Randle, P.H., 1985, El Pensamiento Urbanistico en los Siglos XIX y XX, *Oikos*, Buenos Aires.

Raux, C., 1993, Centralité, Polynuclearité et Étalement Urbain: Application au Cas de l'Agglomeration Lyonnaise. In: Bussiere, Y. & A.Bonnafou (eds), *Transport et Étalement Urbain: les Enjeux. Colloquium Les Chemins de la Recherche.* Programme Rhône-Alpes de Recherche en Sciences Humaines.

Reggazola, T. & J.P. Desgoutte, 1979, Chroniques de la Pendularité, *Transports et Société: Colloque de Royaumont,* April 1978, Economica, Paris.

Ribeill, G., 1986, Le Développement à la Française des Réseaux Techniques, *Metropolis*, 73-74.

Ribeill, G., 1991, From Pneumatics to Highway Logistics: André Michelin, Instigator of the Automobile Revolution, *Flux*, 3, pp. 9-19.

Ribeill, G., 1992, Du Pneumatique à la Logistique Routière: André Michelin, Promoteur de la Revolution Automobile, *Culture Technique*, 19.

Riboud, J., 1981, *La Ville Heureuse*, Le Moniteur, Paris.

Rietveld, P. & J. van Nierop, 1995, Urban Growth and the Development of Transport Networks: The Case of the Dutch Railways in the Nineteenth Century, *Flux*, 19, pp. 31-43.

Roncayolo, M., 1990, *La Ville et Ses Territoires*, Gallimard, Paris.

Rooij, R.M., 2005, *The Mobile City. The Planning and Design of the Network City from a Mobility Point of View*, PhD Thesis under the direction of Paul Drewe, February 2005, TRAIL Thesis Series, T2005/1, Delft (Neth.).

Roos, P., 1992, *L'Automobile*, Economica, Paris.

Rosenbloom, S., 1992, Why Do Working Families Need a Car? In: Wachs, M. & M. Crawford (eds), *The Car and the City: The Automobile, The Built Environment and Daily Urban Life*, University of Michigan Press, Ann Arbor, Michigan.

Roth, G., 1996, *Roads in a Market Economy*, Avebury Technical, Aldershot (UK).

Rouge, M.F., 1953, L'Organisation de l'Espace et les Réseaux. In: *Eventail de l'Histoire Vivante: Hommage à Lucien Febvre*, Armand Colin, Paris.

Rousseau, E., 2001, *La Démotorisation. Comment se Sépare-t-on de sa Voiture?* Rapport de Stage de Mémoire de DEA-Transport, under the direction of Gabriel Dupuy and Laurent Hivert, Université Paris XII-ENPC-INRETS.

Ruppert, W., 1993, Das Auto, Herrschaft über Raum und Zeit. In: Ruppert, W. (ed.), *Fahrrad, Auto, Fernsehschrank: zur Kulturgeschichte der Alltagsdinge*, Fischer Taschenbuch, Frankfurt-am-Main, pp. 119-161.

Rutherford, J., 2004, *A Tale of Two Global Cities: Comparing the Territorialities of Telecommunications Developments in Paris and London*, Ashgate Publishing, Aldershot (UK).

Rutherford, J., A. Gillespie & R. Richardson, 2004, The Territoriality of Pan-European Telecommunications Backbone Networks, *Journal of Urban Technology*, 11 (3), pp. 1-34.

Rutkowski, A.M., 2000, Understanding Next-Generation Internet: An Overview of Developments, *Telecommunications Policy*, 24, pp. 469-476.

S

Sachs, W., 1992, *For Love of the Automobile*, University of California Press, Berkeley.

Sajous, P., 2003, *L'Automobilité Périurbaine en France: Une Façon d'Habiter*, PhD Thesis under the direction of Gabriel Dupuy, Université Paris I.

Salgé, F. & M.N. Sclafer, 1989, *A Geographic Data Model based on HBDS Concepts: The IGN Cartographic Database model*, IGN, Paris.

Salingaros, N.A., 2005, *Principles of Urban Structure*, Series Design/Science/Planning, Techne Press, Amsterdam.

Sansot, P., 1984, L'Eau, *Urbanisme*, 201.

Sansot, P., 1990, Transports Publics, Transports de la Ville, *Transport Public*, 6, p. 102.

Sauvy, A., 1968, *Les Quatre Roues de la Fortune: Essai sur l'Automobile*, Flammarion, Paris.

Savy, M. & P. Veltz, 1989, Le Transport Par Flux Tendus, *Les Cahiers Scientifiques du Transport*, 19.

Scharf, V., 1991, *Taking the Wheel, Woman and the Coming of the Motor Age*, The Free Press, New York.

Scheou, B., 1997, *Modélisation des Déplacements Domicile-Travail en Milieu Périurbain: le Cas de la Région Lyonnaise*, PhD Thesis under the direction of A. Bonnafous, Université Lumière-Lyon II.

Schorske, C., 1984, *Vienne, Fin de Siècle*, Le Seuil, Paris.

Senett, R., 1979, *Les Tyrannies de l'Intimité*, Le Seuil, Paris.

SERC, 1962, Modèles de Trafic, *Note d'information,* 3.

Serratosa, A., 1998, Prologue. In: Dupuy, G., *El Urbanismo de las Redes, Teorías y Métodos*, Oikos-Tau, Barcelona.

Serres, M., 1972, *Hermès II: L'Interférence*, Editions de Minuit, Paris.

Social and Cultural Planning Office of the Netherlands, 1975-1985-1995, *Time Use Survey*, Den Haag.

Soria y Mata, A., 1913 (1979), *La Cité Lineaire, Nouvelles Architectures des Villes*, Ecole Nationale des Beaux-arts, Paris.

Soughir, R., 1984, *L'Enjeu de l'Eau à Sousse, la Production Sociale d'un Déficit*, PhD Thesis under the direction of G. Amar, Institut d'Urbanisme de Paris, Université Paris XII.

Stathopoulos, N., 1990, *Pour une conception territoriale des réseaux: modèles conceptuels, aspects stratégiques et outils d'aide à la decision. Le projet "Autrement Bus" de la RATP*, PhD Thesis, Université Paris IX-Dauphine.

Statistics Iceland, 2000, *Statistical Facts about Iceland*, Statistics Iceland, Reykjavik.

Steinberg, J. & J. Husser, 1988, *Cartographie Dynamique applicable à l'Aménagement*, SEDES, Paris.

Steyer, A. & J.B. Zimmermann, 1996, Externalités de Réseau et Adoption d'un Standard dans une Structure Résiliaire, *Revue d'Economie Industrielle,* 2nd Trimestre, 76, pp. 67–90.

Stiegler, B., 1994, Aménager la Déterritorialisation, *Revista Alliage*, 21.

Stopher, P. R., 1971, *Lectures Notes on Urban Transportation Planning*, Cornell University.

Strizioli, R. (ed.), 1990, *La 500*, Bacchetta Editore, Albenga.

Swan, H.S., 1922, *The Thorougfares and Traffic of PATERSON, A Report of the City Plan Commission*, Paterson, New Jersey.

T

Tarr, J. (ed.), 1979, The City and Technology, *Journal of Urban History*, 5 (3).

Tarr, J., 1984, Evolution of the Urban Infrastructure in the Nineteenth and Twentieth Centuries. In: Hanson, R. (ed.), *Perspectives on Urban Infrastructure*, National Academy Press, Washington D.C.

Tarr, J. & G. Dupuy (eds), 1988, *Technology and the Rise of the Networked City in Europe and America*, Temple University Press, Philadelphia.

Taylor, B.D. & P.M. Ong, 1995, Spatial Mismatch or Automobile Mismatch? An Examination of Race, Residence and Commuting in US Metropolitan Areas, *Urban Studies*, 32 (9), pp. 1453-1473.

Taylor, M.A.P., W. Young & P.W. Bonsall, 1996, *Understanding Traffic Systems: Data, Analysis and Presentation*, Avebury, Sydney.

Terrier, C., 1989, Recherche d'un Espace de Référence pour l'Economie Régionale: d'Un Concept de Territoire à un Concept de Réseau, *Revue d'Economie Régionale et Urbaine*, 3.

Teyssot, G., 1988, *La Métropole en Représentation*, Cahiers du CCI, Paris.

Thiard, P., 2001, *Les Dynamiques du Bassin Parisien (1975-1990): Un Système Spatial entre Mutations du Système Productif et Impact des Politiques Publiques*, PhD Thesis, Université Paris I.

Thibault, S., 1995, The Morphology and Growth of Urban Technical Networks: A Fractal Approach, *Flux*, 19, pp. 17-30.

Triantafillou, C., 1987, *La Dégradation et La Réhabilitation des Réseaux d'Assainissement: France-Angleterre-Etats-Unis*, PhD Thesis under the supervision of Gabriel Dupuy, LATTS, CNRS.

Troy, P.N., 1992, The New Feudalism, *Urban Futures* 2 (2), pp. 36-44.

V

van Kleef, F, 2008, Techniek en Stadsontwikkeling. In: R. Dijkgraaf, L. Fresco & M. van Calmthout, *Betacanon: Wat Iedereen Moet Weten Van De Natuurwetenschappen*, Meulenhoff, Amsterdam.

Vaudoyer, J.L., 1946, *Le Souvenir de Marcel Mallet*, Mallet company, Andrésy/Paris.

Virilio, P., 1984, *L'Espace Critique*, Christian Bourgois, Paris.

Virilio, P., 1987, Cité, Miroir, Agonie, *Les Annales de la Recherche Urbaine*, 34, June-July 1987, pp. 40-42.

Virilio, P., 1988, La machine a descendre le temps, *Liberation*, 11 October 1988.

Virilio, P., 1991, For a Geography of Trajectories, *Flux*, 5, July-September 1991.

Voorhees, A.M., 1956, A General Theory of Traffic Movement. In: *1955 Proceedings, Institute of Traffic Engineers*, New Haven, Connecticut.

W

Wachter, S., J. Theys, Y. Crozet, J.-P. Orfeuil, 2005, La Mobilité Urbaine en Débat, Cinq Scénarios pour le Futur, *Débats*, 46.

Walcott, S.M. & J.O. Wheeler, 2001, Atlanta in the Telecommunications Age: The Fiber-Optic Information Network, *Urban Geography*, 22, pp. 316-339.

Walford R., 1981, *Signposts for Geography Teaching*, Longman, London.

Webber, M.M., 1992, The Joys of Automobility. In: Wachs, M. & M. Crawford (eds), *The Car and the City: The Automobile, The Built Environment and Daily Urban Life,* University of Michigan Press, Ann Arbor, Michigan.

Webster, F.V. & N.J. Paulley (eds), 1990, *Urban Land-Use and Transport Interaction: Policies and Models.* Report of the International Study Group on Land-Use/-Transport Interaction (ISGLUTI), Avebury, Aldershot (UK).

Wenglenski, S. & J.-P. Orfeuil, 2004, Differences in Accessibility to the Job Market according to Social Status and Place of Residence in the Paris Area, *Built Environment*, 30 (2), pp. 116-126.

Whitt J.A., 1982, *Urban Elites and Mass Transportation: The Dialectics of Power,* Princeton University Press, Princeton, New Jersey.

Wiel, M. & Y. Rollier, 1993, La Pérégrination au Sein de l'Agglomération, Constats à Propos du Site de Brest, *Les Annales de la Recherche Urbaine,* 59-60, November 1993, pp. 152-162.

Wilhelm, S.M.A., 1999, The Geography behind the Internet Cloud-Peering, Transit and Access Issues, *Netcom,* 13 (3-4), pp. 235-252.

Williot, J.P., 1990, Nouvelle Ville, Nouvelle Vie: Croissance et Rôle du Réseau Gazier Parisien au XIXe Siècle. In: Caron, F. et al, *Paris et ses Réseaux: Naissance D'Un Mode de Vie Urbain XIX - XX Siecles*, Hotel d'Angouleme-Lamoignon, Paris, pp. 213-232.

Wise, A., 1971, The Impact of Electronic Communications on Metropolitan Form, *Ekistics,* 188, pp. 22-31.

Womack, J.P., D.T. Jones & D. Roos, 1990, *The Machine That Changed the World*, MacMillan, New York.

Wright, F.L., 1923, *Experimenting with Human Lives*, Fine Art Society, Hollywood, CA.

Wright, F.L., 1945, *When Democracy Builds*, University Of Chicago Press, Chicago.

Wright, F.L., 1953, *The Future of Architecture,* Horizon Press, New York.

Wright, F.L., 1958, *The Living City*, Horizon Press, New York.

Y

Yook, S.-H., H. Jeong, & A.-L. Barabási, 2002, Modeling the Internet's large-scale topology, *Proceedings of the National Academy of Sciences,* 99 (21), October 2002, pp. 13382-13386.

Z

Zahavi, Y., 1976, *Travel Characteristics in Cities of Developing and Developed Countries*, World Bank Working Paper 230.

Zahavi, Y., 1982, *Travel Regularities in Baltimore, Washington, London and Reading. UMOT Travel Model Project,* US Department of Transportation, Washington, D.C.

Zimmerman, R. & T. Horan (eds), 2004, *Digital Infrastructures: Enabling Civil and Environmental Systems Through Information Technology*, Routledge, London.

Zook, M., 2000, Internet Metrics: Using Host and Domain Counts to Map the Internet, *Telecommunications Policy*, 24, pp. 613-620.

Index

fixed-line telephony 190, 215, 222, 246

fleet effect 146

flows 19, 25, 27, 31–35, 38, 42, 58, 60, 72, 85, 88, 90–93, 97, 101, 109, 112, 172

Ford 20, 24, 27, 28, 115, 124, 133, 188

forecasting 85–90, 93, 94, 123, 174

fractal 217, 219, 242, 258, 261

frontiers 43

G

garage 23, 65, 66, 124, 237, 238

garden cities 129

gas 23, 66, 77–84, 97, 100, 112, 124, 147, 237, 239, 245

gateway(s) 57, 205, 208, 239, 246

gentrification 168

geographers 41, 209

geographical
  - **areas** 72, 241
  - **characteristics** 183, 194
  - **differences** 216
  - **digital divide** 215
  - **dimensions of the digital divide** 217
  - **disparities** 217
  - **distances** 215
  - **isolation** 183, 193
  - **proximity** 64
  - **scale** 59, 239, 241
  - **space** 20, 22, 34, 217
  - **studies** 131

geography 58, 65, 66, 186, 191, 215, 216, 219, 221, 251

geopolitical 174, 175

global 37, 89, 94, 139, 140, 149, 150, 153, 155, 183, 187–189, 193, 194, 200, 203–208, 215–219, 221, 238, 239, 243–246, 248, 253

governance 176, 189, 190, 193, 195, 203, 249, 255

government 30, 50, 54, 58, 84–89, 92, 100, 105, 108, 140, 162, 163, 171, 174, 189, 190, 199, 201, 204, 207, 208, 222, 227–233, 252

grass-roots actors 118

H

Hall 54, 124, 138, 141, 274

Haussmann 20, 21, 28, 38

heating 45, 52, 124, 258, 259

hierarchy 32, 64, 67, 72, 108, 109, 150, 193, 201, 202, 221

high-speed 117, 138, 177, 194, 195, 211, 212, 215, 229, 239, 246, 247, 258
  - **train** 117

history
  - **of urban infrastructure networks** 97
  - **of urbanism** 19, 28, 30, 33

holistic 54, 82, 109, 176

home 27, 40, 42, 57, 58, 59, 62–66, 78, 97, 103, 106, 118, 121, 124, 128, 131, 134, 144, 165–168, 173, 178, 179, 183–190, 237, 238, 249, 254

hub 111, 116, 188, 194, 198, 203–207, 225, 227, 232, 233

hypermarkets 66, 167

I

ICT 24, 25, 28, 49, 62, 63, 66, 187, 195–203, 206–233, 238–240, 243–248, 252

ICT age 211, 244, 248

identity 40, 41, 78, 101, 112, 130, 134, 143, 184, 185, 208, 221

Ile-de-France 95, 112, 211, 212, 219, 221, 222, 224, 225, 227, 228, 229, 230, 231, 233, 240, 241

immigrants 66, 134, 136

inequalities 44, 175, 221

infrastructure 20, 43–48, 52, 54, 58–66, 72, 80–82, 88, 92, 96–109, 112, 127, 143, 148, 169, 174, 178, 184, 193, 194, 196, 203, 204, 211, 219, 223, 228, 239, 244, 245, 249–255, 260
  - **network** 43–46, 52, 54, 58–62, 65, 66, 72, 80, 81, 97–108, 127, 196, 244, 245, 260

innovation 134, 186, 188, 201, 221, 224, 225, 233, 244, 246, 253

INRETS 60, 174, 175

instantaneousness 19, 25, 57, 251

Insull 22, 23, 27, 28, 68

Internet 19, 24, 74, 183–208, 211, 215–222, 227, 237–247, 254, 257, 261

network(s)
 - strategy 23
 - time 25, 260, 261
 - urbanism 238, 241, 243, 248, 252, 260, 261
 - visualization 74
bus - 101
electricity - 24, 27, 28, 54, 58, 59, 68, 77, 81,
   109, 115, 117, 216, 239, 247, 248
broadcasting - 43, 111, 199
cable TV - 51, 199, 200
consumption - 47, 48
digital public telephone - 184
digital telephone - 195
economic - 188
emergence of - 37, 251
energy - 111
Eurovision - 111-115
hierarchical - 21
information - 63, 109
infrastructure - 43–46, 52, 54, 58–62, 65, 66,
   72, 80, 81, 97–108, 127, 196, 244, 245, 260
Internet - 24, 217 , 190
maximal - 43
modern concept of - 22
optical - 193, 194
personal - 47
physical - 68, 117
polar - 72, 74
premium - 211, 240, 246, 253
production - 47
projected transaction - 42
public utility - 77
radial - 219
railway - 77, 100, 103, 112, 117, 254
random - 257 , 258
real - 41, 44, 45, 46, 47, 50, 54, 72, 260 – see
   also virtual -
road - 32, 35, 49–51, 54, 59, 60, 67, 69, 74, 78,
   87–95, 102, 105, 106, 109, 124, 134, 139, 141,
   144, 148–154, 157, 160, 161, 247, 255
routine - 243
scale-free - 257, 258
seamless - 254
social - 61
technical - 30, 117, 118, 239
telephone - 24, 36, 57, 58, 101, 102, 107, 109,
   148, 184, 195, 200, 204, 239, 245

territorial - 43, 46
travel - 60, 250
urban - 62, 91, 99, 103, 239
utility - 77, 78
virtual - 43, 44, 45, 46, 47, 49, 54, 72 , 193 – see
   also virtual -
new towns 52, 82, 129
node 36, 41, 53, 59, 64, 125, 199, 204
non-car owning households 167
nostalgia 241

O

OECD 138, 184, 190, 193
oil industry 139
oil prices 123, 174
operator 42–54, 57, 67, 68, 74, 77–80, 149, 157, 187,
   199, 200, 204, 208, 211, 227–229, 240, 241, 253,
   258, 260
   level-one - 47, 49–51, 54
   level-three - 49
   level-two - 51, 53
   network - 28, 44, 47–51, 54, 58, 61, 67, 103,
      225, 260
   telecom - 184, 185, 187, 189, 190
origin-destination
 - matrix 149
 - surveys 85, 88

P

paradigm 61, 64, 178, 244
parking 89, 90, 124, 127, 131, 140, 148, 155, 160,
   161, 173, 178, 216, 238, 250, 255
parking policy 160
participation 52, 53, 169, 216
peri-urban 167, 168, 211–213, 243, 247–250
peri-urbanity 133
peri-urbanization 249, 250
periphery 21, 23, 25, 32, 35, 36, 140
Perry 24
planners 25, 38, 41, 43, 49–54, 66, 67, 71–74, 88,
   100, 136, 179, 209, 237–244, 248, 251, 253, 255,
   260, 261

territorial
- adaptation 128, 130, 133, 135, 136
- coverage 216
-ity 31, 43, 46, 52, 53, 61, 63, 64, 65, 66, 81, 114,
116 – *see also* **aterritoriality**
-ization 56, 65
- network 43, 46
territory 19, 22, 23, 25, 28, 42, 46, 50, 53, 58–67, 82,
111, 112, 115–118, 125–136, 157, 172, 176, 179, 180,
197–204, 207, 208, 215, 219, 233, 241, 244, 253
TGV 117
toll 92, 93, 128, 134, 140, 157, 173, 174, 216
toll roads 157
topology 19–22, 24, 30, 32, 35–38, 67, 68, 149, 150,
157, 242, 253, 258, 260, 261
tourism 51, 78, 82, 179, 180, 189, 201, 207, 208, 231
tourists 60, 78, 81, 186
traffic
- flows 33, 85, 88–91, 93
- forecasting 85–90, 93, 94
- models 88, 90, 91, 93, 95
transfer of 'intellectual technology' 85, 91
transportation 19, 20–24, 27, 28, 32, 36, 86–94,
123, 143, 144, 149, 157–161, 239
travel needs 166
trip-chains 167
TV 51, 111, 117, 199, 200

U

ubiquitous 24, 53, 57, 59, 60, 64
UMTS 239, 240, 246
universal adapter 121, 128, 136
urban
- areas 86, 87, 141, 143, 163, 164, 169, 179, 180,
199, 201, 211–213, 221, 225, 229, 233, 240, 247,
249, 250, 251
- centres 28, 44, 101, 130, 227, 228, 239, 247, 249
- form(s) 25, 243 , 249
- fragmentation 253
- network 62, 91, 99, 103, 239
- planners 25, 38, 41, 50, 53, 66, 67, 71, 72, 100,
237, 238, 239, 244, 251
- planning 19, 30, 37, 38, 41, 42, 47–54, 58, 65,
66, 90–94, 126, 136, 163, 237, 241–244, 247,
248, 252

- regeneration 212
- way of life 37
urbanism 19, 20, 28, 30, 33, 34, 37, 38, 211, 238, 241,
243, 248, 251–253, 260, 261
urbanization 31, 49, 74, 86, 88, 93, 94, 98–100, 112,
121, 129, 130, 248–250
utopia 19, 34–37, 47, 175, 215, 243, 247–250
utopianism 248

V

Virilio 20, 25, 27, 28, 65
virtual 19, 28, 42, 43, 44, 45, 46, 47, 49, 50, 54, 72, 193,
201, 202, 212, 260
voiturette 143, 144, 151

W

water 21, 23, 27, 28, 32, 41–46, 50–53, 57–59, 65, 66,
74, 77–84, 96–109, 112, 115, 118, 124, 131, 134,
198, 216, 236–240, 244–246, 251, 261
web-based practices 200
website 200, 201, 205–208, 221, 222, 227, 229
Wi-Fi 211–213, 254, 255
women 128, 129, 134, 135, 158, 166, 167, 198 – *see
also* **feminine territories**
workplace 64, 97, 106, 168, 169, 179
world system 162
Wright 20, 30, 34–41, 47, 52, 134, 248, 249, 250

Y

young people 128, 134–136, 170

Z

Zahavi 162, 178, 284
zoning 19, 20, 22, 23, 38, 50–53, 82, 93
zoning maps 82

Previously published in the series
Design/Science/Planning

Klaasen, I.T., 2004, *Knowledge-based Design: Developing Urban & Regional Design into a Science*

Fernández-Maldonado, A.M., 2004, *ICT-related Transformations in Latin American Metropolises*

Restrepo, J., 2004, *Information Processing in Design*

Salingaros, N.A., 2005, *Principles of Urban Structure*

Hulsbergen, E.D., I.T. Klaasen & I. Kriens (eds), 2005, *Shifting Sense in Spatial Planning - Looking Back to the Future*

Drewe, P., Klein, J.-L., Hulsbergen, E.D. (eds), 2007, *The Challenge of Social Innovation in Urban Revitalization*